IBM® PC AT
User's Reference Manual

IBM® PC AT
User's Reference Manual

Gilbert Held

Hayden Book Company
A DIVISION OF HAYDEN PUBLISHING COMPANY, INC.
HASBROUCK HEIGHTS, NEW JERSEY / BERKELEY, CALIFORNIA

Acquisitions Editor: THERESE A. ZAK
Production Editor: LORI WILLIAMS
Cover design and illustration: JOHN M-RÖBLIN
Text design: DELGADO DESIGN ASSOCIATES
Technical illustrations: JOHN McAUSLAND
Composition: THE MAPLE-VAIL BOOK MANUFACTURING GROUP
Printed and bound by: MALLOY LITHOGRAPHING, INC.

Library of Congress Cataloging-in-Publication Data

Held, Gilbert.
IBM PC AT user's reference manual.

On t.p. the registered trademark symbol "R" in circle appears superscript following "IBM" in the title.
Includes index.
1. IBM Personal Computer AT. I. Title.
QA76.8.I2595H45 1985 004.165 85-21953
ISBN 0-8104-6394-6

Printed in the United States of America

1 2 3 4 5 6 7 8 9

85 86 87 88 89 90 91 92 93 YEAR

Preface

The introduction of the IBM Personal Computer on August 12, 1981, can be considered a milestone in the extension of computer use to the individual. Within a short period of time this computer had become a de facto standard for personal computing and its acceptance by both individual and corporate purchasers resulted in the birth of an industry of hardware and software suppliers offering supplemental products for PC owners. With sales goals constantly being revised upward, the Personal Computer has become almost as common as the office copier in just a few short years since its introduction.

On the third anniversary of the introduction of the PC, IBM has once again extended the scope of computational power by incorporating the latest generation of technology into its Advanced Technology Personal Computer. Although the PC AT has many additional features in comparison to the original PC, by designing it to be highly compatible with the PC, IBM has enabled users to immediately have a library of thousands of software programs available for selection. In addition, a large number of software vendors are developing programs tailored for the multiuser and local area networking capabilities of the PC AT, which should extend its utilization capability beyond its predecessor.

While it is difficult to forecast the future with any degree of certainty, if the past is any guide to the future, one can expect the PC AT to eventually become as popular as the original PC. Thus, schools, businesses, government agencies, as well as home users can be expected to tailor an AT system to meet their computational requirements.

I have written this book to serve as an aid to the effective use of the PC AT. Most of the initial programming examples in this book are limited, by design, to short program segments. By focusing your attention on the utilization of short blocks of code and the use of individual statements, you can increase your foundation of knowledge. Thus, specific applications and major programming examples have been deferred until later chapters. Although I encourage you to try the examples on your PC AT, readers who do not have access to this computer can use the material presented herein as a guide to its effective use if the opportunity should arise.

Gilbert Held
Macon, Georgia

Acknowledgments

The stages involved in preparing a manuscript that gives birth to a book require the cooperation and assistance of many persons. First and foremost, I must thank my family for enduring those long nights and missing weekends while I worked on the manuscript.

Once again, I wish to thank Jeannette A. Maher and Rosemary Morrissey of IBM. With new products for the PC AT being introduced at a rapid rate, the cooperation and assistance furnished to one author among thousands of requests for information are especially appreciated.

Last but not least, one's editors and typist are the critical link in converting the author's manuscript into the book you are now reading. Thus, my special thanks to Therese A. Zak and Lori Williams, as well as the artists, compositors, and production specialists at Hayden Book Company. To Carol Ferrell, who once again has taken my notes and inserts and typed them into a logical order, your fine effort is truly appreciated.

Contents

CHAPTER ONE

Hardware Overview

Unveiled on the third anniversary of the introduction of the IBM PC, the IBM PC AT (Advanced Technology) represents the latest generation of personal computer technology. The PC AT can be used as a stand-alone personal computer or as a multiuser microcomputer since it is capable of simultaneously supporting three users. Although there will probably be no such item as a typical PC AT system, each PC AT system will include a minimum of four major components—a keyboard unit, a system unit containing space for the installation of a variety of adapter boards and storage devices, a monitor, and a printer. Figure 1-1 illustrates a common IBM PC AT system configuration showing the installation of one diskette drive in its system unit.

BASIC AND ENHANCED MODELS

When originally announced, two models of the PC AT were offered. The basic PC AT includes 256K (K representing 1024 units) bytes of random access memory (RAM) and a single 5¼-inch, half-height, double-sided floppy diskette drive capable of storing 1.2 megabytes of information on a diskette, as well as a dual floppy diskette and fixed disk controller installed in the system unit. The enhanced PC AT includes 512K of RAM, a 1.2-megabyte floppy disk drive, a serial/parallel adapter card, and a 20-megabyte fixed disk. Both the basic and the enhanced PC AT models include a keyboard; to display and print information, however, one must obtain a variety of optional equipment to include a monitor, a printer, and appropriate adapter cards that must be installed inside the PC AT's system unit.

Although every IBM PC AT has a keyboard and system unit, the wide variety of equipment available from both IBM and other manufacturers that

Fig. 1-1. IBM Personal Computer AT system. The major components include a keyboard, a system unit, a 25-line by 80-column display, and a printer (not shown). (Courtesy of IBM Corporation.)

can be interfaced to the PC AT may result in your system not looking like the one shown in Fig. 1-1. In fact, even your system unit may look slightly different if you have two diskette drives or two fixed disks. If the second diskette drive is not included in your system unit, a beige backing plate will be installed to cover the slot where the second diskette drive or a second fixed disk can be inserted, as illustrated in Fig. 1-1.

In the remaining portions of this section, we will examine the two components that are common to all IBM PC ATs—the keyboard and system unit—and take a look at some of the optional equipment available from both IBM and non-IBM sources.

KEYBOARD

Operator input to the PC AT is through an 84-key keyboard. Shown in detail in Fig. 1-2, the keyboard contains all the keys found on a normal typewriter as well as special gray keys that will assist you in a variety of tasks such

Fig. 1-2. The PC AT keyboard contains a row of three green LED indicator lights that illuminate when the Caps Lock, Num Lock, and Scroll Lock keys are activated. The keyboard is physically divided into three sections containing function keys, typing keys, and a numeric keypad. (Photo by Douglas Hopkins.)

as programming, editing, updating, and executing programs. At each end of the keyboard is an adjustable leg that can be used to place the unit in either a level or a tilted upright position. The keyboard attaches to the rear of the system unit via a 10-foot-long coiled cord.

The keyboard is physically divided into three sections containing function keys, typing keys, and a numeric keypad. In the upper right-hand portion of the keyboard is a row of three green LED indicator lights that illuminate when the Caps Lock, Num Lock, and Scroll Lock keys are activated. Since the PC AT keyboard has a bidirectional serial interface that only an AT can understand, this keyboard cannot be used with earlier members of the IBM Personal Computer series such as the original PC, the PC XT, and the Portable PC (PPC).

SYSTEM UNIT

The heart of the IBM PC AT is its system unit. When viewed from the front, the window to the right of the IBM logo contains a keylock and two indicators. The first indicator is a power-on light indicator, while the second LED denotes when the 20-megabyte fixed disk is in use. The keylock accepts a hard-to-duplicate "tubular" key, similar to ones used in many home security systems. When the PC AT is placed in a locked position and the key is removed, an operating machine will not accept keystroke input, permitting users to leave their system powered on and to perform a desired activity without having to worry that someone could interrupt the activity. In addition, if the system unit is locked and not powered on, although an unauthorized user could turn the power switch on, he or she could not perform any operations on the AT. Due to the critical importance of the key, it is highly recommended that it be placed in an appropriate location when not required and that its serial number be recorded.

Under the nameplate on the left and extending toward the diskette and optional fixed disk drive housing area is a ventilation grille. Care should be taken to keep this grille uncovered during operation, as it permits an airflow through the interior of the system unit and serves to prevent heat buildup that could cause the electronics inside the system unit to fail.

The diskette and optional fixed disk housing area permits the installation of two half-height devices into the system unit at this location. Standard equipment for both the basic and enhanced PC AT is a half-height, dual-sided, 1.2-megabyte floppy diskette drive that is mounted in the upper portion of that location. Under the 1.2-megabyte high-density floppy diskette drive users can install another 1.2-megabyte floppy diskette drive, a second 20-megabyte fixed disk (if one purchased an enhanced PC AT), or a conventional 360K half-height diskette drive. Although diskettes created on a PC, XT, or Portable PC can be read by the high-capacity 1.2-megabyte diskette drive, users are cautioned not to write to those diskettes when they are in that diskette drive because doing so will make them unreadable by a conventional 360K drive. Thus, users who anticipate creating diskettes to be used on the PC, XT, or PPC should obtain and install a conventional 360K diskette drive for their PC AT.

On the right rear of the system unit is the power switch. Similar to the switch on the original PC, when it is pushed upward the system is powered on.

Figure 1-3 presents a top view showing the interior of the PC AT's system unit after its cover was removed. In the upper right-hand portion of that illustration is the power supply and cooling fan. The power supply converts alternating current (ac) to the direct current (dc) required to operate the various components installed in the system unit. This power supply can be switched for 115- or 230-volt operation and thus permits the PC AT to be used worldwide. You can select either voltage by toggling a recessed switch on the back panel of the system unit. The cooling fan expels excess heat generated by the electrical operation of the components in the system unit and prevents a heat buildup that could adversely affect your computer.

In the lower right portion of Fig. 1-3 is the housing for the 1.2-megabyte floppy diskette drive and an optional 20-megabyte fixed disk, another 1.2-megabyte floppy diskette drive, or a 360K floppy diskette drive. The latter optional device permits the user to create diskettes that can be read by the diskette drives installed in the IBM PC, XT, and PPC. A high-capacity 1.2-megabyte floppy diskette drive is installed in the top part of the housing in both the basic and enhanced models of the PC AT, while any of the three optional devices previously mentioned can be installed in the lower part of this housing area.

In the enhanced model of the PC AT a 20-megabyte fixed disk is installed to the left of the previously discussed housing area. This device is also illustrated in Fig. 1-3.

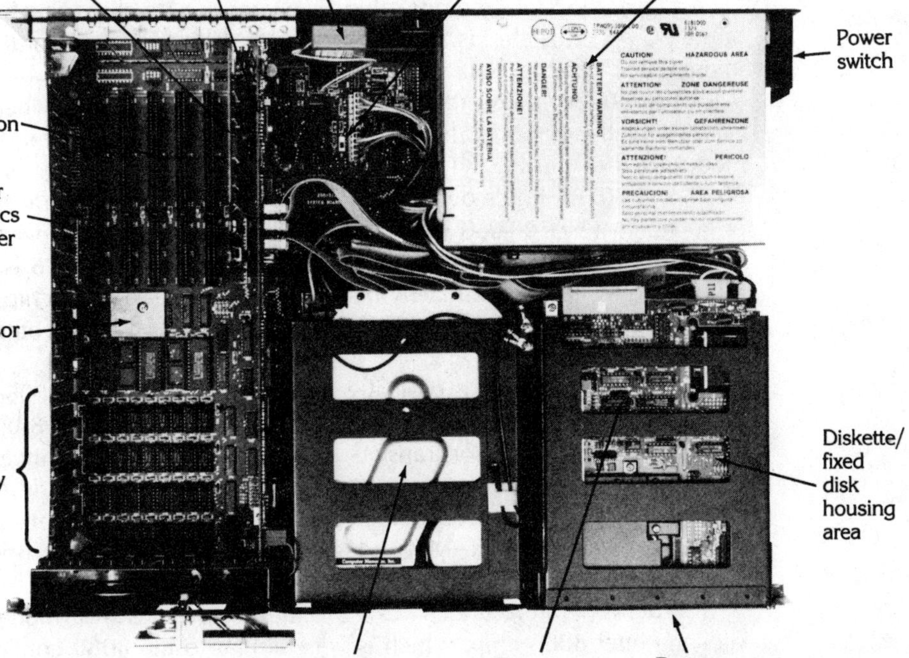

Fig. 1-3. The interior of the system unit, housing the memory, disk and diskette storage devices, microprocessor, and up to eight adapter boards that provide the means for customizing the functionality of the PC AT. (Photo by Lou Odor; IBM equipment courtesy of In*Sight Computer Center.)

The lower left portion of the system unit contains the Intel 80286 microprocessor, read-only memory (ROM), and random access or read/write memory (RAM). Probably due to unavailability in sufficient quantities or the cost of 128K RAM chips, IBM used a piggyback arrangement of two 64K bit chips for RAM memory in the initial versions of the basic and enhanced models of the PC AT. As previously discussed, the basic system contains 256K of RAM, whereas the enhanced model contains 512K bytes. The three rows of nine piggyback chips illustrated in the lower left portion of Fig. 1-3 shows a fully populated system board on an enhanced model of the PC AT containing 512K of RAM. Once the system board is fully populated, users can expand the PC AT's memory to a maximum of 3 megabytes by installing five 512K memory expansion cards into the system expansion slots located in the upper left portion of the system unit.

Above the RAM memory chips are the ROM chips that contain built-in instructions that govern the initial power-on self-test of the AT that occurs when one activates the system. In addition, these ROM chips contain a built-in version of the BASIC programming language and other specialized diagnostic and control information.

Above the ROM memory chips is a large square chip, which is the brain of the PC AT. This chip is the Intel 80286 16-bit microprocessor that has both internal and external data buses 16 bits wide.

The 80286 microprocessor operates at 8 million cycles per second (8 MHz), which is considerably faster than the 4.77 MHz rate of the earlier 8088 model used in the PC, XT, and PPC. In addition to operating faster than the 8088, the 80286 holds over six times the number of transistors as the 8088, or approximately 120,000 such devices. By integrating many devices onto one chip where previously several chips were required, the 80286 is capable of running software approximately five times as fast as an 8088 chip, permitting programs to operate considerably faster on the AT than on the other members of the PC family.

Although this chip is basically compatible with the Intel 8088 that powers the PC, XT, and PPC, unlike the 8088 that transfers data in 8-bit segments, the 80286 microprocessor transfers data in 16-bit segments (since it is a true 16-bit microprocessor). In addition, the 80286 has a 24-bit address bus that permits the microprocessor to address and directly communicate with 2^{24}, or about 16 megabytes of RAM, although physical constraints and operating system software permit a lessor amount of memory to be used.

When operating under PC-DOS, the 80286 runs in a mode that emulates the Intel 8086 chip, which is very similar to the 8088 contained in the PC, XT, and PPC. In this mode, the PC AT can only access 640K of memory directly, which is the addressing limit of earlier members of the IBM PC series. When used with the multiuser operating system known as XENIX, the 80286 can directly access up to 16 megabytes of memory, although presently only 3 megabytes can be physically installed.

In the upper left-hand portion of Fig. 1-3 are eight system expansion slots into which one can install a variety of adapter cards. Numbered 1 to 8 from left to right, expansion slots 2 through 6 and slot 8 have two connectors. One connector is the standard 62-pin IBM PC expansion slot connector used in the PC, XT, and PPC. To the rear of this connector, in expansion slots 2 through 6 and slot 8, is a 36-pin connector that supports the extra data and address lines of the 80286's microprocessor. Expansion slots 1 and 7 contain only one connector, the standard 62-pin IBM PC expansion slot connector that is standard on the PC, XT, and PPC. These two expansion slots permit users to install adapter cards that contain an extension of the circuit board down to its lower edge, known as a "skirt." As adapter cards with skirts cannot fit into expansion slots 2 through 6 and slot 8 because the skirt would bump the second connector, one is limited to using only two such adapter boards in the PC AT. Currently, the IBM monochrome display and parallel printer adapter board and the IBM color graphics board represent two popular add-on boards that can be used in expansion slots 1 or 7.

The IBM color graphics card illustrated in Fig. 1-4 shows the skirt on the card that precludes its insertion into expansion slots 2 through 6 and slot 8. The adapter card illustrated in expansion slot 8 of Fig. 1-3 is a single controller card designed to support a mixture of up to two floppy diskette drives and

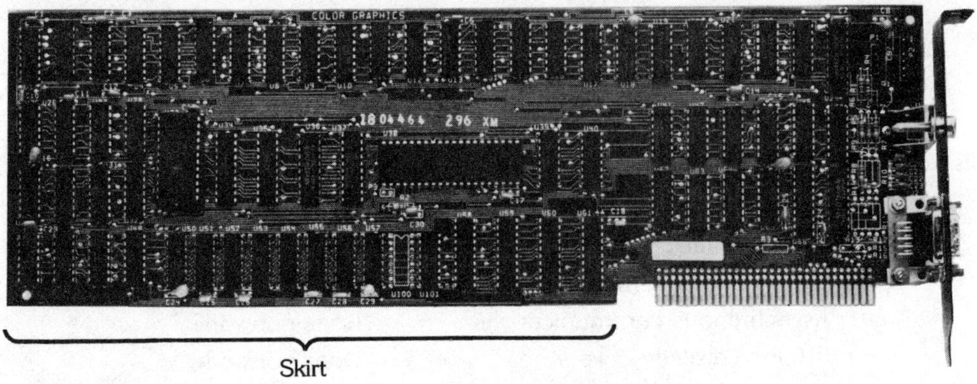

Fig. 1-4. Color graphics card. Because of the skirt behind the connector edge, the color graphics card must be installed in either expansion slot 1 or expansion slot 7. (Courtesy of IBM Corporation.)

two fixed disks. These boards will be discussed in more detail later in this chapter.

To the right of expansion slot 8 on the back wall of the system unit is a battery pack that provides power to a clock/calendar and 64K of complimentary metallic oxide semiconductor (CMOS) RAM. This low-power consumption RAM stores the system configuration data that one enters during the installation process and serves as a replacement for the hard-to-access dual in-line package (DIP) switches found on the PC, XT, and PPC. The only switch in the system unit is used to set the default for the type of display one wishes to use—monochrome or color graphics.

EXPANSION/ADAPTER CARDS

A variety of expansion/adapter cards are available from IBM and other manufacturers and provide the ability to enhance the functionality of the PC AT. Care must be taken, however, to ascertain which expansion slots an adapter card can be inserted into, since many cards cannot operate in expansion slots 2 through 6 and 8 even if they do not have skirts and can be inserted into those slots.

PC INCOMPATIBILITY

For AT users and owners who have access to earlier PC systems, Table 1-1 will serve as a compatibility guide indicating which IBM PC, XT, and PPC adapters can be used with the PC AT and which will not work. The adapters listed in Table 1-1 that do not work on the PC AT are incompatible because the Intel 80286 microprocessor addresses 16 bits at a time, and those cards are designed to operate with the 8-bit data transfer used with the 8088 microprocessor that powers the PC, XT, and PPC.

As an example of this incompatibility, consider the 5¼-inch disk drive adapter that controls the floppy disk drives on the PC, XT, and PPC. This disk

Table 1-1. PC Adapter Compatibility Guide

ADAPTER CARDS	COMPATIBILITY WITH PC AT
Monochrome display and parallel printer	Works in expansion slot 1 or 7
Color/graphics	Works in expansion slot 1 or 7
Parallel printer	Does not work
64K to 256K memory	Does not work
Asynchronous communications	Does not work
5¼-inch diskette drive	Does not work
Game control	Works in expansion slot 1 or 7

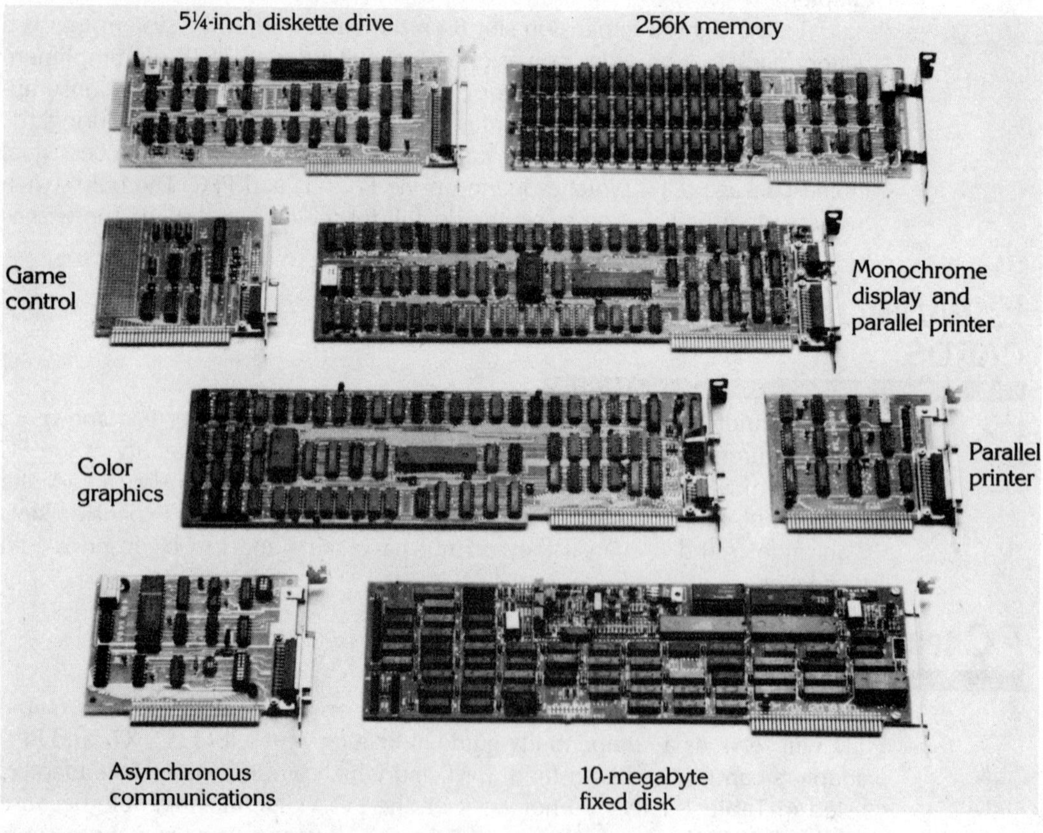

Fig. 1-5. Common adapter cards used in the PC, XT, and PPC. From top to bottom, left to right, the following adapter cards are illustrated: 5¼-inch diskette drive, 256K memory, game control, monochrome display and parallel printer, color graphics, parallel printer, asynchronous communications, and 10-megabyte fixed disk. (Courtesy of IBM Corporation.)

drive adapter is designed to work with the 8088 microprocessor that receives data from a disk drive 8 bits at a time, processes it internally in a 16-bit register, and then sends the result back to the drive in an 8-bit form. Since the 80286 inputs and outputs data using a 16-bit bus containing 16 wires, this disk drive adapter cannot work with the 80286. Figure 1-5 illustrates the eight most common IBM PC adapter cards and can be used as a visual reference in conjunction with the data contained in Table 1-1 to ascertain which adapters that operate with the PC, XT, or PPC can be used with the AT.

AT ADAPTER CARDS AND OTHER OPTIONS

Table 1-2 lists the PC AT adapter cards and other optional equipment that can be installed inside the system unit.

The 256K memory expansion module is sold in kit form and is inserted into the system board of a basic AT model to increase its on-board memory to 512K bytes. The 128K RAM adapter card increases a 512K system to 640K, which is the maximum amount of memory that can be addressed under the AT's primary single user operating system, PC-DOS.

Table 1-2. IBM PC AT Adapter Cards and Options

ADAPTER CARD/OPTION	FUNCTION
128K memory adapter card	Increases system unit memory by 128K after on-board memory totals 512K
256K memory expansion module	Increases on-board system unit memory by 256K
512K expansion adapter card	Increases system unit memory by 512K after on-board memory totals 512K
Serial/parallel adapter card	Contains the interface for one serial and one parallel device
Serial adapter connector	Converts the DB-9 connector on the serial interface of the serial/parallel adapter card to a more common DB-25 connector
1.2-megabyte floppy diskette drive	Reads diskettes in 160/180K, 320/360K, and 1.2-megabyte mode; writes to diskettes in 1.2-megabyte mode
Diskette drive and hard disk adapter	Provides signal interfacing for up to four devices, but only three can be installed within the system unit

Table 1-2. IBM PC AT Adapter Cards and Options (cont.)

ADAPTER CARD/OPTION	FUNCTION
Monochrome display and parallel printer adapter	Has dual function of providing a parallel printer interface as well as the interface necessary to drive the IBM monochrome display; must be installed in expansion slot 1 or 7
Color/graphics monitor adapter	Permits attachment of a wide variety of TV frequency monitors and TV sets via a user-supplied RF modulator (including a light pen interface); must be installed in expansion slot 1 or 7
Enhanced graphics adapter	Can be used with both the IBM monochrome display and the color display: provides the monochrome display with graphics capability that is unattainable with the monochrome display and parallel printer adapter; improves the resolution on the color screen when used with a color display

Serial/Parallel Adapter

A combination serial/parallel adapter card contains a serial and parallel interface that can be used to transfer data to serial or parallel devices. Serial devices that can be connected to this card include modems and acoustic couplers, as well as serial printers and other serial interfaced devices. The parallel interface on this card will most likely be employed by users to drive a parallel interfaced printer.

Up to two serial/parallel adapter cards can be installed inside the PC AT and, thus, limits the multiuser operating system to the support of two serial terminal devices and the AT user, for a total of three users. The parallel interface on this card is a DB-25 connector, which is the same as that used in the parallel interface card on the original PC. The serial interface on this card uses a male-headed DB-9 connector that requires one to purchase a special DB-9/DB-25 serial adapter connector in order to use a standard cable to connect the serial interface to a serial device.

1.2-Megabyte Floppy Diskette Drive

The 1.2-megabyte high-capacity floppy diskette drive can read diskettes formatted on the PC, XT, or PPC. Although this drive will determine prior to reading a diskette whether it is a 160K, 180K, 320K, 360K, or 1.2-megabyte diskette, it does not make this determination when it writes onto a diskette. Any modifications made by an AT to a non-1.2-megabyte formatted diskette to include renaming or erasing a file will make the diskette unreadable by other members of the PC series product line. Thus, to provide a mechanism to exchange data with other members of the IBM PC series, one must install a 360K floppy disk drive into one's AT.

360K Floppy Diskette Drive

The 360K floppy diskette drive permits data to be recorded onto diskettes in a format compatible with other members of the IBM PC family. This drive will be mounted in the lower portion of the disk housing area inside the system unit and has a star in its lower right corner to distinguish it from the 1.2-megabyte floppy diskette drive.

Diskette Drive and Hard Disk Adapter

This adapter card provides the signal interface to attach up to three diskette drives and hard disks. Although many AT users will attach one hard disk and a 1.2-megabyte floppy diskette drive and a conventional 360K drive to this card, a total of 41.2-megabytes of on-line storage can be supported by this device. This is accomplished by installing two hard disks and one 1.2-megabyte high-capacity diskette drive in one's PC AT and connecting the three devices to the diskette drive and hard disk adapter card. This device is standard on both versions of the AT, although the enhanced version only permits one additional device to be attached to the card since two storage devices are standard with that model.

MONITORS

Four IBM monitors are presently available for use with the PC AT—the IBM 5151 monochrome display, the IBM 5153 color display, the IBM 5175 PC professional graphics display and controller, and the IBM 5154 color display. In addition, a variety of third party monitors as well as standard television sets can be connected to the AT.

IBM 5151 Monochrome Display

The IBM 5151 monochrome display illustrated in Fig. 1-1 is a high-resolution, green phosphor display. The screen of the display features an 11½-inch-wide surface with an anti-glare coating and displays 25 lines of 80 characters. Using a 9 by 14 dot matrix to form characters, it supports 256 different letters, numbers, and special characters. The character set supported is listed in Appendix A.

To use the IBM monochrome display requires the installation of the monochrome display and printer adapter option into slot 1 or 7 of the system expansion slots in the system unit. The monochrome display and printer adapter card is illustrated in Fig. 1-6. The end of the adapter card that fits into one end of the system expansion slot facing the rear of the system unit contains two connectors. The upper connector on the adapter card is a 9-pin video connector to which the cable from the monochrome display will be attached. The lower connector is a 25-pin printer connector that can be used to connect the system unit to a printer that has a parallel interface.

Note that the monochrome display can obtain power from the system unit by connecting the display's power plug to the electrical receptacle at the left rear part of the system unit. In addition to reducing the requirements for wall outlets to power the entire computer system, it allows the system unit's power on/off switch to control the display unit.

Fig. 1-6. IBM monochrome display and parallel printer adapter. The upper connector on the adapter card is a 9-pin video connector to which the cable from the monochrome display will be attached. The lower connector is a 25-pin printer connector that can be used to connect the system unit to a printer with a parallel interface. (Courtesy of IBM Corporation.)

IBM 5153 Color Display

The IBM 5153 color display is used to display text and graphics output on a 13-inch-diagonal high-resolution color monitor. The display format is 25 lines by 80 characters and permits 16 colors (two shades of gray, red, green, blue, magenta, and cyan; and one shade of yellow, white, brown, and black. to be displayed at any one time. This display must be connected to a color/graphics monitor adapter card installed in the system unit of the PC AT.

Color/Graphics Monitor Adapter

The color/graphics monitor adapter card is shown in Fig. 1-4 and has several video interfaces as well as a light pen connector. Both a 9-pin "D" type shell RGB connector and a composite phono jack hookup are available to directly interface a monitor. To the rear of the retaining bracket of the adapter card is a 4-pin Berg strip that can be used to connect the adapter card to a radio frequency (RF) modulator. The RF modulator, in turn, can be connected to a standard TV. Normally, the output from the RF modulator is connected to a switch box, which in turn is connected to the TV's antenna connector. The slide switch on the switch box can be placed in one of two positions. In the position labeled "TV," the TV set is connected via the switch box to its antenna or perhaps a cable TV hookup. When the switch is moved to the position marked "game" (on some switch boxes the position is marked "computer"), the TV will be directly connected to the PC AT. Neither the 4-pin Berg strip for the RF modulator nor a similar 6-pin strip connection to a light pen uses pin 2, which is missing its prong on both pin strips.

The key differences between using the IBM monochrome display and a TV set or monitor are in the areas of data output representation and display color. The IBM monochrome display can only operate in a noncolor text mode of 25 lines of 80 characters per line. TVs and monitors can operate in color and both text mode and two graphics modes—medium-resolution graphics of 320 by 200 picture elements (pixels) and high-resolution graphics of 640 by 200 pixels.

The lower resolution and bandwidth display clarity of standard TVs in comparison to monitors normally limit the former to displaying 40 characters per line in text mode and medium-resolution graphics. Since high-resolution graphics is in black and white, if you wanted to use this capability of the AT exclusively, a black-and-white monitor would suffice. For color text display and medium-resolution graphics, either a color TV or color monitor may be used; however, a color monitor would provide greater clarity as well as the ability to clearly display 80 characters of text per line. Both the number of characters displayed per line as well as the graphics mode one is operating in are controlled via software.

The use of the color/graphics monitor adapter permits black-and-white or color operation. The two basic modes of operation of the adapter card are alphanumeric (A/N) and all points addressable (APA) graphics. Within each mode, several display character widths or pixel sizes are available for selection.

In the A/N mode, the display can be operated in a 40-character by 25-line mode if you are using a low-resolution monitor or TV. The AT can be operated in an 80-character by 25-line mode if you have a high-resolution monitor attached to the color/graphics monitor adapter card. Character blinking and highlighting as well as reverse video are available for display under program control when your PC is in the black-and-white mode of operation. In the color mode of operation, a total of 16 foreground colors and eight background colors can be selected for each displayed character. In addition, under program control, individual characters can be blinked.

The color/graphics monitor adapter card contains 16,384 bytes (16K) of RAM storage. If a 40-character by 25-line screen display is used, 1,000 bytes are employed to store character information (40 by 25), while an additional 1,000 bytes are employed to contain the attribute/color information required for each character. With a total of 2,000 bytes required to display a 40 by 25 screen, up to eight pages of screens can be stored in the adapter's memory. If an 80 by 25 screen size is employed, up to four screens can be stored in the adapter. The direct addressability of the color/graphics monitor adapter via the Intel microprocessor permits a large degree of software flexibility for managing the data on the screen. This is particularly important for animation and graphic image displays.

In the APA mode of operation, two graphics resolution modes are available—320 by 200 pixels and 640 by 200 pixels. In the 320 by 200 pixels graphics mode each pixel can have one of four colors, while the 640 by 200 pixel mode is only available in black and white, since it requires all of the adapter cards' memory to define the on or off state of each pixel.

IBM 5154 Color Display

The IBM 5154 is an enhanced version of the 5153 color display. It is similar in size to the 5153 but provides a greater bit-mapped display (640 by 350 pixels on the 5154 versus 640 by 200 pixels on the 5153). Like the 5153, 16 colors can be displayed simultaneously, chosen from a palette of 64 colors. The IBM 5154 incorporates a dark, etched screen for high contrast and reduced glare. Like the 5153, brightness and contrast controls are provided on the front of the display.

IBM 5175 PC Professional Graphics Display and Controller

The IBM 5175 graphics display and professional graphics controller enable engineers, scientists, technicians, and designers to use the PC AT as an integrated work station. The display and controller offer a variety of advanced graphics functions to include computer-aided design (CAD), computer-aided manufacturing (CAM), computer-aided engineering (CAE), and business presentation graphics.

The graphics display is attached to a controller, which occupies two adjacent expansion slots. The controller—a set of cards that includes an Intel 8088 microprocessor, 320K memory, and 64K ROM—provides many graphics functions that reduces the need to load software subroutines for most graphics activities. The controller provides for the following key functions:

- Two- and three-dimensional capabilities for drawing, rotating, translating, and scaling
- Moving and drawing with absolute or relative coordinates
- User-selectable character sizes
- User-redefinable color selection
- User-programmable character set
- Vector and polygon drawing and polygon fill

The IBM PC professional graphics display has the same physical dimensions as the IBM 5153 color display but has a darkened screen to enhance contrast. Up to 256 colors can be displayed simultaneously, with the colors selected from a palette of 4,096 colors, and the bit-mapped display provides a resolution of 640 by 480 pixels.

PRINTERS

Several types of printers are available from IBM for use with the PC AT. These printers range from the IBM graphics printer (a dot matrix printer originally developed for use with the PC) to several low-cost letter quality printers and typewriters that can be linked to the PC AT and used as a printer as well as a printer than can print up to eight colors.

The IBM graphics printer illustrated in Fig. 1-7 is an 80-character-per-second (cps), bidirectional, dot matrix printer manufactured by Epson. This printer has a nine-wire print head that allows it to print characters and graphic symbols in a 9 by 9 dot matrix.

Under program control, a variety of printing options can be exercised to obtain 40, 60, 80, or 132 characters per line, enlarged font printing of 66 characters per line, double-size character printing and double striking, and double-dotted character printing. The basic matrix printer uses the American Standard Code for Information Interchange (ASCII): 96 uppercase and lowercase character sets as well as 64 special block graphic characters. A special graphics chip can be added to printers sold before mid-1983 to obtain dot-addressable graphics capability.

This printer can be attached to the system unit of the AT via the parallel connector on the serial/parallel adapter card, or it can be connected to the monochrome display and parallel printer adapter card.

The IBM Quietwriter can be used to print data processing reports, graphics, and letters, while the IBM 5216 Wheelprinter can be used for letter quality

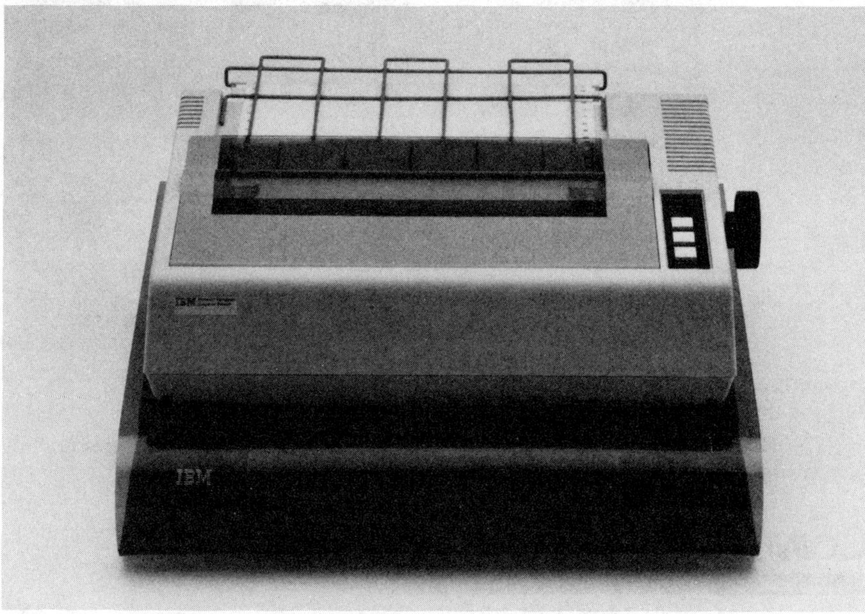

Fig. 1-7. The IBM graphics printer is an 80-character-per-second, bidirectional, dot matrix printer. (Courtesy of IBM Corporation.)

text printing. The Quietwriter employes "resistive ribbon" print technology consisting of three key components: an electronic type font, an electronic printhead containing 40 electrodes, and a ribbon that releases ink in response to pinpoints of heat generated by a current from the printhead. This technology results in a painting effect that causes print quality to resemble that of higher priced impact printers. The Quietwriter printer has a 252-character font in the IBM PC series character set that permits images of every PC AT character to be printed.

Both the IBM graphics printer and the Quietwriter printer can be attached to the system unit via the combination monochrome display and parallel printer adapter card or via a connection to the parallel interface on the serial/parallel adapter card. Other printers that have a serial interface can be connected to the system unit via the serial interface on the serial/parallel adapter card.

The IBM color printer illustrated in Fig. 1-8 can print up to eight colors under program control. This printer operates at speeds up to 200 characters per second and can accommodate single sheet, fanfold, and continuous roll paper.

Fig. 1-8. The IBM PC color printer can print up to eight colors under program control at speeds up to 200 characters per second. (Courtesy of IBM Corporation.)

COMMUNICATIONS

A wide variety of acoustic couplers and modems can be connected to the system unit of the PC AT via the serial interface on the serial/parallel adapter card. As noted earlier in this chapter, one must obtain a DB-9/DB-25 serial adapter connector in order to use a standard cable to connect a serial device to this serial interface.

The serial interface on the serial/parallel adapter permits the PC AT to communicate with another PC AT, an information network, or another personal computer or mainframe computer at data rates between 50 and 9600 bits per second (bps). While the PC AT can be directly connected (via a short cable) to another computer and can transmit and receive data at speeds up to 9600 bps, its maximum communications data rate for remote communications operations is typically limited to 1200 or 2400 bps due to asynchronous communications modulation limitations. Since up to two serial/parallel adapters can be installed in the AT's system unit, one can be used to interface a serial printer while the second can be used for data communications. The Cermetek 1200 modem illustrated in Fig. 1-9 represents one of the many intelligent automatic-dialing modems that can be used with the AT. This modem operates at 110/300/1200 bps and is Bell System 212A and 103 compatible, permitting communications with a large base of equivalent devices.

Fig. 1-9. The Cermetek 1200 modem operates at three distinct data rates: 110, 300, and 1200 bits per second. Since it is Bell System 212A and 103 compatible, it can be used to communicate with a large base of equivalently equipped personal computers and mainframe computer systems. (Courtesy of Cermetek Corporation.)

OTHER EQUIPMENT

Although the PC AT is a tremendously capable microcomputer-based system, no efficient method of backup is provided for the 20-megabyte hard disk. To back up the contents of a single 20-megabyte disk requires 17 high-capacity 1.2-megabyte diskettes. While this is not an unreasonable number of floppy diskettes, if compatibility with the PC, XT, or PPC is desired by installation of a 360K diskette drive, backup would then require 55 diskettes. If two 20-megabyte hard disks are installed, one disk could be used as a backup for the other; this, however, would be costly and limit the user to one diskette drive, because only three devices can be supported by the diskette drive and fixed adapter card.

Since IBM continued a policy of open architecture for third-party vendors, one of the first products third-party suppliers furnished for use in the AT was a controller board and cartridge tape drive to provide a mechanism for hard disk backup. While some third-party vendors manufacture a stand-alone tape subsystem that is self-contained and connected to an adapter inserted into the AT's system unit, other vendors offer a tape unit that is designed for insertion into the system unit itself.

Figure 1-10 illustrates the Maynstream high-capacity cartridge backup system manufactured by Maynard Electronics. This cartridge tape system can back up 10-megabytes of fixed disk storage in less than three minutes and uses conventional 20-megabyte or 26-megabyte tape cartridges. Although one must install an interface card into the system unit of the AT to operate Maynstream, a quick release cable permits this unit to be easily detached from one system and attached to another PC, XT, PPC, or AT system. This portability can be a most economical asset because it permits one cartridge system to easily back up numerous fixed disk systems as long as each system contains an interface card installed in its system unit.

Another storage device that may warrant reader consideration, especially in a business environment requiring large data storage, is the U.S. Design Corporation CSS-800 Winchester hard disk subsystem. This subsystem is

Fig. 1-10. Maynstream cartridge backup system. (Courtesy of Maynard Electronics.)

Fig. 1-11. U.S. Design Corporation CSS-800 Winchester storage system. (Courtesy of U.S. Design Corporation.)

illustrated in Fig. 1-11 and consists of a controller card installed in one of the PC AT's system expansion slots and the Winchester storage unit. The latter device contains a 70-megabyte Winchester disk drive that is expandable to 280 megabytes of on-line storage as well as a 22-megabyte tape backup unit.

Multifunction Boards

Although the PC AT has eight expansion slots in its system unit, only seven are actually available, since both models are shipped with the diskette and fixed disk controller installed in one expansion slot. After adding a display adapter, a serial/parallel adapter, and perhaps a few memory cards, one may rapidly run out of expansion slots. To alleviate this situation many third-party vendors have introduced multifunction boards that contain several functions on one card and only require the use of a single expansion slot.

Figure 1-12 illustrates the first multifunction board developed for the PC AT. Marketed under the name Advantage, this multifunction board from AST Research can expand the AT's memory to 3 megabytes as well as provide up to two serial ports, a parallel port, and an optional game port. Each Advantage board can be populated with 64K or 256K memory chips and can round out the AT's system board memory to 640K and then continue memory expansion 1 megabyte at a time, permitting up to 3 megabytes of memory to be obtained through the use of a single expansion slot.

Although better known as a video display board, the STB Graphix Plus II can also be classified as a multifunction board. This device, which is illus-

Fig. 1-12. AST Advantage multifunction board. (Courtesy of AST Research, Inc.)

trated in Fig. 1-13, supports both RGB color and monochrome displays, yet occupies only one expansion slot in the PC AT. This board provides full-screen monochrome as well as 16-color graphics for most popular software and software drivers for Lotus 1-2-3, Symphony, and Framework. With the Symphony driver, AT users are provided with 44 lines of text display on their monitor. A

Fig. 1-13. STB Graphix Plus II video board. This board provides AT users with three display modes: 64 by 352 monochrome graphics, 640 by 200 by 4 color graphics, and 320 by 200 by 16 color graphics. (Courtesy of STB Systems, Inc.)

dual monitor support is provided by software that permits users to switch to the appropriate monitor. The board also includes a parallel port or a hard disk controller interface.

Switch versus Expansion

Another interesting device many personal computer users have obtained is what is known as an AB or fallback switch. One such switch, put out by Western Telematic, is illustrated in Fig. 1-14. This instrument switches a common 25-pin connector input to one of two outputs, allowing the user to connect a parallel port from the AT to two printers and to switch from one printer to the other as the need arose. Similarly, we could attach two ATs or an AT and a PC to a common printer if we wished to share a printer between two computers.

Fig. 1-14. Western Telematic AB Switch. An AB or fallback switch permits a common adapter card to share access to two printers or two personal computers to share access to a common printer. (Courtesy of Western Telematic, Inc.)

CHAPTER TWO
System Setup

For most systems, assembling the components of your PC AT in a work area four to six feet from a dual power receptacle will provide adaquate access to power. If many options that are independently powered (such as an acoustic coupler or modem or a printer) are to be added to the system, additional power outlets will be needed. A power strip can be connected to your household receptacle to obtain several additional outlets, or you can use an extension cord. A standard six-plug power strip is recommended, since most include circuit breaker protection against overloads and have a built-in reset button, making it a safer, neater alternative to dangling extension cords.

ISOLATORS AND SURGE PROTECTORS

The electrical environment in which you will install the PC AT may warrant the use of an electronic isolator. Illustrated in Fig. 2-1, the electrical isolator or surge suppressor provides high-voltage spike suppression against possible equipment damage from lightning or motorized machinery as well as such potential surge sources as air conditioners, heaters, and fluorescent light ballasts. A filter-isolator in the device isolates your equipment from potential disruptive efforts of power line noise, and the device itself typically plugs into any standard 120-volt outlet. Thereafter, you can plug the power cords from the AT and its peripheral devices into the sockets on the isolator.

Isolators can be obtained with different amounts of amperage and varying numbers of three-prong sockets. For most PC AT applications, a 15-A, three-prong socket isolator will be sufficient.

Fig. 2-1. Three-socket super isolator. (Courtesy of Electronic Specialists, Inc.)

POWER-ON SELF-TEST

If you wish to immediately ascertain the status of your system unit and keyboard prior to installing any optional equipment, this can be done by performing what is known as the power-on self-test. To accomplish this test you should connect your keyboard to the circular receptacle in the rear of the system unit as illustrated in Fig. 2-2. Next, check the 115V-230V selector switch located above the two power receptacles on the rear of the system unit to ensure that it is in the correct position. For the United States and Canada, this switch should be set at 115V. As indicated in Fig. 2-2, a screwdriver can be used to place the voltage selector switch to its correct position.

If your system unit is in the locked position, insert the tubular key into the lock on the front of the system unit. Turning the key counterclockwise will unlock the system unit. If you are using your system unit for the first time check each diskette drive for the presence of a shipping insert and remove them from each drive prior to their use.

If you are using the IBM monochrome display, its power cord can be connected to the lower left power receptacle on the rear of the system unit,

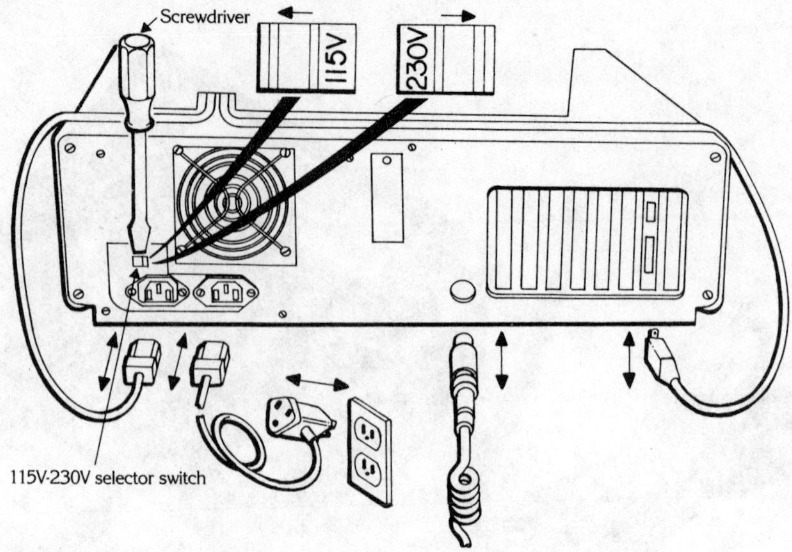

Fig. 2-2. Connecting the keyboard and power cords to the system unit and setting the voltage selector switch.

permitting the system unit power switch to provide power to both the system unit and the monitor as illustrated in Fig. 2-2. The three-prong receptacle at the right is for attaching one end of the system unit's power cord, while the other end of the cord should be connected to a wall outlet, electrical isolator, or power strip. Before you do this, make sure that the power switch on the system unit is in the Off position. If everything is ready, when you turn the power switch on the system unit to the upright, On position, three things will happen. First, the keyboard status lights will blink on and off. Next, a memory test will occur and the amount of memory installed in your system unit followed by the letters "OK" should be displayed in the upper left corner of your screen. After the power-on self-test is completed you should hear one short beep, indicating that your system unit has completed its self-test.

The time required to perform the self-test depends on the amount of memory installed in the system unit and can vary between 13 and 90 seconds. If you did not hear one short beep, there is a high probability that your system unit contains a defect and you may wish to contact the place where you purchased it or try to run the diagnostic diskette contained in the IBM Guide to Operations Manual.

If you purchased your AT system from a dealer who did not install optional equipment you will be required to disassemble the system unit. If your dealer assembled your AT system you may still have to run a setup program if this program was not previously run by the dealer, since this program is required to set the date, time, and installed options. Once setup is run, this information is stored in the CMOS RAM previously described in Chapter 1.

SETUP

When you install your system for the first time, or install certain options in your system unit, or replace the AT's battery, you will have to set the date, time, and installed options. This setup is accomplished by the use of the diagnostic diskette, which configures your system to reflect the equipment installed. To use this diskette you should first power-off all external devices such as printers and TVs, as well as your system unit. After the diagnostic diskette is inserted into drive A (which is the top diskette drive) and the drive lever is closed, turn on all externally attached devices and then turn on the power. Once the power-on self-test is performed, a menu of options will appear on your screen, from which you can select the SETUP option. To successfully run this program you must know what options were installed in your system unit. If your dealer did not furnish you with a list of installed options, you can ascertain what is installed by removing the cover on the system unit. This process is described in the following section, since you must remove the cover to add memory, adapter cards, or additional storage devices as well.

ADDING SYSTEM UNIT OPTIONS

Prior to disassembling the system unit, you should disconnect the keyboard and set it aside. Next, you should ensure that the system unit power switch is off and then disconnect the power cord and all cables from the back of the unit. As a safety precaution, also disconnect the power cord plug from the wall outlet, power strip, or surge protector.

Turning the system unit to allow easy access to the rear, use a flat blade screwdriver to remove the five cover mounting screws as illustrated in the top part of Fig. 2-3. After the screws are removed, set them aside in a convenient place, since they will be needed to fasten the cover when the unit is reassembled. Next, gently lift the system unit and turn it so the front panel with the IBM label is facing you and lower it onto your work area. Then, slide the system unit cover away from the rear and toward you until it slides off the base. This process is illustrated in the bottom part of Fig. 2-3. Set the cover aside.

Inside the system unit there should be at least one expansion card in the eight system expansion slots, since each AT is shipped with a diskette and fixed disk adapter installed in slot 8. In addition, the high-capacity diskette drive comes installed as drive A. Now, turn to the fold-out at the back of the IBM PC AT Installation and Setup manual to record the equipment installed in your system unit (if you haven't previously done so), as well as to denote any additional equipment you will install. This information is required to successfully run the setup program on the Diagnostic diskette, which configures your system for use.

At the rear of the system unit to the right of expansion slot 8 is the battery, which should be connected to the system board connector if not done

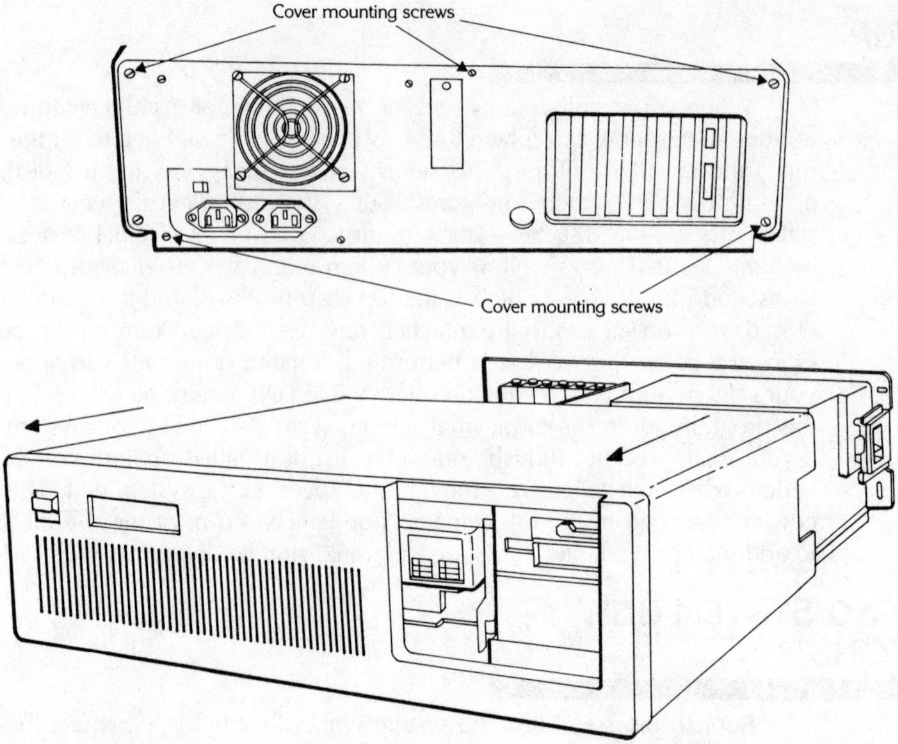

Fig. 2-3. To remove the system unit cover, first remove the five cover mounting screws and then slide the cover forward.

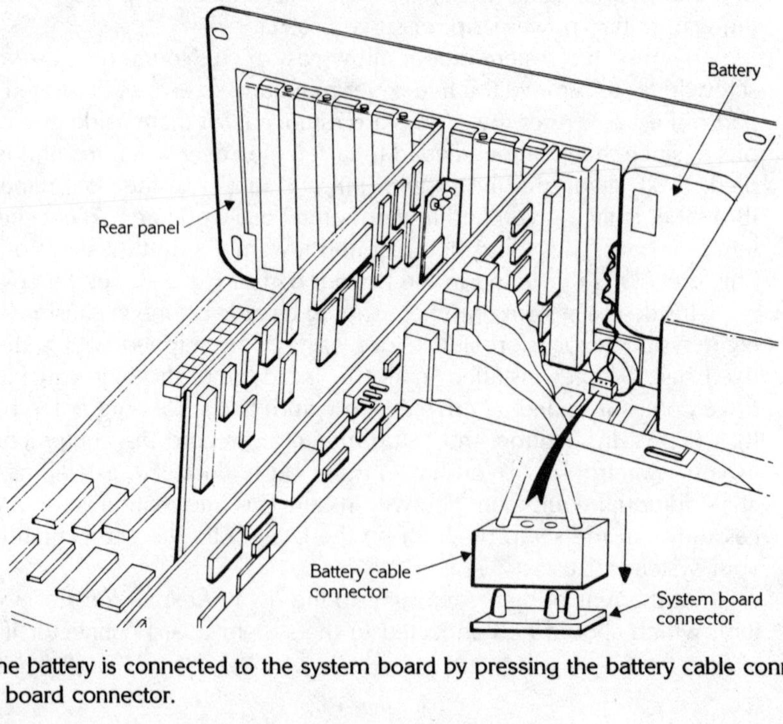

Fig. 2-4. The battery is connected to the system board by pressing the battery cable connector into the system board connector.

so by your dealer. To connect the battery requires you to locate the battery cable connector attached to the battery and to press it into the system board connector as shown in Fig. 2-4.

On-Board Memory Expansion

The minimum on-board RAM is 256K bytes, since this is the amount of memory installed in the basic model of the AT. In the lower left portion of the system unit you will find either two or four rows of nine memory modules. If only two rows are installed, you have a 256K system, while four rows means the maximum 512K bytes of on-board RAM is installed.

To install the 256K RAM memory kit to bring on-board memory up to 512K will require the removal of any adapters installed in expansion slots 1 through 6. Before you do this, however, you should ground yourself by touching a metal part of the system unit or another device to prevent static damage from occuring.

If you have adapters installed in slots 1 through 6, they can be removed by first turning the screws that hold the adapters in place in a counterclockwise direction as illustrated in Fig. 2-5. After the screws are removed from each adapter, they should be placed in a convenient location, since they will be required to refasten each adapter to its system expansion slot when the adapter is reinstalled. Once the screw is removed, the adapter can be removed from the expansion slot by grasping it at the top and lifting it upward.

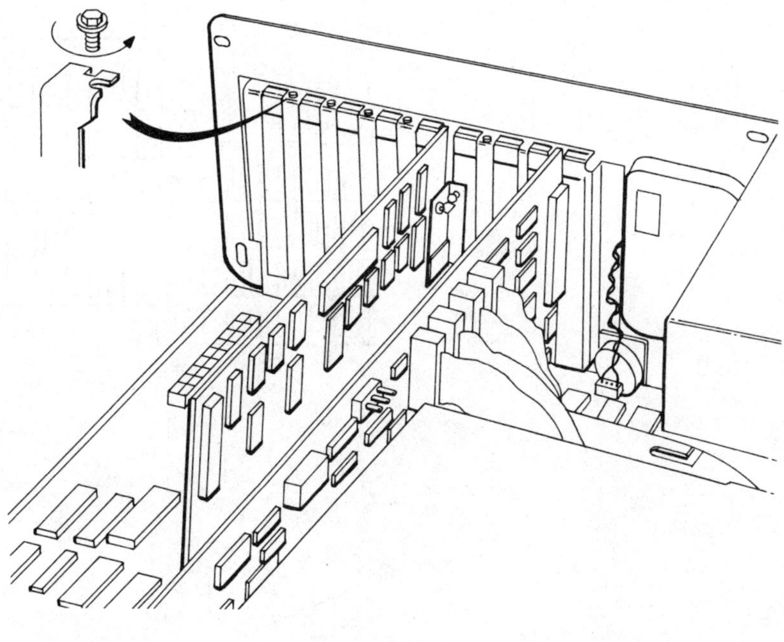

Fig. 2-5. Adapter cards can be removed by unfastening and removing the screws that hold the adapters in place.

Make a note as to which slot it was removed from and place the adapter in a safe place (they can be damaged if they should fall).

Once the adapters are removed, you are ready to insert your memory modules. Each module has a notch that must be aligned with the notch of the connector on the system board to be properly installed as illustrated in Fig. 2-6. Nine memory modules are required for each 128K addition, since each memory byte on the AT includes a parity bit for memory error-status checking. In Fig. 2-6 note the location of the factory-installed memory kit of 256K bytes, which is standard on all ATs. Once you have added your 256K memory kit, your on-board memory will be 512K bytes.

The pins on the modules are easily bent and must be aligned with the connector before pressing into place. The left part of Fig. 2-6 shows a memory module being inserted into a connector on the system board. Note that if you fail to properly align the module when you insert it into the connector, you can remove the module with a device known as a module puller or "dip puller." This tweezer type device can be purchased at most electronics stores.

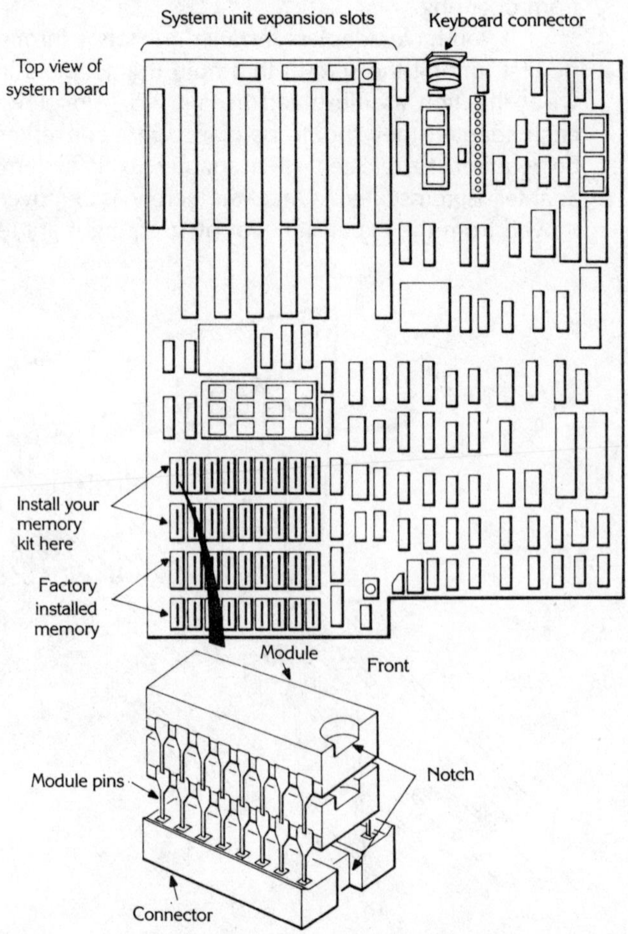

Fig. 2-6. The notch in each memory module should be aligned with the notch on the system board to be properly installed.

It is placed over each end of the module and can be gently tilted back and forth to remove the module from the connector it was inserted into. If any pins are bent, you can use a pair of regular tweezers to carefully straighten them prior to reinserting the module into the connector. You can also use a small flat-blade screwdriver to remove a module by inserting it under the module and gently lifting it up.

Once the memory modules are installed, you should install any adapters you previously removed by holding the adapter by the top of the card and pressing it firmly into its expansion slot. When it is in its expansion slot, fasten it to the system unit by installing the adapter mounting screw you previously removed.

DISPLAY ADAPTERS

Two of the more common display adapters used with the AT are the IBM monochrome display and printer adapter and the IBM color/graphics monitor adapter. Each of these display adapters must be installed in expansion slot 1 or 7. Since your PC AT comes with support brackets installed for all expansion slots except slot 1, you may first have to remove an expansion slot cover if you wish to insert your display adapter into slot 7. This is accomplished by removing the screw that holds the expansion slot cover in place by turning it counterclockwise as illustrated in Fig. 2-7.

After the expansion slot cover is removed, you should save it so that if you remove the adapter from that slot at a later date, you could recover the gap. Otherwise, the cover will not be needed. After the cover is removed, grasp the adapter by the top of the card and press it firmly into the expansion slot, ensuring that the adapter falls into the support bracket. Then install the screw you previously removed to fasten the adapter.

Once your display adapter or adapters are installed, you should then set

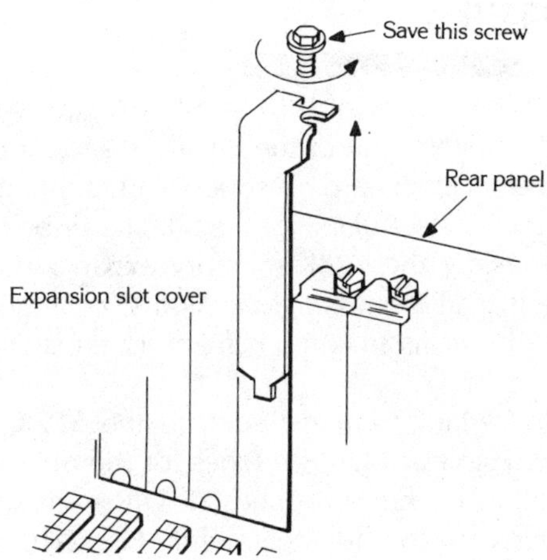

Fig. 2-7. Expansion slot covers can be removed by removing the screw that holds the slot cover in place.

the display switch on the system board. The setting of this switch will govern the display adapter that will be used when you turn the system unit power on. If the monochrome display and printer adapter is to be the primary display, the switch should be pushed to the rear of the system unit as indicated in Fig. 2-8. If the color/graphics is to be the primary display, the switch should be pushed in the opposite direction.

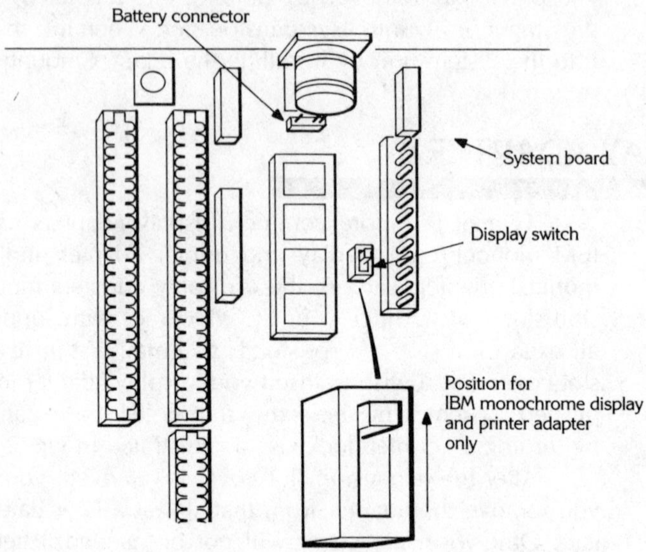

Fig. 2-8. The display switch should be pushed toward the rear of the system unit if the monochrome display and printer adapter is to be the primary display. If the color/graphics adapter is to be the primary display, the switch should be pushed in the opposite direction.

OTHER ADAPTERS

A wide variety of IBM and third-party vendor adapters can be installed inside the system unit of the AT. Care should be taken to ascertain which expansion slots each card must be inserted into and any configuration rules that govern the successful use of the adapter to be installed. As an example of this, let us consider the 128K memory expansion option adapter card. This card must be installed only in expansion slots 2 through 6 and requires the system board to be at its maximum memory capacity of 512K bytes prior to its installation.

On certain adapters, such as the 512K memory expansion cards, you must set a series of DIP switches for the option to work. Figure 2-9 illustrates the location of the two banks of DIP switches contained on the IBM 512K memory expansion adapters, while Fig. 2-10 indicates the switch settings for each adapter one can install. A ball-point pen or similar object can be used to set the correct position of each switch.

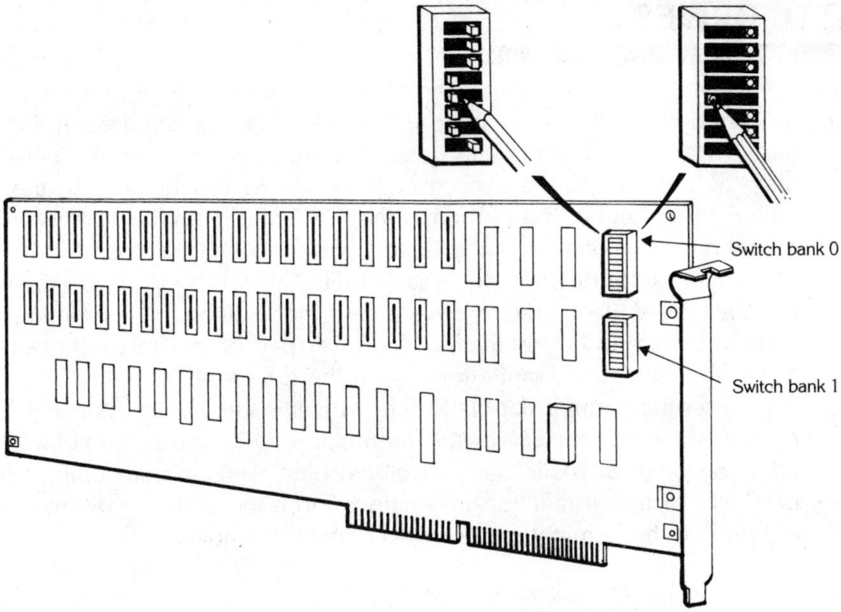

Fig. 2-9. The installation of the IBM 512K memory expansion adapter requires the setting of two banks of DIP switches.

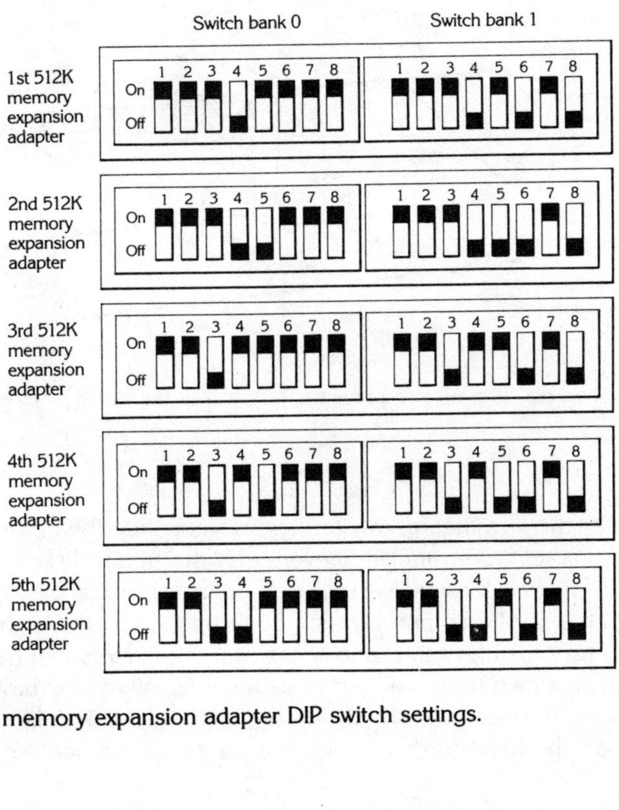

Fig. 2-10. 512K memory expansion adapter DIP switch settings.

Diskette Drives

You can install a second high-capacity diskette drive or a double-sided diskette drive in the lower portion of the storage housing area in the system unit. To install either diskette drive, you must first remove the beige cover plate by unscrewing the two cover plate screws that fasten it to the system unit as shown in Fig. 2-11. Then, remove the four mounting screws and three mounting clips, of which the upper two screws fasten the standard high-capacity diskette drive to the system unit. This will enable you to slide the previously installed diskette drive a few inches forward, permitting you to cable the drive to be installed in the lower part of the storage housing area. Next, locate the terminating resistor on the drive to be installed and remove it by inserting a small flat-blade screwdriver under the resistor and lifting it off. On some diskette drives this terminating resistor may be colored black, while on other drives it may be colored blue. Thus, it is recommended that one refer to the installation instructions furnished with the diskette drive to ensure that the terminating resistor is correctly removed.

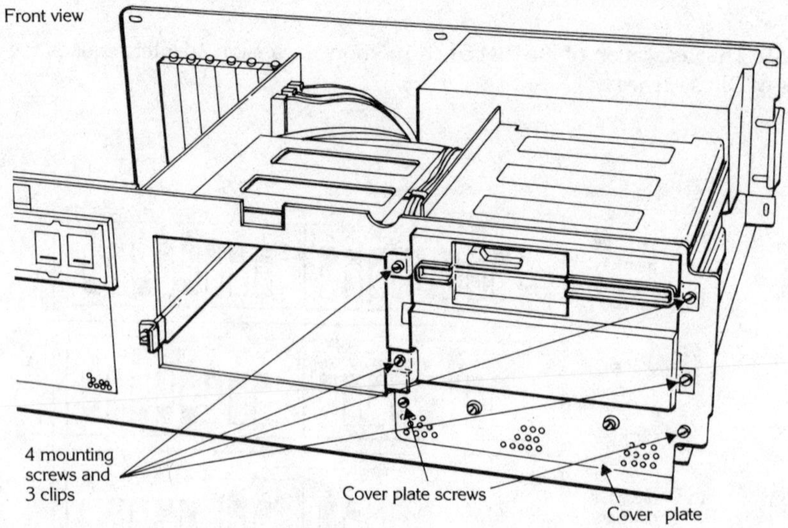

Fig. 2-11. To install a second diskette drive requires the removal of the cover plate from the system unit base.

Once the terminating resistor is removed, slide the drive into the center slot of the system unit until it is even with the upper diskette drive that was previously moved forward several inches. Next, locate the signal cable that connects the hard disk and diskette drive adapter to the high-capacity fixed disk. As Fig. 2-12 illustrates, one of the four connectors will be labeled B and must be connected to the second diskette drive. When you have identified the appropriate drive connector, you should align its locating key with the locating slot on the diskette drive, which is an edged surface area on the upper

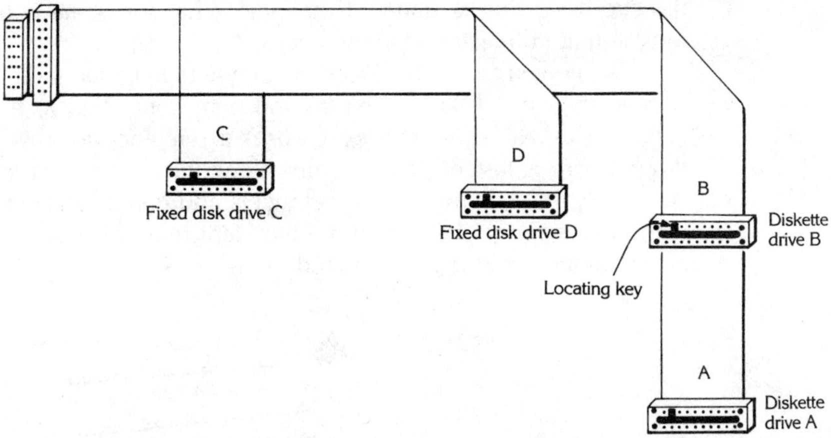

Fig. 2-12. The connector on the signal cable labeled B must be used to connect the second diskette drive to the diskette and fixed disk adapter.

right-hand portion of the drive. Once they are aligned, press the connector firmly into place as shown in Fig. 2-13.

After the signal cable is attached, a power connector must be attached to operate the diskette drive. The power cable has a four-hole connector labeled P12 and is connected to four wires that run back to the power supply. The P12 connector should be inserted into the four-prong connector located on the upper right corner of the diskette drive. Since the high-capacity

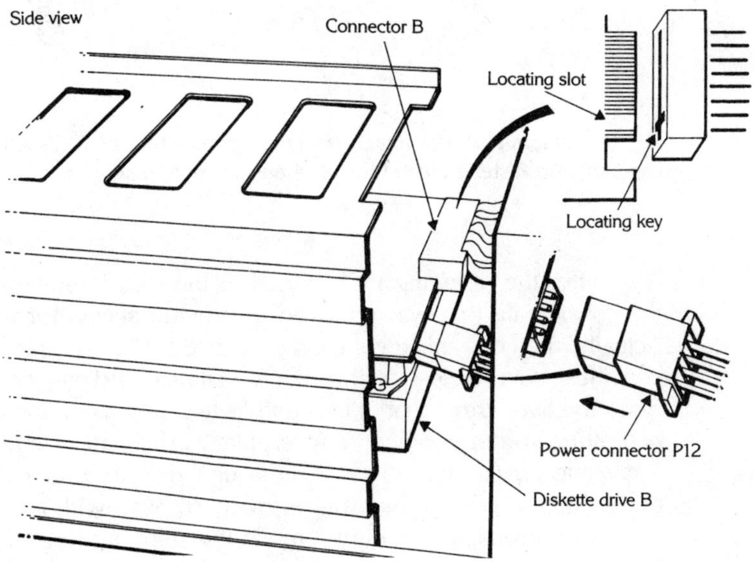

Fig. 2-13. The signal cable connector labeled B and the P12 power connector must be attached to the second diskette drive.

diskette drive that is standard equipment has the same connector, you can look at that connector as a reference.

Before you fasten the drives to the system unit, you must connect a ground wire to the new diskette. The ground wire connected to the standard high-capacity diskette drive can be used as a reference for this installation. This ground wire is fastened to and runs along the system unit to the left of drive A. Once the following wire attachments and connectors are made, both diskette drives should be slid into the system unit and fastened with four clips and mounting screws as illustrated in Fig. 2-14.

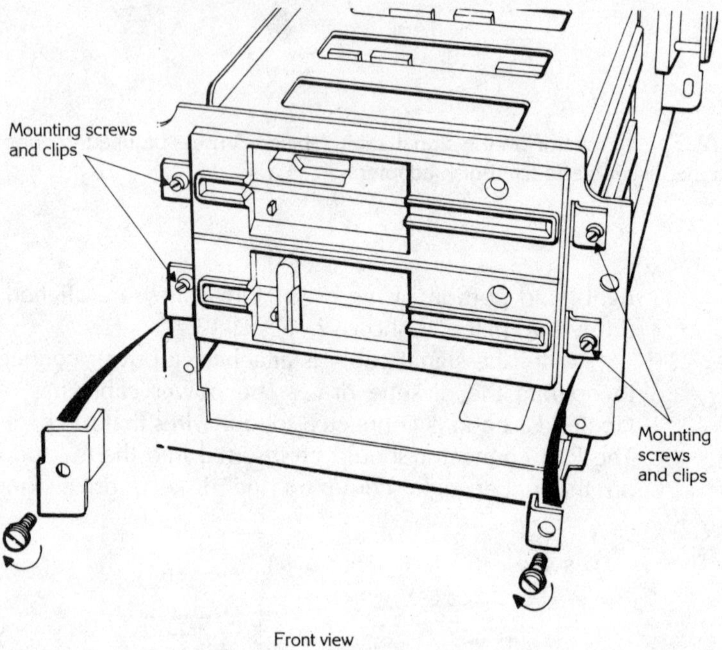

Fig. 2-14. After the connectors and wire attachments are completed, both diskette drives should be slid into the system unit and fastened with four clips and mounting screws.

After the diskettes are fastened to the system unit, you can then install the cover plate that was removed to provide access for the second diskette. Actually, the cover plate contains a diskette face plate and a cover plate. Since you must have access to the newly installed diskette drive, you should remove the two screws that hold the diskette face plate to the cover plate, thereby permitting you to remove the face plate as shown in Fig. 2-15. Then you can screw the cover plate to the system unit directly under the second diskette drive. Since diskette drives are normally shipped with an insert to protect the read/write heads, you should remove the shipping insert from the drive prior to its use.

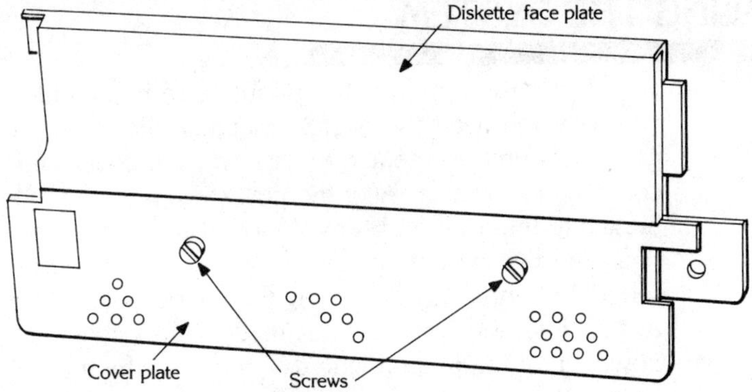

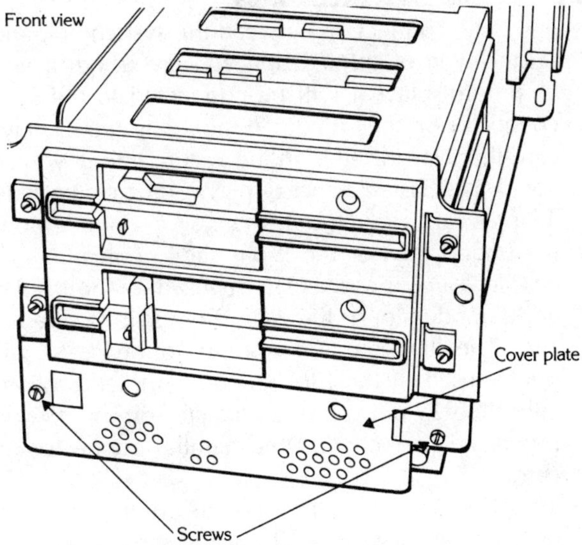

Fig. 2-15. After the diskettes have been fastened to the system unit, remove the diskette face plate from the cover plate and fasten the cover plate to the system unit.

FIXED DISK DRIVE

Up to two fixed disk drives can be installed in your system unit. When installing a fixed disk drive, it is very important to handle it with the utmost care, since dropping, shaking, or rough handling could damage the drive and void the warranty. You should carefully read the installation instructions furnished with the fixed disk before you install it. Because of the sensitivity of this device to shock and vibration, it is recommended that the novice seek professional assistance for the installation of the drive.

CABLING THE SYSTEM

Once the appropriate options have been added to your system unit or you have removed its cover to ascertain the options for use in the setup program, it is time to replace the system unit cover and cable the major system components together. After the cover is replaced, the entire system unit should be gently lifted up and turned so that the back of the unit faces you. At this time, the five mounting screws that were previously removed should be inserted and tightened by turning them clockwise with a flat-blade screwdriver. At this time, the system unit is ready to be cabled to your peripheral devices, powered on, and reconfigured if necessary by the use of the setup program.

Device Connection

The connection between the system unit and your display will be based on the type of display unit you are using. If you are using the IBM monochrome display, it will be connected to the system unit via the 9-pin shell connector on the combined monochrome display and parallel printer adapter card that was installed in the system unit. If you are using the IBM color monitor or a television, either display can be connected to the color/graphics monitor adapter card mounted in the system unit. A monitor can be cabled to either the phono jack or the 9-pin shell connector on the color/graphics monitor adapter card. If a television is used as the display, it must be connected via an RF modulator to the 4-pin Berg strip on the card.

The attachment of a printer to the PC AT will vary, based on the type of printer used. If the IBM graphics printer is obtained, you can connect it to either the 25-pin printer connector on the monochrome display and parallel printer adapter card or the parallel connector on the serial/parallel adapter card.

If you wish to use a serial printer, you must interconnect that type of device to the system unit via the serial connector on the IBM serial/parallel adapter. As previously discussed in Chapter 1, you will require a cable to connect this 9-pin connector to a standard 25-pin connector commonly used on cables. This adapter card generates the serial bit stream required to operate a serial printer. Other devices that require a serial bit stream include a modem or coupler, as well as a graphic tablet. Such devices will also be connected to the system unit via a cable connection to the serial connector on the IBM serial/parallel adapter card.

After the PC AT is cabled and powered on, the power-on self-test will be initialized. A cursor will appear on the screen and a beep will indicate the successful operation of all components, after which a message asking you to enter the date or displaying the message "IBM Personal Computer" will appear on your display. If one or more actions of this three-sequence operation fail to materialize, a problem may exist with your system. To assist you in resolving operational or system failures, you should refer to the IBM Guide to Operations for the appropriate instructions concerning the use of the IBM diagnostic programs.

MOVING THE SYSTEM

If you have an enhanced AT with a fixed disk you should execute the IBM diagnostic program and select option 3, "Preparing System for Moving." This program "parks" the read/write heads of the fixed disk at a predefined location to prevent the loss of data due to vibrations in moving the system.

MIXING SYSTEMS

Although the preceding discussion focused on the installation of IBM components into the AT's system unit, any plug-compatible adapter card, monitor, or printer can be added to the PC AT. In mixing and matching hardware in your system unit, it is recommended that you first ascertain whether the addition of non-IBM hardware will invalidate your IBM warranty.

CHAPTER THREE

Storage Media and Keyboard Operation

The IBM PC AT uses 5¼-inch diskettes and fixed disks for storing information. Figure 3-1 shows the 5¼-inch diskette with its protective jacket, which shields the uncovered index hole and exposed recording surface during storage. Since every AT has at least one diskette drive, and diskettes provide us with a mechanism to exchange information with other personal computer users, we will examine diskette storage in this chapter.

DISKETTES

The top section of Fig. 3-2 illustrates the various parts of the diskette with respect to its permanent protective jacket. The lower part provides a detailed view of the contents of the diskette.

The diskette is inserted into the diskette drive so that the end with the dual notches enters forward with the label side of the diskette facing upward. When the diskette is being read or information is being recorded on it, the diskette will spin inside its jacket. The read/write head of the diskette drive will come into contact through the head aperture, which is a slot in the protective jacket through which reading or recording of information occurs.

Tracks, Bytes, and Sectors

Information in the form of data or programs is written onto and read from the diskette along concentric circles called tracks as illustrated in Fig. 3-3. There are 40 tracks on a conventional diskette that are numbered from 0 to 39, while a high-capacity diskette contains 80 tracks, numbered from 0 to 79. Depending on the type of diskette drive used to format the diskette and the personal computer users FORMAT command specification, each track can be subdivided into 8, 9, or 15 sectors, and each sector can store 512 8-bit bytes of

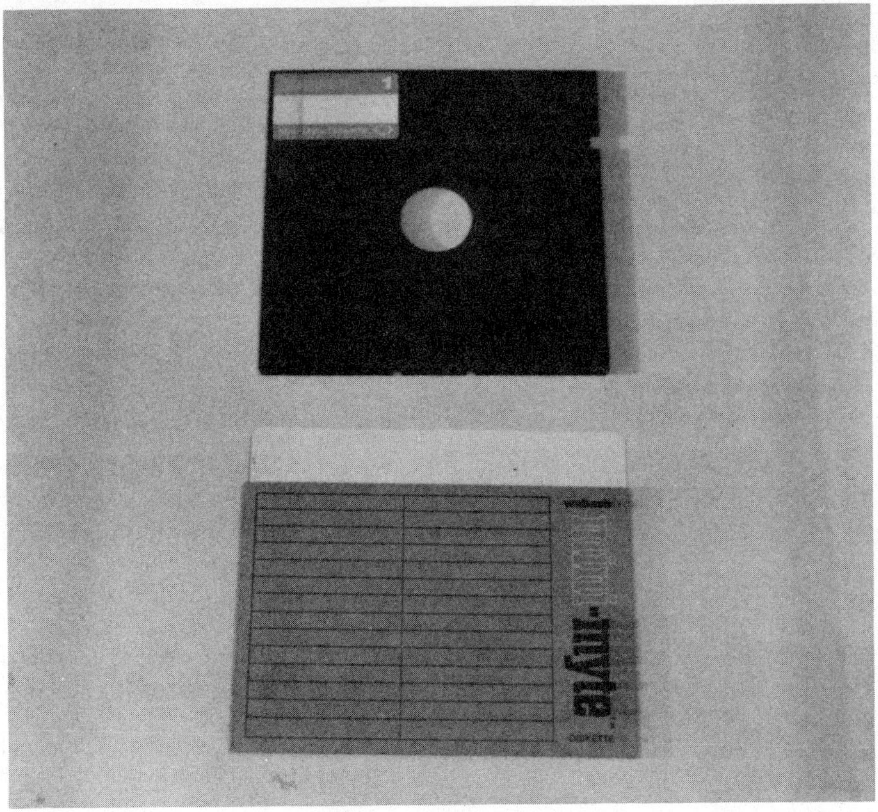

Fig. 3-1. A 5¼-inch diskette.

information, where a byte represents 8 bits or one character of data. Each time the computer reads information from or writes information onto a diskette, a minimum of one sector's worth of information is read or written. The FORMAT command prepares a diskette to receive information, checks the diskette for bad spots, and builds a directory to hold information about the files that will eventually be written onto it. This command, as well as other operating system commands, will be covered in Chapter 4.

Diskette and Drive Compatibility

Both double-sided and high-capacity diskette drives can be installed in the PC AT. The double-sided drive can read and write to single-sided and double-sided diskettes but cannot read or write to high-capacity diskettes. Although the high-capacity diskette drive can read data contained on single- and double-sided diskettes, if you write on any of these two diskette types using a high-capacity diskette drive you may not be able to read the diskette in a standard double-sided drive. Thus, it is recommended that high-capacity diskettes be used in the high-capacity diskette drive if you wish to write in-

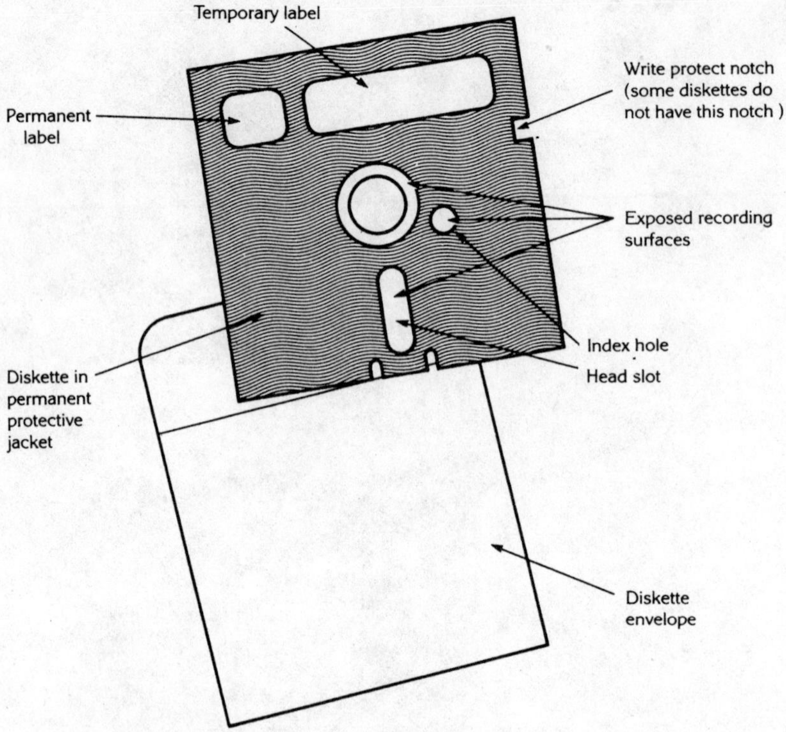

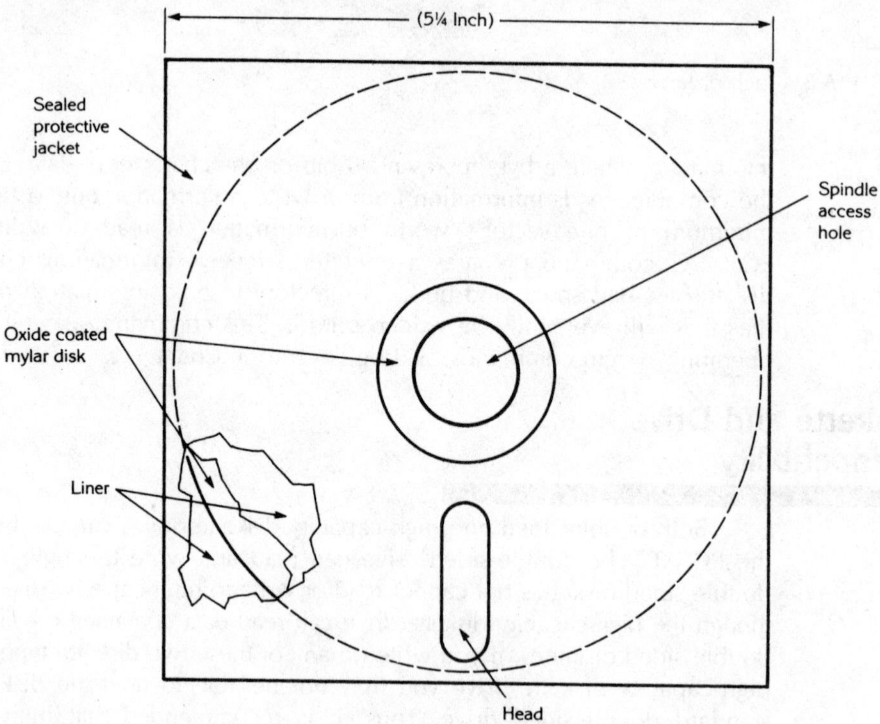

Fig. 3-2. The parts of a diskette.

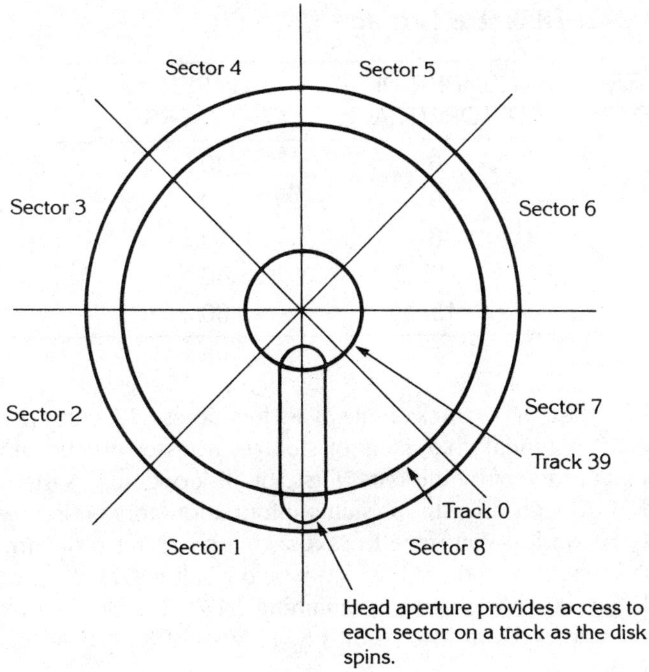

Fig. 3-3. Diskette format.

formation onto a diskette using that drive. Table 3-1 summarizes the diskette and drive compatibility between double-sided and high-capacity drives.

Table 3-1. Diskette and Drive Compatibility Reading/Writing

DOUBLE-SIDED DRIVE	HIGH-CAPACITY DRIVE
Single-sided diskette	Single-sided diskette*
Double-sided diskette	Double-sided diskette*
	High-capacity diskette

*If you write on any of these diskette types using a high-capacity drive you may not be able to read the diskette in a single- or double-sided drive.

Storage Capacity

The theoretical storage capacity of a diskette will depend on the number of formatted sectors per track, while the actual storage on the diskette will be based upon the manner in which data is written onto the diskette. Table 3-2 indicates the theoretical storage capacity of single- and double-sided diskettes. Note that only a high-capacity diskette drive is capable of writing 15 sectors per track and should only do so when a high-capacity diskette is installed in that drive.

As an example of how the actual quantity of data stored on a diskette can be less than the theoretical storage capacity let us consider a single-sided

Table 3-2. Diskette Storage Capacity

NUMBER OF SIDES	NUMBER OF SECTORS/TRACK	NUMBER OF TRACKS	STORAGE CAPACITY BYTES
1	8	40	163,840
1	9	40	184,320
2	8	40	327,680
2	9	40	368,640
2	15	80	1,228,800

diskette. Although 40 tracks times 8 sectors times 512 bytes per sector results in 163,840 potential characters of storage, a lesser number normally results from actual usage of the diskette. First, the disk operating system uses portions of track 0 of each diskette for status information concerning the files on that diskette. Second, if you were to save a one-character program, one sector of 512 bytes would be required, which would result in 511 bytes of storage being wasted. Similarly, a program containing 513 characters would require two sectors for storage and also result in 511 wasted 8-bit byte locations on that diskette.

To find a particular track, the diskette drive will move its read/write head to a point on the diskette where the desired track is located. Two methods are used by most diskette drives to locate a specific sector on the track. Each method uses a hole punched in the diskette jacket that is known as the index hole. When the diskette spins in its jacket, the diskette will pass under the index hole once every revolution. A light source in the diskette drive will focus through the diskette's index hole and serve as a sensor to denote when the index hole is aligned with the hole in the jacket. This position will mark the first sector on a track, and each additional sector on the track will be a function of the diskette's rotation time. The use of one index hole in the diskette is known as "soft sectoring." The second method of locating sectors is by placing a hole on the diskette before each sector. Here, the position of a particular sector on a track would be obtained by counting the number of holes that pass under the index hole opening on the jacket. This method of sector location is called "hard sectoring." The drives on the IBM PC AT use soft-sectored, single-sided, single-density (SSS); soft-sectored, double-sided, single-density (SDS); and soft-sectored, double-sided, high-density (SDH) floppy diskettes. The latter diskettes would be used with the high-capacity double-sided diskette drives that operate with the PC AT.

Care and Handling

Information on the diskette can be located quickly by the disk operating system reading track 0 to obtain the track and sector number that defines the location where a particular program or data file resides. If the head aperture opening on the diskette should become dirty, it may not only prevent access to a particular program but could also prevent access to all the information on the diskette if track 0 became unreadable. Therefore, you should be extremely careful when handling and storing diskettes. If possible, always consider the following factors with respect to diskette handling and storage.

- Never touch the exposed recording surfaces of the diskette formed by the head aperture and index hole.
- Due to the fragile nature of diskettes, always try to store them in an upright position in their envelope to ensure that they do not bend or sag.
- Never place heavy objects on top of your diskettes.
- As soon as you remove your diskette from the drive, place it in its envelope to prevent the accumulation of dust from occuring on its head slot.
- Store your diskettes in appropriate storage boxes away from sunlight and other heat sources as well as such magnetic field sources as telephones, electronic calculators, and other electronic equipment.
- If you label the information on your diskette, do so only with a felt tip pen to avoid damaging the diskette. Write on the labels, whenever possible, before putting them on the diskette.

Write Protection

The write protect notch (Fig. 3-1, top) provides the mechanism to safeguard information recorded on your diskette from accidental erasure. In order to use this feature, you must place a tab over the notch so that data already recorded on the diskette cannot be erased or recorded over. Many purchased programs such as the IBM disk operating system come without this notch, so that you don't have to take any action to protect the information stored on these diskettes; the protection is built in. Be aware, however, that some purchased programs do have the write protect notch, and you will have to cover it to protect data. If your requirements for protection change at a later date, you can always peel the tab off the notch to permit new data to be recorded onto the diskette.

KEYBOARD USE

The AT's keyboard contains 84 keys and is divided into three sections as illustrated in Fig. 3-4. The left-hand section is comprised of 10 function keys, while the typewriter key area is in the middle section. A numeric keypad is in the third section on the right-hand side of the keyboard. In the upper right corner are three status lights that display the status of the Capitals (Caps) Lock, Numeric (Num) Lock, and the Scroll Lock keys.

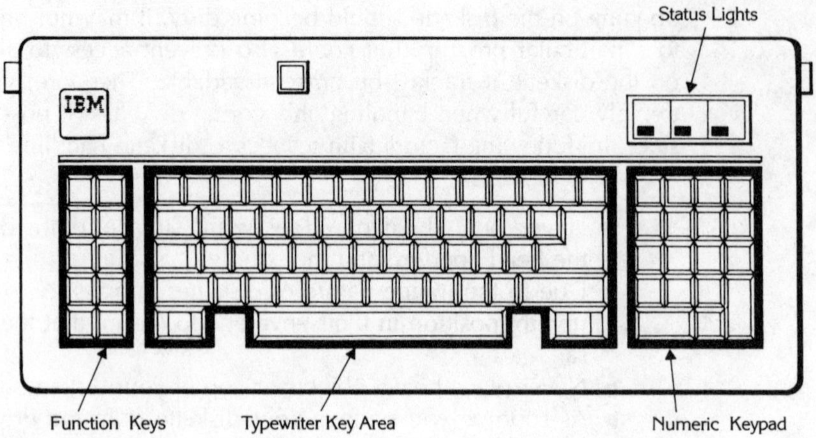

Fig. 3-4. Keyboard unit.

Function Keys

Examine the keyboard illustrated in Fig. 3-4. On the left-hand side of the keyboard are two columns of five keys labeled F1 through F10. These keys are known as program function keys and can be used to make your PC AT perform predefined commands. If unaltered by programming, the function keys have been assigned for use with your IBM BASIC program to generate the predefined commands listed in Table 3-3 when depressed.

Table 3-3. Function Key Commands

KEY	COMMAND	DESCRIPTION
F1	LIST	Displays the lines of the program on the monitor display or television
F2	RUN	Causes the program to begin execution from the first line of the program
F3	LOAD	Reads designated program from auxiliary storage and stores it in main memory
F4	SAVE	Stores your program on the diskette or fixed disk
F5	CONT	Restarts a program after it has been interrupted by a Stop or Ctrl Break
F6	LPT1:	Refers to line printer and transfers data from the screen to the printer
F7	TRON	Means trace on and causes the line numbers of the program to be displayed as each program line is executed
F8	TROFF	Means trace off and cancels command F7
F9	KEY	Changes the function of other function keys
F10	SCREEN	Returns the program to character mode from graphics mode and turns off color

Programming Assistance Keys

Surrounding the normal typewriter keys in the middle section of the keyboard is a series of keys that can be used for assistance in writing, updating, and executing programs. These keys are listed in Table 3-4 along with a description of their operation. Examples of the effective use of most of these keys will be covered shortly; however, read the description of the result of each key command operation to become familiar with the usage of each key.

Table 3-4. Programming Assistance Keys

KEY	MEANING	DESCRIPTION
|← →|	Tab	Performs a tab function similar to a typewriter; tabs are set every eight characters
Ctrl	Control	Always used with a second or third key to perform a function or command
⇧ Shift	Shift	Changes lowercase letters to capitals or capitals to lowercase letters
Alt	Alternate	Used with alphabetic keys to generate BASIC key words from abbreviated data entry
←	Backspace	Moves the cursor to the left and removes one character for each key stroke
Enter ↵	Enter	Indicates the logical end of a line of input by moving the cursor from the last character on one line to the first character of the next line
	Space	Moves the cursor one position to the right
Caps Lock	Capitals Lock	A toggle key that causes letters to be typed in upper case (capitals); pressing the key again causes a return to lower case

Numeric Key Pad

When the Num Lock key is pressed, the numeric key pad will become activated. This will cause the cursor keys to switch to number keys and the shift keys to work in reverse. This key pad is arranged like a calculator and permits the easy entry of large quantities of numeric data.

With the Num Lock key activated, keys 1 through 9 on the numeric key pad produce the digits 1 through 9, while the [. Del] key produces a "decimal point" and the [0 Ins] key results in a "zero."

Cursor Control and Editing

When the Num Lock key is not activated, the numeric key pad keys take on alternate meanings and function as a cursor control and screen editing mechanism. The alternate meanings of the numeric key pad keys are indicated in Table 3-5.

In addition to the previously discussed keys on the numeric key pad, there are several additional keys that can be used to perform special functions.

Table 3-5. Alternate Numeric Key Pad Functions

KEY	DESCRIPTION
7 Home	"Home" repositions the cursor to the first character of the top line of the screen
8 ↑	Moves the cursor up one line for each key stroke
4 ←	Moves the cursor to the left one character position for each key stroke
6 →	Moves the cursor to the right one character position for each key stroke
2 ↓	Moves the cursor down one line for each key stroke
1 End	"End" positions the cursor at the last character on the current line
Del	"Deletes" the character where the cursor is positioned
0 Ins	"Insert" sets the keyboard to the insert mode of operation; other keys entered to the right of the cursor and all data to the right will move to the right; terminate the insert mode by pressing the Ins key again or press the Enter key if all line modification has been completed

Table 3-6. Multi-Key Program and Screen Control

KEY	FUNCTION	DESCRIPTION
Ctrl + Scroll Lock/Break	Break	Causes the execution of a program to terminate and identifies the line where it stops
Ctrl + Num Lock	Pause	Suspends program execution; press any key to continue program execution
Ctrl + →|	Tab	Moves the cursor to the next word on the current line
Ctrl + |←	Reverse Tab	Moves the cursor to the previous word on the current line
Ctrol + Home	Clear Screen	Moves all information from the screen and moves the cursor to the first character position on the first line
Ctrl + Alt + Del	System Reset	Causes a reload from the diskette or fixed disk
Shift + PrtSc	Print Screen	Causes all data on the screen to be printed

The Escape (Esc) key will perform functions defined in your operating system or by the application program used when depressed. Normally, this key is used to remove the line that the cursor is on for corrections, but does not delete the line from memory.

When the Scroll Lock key is pressed, the Scroll Lock light will be illuminated on your keyboard. When this key is pressed once, the cursor up and cursor down keys will move text up or down one line and lock the cursor to the line it is on. This key can also be used in conjunction with the Control (Ctrl) key to stop a job, as indicated in Table 3-6. Once the Scroll Lock light is on, it can be turned off by pressing the Scroll Lock key again, which will also turn off the Scroll Lock mode of operation.

In the upper right-hand portion of the numeric key pad is the System (Sys) key. Like the Esc key, this key has its functions defined by the operating system or through the application program you are using.

Just under the Sys key on the numeric key pad is a key labeled PrtSc. The Print Screen (PrtSc) key will display an asterisk (*) when depressed; however, if you press and hold a shift key and then press this key, the data that is displayed on your screen will be printed.

Multi-Key Operational Combinations

The depression of two or three keys simultaneously can be employed to perform a series of unique program control and screen control functions. These functions are listed in Table 3-6. Additional multi-key operational combinations are applicable only to the use of IBM's disk operating system and are described in Chapter 4.

SYSTEM SETUP

Once you have connected the battery in the system unit and installed any optional devices, you are ready to perform the system setup. The system setup requires the installation of the diagnostic diskette and allows you to set the date and time as well as to denote the equipment installed in the system unit.

With power to the system off, insert the diagnostic diskette in diskette drive A, which is the top drive in each PC AT system. After power is turned on, the following display will appear on the screen.

```
The IBM Personal Computer
DIAGNOSTICS
Version 1.00
(C)Copyright IBM Corp.
   1981,1982,1983,1984

SELECT AN OPTION

0 - SYSTEM CHECKOUT
1 - FORMAT DISKETTE
2 - COPY DISKETTE
3 - PREPARE SYSTEM FOR MOVING
4 - SETUP
9 - END DIAGNOSTICS

SELECT THE ACTION DESIRED
?
```

Once option 4 is selected, you will be prompted to set or verify the time, date, and options installed in the system unit. If this is the first time you have used SETUP, set the preceding items and subsequent uses of SETUP will allow you to verify or reset those items.

CHAPTER FOUR

The Disk Operating System

The disk operating system (DOS) can be viewed as a collection of programs that permits a computer system to supervise its own operations, automatically or under operator control, calling in program routines, languages, and data as required for a continuous throughput of a series of jobs. It is the central nervous system of the computer. Normally, an operating system consists of a nucleus of three elements—control programs, processing programs, and data management programs. The control programs provide for an automatic or enhanced operator control of the resources of the computer and permit an orderly and efficient flow of jobs through the computer system.

The processing programs are invoked as required by the control programs and consist of language processors such as compilers or interpreters that compile or interpret source programs as well as service programs that perform linkage between programs.

Data management programs are used by the operating system to control the organization and access of data used by the application programs you will develop or purchase. As an entity, the programs that make up the operating system provide significant advantages not only in the operating efficiency area but also as an aid to programmers. In the latter case, the operating system provides easy access and usage of the higher level languages, diagnostic aids, and libraries of programs you may wish to use.

The IBM DOS is a collection of programs on a 5¼-inch diskette designed to facilitate running programs, create and manage files, and simplify functions using such devices as the line printer and diskette drives that may be attached to your computer.

Storage Device Designators

Before you can start DOS, you must first consider the designator or specifier used for each storage device. This is because the manner in which DOS is started will depend on the storage devices attached to your system.

The high-capacity diskette drive is referred to as drive A by the disk operating system, while the first fixed disk is referenced by drive specifier C. If you have a second diskette drive installed in your system unit, its specifier will be the letter B, while a second fixed disk will be referenced by the letter D.

Bringing up DOS from Drive A

There are two ways to start DOS. If power to the system unit is off, you can insert DOS in drive A and close the drive's slot cover. After turning power on, DOS will be automatically loaded into memory after the internal power-on self-test is performed. If your system already has power on, you can perform what is known as a system reset to load DOS. This is accomplished by inserting the DOS diskette into drive A, closing the drive's slot cover, and then pressing the Del key while holding down the Ctrl and Alt keys.

Once DOS is loaded, it will automatically search its diskette for a file named COMMAND.COM and proceed to load this file into memory. This file is a command processor that will accept and process the DOS commands you enter from the keyboard or from a "batch" file containing a list of DOS commands.

After the DOS command processor is loaded, the following message will appear on your screen. Note that the execution of the setup program (contained on the diagnostic diskette) prior to bringing up DOS would result in the current date being the correct date, since the AT's clock/calendar is powered by the battery in the system unit.

```
Current date is Tue 1-01-1980
Enter new date:
```

You may enter any month, day, and year as long as they fall within the following ranges:

month (m) is 1 or 2 digits from 1 to 12
day (d) is 1 or 2 digits from 1 to 31
year (y) is 2 digits from 80 to 99 or 4 digits from 1980 to 2099

The delimiters between the month, day, and year must be either a slash (/) or hypen (-). If you enter an invalid date or delimiter, DOS will repeat the message as shown below.

```
Enter new date: 11-23/84
Enter new date: 11-23-84
```

Once an acceptable date has been entered, DOS will display a message similar to this:

```
Current time is 0:01:49.85
Enter new time:
```

Note that the time is displayed as follows:

hours:minutes:seconds.hundredths of a second

You may enter any time as long as it falls within the following ranges:

hours is 1 or 2 digits between 0 and 23
minutes is 1 or 2 digits between 0 and 59
seconds is 1 or 2 digits between 0 and 59
hundredths of a second is 1 or 2 digits between 0 and 99.

When entering the time, be sure to enter a colon (:) after each time element except hundredths of a second, where you must enter a period—a slash (/) or a hyphen (-) will not work.

Since time is entered in military fashion, with 1 p.m. expressed as 13 hours, be sure to convert the appropriate hour of the day to military time format. You should also note that you may enter no time at all, just the hour or additional time information down to hundredths of a second.

Once DOS is ready, two lines of information concerning the version of DOS and a copyright notice will appear and the prompt A> will be displayed. The character A signifies that DOS will look at the diskette in drive A to process any file reference commands that are entered without a specified device name. The complete DOS initialization procedure is shown below.

```
Current date is Thu 11-01-1984
Enter new date (mm-dd-yy):
Current time is 21:12:53.73
Enter new time:

The IBM Personal Computer DOS
Version 3.00 (C) Copyright IBM Corp 1981, 1982, 1983, 1984

A>
```

DOS version 3.00 was the initial version of DOS shipped with the PC AT. DOS version 3.10 is very similar to version 3.00 except that it includes networking programs that permit the AT to be used in this type of environment.

When you load DOS for the first time, you need to select the keyboard layout you wish to use, as well as the country whose date and time format you wish to use. These two tasks can be accomplished by the use of the

SELECT program on the DOS diskette. To use the SELECT program requires both the DOS diskette and a new blank diskette. If you have a one-diskette drive system, insert the DOS diskette in drive A and perform a system reset if power was already on, or turn on power if it was not on. At the DOS prompt A>, enter the SELECT command, followed by the country code and keyboard code. For the United States, you would enter SELECT 001 US. Other country and keyboard codes are described in IBM's DOS User's Guide.

Once the SELECT command is entered, you will be prompted to enter and remove the DOS diskette and the blank diskette until the message "Copy another (Y/N)?" is displayed. This results in the generation of a copy of your DOS diskette that is set up for the keyboard code and the country code you selected. By entering N in response to the preceding message, you will again be prompted to insert and remove the original DOS diskette and the newly created copy of DOS because the SELECT command will now perform a comparison of the contents of both diskettes. If you have a two-drive system, you would have placed DOS in drive A and the blank diskette in drive B.

BRINGING UP DOS FROM DRIVE C

If you have a fixed disk on your AT, you will normally prefer to bring up DOS from that device. This will allow you, upon power-up or a system reset, to forgo placing a DOS diskette into drive A, since once DOS is placed on your fixed disk, that drive will be automatically searched for DOS when no diskette is in drive A, causing DOS to be loaded from drive C. To bring up DOS from drive C, you first have to bring up DOS from drive A and use a program on the DOS diskette to partition your fixed disk. Then you must format your DOS partition and transfer the files from your DOS diskette to the fixed disk.

After DOS is loaded from drive A, the DOS prompt A> will be displayed on your screen. To partition your fixed disk will require you to execute the fdisk program by entering the name of the program as follows. Note that for all DOS commands you can enter the commands in either uppercase or lowercase letters.

```
A>fdisk
```

After you press the Enter key, the main menu of the fdisk program will be displayed as illustrated here.

```
IBM Personal Computer
Fixed Disk Setup Program Version 3.00
(C) Copyright IBM Corp. 1983,1984

FDISK Options


Choose one of the following:
```

```
1. Create DOS partition
2. Change Active Partition
3. Delete DOS Partition
4. Display Partition Data


Enter choice: [1]


Press Esc to return to DOS
```

If you have two fixed disks on your system, a fifth choice would appear on the main menu of the program. This choice would permit you to select the next fixed disk drive. Since the AT is constructed to search drive C upon power-on or a system reset if there is no diskette in drive A, you would normally use a second fixed drive for additional storage capacity while placing DOS and programs and data on drive C.

If DOS is the only operating system you intend to use with your fixed disk, after entering 1 to create a DOS partition, you would respond to the prompt, "Do you wish to use the entire fixed disk for DOS (Y/N) . . . ?" with the letter Y. This would permit the entire fixed disk to be used by DOS. If you wish to use several operating systems, you would respond by entering the letter N. This would result in the program prompting you for the partition size to reserve for DOS.

Once your DOS partition is created, you must format it to prepare it for use. To do so you will use the format program on the DOS diskette which was previously installed in drive A. Here at the DOS prompt A> you would enter the command:

```
A>format c:/s/v
```

The letter C followed by a colon (:) informs the format program that drive C is to be formatted. The /s and /v are optional parameters in the format command that are passed to the program. The /s parameter causes the system files from the DOS diskette to be copied to drive C, while the /v parameter will cause the format program to prompt you to enter a volume label (identifier) of up to 11 characters after the formatting process is completed. Since formatting will cause any previously recorded data to be destroyed, the program will issue a warning and prompt you to proceed or to cancel the format request as indicated below.

```
A>format c:/s/v
WARNING, ALL DATA ON NON-REMOVABLE DISK
DRIVE C: WILL BE LOST!
Proceed with Format (Y/N)?
```

Since you wish to format your DOS partition, you would enter the letter Y. This will cause the red indicator light on the fixed disk to come on and the message "Formatting . . ." to be displayed. After several minutes, the message "Format complete" and "System transferred" will be displayed. The message "System transferred" will be displayed because you included the /s parameter in the format command, causing a copy of three operating system files to be placed in the DOS partition on drive C. Next you will be prompted to enter a volume label, or you can press the Enter key if you do not wish to give an identifier to the fixed disk. Normally, you will use volume identifiers on diskettes and on a fixed disk when it is subdivided into many partitions.

Once you have partitioned and formatted your fixed disk, you are ready to copy DOS to the DOS partition on drive C. With the DOS diskette in drive A, at the DOS prompt A> you would enter:

```
A>copy a:*.* c:
```

Here, copy is a DOS command used to transfer files. The asterisk (*) characters are global file specifiers that will be covered later in this chapter. For the present, it is enough to know that their use in the command results in all files on the diskette in drive A being copied to drive C.

Once the copy command is entered, each file on the diskette in drive A is transferred to the fixed disk. At the same time, the drive specifier designating from where the file is being copied and the name of the file being copied are displayed on your screen. At the end of the copy process, the number of files copied will also be displayed and the prompt A> will then reappear. A portion of the display indicating this process is illustrated below.

```
A:SELECT.COM
A:GRAPHICS.COM
A:RECOVER.COM
A:EDLIN.COM
A:GRAFTABL.COM
        34 File(s) copied

A>
```

To verify that you can bring up DOS from the fixed disk, remove the DOS diskette from drive A and perform a system reset by pressing the Del key while holding down the Ctrl and Alt keys. First, the system will search drive A for a diskette, and since none is there, it will bring up DOS from the fixed disk (drive C). This will cause the date and time messages to be displayed, as well as the DOS version and a copyright notice. The only difference between bringing up DOS from the fixed disk instead of a diskette drive is that after the copyright notice, the prompt C> is displayed instead of the prompt A> as shown below.

```
Current date is Thu 11-01-1984
Enter new date (mm-dd-yy):
Current time is 21:22:58.95
Enter new time:

The IBM Personal Computer DOS
Version 3.00 (C) Copyright IBM Corp 1981, 1982, 1983, 1984

C>
```

Here the C> prompt indicates that the fixed disk is the default drive.

Default Drive

The C in the last prompt illustrates what is known as the default drive. DOS searches the default drive to locate any commands or file names you enter, unless you specify another drive in the file specification. Since many PC AT systems may have only one disk drive, a logical question is how can one perform operations that require two disk drives, such as copying disks? The answer to this question is that DOS treats one drive as both drive A and drive B. When you perform an operation that normally requires two drives, DOS will prompt you to exchange diskettes in your single disk drive. For most operations that require copying of disks, DOS will prompt you when to insert the "source" diskette and when to insert the "target" diskette. All you will then have to remember is that the source is the original diskette and the target is the backup diskette.

You can also change the default drive designation prompt by entering the new drive designation letter, followed by a colon as shown below.

```
A>    (original prompt)
A>B: (change drive designation)
B>    (new prompt)
```

Now, B will be the drive DOS will search for any commands or file names you enter. For ATs that have only one diskette drive, changing the drive designation from A to B has no effect on which physical drive will be searched for commands or file names.

BACKING UP DOS

One of the first things you will want to do is to make a copy of your DOS diskette as a backup in case the original is damaged. Although the SETUP command discussed earlier in this chapter produces a copy of DOS, if SETUP was conducted by your dealer, you probably were not furnished with the copy. The diskette you use to copy onto must not have its write protect notch covered, since the AT will not be able to write on the diskette. Normally, you will want to use a brand new, blank diskette for the DOS backup. If the diskette was previously used for data storage, you should double check its contents, since the backup procedure will destroy any information that was previously stored. To check the contents of a previously used diskette in drive A you can use the DIR command. Thus, you would enter DIR A: in response to the prompt C> (C>DIR A:) if drive C was the default drive, and DIR in response to the prompt A> (A>DIR) if you previously changed the default drive from C to A or if you have an entry model AT.

The directory command will be discussed in more detail when DOS commands are covered later in this chapter. Entering the command DIR in response to the DOS prompt causes the volume identifier of the diskette, if previously assigned, to be listed as well as all directory entries on the diskette in the drive A. For each file on the diskette, you obtain information concerning its name and extension, file size in bytes, and its date and time of creation or last modification. If one or more files on the diskette warrant retention, you should place the diskette aside and use a different diskette to create your DOS backup.

If you are using a diskette that previously had data recorded on it, it was already formatted and you could skip reformatting the diskette. Since the format command not only initializes the diskette to a recording format acceptable to DOS but also analyzes the diskette for defective tracks and prevents such tracks from being used, it is recommended that you format any diskette that will be used as a DOS backup. If you are going to use a new diskette, you must format it prior to its use, since the format command will prepare the diskette to accept DOS files. This is accomplished by the format command initializing the diskette's directory as well as performing several other initialization functions. The steps required for formatting a diskette will vary, depending on whether you have one or two diskette drives and whether or not you have a fixed disk containing DOS.

One-Drive Backup Procedures

After DOS is initialized and the prompt A> is displayed, you can invoke the format process by entering the following command.

```
A>FORMAT A:
```

If you have a fixed disk to which DOS was previously transferred and drive C is the default drive, you would enter the same command after the prompt C>.

If you wish to enter a label onto the diskette you are formatting you should enter the /V parameter in the command line. Thus, your command could become:

```
A>FORMAT A:/V
```

On the PC AT, the disk drive is dual-sided, so the command FORMAT A: will create a diskette for dual-sided use only. If you wish to format a diskette that can be used in a single-sided drive similar to those found on some PCs, then enter:

```
FORMAT A:/1
```

Here the /1 parameter formats a diskette for single-sided use regardless of the type of drive the diskette is in.

Once the format command is entered, the following message will be displayed.

```
Insert new diskette for drive A:
and strike any key when ready
```

When you use multiple diskettes, it is often convenient to think of the primary diskette as the source diskette and the diskette that is to receive information as the target diskette. Then, the DOS diskette will be considered as the source diskette while the diskette you wish to format will be the target diskette. This is because you will place information on that diskette by first formatting it and later copying the contents of DOS onto it.

After the "insert new diskette for drive A:" message is displayed, you should remove your source (DOS) diskette and insert your target (backup) diskette into drive A. Remember, if you have one drive, DOS will require you to exchange diskettes each time DOS prompts you to do so. Now, you can press a key, which serves to inform DOS that the diskettes have been changed. Once any key is pressed, the message "Formatting . . ." will be displayed and drive A will become active as the diskette in that drive is formatted. After the formatting of the target diskette is completed, the rest of the formatting message will appear as shown below.

```
Formatting . . . Format complete
xxxxx bytes total disk space
xxxxx bytes available on disk
Format another (Y/N)?
```

If you want to make multiple copies of DOS, you could format additional diskettes at this time by entering the character Y and following the previously discussed procedure once the "Format another" message is displayed. Instead of removing the DOS diskette, you would remove the formatted diskette and insert an unformatted diskette into drive A. Then, after the formatting process is completed, you could continue to remove the previously formatted diskette and insert a new diskette, entering the character Y to continue the formatting process.

Once you have formatted your diskette or diskettes, you should enter the character N and remove the last formatted diskette from drive A and reinsert the DOS diskette into that drive. Now you are ready to copy the contents of the original DOS diskette onto the diskettes you just formatted. To do so you will use the DISKCOPY command by typing DISKCOPY and pressing the Enter key in response to the prompt A>.

Once that command is entered, the following message will be displayed.

```
Insert source diskette in drive A
Strike any key when ready
```

You do not have to exchange diskettes, since the DOS diskette is your source diskette and is already in drive A. You can simply press any key when you wish to commence the copying process. Once you press a key, a portion of the contents of the DOS diskette will be read into memory from drive A and the following message will be displayed:

```
Insert target diskette in drive A
Strike any key when ready
```

The DISKCOPY command will attempt to keep the number of diskette insertions and removals to a minimum. This is accomplished by reading the maximum amount of data from the diskette in drive A into the memory installed in your AT.

Prior to pressing a key, you must remove the DOS diskette and insert the target diskette, which you want to become your DOS backup. Once you press a key, that portion of the source diskette previously read into memory will be written onto the target diskette and you will again be requested to insert the source diskette back into drive A as illustrated below.

```
Insert source diskette in drive A
Strike any key when ready
```

After you remove the target diskette and reinsert the source diskette, pressing a key will cause another group of tracks to be read into memory from the DOS diskette. Again, the precise number of tracks read will depend on the amount of memory installed in your system unit. Once another group of tracks on the source diskette is read into memory, you will again receive the message to insert the target diskette so that the "new" contents of memory can be recorded onto that diskette. You will continue to repeat this process of removing the target diskette and reinserting the source diskette until the following message appears:

```
Copy complete
Copy another (Y/N)?
```

If you have a fixed disk to which you previously copied DOS, you could easily copy DOS from drive C to the formatted diskette in drive A. Since the DISKCOPY command only works with diskettes, you should use the COPY command as follows:

```
A>COPY C:*.* A:   (if A is the default drive)
A>COPY *.* A:     (if C is the default drive)
```

If you made only one backup copy of DOS, you will type the character N without using the Enter key. This will bring you back to the DOS command level and the prompt A> will be displayed if you copied DOS from the DOS diskette. You can verify that the contents of the backup diskette have been correctly copied from the source (DOS) diskette through the use of the DISKCOMP command. This command is used to compare the contents of two diskettes on a track-for-track basis and will issue a message indicating the track number when they are not equal. Note that you can only use this command to compare single-sided diskettes to single-sided diskettes, double-sided diskettes to double-sided diskettes, and a high-capacity diskette to another high-capacity diskette. This command can be invoked by typing DISKCOMP and pressing the Enter key. Once invoked, the following message will be displayed:

```
A>DISKCOMP
Insert first diskette in drive A
Strike any key when ready
```

Similar to the DISKCOPY command, DISKCOMP will attempt to reduce the number of diskette insertions to a minimum. This is accomplished by reading the maximum number of tracks of information into your system unit's memory prior to comparing the data stored in memory with a portion of the contents of the next diskette. Once a portion of the first diskette is read into memory the following message will be displayed:

```
Insert second diskette in drive A
Strike any key when ready
```

After you follow the requested actions by removing the first diskette from drive A and inserting the second diskette, the contents of memory representing a number of tracks of information from the first diskette will be compared against a similar number of tracks of information contained on the second diskette. When this comparison is completed, you will be requested to insert the first diskette back into drive A and again strike any key when you are ready for the comparison to continue. The insertion of the first and second diskettes will be alternately requested until the comparison is completed and the following message is displayed.

```
Diskettes compare ok
Compare more diskettes (Y/N)?
```

If you made only one backup copy of DOS, you will type N and the DOS prompt A> will be displayed. This backup copy of DOS should be labeled accordingly. You should use a felt tip pen or write on a label that can be peeled off paper and placed onto the backup diskette.

Two-Drive Backup Procedures

If you expanded your PC AT to two diskette drives, formatting, copying, and verification of the copying process will be much simpler than for one-drive systems. After DOS is brought up in drive A, the prompt A> will be displayed. Next, insert the backup diskette you wish to format into drive B and enter the FORMAT command as shown below.

```
A>FORMAT B:
```

Note that you've specified the device address as B: since you wish to format the diskette in drive B. Later in this chapter, we will cover in detail the syntax of DOS commands.

If you forget to close the drive cover or improperly insert the diskette, you will receive an error message as shown below:

```
A>FORMAT B:

Not ready error reading drive A
Abort, Retry, Ignore? A
```

In this example, you aborted the FORMAT request by entering the character A. Once the command FORMAT B: is entered, you will see the message:

```
Insert new diskette for drive B:
and strike any key when ready
```

Since the backup diskette has already been inserted into drive B, pressing a key on the keyboard will display the first part of the formatting message, "Formatting . . ." After approximately 45 seconds, the remainder of the formatting message will appear and you will be asked if you wish to format another diskette as shown below.

```
Formatting . . . Format complete
xxxxxx bytes total disk space
xxxxxx bytes available on disk
Format another (Y/N)?
```

If you previously entered the /V parameter into the format command, you would be prompted to enter a volume label up to 11 characters in length, which can be used as a diskette identifier.

If you only want one backup copy of DOS, the formatting of one diskette should suffice. If you would like to make multiple backup copies of DOS, you may wish to format several additional diskettes at this time. If you wish to format additional diskettes, you will respond to the "Format another (Y/N)?" question with the character Y. If Y is entered, you will be told to insert a new diskette into drive B and to strike a key when you are ready for formatting to commence. After you have formatted your diskettes, you will type the character N in response to the "Format another?" question and the DOS prompt A> will again be displayed. Now you are ready to copy the information from the DOS diskette onto one or more of the diskettes you just formatted.

With the DOS diskette in drive A and the formatted backup diskette in drive B, you can copy the contents of the diskette in drive A onto the diskette in drive B through the use of the DISKCOPY command. This is shown below.

```
A>DISKCOPY A: B:
```

Note that in the above command the device name A: specifies from where you will copy, while the device name B: specifies where the information will be copied to. Once the enter key is pressed, the following message will be displayed:

```
Insert source diskette in drive A
Insert target diskette in drive B
Strike any key when ready
```

Since the source (DOS) and target (backup) diskettes are already inserted into their correct drives, you will initiate the copying process by pressing any key on the keyboard. This will cause the entire contents of the diskette in drive A to be copied onto drive B.

Similar to using DISKCOPY on a one-drive system, a variable number of tracks will be read into memory that will depend on the amount of memory installed in the system unit. Unlike a one-drive system, using dual drives will alleviate the requirement for multiple insertions and removal of diskettes as segments of the DOS diskette will be read into memory and written onto the diskette in drive B until the copying process is completed, without any human intervention being required.

After the copy has been made, a "copy complete" message will be displayed as well as the question, "Copy another? (Y/N)" If you wish to make multiple copies of DOS, you can remove the first backup diskette from drive B and insert another formatted diskette into that drive. Once you have done so, you would enter the character Y to copy DOS from drive A onto the diskette in drive B. After you have completed making the required number of backup copies of DOS, you would enter the character N in response to the "Copy another? (Y/N)" question. This will result in the DOS prompt A> being displayed.

The entire process required to copy the contents of a diskette in drive A onto a formatted diskette in drive B is shown below. Note the simplicity of this operation when your system has two drives in comparison to the insertion and removal of diskettes required for DISKCOPY operation when you have only one drive.

```
A>DISKCOPY A: B:

Insert source diskette in drive A

Insert target diskette in drive B

Strike any key when ready
X
Copy complete

Copy another? (Y/N)
N
A>
```

To verify that DOS has been correctly copied onto the backup diskette, you can enter the DISKCOMP command as follows:

```
A>DISKCOPY A: B:
```

Once the preceding command is entered, the following message will be displayed:

```
Insert first diskette in drive A
Insert second diskette in drive B
Strike any key when ready
```

With the original copy of DOS in drive A and the backup copy in drive B, pressing any key will cause a track-by-track comparison of the contents of the two diskettes to be conducted. When the comparison shows that both diskettes have exactly the same contents, the following message will be displayed:

```
Diskettes compare ok
Compare more diskettes (Y/N)?
```

If you made only one backup copy of DOS, you would enter the character N. Otherwise, you would remove the first backup DOS diskette from drive B and insert the next diskette you wish to verify. Then, you would enter the character Y. After you successfully complete a comparison operation, you should label each backup DOS diskette and insert it into its protective envelope.

EDITING KEYS AND CONTROL FUNCTIONS

When DOS is initialized, you will notice the absence of data on the 25th line, which is known as the soft key display. This results from the fact that the function keys take on different meanings when you are at the operating system level. In addition to new meanings assigned to the function keys, there are several DOS editing keys that can be used to make corrections to input lines and commands as they are being entered. The DOS editing keys are used to edit within a line while the line editor program known as EDLIN permits operations on complete lines or groups of lines within a file or document. In addition to permitting operations on complete lines, EDLIN serves as a text editor that permits us to search for text, replace text, list segments of a document, and perform various additional functions common to most text editors. The use of EDLIN will be covered in the last section of this chapter.

Editing Keys

A summary of the DOS editing keys and the functions associated with the use of each key are listed in Table 4-1. In addition to these function keys, the backspace key can be used for editing purposes; however, the normal cursor control keys will be disabled.

When we enter data from the keyboard, it is placed into an input buffer and will not be processed until entered by pressing the Return key. A line of data will remain in the input buffer and can be modified or repeated via the

Table 4-1. DOS Editing Keys

KEY	FUNCTION PERFORMED
Del	Deletes one character in the retained line (the cursor does not move)
Esc	Cancels the line currently displayed (the retained line remains unchanged)
F1 or →	Redisplays one character from the retained line and displays it
F2	Redisplays all characters up to a specific character
F3	Redisplays all remaining characters from the retained line to the screen
F4	Skips over all characters up to a specified character (this is the opposite of F2)
F5	Accepts the edited line for continued editing; the currently displayed line becomes the retained line, but it is not sent to the requesting program
Ins	Inserts characters

DOS editing keys or an entirely new line can be entered. The following examples illustrate the use of the DOS editing keys. Assume that the line in the input buffer was typed and entered to the system as follows in response to the DOS prompt.

```
A>DISKCOPY A: B:
```

Now, use the backspace key to erase the line from the display. Although erased from the display, the line is still in the input buffer.

By pressing the F1 key, one character from the buffer would be copied to the screen as shown below:

```
A>D
```

Each time the F1 key is pressed, one additional character from the input buffer will be displayed.

The F2 key is similar to the multiple use of the F1 key. The F2 key should be pressed followed by a single character, which is used as a delimiter. This delimiter character tells how many characters from the input buffer up to but not including the first occurrence of the delimiter will be copied to the screen. If we type the F2 followed by a Y, the screen would appear as follows:

```
A>DISKCOP
```

The F3 key can be used to copy all of the remaining characters in the input buffer onto the screen. If you should press the enter key, only the characters on the screen would be sent to the computer. Typing the F3 key would result in the remainder of the command being displayed as follows:

```
A>DISKCOPY A: B:
```

The F4 key must also be followed by a delimiter. In this instance, the character after the F4 key is pressed specifies that all characters up to but not including the first occurrence of the delimiter character will be skipped, and the remainder of the input buffer contents will be displayed. If the specified character is not present in the input buffer, no characters will be skipped over. Suppose your input buffer appears on the screen as follows:

```
A>DISKCOPY A: B:
```

You can reposition your cursor next to the greater-than sign by using the backspace key. Each time you press that key, one of the characters shown on the screen will be temporarily erased from the display. Once the cursor is repositioned to the left of the greater-than (>) character, if you press the F4 key followed by the letter "A," the first nine characters in the input buffer will be skipped. If you follow the preceding sequence by the F3 key, the remainder of the line will be copied to the screen as shown below:

```
A>A: B:
```

You could move the cursor back to the left using the backspace key until it is next to the greater-than character and press the Ins key to enter the insert mode. Unfortunately, at the operating system level, the cursor will remain as an underline when you are in the insert mode of operation. By typing DISKCOMP, each character will be inserted into the line and all characters to the right of and including the second A will be moved to the right. By pressing the Ins key a second time, we will leave the insert mode. When you enter the F3 key, the remainder of the line will be displayed as shown below.

```
A>DISKCOMP A: B:
```

You can now either press the enter key to make this final revision line replace the data in the input line and send it to the system or you can press the F5 key. Pressing the F5 key would put the displayed line into the input buffer for further editing, but it would not send the line to the system to process. This action would be signified by the character @ being displayed at the end of the line, and the cursor would be moved to the first position of the next line.

In the following example, we started to enter the command DISKCOMP into the system. Due to some doubt about whether or not we wanted to use that command, we pressed the F5 key after the character P. This placed the command in the input buffer as signified by the character @ at the end of the top line.

With the cursor one line directly under the character D, we can now press other function keys to change the contents of the input buffer. Pressing

F2 followed by the character M and the F5 key resulted in the second line shown below. On the third line we can press the F1 key down to generate DISKCO and then type the remaining part of the line and enter the data as shown below.

```
A>DISKCOMP@
  DISKCO@
  DISKCOPY A: B:

Insert source diskette in drive A

Insert target diskette in drive B

Strike any key when ready
```

Control Functions

When DOS is invoked, three additional predefined control functions can result from multi-key combinations.

Pressing Ctrl + Num Lock will result in the suspension of the system's operation. Normally, this key combination is used to freeze the screen so you can read it or to suspend an invoked operation that you want to think about before allowing it to continue. You can press any key to have the operation continue or you can enter Ctrl + Break to stop the command from further action.

Suppose after initiating the DISKCOPY command you decided you really didn't want to perform that particular operation. As shown by the following example, using the Ctrl + Break keys during the execution of a DOS command causes you to return to the DOS command level where the prompt message (A>) is generated. Here, instead of striking any key when ready, we pressed the Ctrl + Break keys to suspend this operation.

```
A>DISKCOMP@
  DISKCO@
  DISKCOPY A: B:

Insert source diskette in drive A

Insert target diskette in drive B

Strike any key when ready  (Ctrl+Break Pressed)

A>
```

The last multi-key control function is the Ctrl + PrtSc combination. This key combination echoes and prints whatever you type and what the system displays until you press this pair of keys again. This multi-key combination can be a very handy device to produce a hard-copy historical log of operational procedures, error messages, and the like for future reference. One word of caution is in order, however, If you press this key sequence and your printer is not in the select mode of operation, no error message will be initially generated. As you attempt to enter a command you will notice that DOS will not accept further input. As soon as you place your printer in the select mode, the message "Printer fault" will be generated followed by a backslash on the next line. After you receive the DOS prompt, you can then enter your command as is shown below.

```
A>D
Printer fault
\

A>DIR
```

These DOS keys and their resulting functions are summarized in Table 4-2.

Table 4-2. DOS Control Function Multi-Key Operations

KEYS	OPERATION
Ctrl+Num Lock	Suspend
Ctrl+PrtSc	Echo to printer
Ctrl+Break	Break

DOS Commands

A summary of commonly used DOS commands is listed in Table 4-3. Those commands preceded by an asterisk will be covered in this chapter.

There are two types of DOS commands. Internal commands that are represented by an "I" in the "Type" column of Table 4-3 are executed immediately after they are entered, since they reside in memory. Thus, these commands are also referred to as resident commands. External commands that are represented by an "E" in the "Type" column in Table 4-3 reside on the DOS diskette as program files. When an external command is invoked, the program file must be read from the diskette before the command can be executed. Under DOS, any file with a file name extension of .COM or .EXE is considered to be an external command. This concept permits you to develop your own unique program files and execute those files with your own commands. If you list the files on the DOS diskette with the DIR command, you will notice the FORMAT.COM program file. The contents of this program are automatically loaded and executed when you enter the FORMAT command, which loads and executes this program file. When you enter an external command, it should be noted that the filename extension is not included.

In the format column of Table 4-3, we have purposely omitted what is known as a path from each command format. A path is used in a tree structured directory to obtain a more efficient organization of a fixed disk and in certain cases a diskette. In the next chapter, we will cover tree structured directories and examine how we can modify the formats listed in Table 4-3 to include path specifiers.

Table 4-3. Commonly Used DOS Commands

COMMAND	TYPE	ACTIVITY PERFORMED	FORMAT
*ASSIGN	E	Routes disk I/O requests from one drive to another	[d:]ASSIGN[x[=]y[...]]
*ATTRIB	E	Sets the attribute byte of a file to read only or displays its status	[d:]ATTRIB[+/−R][d:]filename[.ext]
BACKUP	E	Backs up one or more files from one disk to another	[d:]BACKUP d:[filename[.ext]] d:[/S][/M][/A][/D:mm-dd-yy]
(Batch)	I	Executes commands contained in a specified file	[d:]filename[parameters]
*BREAK	I	Instructs DOS to check for Fn + Break whenever a program requests DOS to perform any function	BREAK[ON/OFF]
*CHKDSK	E	Checks the diskette and issues a status report about the diskette and memory	[d:]CHKDSK[d:][filespec][/F][/V]
*CLS	I	Clears the display screen	CLS
*COMP	E	Compares files	[d:]COMP[filespec][d:][filename.ext]
*COPY	I	Copies the files specified to the same or another diskette or fixed disk	COPY filespec[d:][filename.ext][/V]
*DATE	I	Lets you store a date in the computer	DATE[mm-dd-yy]
*DIR	I	Lists the file names on a diskette or fixed disk that matches your specifications	DIR[d:][filename[.ext]][/P][/W]
*DISKCOMP	E	Compares diskettes	[d:]DISKCOMP[d:][d:][/1][/8]
*DISKCOPY	E	Copies the contents of one diskette onto another	[d:]DISKCOPY[d:][d:][/1]
*ERASE	I	Deletes specified files	ERASE filespec
FIND	E	Searches for strings of text	[d:]FIND[/V][/C][/N] string [[d:]filename[.ext]...]
*FORMAT	E	Prepares a new diskette for use and optionally copies DOS to it	[d:]FORMAT[d:][/S][/1][/8][/V][/B][/4]
*GRAPHICS	E	Permits the contents of a graphics display screen to be printed	[d:]GRAPHICS[printer type][/R][/B]

*Indicates commands covered in this chapter.

Table 4-3. Commonly Used DOS Commands (cont.)

COMMAND	TYPE	ACTIVITY PERFORMED	FORMAT
*LABEL	E	Creates, changes, or deletes a volume label on a disk	[d:]LABEL[d:][volume label]
*MODE	E	Sets the way a printer, color/graphics adapter, or communications adapter operates and permits the switching of display adapters	[d:]MODE[LPT#:][,n] [,m][,P]] [d:]MODE n [d:]MODE[n], m[,t] [d:]MODE COMn[:]baud [,parity[,databits[,stopbits [,P]]]] [d:]MODE LPT#[:]=COMn
MORE	E	Sends one screen of output to the output device and pauses with the message "More"	[d:]MORE
PAUSE	I	System wait	PAUSE[remark]
*PRINT	E	Prints a list of files on the printer while you are doing other tasks	PRINT[[d:][filespec][/T] [/C][/P]...]
*PROMPT	I	Sets a new DOS prompt	PROMPT[prompt-text]
REM	I	Displays remarks contained in a batch file	REM[remark]
*RENAME	I	Lets you change the name of a file or group of files	RENAME filespec filename[.ext]
RESTORE	E	Restores one or more files placed on a source disk by the BACKUP command	[d:]RESTORE d:filename[.ext][/S][/P]
SORT	E	Sorts text data	SORT[/R][/+n]
*SYS	E	Transfers the operating system files from the default drive to the specified drive	SYS d:
*TIME	E	Lets you set the clock in the computer	TIME[hh:mm:ss.xx]
*TYPE	I	Displays the contents of the specified file on the screen	TYPE filespec
*VER	I	Displays the version of DOS you are working with	VER
*VERIFY	I	Verifies that data written onto a disk is correctly recorded	VERIFY[ON/OFF]
*VOL	I	Displays the disk volume label of the specified drive	VOL[d:]

*Indicates commands covered in this chapter.

Command Syntax (Format)

A common format notation will be used in discussing each of the DOS commands.

- Words in capital letters are keywords. The specific characters in the keyword must be entered, although any combination of upper- and lowercase characters can be used.
- The items shown in lowercase letters are to be supplied by you when you enter the command.
- All items in square brackets ([ ]) are optional and may or may not be included in a command.
- Items that may be repeated as many times as you wish are indicated by ellipses (. . .).
- With the exception of square brackets, all punctuation characters such as commas, equal signs, slashes, and so on must be included as indicated by the format.

Command Parameters

d: —The drive letter followed by a colon will be used to specify the drive. Currently, DOS supports diskette drives A and B and fixed disk drives C and D. If the drive parameter is omitted, the default drive is assumed. If you do not have a fixed disk, when DOS is initialized, the prompt A> indicates that drive A is the default drive and that the system is waiting for you to enter a command. If you have a fixed disk to which DOS was transferred, the prompt C> will be displayed when DOS is initialized. You can change the default drive by entering a new designation letter followed by a colon as shown below.

```
A>      (original prompt)
A>B:    (new drive designator)
B>      (new prompt)
B>C:    (new drive designator)
C>      (new prompt)
```

Each of the commands listed in Table 4-3 that contains one or more drive designators (d:) can have a path specified after the designator. As previously mentioned in this chapter, paths are used in tree structured directories that are mainly used with fixed disks. This will be discussed in detail in the next chapter.

filename —Filenames can be up to eight characters in length and may be followed by a period and a filename extension. Valid characters in the filename include all alphanumeric characters and special characters with the exception of the following, which have special meanings and cannot be used in filenames.

. " / \ [ ] : | < > + = ; ,

If you wish to direct the results of a DOS command to a specific physical device, you can do so by using the device name in place of the filename. These reserved names cannot be used as diskette filenames, since the system assumes that they are assigned to the indicated devices. For the following device names, the colon is optional and any drive parameter or file name extension erroneously entered with the name will be ignored.

CON:—Console keyboard/screen. If the console is used as an input device, the F6 key followed by the Enter key can be used to generate an end-of-file indication to terminate its use as an input device.

AUX: or COM1:—First asynchronous communications adapter port.

LPT1: or PRN:—Printer (as an output device only).

LPT2: or LPT3:—Second and third parallel printer ports (output device only).

NUL:—A dummy (nonexistent) device for test purposes. If used as an input device, an immediate end-of-file is generated. When used as an output device, the write operations are simulated, but no data is actually tranferred.

.ext —The optional filename extension consists of a period followed by up to three characters. Valid characters in the extension are the same as for the filename. If a filename is followed by an extension, you must use both parts when referencing the file. Table 4-4 lists 11 of the most commonly used extensions.

filespec —The file specification can include the device name, file name, and extension as indicated below.

[d:] filename[.ext]

$format_{DOS}$ —We will use the term $format_{DOS}$ to indicate the format of DOS commands.

If drive A is the default drive, and you wish to access the file XRAY.BAS on the diskette in that drive, you would enter the following file specification.

```
XRAY.BAS
```

Note that you can eliminate the drive parameter, since the file you wish to access is on the default drive.

Table 4-4. Filename Extension and File Types

EXTENSION	FILE TYPE
.ASM	Assembly language program in source code
.BAK	Backup file
.BAS	BASIC language program
.BAT	Batch processing program
.BIN	Binary coded file
.COM	Command or program directly executable by DOS
.DAT	Data file
.EXE	Program directly executable by DOS
.PIC	Screen image display
.TMP	Temporary file
.TXT	Text file

Global File Name Characters

The question mark (?) and asterisk (*) characters take on special significance when used in a filename and its extension. A ? in a filename or a filename extension means that any character can occupy that position. As an example of the use of the question mark character consider the following command.

```
DIR A:STAT?.BAS
```

Entering the above command would cause all directory entries on drive A with filenames that begin with STAT and are five characters in length and have an extension of BAS to be listed. The result of the preceding command could produce a listing of statistical files we programmed in BASIC, their size, and the date they were stored as follows:

```
STAT1     BAS       512  06-23-82
STAT5     BAS      3712  08-04-82
STAT7     BAS      1920  05-23-82
```

The use of the asterisk (*) in a file name or a filename extension means that any character can occupy that position as well as all the remaining positions in the filename or extension.

Suppose you changed the preceding command as follows:

```
DIR STAT*.BAS
```

This would result in all directory entries on the default drive with filenames that begin with STAT and have an extension of BAS to be listed. In this case, all files from four to eight characters in length beginning with the letters STAT and with an extension of BAS will be listed.

From the preceding discussion, it should be apparent that the asterisk (*) character serves as a shorthand method of entering many question mark (?) characters. The following examples illustrate how these characters can be used to perform equivalent file specification notations.

```
DIR A:STAT????.???
```

is equivalent to

```
DIR A:STAT*.*
```

The preceding examples will list all directory entries for all files on the diskette in drive A, beginning with STAT, regardless of their file extension. Either of the following examples will list all files on the diskette in the default drive with a file extension of BAS.

```
DIR *.BAS
```

or

```
DIR ????????.BAS
```

If your DOS diskette is in drive A, you can list all executable files on that diskette by entering DIR *.EXE. The entering of this command with the global * character and its response is shown below.

```
A>DIR *.EXE

 Volume in drive A is BACKUPDOS
 Directory of A:\

SORT        EXE       1632      8-14-84      8:00a
SHARE       EXE       8544      8-14-84      8:00a
FIND        EXE       6363      8-14-84      8:00a
ATTRIB      EXE      15123      8-14-84      8:00a
        4 File(s)      965120 bytes free
A>
```

Another term often used to reference the global filename characters is "wild card." This is because the term wild card is synonymous with the term global when used for searching.

Resident DOS Commands

These commands are available for use once DOS is initially loaded without having to reinsert the DOS diskette and are signified by the letter "I" in the "Type" column of Table 4-3. In this section, 11 such resident or internal commands will be reviewed. A discussion of several commands will be deferred for the time being.

Like all DOS commands, these resident commands can be issued after the DOS prompt A> or C> occurs. At that time, you can type the command followed by the Enter key to issue the command to DOS.

BREAK Command

The BREAK command allows you to tell DOS to check for the Ctrl key followed by the Break key sequence whenever a program requests DOS to perform a function. The format of this command is:

$$\text{format}_{\text{DOS}}\text{: BREAK } \left[\begin{Bmatrix}\text{ON}\\\text{OFF}\end{Bmatrix}\right]$$

When ON, this command allows you to break out of a program that performs few device operations, since DOS only checks for the key sequence during those operations if BREAK is set to OFF. If the command is entered without any parameters, DOS will display the current state of BREAK checking.

CLS Command

The CLS command can be used to clear the display screen of data previously displayed. This command is useful if you wish to print a copy of some screen activity and first wish to remove previous activity from the screen. The format of this command is:

format$_{\text{DOS}}$: CLS

COPY Command

The COPY command allows you to copy one or more files to the same or to another diskette or the fixed disk. If you copy files to a different diskette or fixed disk, you can give the copies different names. When you copy files to the same device, you must give the copies different names or the copying will not be permitted. This is because you cannot have duplicate file names on one storage device.

The general format of the COPY command is as follows:

format$_{DOS}$: COPY filespec [d:] [filename[.ext]][/V]

The /V parameter causes DOS to verify that information written onto the target diskette is recorded properly.

By including only the file specification in the COPY command, you can copy a file to the default drive. Assuming the default drive is A, several examples of the use of the COPY command are shown below:

```
A>COPY B:STAT.BAS
A>COPY B:*.*
A>COPY B:STAT.*
```

In the first example, the file STAT with the file extension BAS will be copied from the diskette in drive B to the diskette in drive A. The second example would result in the copying of all files on the diskette in drive B to the diskette in drive A, while the third example would result in the copying of all files named STAT, regardless of their file extension.

A word of caution is in order concerning the use of the COPY command. If you are attempting to copy a single file and there is insufficient room on the target diskette, DOS will provide an appropriate message that will indicate you were unsuccessful as shown below.

```
A>COPY B:SHIP.BAS
Insufficient disk space
        0 File(s) copied
```

If there is insufficient disk space when you attempt to copy multiple files, DOS will not inform you as to which files were successfully copied. This is shown by the following attempt to copy all files on the diskette in drive B to the diskette in drive A when space was only available to copy one file.

```
A>COPY B:*.*
Insufficient disk space
        1 File(s) copied
```

What you have to do is use the DIR command. You can use this command to scan the directory to determine what files were copied to the diskette in drive B.

If you wish to copy files from drive A to drive B and drive A is the default drive, the following commands could be issued.

```
A>COPY STAT.BAS B:
A>COPY *.* B:
A>COPY STAT. * B:
```

In each of the above examples it was assumed that the appropriate files to be transferred reside on the diskette in drive A.

If there is not enough room on the target diskette for the file to be copied to, you will receive the message "Insufficient disk space," followed by the number of files actually copied, if any.

If you wish to copy a file and simultaneously change the name of that file, you must include both the file specification of the file and the filename it is to be changed to. This is illustrated by the following example, assuming the default drive is A.

```
A>COPY CONFIG.SYS B:NEWFIG.SYS

Insert diskette for drive B: and strike
any key when ready

        1 File(s) copied

A>
```

Note in the preceding example, DOS issued the prompt "Insert diskette for drive B: and strike any key when ready." This prompt will appear when you have one diskette drive on your AT and wish to perform a two-diskette drive operation. In such situations, DOS will consider physical drive A as both logical drives A and B and prompt you to insert diskettes as required.

When the COPY command is successfully executed, you will receive a message indicating the number of files copied as shown in the previous example.

If the file does not exist, a "0 File(s) copied" message will be displayed.

By using reserved device names, you can copy files to the screen, which in effect serves to display the file, to the line printer, which serves as a mechanism to obtain a hard copy printout of the file, or to other device names to perform additional functions. Several examples using device names within a COPY command are shown below. In these examples, drive A is again shown as the default drive.

```
A>COPY B:STAT.BAS LPT1:
A>COPY STAT.BAS CON:
```

The first example would cause the file STAT.BAS on the diskette in drive B to be listed on the line printer. In the second example, the file STAT.BAS on the diskette in the default drive would be displayed on the screen. The use of device names at the DOS command level provides you with a mechanism to perform many functions without reverting to a program language level to perform the required function. Thus, copying a file to the console under DOS will perform the equivalent function of loading a file into memory and then listing the file under BASIC.

Another word of caution is in order when copying files to the console or printer. Only files stored in ASCII will be meaningful when printed or displayed using the COPY command. Since BASIC programs are stored on diskette in a tokenized format unless specifically delimited in a SAVE command to be stored in ASCII, printing or displaying the contents of such a file may produce a jumble of special characters that are not meaningful. This is shown by the following example where we will COPY the file TEST.BAS to the console. In this example, drive B was used as the default drive.

```
B>COPY TEST.BAS CON:
S
    Lg Y ; t : "TEST.BAS"    AS # (   #() M >      2 0   #,X$ #<   "
REC#";L -F LgLi @P  Ig L (X$) rU  ((X$,I,))h o ((X$,I,))f2
 M   W  Pg<<X$,I,>>  Z      Pfg                1 File(s) copied
B>
```

DATE Command

The DATE command permits you to enter a date or to change the date previously entered when DOS was initialized. The format of this command is shown below.

format$_{DOS}$: DATE[mm-dd-yy]

In addition to the preceding format, the date can also be entered as (dd-mm-yy) or (yy-mm-dd), depending on the country code selected with the SELECT command.

Once entered, the DATE command will result in the display of a prompt message telling you the current date and requesting the entry of the new date as shown below.

```
C>DATE
Current date is Sat 11-03-1984
Enter new date (mm-dd-yy):
```

If the date displayed is correct, you can press the Enter key to leave it unchanged. If you wish to enter a new date, the following constraints must be adhered to or an "Invalid date" message will be displayed.

m must be 1 or 2 digits from 1 to 12
d must be 1 or 2 digits from 1 to 31
y must be 2 digits from 80 to 99 or 4 digits from 1980 to 2099

The delimiters within the date can be the hyphen (-) or the slash (/). The following examples illustrate the use of this command.

```
C>DATE
Current date is Sat 11-03-1984
Enter new date (mm-dd-yy): 7-15-86

C>DATE
Current date is Tue 7-15-1986
Enter new date (mm-dd-yy): 11-03-84
```

One practical use of the DATE command is as a mechanism to determine the day of the week of a particular date if a calendar is not handy. Thus, entering 7-15-86 in the preceding DATE command and issuing it a second time tells you that the date was a Tuesday.

```
A>DATE
Current date is Sun 7-15-1984
Enter new date: 16-07-84

Invalid date
Enter new date:
```

In the first example, the date was changed from 11-03-1984 to 7-15-1986, while the second example reset the date to its previous value. In the third example, the date was initially entered incorrectly, which resulted in the generation of the "Invalid date" message and the prompt to "Enter new date:".

DIRECTORY Command

The DIRECTORY command permits you to obtain information about all or a group of specified files on a diskette. The format of the command is as follows:

format$_{DOS}$: DIR [d:][filename[.ext]][/P][/W]

In the preceding example, the /P parameter will cause the display to pause when the screen is filled. This parameter is valuable when you have many files on a diskette; otherwise, the information would rapidly fill the screen and information would then scroll off the screen from view. When the /P parameter is used and the screen fills, you can press any key to continue with the directory listing.

The /W parameter results in a wide display of the directory, where each line displayed will contain five names. It is recommended that this parameter be used only if you have 80-column display capability.

The following examples show the use of this command to list all directory entries from the default drive or from a designated drive.

A>DIR
C>DIR A:

We can obtain information about a specific file or a group of files by using a file name and the special characters ? and * in the filename and file extension parameters. This is shown by the following examples, again assuming the default drive is drive A.

A>DIR STAT*.*
A>DIR B:STAT.*
A>DIR C:*.BAS

The first example would provide a listing of all directory entries on the diskette in the default drive of files beginning with the name STAT, regardless of their file extension. The second example would list all directory entries on the diskette in drive B of files named STAT, regardless of their file extension. In the third example, all directory entries on the fixed disk would be listed that have the extension BAS.

If you request information about a specific file or group of files and they do not exist on the referenced diskette, DOS will return the message "File not found."

ERASE Command

The ERASE command permits you to delete the file with the specified file name from a designated drive or from the default drive. The format of this command follows:

format$_{DOS}$: ERASE filespec

Some examples of the use of this command are shown below, with drive A used as the default drive.

```
A>ERASE STAT.BAS
A>ERASE B:STAT.BAS
A>ERASE *.*
A>ERASE B:*.*
```

In the first example, the file STAT.BAS will be deleted from the diskette in the default drive. In the second example, the same file will be deleted from the diskette in drive B. The third example shows how you could delete all files on the diskette in the default drive, while the fourth example shows how you could delete all files on the diskette in drive B.

If you attempt to ERASE a file that does not exist on the designated drive, DOS will return the message:

```
File not found
```

You can erase all the files except the system files IBMBIO.COM, IBMDOS.COM, and BADTRACK. The first file is an I/O device handler program that is on your DOS diskette. This program provides the interface between the computer's memory and the devices attached to it. The second file is a program that acts as a manager and provides a series of service functions that can be used by any program that runs under DOS's control. During the formatting process, any defective tracks that are encountered are allocated to a file named BADTRACK. Due to the importance of these three files, the system will not permit their erasure.

PROMPT Command

The PROMPT command provides you with a mechanism to set a new DOS prompt. The format of the command is:

format$_{DOS}$: PROMPT[prompt-text]

where prompt-text can be text to be displayed as the new system prompt and can contain special meta-strings in the form of $c, whose meanings are defined in Table 4-5.

Table 4-5. Meta-String Meanings

META-STRING	MEANING
$	The "$" character
t	The time
d	The date
p	The current directory of the default drive
v	DOS version number
n	Default drive letter
g	The ">" character
l	The "<" character
b	The ":" character
q	The "=" character
h	A backspace; the previous character is erased
e	The Escape character
-	The CRLF (carriage return line feed) sequence, which causes you to go to the beginning of a new line on the display

To illustrate the use of the PROMPT command, enter the command PROMPT COMMAND? after the normal DOS prompt. As illustrated below, this changes the DOS prompt to "COMMAND?".

```
A>PROMPT COMMAND?

COMMAND?
```

A return to the normal DOS prompt can be accomplished by entering the command PROMPT without any parameters. To see how you can use the meta-strings, consider the following example that appended the characters SQ to the previous PROMPT command. This causes the text "COMMAND?" to be displayed, followed by the "=" character, which was generated by the meta-string $Q.

```
A>PROMPT COMMAND?$Q

COMMAND?=
```

By using a combination of meta-strings and text you can structure the DOS prompt to fit a variety of possible requirements. In the next example, we will first display the time and then go to the beginning of a new line where we will display "COMMAND?=".

```
A>PROMPT $T$_COMMAND?$Q

14:40:39.09
COMMAND?=
```

Now, each time you enter a DOS command the time will be displayed followed by the text "COMMAND?=" on a new line.

TIME Command

The TIME command allows you to enter or change the time from the keyboard or from within a batch file. The format of the command is shown below.

format$_{DOS}$: [hh:mm:ss.xx]

Once the command is entered, the following prompt message will be generated:

```
Current time is hh:mm:ss.xx
Enter new time _
```

where hh is 1 or 2 digits from 0 to 23 that represents hours; mm is 1 or 2 digits from 0 to 59 that represents minutes; ss is 1 or 2 digits from 0 to 59 that represents seconds; and xx is 1 or 2 digits from 0 to 99 that represents hundredths of a second.

If you desire to leave the time as currently displayed, you can just press the Enter key without changing any parameters. If after entering one field of information you press the Enter key, the remaining fields will be set to zero. Some examples of the use of this command are shown below.

```
A>TIME
Current time is 00:26:54.53
Enter new time:
A>TIME
Current time is 00:27:22.38
Enter new time: 21:30
A>TIME
Current time is 21:30:05.83
Enter new time: 21:35:30
A>TIME
Current time is 21:35:32.75
Enter new time:
A>
```

In the first example the TIME command was used merely as a mechanism to ascertain the system time setting, and the Enter key was pressed to leave its setting unchanged. In the second example, the time was changed to 9:30 p.m., which is denoted as 21:30 hours, since noon is 12 and 1 p.m.

becomes the thirteenth hour of the day and so on. In the third example, the clock was advanced to 9:35 and 30 seconds and then its setting was verified by the fourth TIME request. Note that you were pretty fast with your fingers on the keyboard as only 2 and 75 hundredths of a second elapsed between entering the time as 21:35:30 and obtaining the response to issuing the TIME command.

RENAME Command

The RENAME command provides you with the ability to change the name of a file or group of files. The format of this command is shown below.

format$_{DOS}$: RENAME filespec filename[.ext]

Some examples of the use of this command are shown below.

A>RENAME STAT.BAS HISTGM.BAS
A>RENAME B:STAT.BAS HISTGM.BAS
A>RENAME STAT.BAS *.XYZ

In the first example, the file named STAT.BAS on the diskette in the default drive is renamed HISTGM.BAS. The second example renames the file on the diskette in drive B, while the third example shows how one of the special global characters can be used in the parameter. In this example, the file STAT.BAS on the diskette in the default drive will have its file extension changed to XYZ.

The following example shows the effect of the RENAME command on your file directory.

```
A>DIR *.SYS

 Volume in drive A is BACKUPDOS
 Directory of A:\

ANSI        SYS      1641      8-14-84      8:00a
VDISK       SYS      3080      8-14-84      8:00a
CONFIG      SYS        14     11-02-84     10:43p
NEWFIG      SYS        14     11-02-84     10:43p
         4 File(s)     964608 bytes free

A>RENAME NEWFIG.SYS OLDFIG.SYS

A>DIR *.SYS

 Volume in drive A is BACKUPDOS
 Directory of A:\

ANSI        SYS      1641      8-14-84      8:00a
VDISK       SYS      3080      8-14-84      8:00a
CONFIG      SYS        14     11-02-84     10:43p
OLDFIG      SYS        14     11-02-84     10:43p
         4 File(s)     964608 bytes free

A>
```

In the preceding example, the directory of files containing the extension SYS on the diskette in drive A is listed first. Then, the name of the file was changed from NEWFIG.SYS to OLDFIG.SYS, and the directory was listed again to verify the name change.

If you attempt to RENAME a file with a name that already exists on the directory or if the file you wish to rename does not exist on the designated diskette, DOS will display the message shown in the example below.

```
A>RENAME CASH.BAS CARY.BAS
Duplicate file name or file not found
```

TYPE Command

The TYPE command provides you with another method to display the contents of a file on the screen. The format of this command is shown below.

format$_{DOS}$: TYPE filespec

If you desire to have the contents of the file printed as it is being displayed, you can initiate printing by pressing Ctrl + PrtSc. The legibility of the file will depend on the method used to originally store it on the diskette. BASIC programs stored as ASCII characters and other text and data files will appear in a legible format. Other files such as BASIC programs stored in tokenized format and object program files will appear unreadable due to the presence of nonalphanumeric characters. This is similar to the problem previously discussed concerning using the COPY command to copy a file to the printer or screen.

Several examples of the use of the TYPE command using drive A as the default drive are shown below.

```
A>TYPE MEMO.TXT
A>TYPE B:SPACE.XYZ
```

In the first example, the file MEMO.TXT on the diskette in the default drive will be displayed. The second example will result in the file SPACE.XYZ being listed on the screen. If the file does not exist on the reference diskette, DOS will return the message "File not found."

VER Command

The VERsion command causes the DOS version number you are currently using to be displayed. The format of this command is:

format$_{DOS}$: VER

```
C>VER

IBM Personal Computer DOS Version 3.00

C>
```

VERIFY Command

The VERIFY command causes data that have been written onto a diskette to be verified by performing a Read after each Write operation. If the command is entered without a parameter, the present state of the command will be displayed. The format of this command is:

format$_{\text{DOS}}$: VERIFY $\left[\begin{Bmatrix}\text{ON}\\\text{OFF}\end{Bmatrix}\right]$

VOL Command

The VOLume command causes the disk volume of the specified drive to be displayed. The format of this command is:

format$_{\text{DOS}}$: VOL

The following example illustrates the use of this command.

```
A>VOL

 Volume in drive A is BUDGET84

A>
```

NONRESIDENT COMMANDS

Nonresident commands are those commands that are actually programs on the DOS diskette. Prior to using these commands, the DOS diskette must reside in one of your drives or on your fixed disk.

Since nonresident or external commands have to be loaded into memory, you must either have the program for that command on the default drive or prefix the command with the drive designator where it is located. The following example illustrates this concept through the use of the LABEL command, which is an external command whose use will be covered later in this chapter. If you have a diskette in drive A that does not contain the LABEL program, entering the command after the prompt A> causes an error message, since the diskette in drive A did not contain the program. This is illustrated below.

```
A>LABEL
Bad command or file name
```

If DOS is on the fixed disk, then that device will contain the LABEL program. Thus, prefixing the command with the drive designator C: will cause the fixed disk to be searched for the program, which, when located, is loaded into memory. This is illustrated by the following example.

```
A>C:LABEL

Volume label (11 characters, ENTER for none)?
```

ASSIGN (Drive) Command

The ASSIGN command causes DOS to route disk I/O requests for one drive into disk I/O requests for another drive, which you specified in the command. The format of this command is illustrated below.

format$_{DOS}$: [d:]ASSIGN[x[=]y[. . .]]

The [d:] before the ASSIGN statement permits you to specify the device that contains the ASSIGN command file. Thus, if you were currently "logged onto" drive B and DOS was on your fixed disk you would prefix the ASSIGN command with C:. The letter x in the command is replaced by the drive letter that current disk I/O requests are sent to, while the letter y is replaced by the drive letter that you want disk I/O requests to be sent to. Normally, you would use this command with programs that were written to perform I/O operations on diskette drives (A and B) that you now wish to operate on the fixed disk (C and D).

In the following example, you will first assign diskette drive B I/O references to the fixed disk, drive C. Next, when you issue a DIR command for drive B, it is obvious that physical drive C was used because no diskette could have over 17 million bytes of storage available.

```
A>ASSIGN B=C

A>DIR B:*.EXE

 Volume in drive B has no label
 Directory of B:\

SORT       EXE      1632     8-14-84     8:00a
SHARE      EXE      8544     8-14-84     8:00a
FIND       EXE      6363     8-14-84     8:00a
ATTRIB     EXE     15123     8-14-84     8:00a
        4 File(s)     17518592 bytes free

A>
```

ATTRIB (Attribute) Command

The ATTRIB command provides you with the capability to set the read attribute of a file to read-only, or to display the present setting of the attribute of a specified file. The format of this command is illustrated in the following:

format$_{DOS}$: [d:]ATTRIB[+/−R][d:]filename[.ext]

In the preceding command the parameter +R is used to set the attribute of a file to read-only, while the parameter −R removes the read-only attribute. Once the read attribute is set, the file cannot be modified or deleted. This is illustrated by the following example, where you first set the attribute of the file OLDFIG.SYS on the diskette in drive A to read-only. Next, attempt to erase that file and you receive the message "Access denied."

```
C>ATTRIB +R A:OLDFIG.SYS

C>ERASE A:OLDFIG.SYS
Access denied

C>
```

Knowing that something about the file is different since you could not delete it, check its attribute.

```
C>ATTRIB A:OLDFIG.SYS
R      A :\OLDFIG.SYS
```

The response to the preceding ATTRIB command entered without a +R or −R parameter causes the attribute of the file to be displayed. Here the R indicates that the read-only attribute is set.

Now, remove the read-only attribute of the file OLDFIG.SYS on the diskette in drive A, check the attribute of the file, and, since it has been removed, proceed to erase it. This is accomplished by the following three commands.

```
C>ATTRIB -R A:OLDFIG.SYS

C>ATTRIB A:OLDFIG.SYS
        A:\OLDFIG.SYS

C>ERASE A:OLDFIG.SYS

C>
```

In addition to preventing the deletion of a file by mistake, the ATTRIB command is a valuable mechanism to prevent other users of the AT from modifying a file.

CHKDSK (Check Disk) Command

The CHKDSK command allows you to analyze the directory and file allocation table on a diskette. The result of the execution of this command is a display of the number of disk files currently stored on the diskette as well as a status report of disk space and memory availability status.

If you specify a file name defined by the file and an optional extension, this command will display the number of non-contiguous areas occupied by the file. You can also use global identifiers in the command to check several files.

The /F parameter causes the command to fix any errors encountered in the directory or file allocation table. The /V parameter will cause the command to display a series of messages indicating its progress, as well as providing detailed information concerning any errors it encounters. The format of this command is illustrated below.

format$_{DOS}$: [d:]CHKDSK [d:][filespec][/F][/V]

To analyze the diskette in the default drive, you can omit specifying the device name as shown in the following example:

```
A>CHKDSK
Volume BACKUPDOS created Nov 3, 1984 2:02p

    1213952 bytes total disk space
      37376 bytes in 3 hidden files
     211968 bytes in 36 user files
     964608 bytes available on disk

     524288 bytes total memory
     484384 bytes free
```

Since 1.2 million bytes of total disk space are shown, the diskette is obviously a high-capacity diskette. If you have a one-diskette drive system, entering CHKDSK B: would cause DOS to prompt you to insert a new diskette into physical drive A. This is shown in the following example.

```
A>CHKDSK B:

Insert diskette for drive B: and strike
any key when ready

    362496 bytes total disk space
     22528 bytes in 3 hidden files
    107520 bytes in 22 user files
    232448 bytes available on disk

    524288 bytes total memory
    484384 bytes free

A>
```

In the last example, the diskette had 362K bytes of total disk space, which indicates that it is a conventional dual-sided diskette. Although you entered the command CHKDSK B:, if your system only has one diskette drive you could have removed any diskette in drive A and entered CHKDSK if A was the default drive.

Note that the status report provides the decimal integer values for the number of disk files, disk space, and memory status. If an error condition is encountered, an error message or messages will be displayed prior to the status report. As an example, if the diskette has not been formatted and the CHKDSK command is entered, the directory and file allocation table will not be recognizable and the error message "Diskette not initialized" will be displayed.

COMP (Compare Files) Command

The COMP command permits you to compare the contents of two files. The format of this command is indicated below.

format$_{DOS}$: [d:]COMP [Filespec] [d:] [Filename].ext]]

Files to be compared can be on the same disk or diskette or on different disks or diskettes. While the filenames are optional within the command, if they are omitted you will be prompted to enter them when the command is invoked. Some examples of the use of this command, again using drive A as the default drive, are shown below.

```
A>COMP STAT B:STAT
A>COMP STAT.BAS B:MATH.BAS
A>COMP SPACE.BAS GAME.BAS
```

In the first example, the file STAT on the diskette in the default drive will be compared to the file STAT on the diskette in drive B. The second example compares the file STAT.BAS on the diskette in the default drive to the file MATH.BAS on the diskette in drive B. In the third example, the files GAME.BAS and SPACE.BAS, both residing on the diskette in the default drive, will be compared.

After the COMP command is entered, the message "Insert diskette for drive B: and strike any key when ready" will be returned by DOS if you have a one-diskette drive system and wish to compare files on two diskettes. Once a key is pressed, a byte-by-byte comparison of the two files will be conducted. If the files compare, an appropriate message will be generated, and you can terminate the comparison with the Enter key or enter another file pair to compare. In the following example, the files named CONFIG.SYS and NEWFIG.SYS on the same diskette are compared.

```
A>COMP CONFIG.SYS NEWFIG.SYS

A:CONFIG.SYS and A:NEWFIG.SYS

Files compare ok

Compare more files (Y/N)? N
```

In the next example, the same files on two different diskettes are compared.

```
A>COMP CONFIG.SYS B:NEWFIG.SYS

Insert diskette for drive A: and strike
any key when ready
```

```
A:CONFIG.SYS
Insert diskette for drive B: and strike
any key when ready
```

```
and B:NEWFIG.SYS
```

```
Files compare ok
```

The COMP command results in the designated files being compared on a byte-for-byte basis. If the comparison is not equal, an error message showing where the unequal bytes occurred will be printed. This message gives the hexadecimal offset into the file where the unequal comparison occurred and the bytes that were compared. After 10 unequal comparisons, COMP assumes further comparing is of no use and generates the following message:

```
10 Mismatches—aborting compare
```

DISKCOMP (Compare Diskette) Command

The DISKCOMP command is used to compare the contents of entire diskettes. Normally, this command is used to verify the results of a DISKCOPY operation. The format of this command is illustrated below.

format$_{DOS}$: [d:]DISKCOMP [d:] [d:] [/1][/8]

If the /1 parameter is included in the command, DISKCOMP will compare only the first side of the diskettes, even if they are double-sided. The /8 parameter will cause the command to compare diskettes on an 8-sectors-per-track basis, even if the first diskette contains 9 or 15 sectors per track. With one diskette drive, you can compare two diskettes by entering the command DISKCOMP A:. The program invoked will automatically prompt you to insert the required diskettes at the appropriate times. For a dual-drive system, the command DISKCOMP A: B: would compare the diskette in drive A with the diskette in drive B. If you have a fixed disk with DOS on it, you can compare two diskettes without inserting a diskette containing the DOS DISKCOMP program by entering the command A>C:DISKCOMP A: B: or B>C:DISKCOMP A: B:, depending on which device was the default drive.

When the DISKCOMP command is invoked, all tracks of each diskette are compared on a track-by-track basis. A message indicating the track number of unequal tracks will be displayed, and a beep will be generated each time a track comparison results in a compare error. An example of the comparison message generated when tracks of two diskettes are not equal is shown below.

```
Compare error(s) on track 12
Compare error(s) on track 13
```

After the comparison is completed, the following message will be displayed.

```
Compare more diskettes (Y/N)?
```

Entering the character N will cause the command activity to terminate. If the character Y is entered, the next comparison will occur on the same drives after prompt messages are displayed concerning the insertion of the appropriate diskettes.

DISKCOPY (Copy Diskette) Command

This command can be used to copy the entire contents of one diskette onto a second diskette. The format of this command is shown below.

format$_{DOS}$: [d:]DISKCOPY [d:] [d:][/1]

If the /1 parameter is specified, DISKCOPY will copy only the first side of the diskette, even if a double-sided diskette is used.

As discussed in the beginning of this chapter, if you have only one diskette drive, when this command is invoked it will prompt you to insert the target and source diskettes at the appropriate times. If both device name parameters are omitted, a single drive copy operation will be performed on the default drive. If the second parameter is omitted, the default drive will be used as the target drive, and the other drive will serve as the source drive. If we have a single drive system, all prompt messages displayed will be for drive A, regardless of the drive specifier entered.

FORMAT Command

As discussed in the beginning of this chapter, the FORMAT command must be used to initialize diskettes and fixed disks to a recording format that is acceptable to DOS. In addition to initializing diskettes and fixed disks, the FORMAT command will analyze the entire storage media for defective tracks and prepare the media to accept DOS files by initializing the directory, file allocation table, and the system loader. All new diskettes must be formatted prior to being used by DOS. Since formatting destroys all data on the recording media, you should be very careful prior to formatting any disk, and especially a fixed disk. The format of this command is shown below.

format$_{DOS}$: [d:]FORMAT [d:][/S][/1][/8][/V][/B][/4]

If the /S option is specified, after formatting, three operating system files will be copied from the default drive to the diskette in the designated drive in the following order.

IBMBIO.COM
IBMDOS.COM
COMMAND.COM

The /1 parameter will cause the target diskette to be formatted for single-sided use only, while the /8 parameter will format that diskette on the basis of 8 sectors per track. Note that when the /1 parameter is omitted, both sides of the diskette will be formatted and the omission of the /8 parameter results in 9- or 15-sectors-per-track formatting, with 15 sectors per track occurring when the diskette is formatted in a high-capacity diskette drive. This increases the storage capability of the diskette and will normally be used by AT users. Upon occasion, you may wish to use the /1 and /8 option parameters if you intend to use your diskette on a PC that has a single-sided drive and operates under some version of DOS other than DOS 3.0.

If you specify the /V parameter, FORMAT will prompt you for a volume label that serves to identify the diskette. When entered, the volume label will be written onto the diskette. The /8 and /V options are mutually exclusive, since the operating system that previously worked only on an 8-sectors-per-track basis on the original IBM PC did not recognize a volume label.

The /B parameter results in FORMAT, creating an 8-sectors-per-track diskette with space reserved for two system files known as IBMBIO.COM and IBMDOS.COM. Use this parameter only to create a diskette upon which you later wish to transfer another DOS set of system files through the SYS command.

The /4 parameter is used to format a conventional double-sided diskette in a high-capacity drive. Since diskettes formatted using the /4 parameter may not be reliably read in a conventional single- or double-sided drive, you may prefer to install a conventional 320K diskette in your AT. Then, diskettes formatted in this drive can be read by a single- or double-sided drive without the potential for problems that formatting in the high-capacity diskette drive can cause.

Since the formatting process destroys any data previously recorded on the diskette, you should double check the diskette's contents with the DIR command prior to formatting if you are unsure of its contents. When a diskette is formatted, defective tracks will be allocated to a file called BADTRACK, which will prevent them from being used for data storage.

The following example shows how to format the diskette in drive A, copy the operating system files, and assign a volume label to the diskette.

```
C>format a:/s/v
Insert new diskette for drive A:
and strike ENTER when ready

Formatting. . .Format complete
System transferred

Volume label (11 characters, ENTER for none)? BUDGET85

    1213952 bytes total disk space
      59904 bytes used by system
    1154048 bytes available on disk

Format another (Y/N)?N
C>
```

In the preceding example we have formatted a single-sided diskette, copied the operating system files to it, and assigned BUDGET85 as the volume label.

Note that if you attempt to format the fixed disk, the FORMAT program will issue a warning and permit you to cancel the format operation as illustrated by the following example.

```
C>FORMAT
WARNING, ALL DATA ON NON-REMOVABLE DISK
DRIVE C: WILL BE LOST!
Proceed with Format (Y/N)?N
C>
```

Since formatting the fixed disk will erase any previously stored data, you should carefully think over any format operation on that device. Otherwise, you might wipe out weeks or months of effort.

The data in Table 4-6 denotes the permitted utilization of the format parameters based on the disk type to be formatted.

Table 4-6. Format Parameter Usage

DISK TYPE	PARAMETERS ALLOWED
320/360K	/S,/V,/1,/8,/B,/4
1.2 megabytes	/S,/V
Fixed disk	/S,/V

GRAPHICS Command

The GRAPHICS command permits the contents of a screen containing graphics picture elements (pixels) as opposed to text to be printed on the IBM graphics printer or a specified printer when the Shift+PrtSc keys are pressed. The format of this command is:

format$_{DOS}$: [d:]GRAPHICS[printertype] [/R] [/B]

The printer type option permits you to specify the following types:

COLOR1	IBM PC color printer with black ribbon
COLOR4	IBM PC color printer with red, blue, black ribbon
COLOR8	IBM PC color printer with cyan, magenta, yellow, black ribbon

COMPACT	IBM PC compact printer
GRAPHICS	IBM PC graphics printer

If the printer type is not specified, the GRAPHICS printer will be used.

The /R parameter causes black to be printed as black and white as white. If not specified, black is printed as white and white as black.

The /B parameter is required to print the background color and is only applicable to printer types COLOR4 and COLOR8. If this parameter is not specified, the background color is not printed.

When the command is invoked, the resident size of DOS in memory is increased by the size of the program required to dump the pixels to the specified printer. It should be noted that all text on the screen, as well as the graphics picture elements, will be printed on the printer when this command is invoked.

LABEL (Volume Label) Command

The LABEL command provides you with the ability to create, change, or delete a volume label from a diskette or fixed disk. The format of this command is:

format$_{DOS}$: [d:]LABEL[d:][volume label]

The volume label can be up to 11 characters in length. The following example illustrates the use of this command.

```
C>DIR A:

 Volume in drive A is BUDGET85
 Directory of A:\

COMMAND     COM     22042     8-14-84     8:00a
             1 File (s)    1154048 bytes free

C>LABEL A:CASHFLOW

C>DIR A:

 Volume in drive A is CASHFLOW
 Directory of A:\

COMMAND     COM     22042     8-14-84     8:00a
             1 File(s)    1154048 bytes free

C>
```

In the preceding example, the directory command was used first, which showed that the label of the diskette in drive A is BUDGET85. Next, the LABEL command was used to change the diskette's label to CASHFLOW and verified this by using the directory command again. It should be noted that entering the command followed by the drive letter without a volume label will cause any existing label to be deleted. This is illustrated by the next example and shows that one should use the DIR command to verify volume labels or the VOL command, which is actually better suited since no files are listed when that command is used.

```
C>DIR A:

 Volume in drive A is CASHFLOW
 Directory of A:\

COMMAND      COM      22042      8-14-84      8:00a
         1 File(s)      1154048 bytes free

C>LABEL A:

Volume label (11 characters, ENTER for none)?

C>DIR A:

 Volume in drive A has no label
 Directory of A:\

COMMAND      COM      22042      8-14-84      8:00a
         1 File(s)      1154048 bytes free

C>
```

MODE Command

The MODE command lets you change the amount of information to be displayed on the screen or printed on the printer. The general format of this command is shown below.

format$_{DOS}$: [d:]MODE [LPT#:][n][,m][,P]

The following version of the command is used to change the mode of operation of a printer attached to the PC AT.

format$_{DOS}$: [d:]MODE LPT#:[n][,m][,P]]

where # is 1,2, or 3 that designates the printer number; n is 80 or 132 characters per line (note that an 80-column printer capable of compressed printing can work with n specified as 132); and m is 6 or 8 lines per inch vertical spacing. The P parameter will cause continuous retries if a printer time-out error occurs.

The power-on default options of printers attached to the AT are 80 characters per line and 6 lines per inch. In the following example, you would change the printer to 132 characters per line and 6 lines per inch, assuming the default drive is drive A.

```
A>MODE LPT1:132,6
```

The second use of the MODE command permits you to switch display adapters as well as to shift the color/graphics display 1 or 2 characters to the left or right for readability. When used to switch the display, the format of this command is as follows:

format$_{DOS}$: MODE[n][,m][,T]

where n is 40 or 80 characters per line—BW40, BW80, CO40, CO80, or MONO (BW40 sets the display to black and white with 40 characters per line, while BW80 performs the same function with 80 characters per line; CO40 enables color and sets the display width to 40 characters, while CO80 performs a similar function, with the display width set to 80 characters per line; if you are using DOS 3.0 on the IBM AT, MONO will switch to the monochrome display adapter that has a width of 80 characters per line); m is R or L to signify shifting the display to the right or to the left; and T requests a test pattern that can be used to align the display.

If the screen is set to 40 columns, the display will be shifted one character position. If the display is set to 80 columns, it can be shifted two character positions. If the character T is entered, after the test pattern is generated you will be asked if the screen is aligned properly. If you respond by entering the character Y, the command will end. If you enter the character N, the shift requested will be repeated followed by the same prompt message. Let us examine the use of this command and its effect on the display.

```
A>MODE 80,R,T
```

Entering the preceding command causes the output to the display to be set at a width of 80 characters, and you can shift the output two positions to the right if you cannot observe the test message correctly. The inclusion of the character T causes a test pattern of 80 characters to be generated, and you are asked if you can see the leftmost 0. Since the test message appears correctly, entering the character Y will terminate the MODE command as illustrated below. This will return you to the DOS prompt level.

```
01234567890123456789012345678901234567890123456789012345678901234567890123456789

Do you see the leftmost 0? (Y/N) Y
A>
```

PRINT Command

The PRINT command provides you with the capability to queue up to ten files to include files defined by global characters. These files will be printed concurrently with other computer tasks. The format of this command is:

format$_{DOS}$: [d:]PRINT [d:][filename[.ext]][/T][/C][/P...]

The /T parameter terminates the printing of any files currently in the print queue. The /C parameter results in the preceding and any following file names being cancelled from the print queue until a /P is found or the Enter key is pressed. The /P parameter results in the preceding and any following file names being added to the print queue until a /C is found on the line or the Enter key is pressed. If the command is entered without parameters, the files currently queued for printing will be displayed. The use of this command is illustrated in the following example:

```
A>PRINT B:SOFTG.BAS B:GRAPH.BAS

          B:SOFTG  .BAS is currently being printed
          B:GRAPH  .BAS is in queue
```

A word of caution is in order concerning the printing of BASIC program files. If the file was not saved in ASCII format, the tokenized characters in BASIC will be interpreted as various printer control codes and will produce interesting but not desired results.

SYS (System) Command

The SYS command provides you with a mechanism to transfer the operating system files from one diskette onto another diskette. SYS is normally used to transfer a copy of DOS onto application program diskettes that are designed to use DOS but are sold without it. The format of this command is shown below.

format$_{DOS}$: [d:]SYS d:

The use of this command to transfer the operating system files from a DOS diskette in drive A to a diskette in drive B is shown below:

```
A>SYS B:
System transferred
```

When this command is invoked, the files IBMBIO.COM and IBMDOS.COM will be transferred from the default drive to the specified drive in sequence. The diskette these files will be transferred to must have been previously formatted by a FORMAT d:/S command. If not formatted in that manner, the files will not be transferred because the specific diskette locations required for the system files were not allocated. This is shown by the following example where a diskette previously formatted without using /S is used as the target diskette for transferring the system files. Since the formatting process did not allocate room for the system files, the error message is self-explanatory.

```
A>SYS B:
No room for system on destination disk
```

THE LINE EDITOR (EDLIN)

Resident on the DOS diskette, EDLIN is a text editor that can be used to create, alter, and display ASCII program files or text files. To invoke EDLIN, the following command format is used:

format: EDLIN [d:]filespec

If the entire file cannot be loaded into memory due to its size, EDLIN will automatically load a portion of the file until memory is 75% full and issue an asterisk (*) as a prompt. If the entire file can be loaded into memory, both a message and the prompt character will be displayed. This is illustrated by the following example where EDLIN is invoked to edit the file named SHIP.BAS located on the diskette in drive B.

```
A>EDLIN B:SHIP.BAS
End of input file
*
```

If the entire file was loaded into memory, you can edit the file without future reference to the diskette. If only a portion of the file was loaded, you can only edit that part of the file that resides in memory. To edit the remainder of the file will require you to direct a portion of the file in memory to be written to a diskette. This will free memory for unedited lines to be loaded from the diskette, and they will be appended to the portion of the file resident in memory.

EDLIN will dynamically generate and display line numbers during the editing process; however, these lines only serve as an operational reference and will not be included in the actual file. Thus, if you are editing a program file, it will appear awkward at first, since you will see two line numbers on every line. The first line number will be generated and displayed by EDLIN but will not actually be included in the file. This line number will be used as the reference line for editing purposes. This is shown by the following example where the EDLIN command was entered to list the first five lines of the file SHIP.BAS. Later in this section, the format of each EDLIN command will be covered in detail; however, as indicated below, most EDLIN commands are very easy to use. In this example we entered 1,5L to list the first five lines of the file.

```
A>EDLIN B:SHIP.BAS
End of input file
*1,5L
       1:*5 KEY OFF
       2: 10 SCREEN 1,0
       3: 20 COLOR 7,0
       4: 30 CLS
       5: 35 LOCATE 1,15
*
```

The asterisk in EDLIN line 1, which is line 5 of the program file, indicates the position of the current line. The current line is a reference or baseline for making changes to a file.

When you insert lines, all line numbers generated by EDLIN following the inserted text will be automatically advanced by the number of lines inserted. If you delete lines from the file, all line numbers generated by EDLIN that follow the deleted text will be automatically decreased by the number of lines deleted.

When your editing session is completed, the original and the updated or newly created file can be saved. The original file will be renamed by EDLIN with an extension of .BAK. This will denote it as the backup file in the event you wish to maintain the previous version of the file. The new file will have the file name and extension as specified in the EDLIN command. The EDLIN file manipulation process is illustrated in Fig.4-1. Note that the backup file will only be created if you make a change to the original file you are editing.

A summary of the EDLIN commands is listed in Table 4-7. When the format of EDLIN commands is discussed, the term format_E will be used to distinguish their format as such.

The use of EDLIN will be examined by first creating a file and then performing selective editing of its contents.

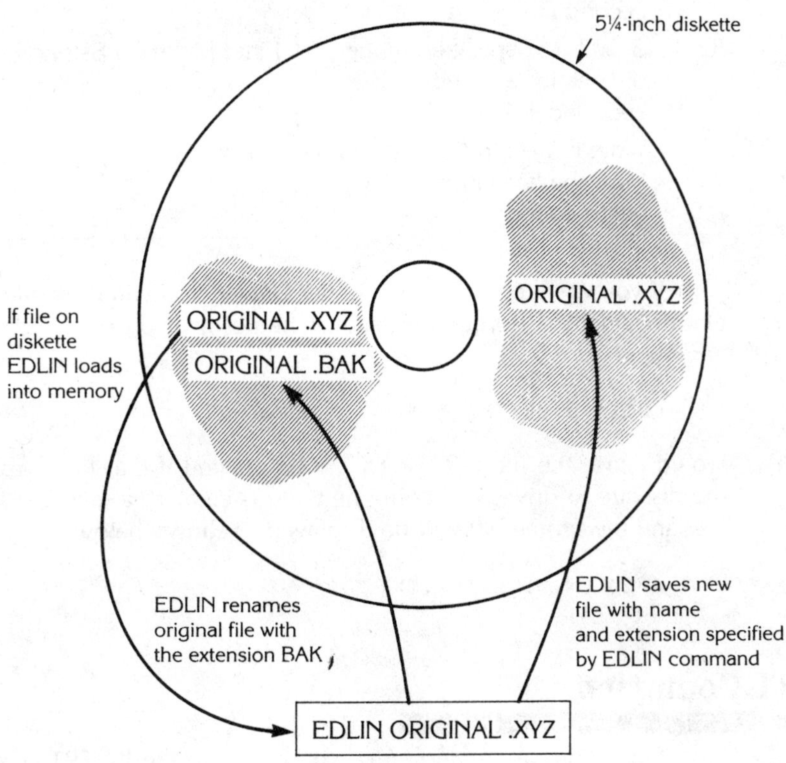

Fig. 4-1. EDLIN file manipulation.

Table 4-7. EDLIN Command Summary

COMMAND	PURPOSE	EDLIN FORMAT
APPEND	Add lines from diskette to file in memory	[n] A
DELETE	Delete the specified range of lines	[line] [,line] D
EDIT	Display line to be edited	[line]
END EDIT	End EDLIN and save the updated file	E
INSERT	Insert lines of text immediately before the specified line	[line] I
LIST	Display the specified range of lines	[line] [,line] L
QUIT EDIT	Quit the editing session without saving changes	Q
REPLACE TEXT	Replace all occurrences of the first string in the specified range of lines by the second string	[line] [,line] [?] Rstring[<F6>string]
SEARCH TEXT	Search the specified range of lines for a match of the specified string	[line] [,line] [?] Sstring
WRITE LINES	Write n lines to the diskette from the lines in memory being edited	[n] W

If you wish to create a file under EDLIN, you will use a file specification that does not exist on the diskette in the designated drive. Thus, entering the command

```
EDLIN B:LETTER.TXT
```

would cause the file LETTER.TXT to be created if that file does not exist on the diskette in drive B. When a new file is created, a message signifying this fact and the prompt (*) will be displayed as shown below.

```
A>EDLIN B:LETTER.TXT
New file
*
```

INSERT Command

Since you are creating text, you must use the INSERT command to reserve space for the lines of text you wish to enter before a particular line in a file. The format for the INSERT LINE command is shown below.

format$_E$: [line]I

EDLIN will display each line number sequentially, starting with 1 as your prompt for data entry, since you are creating a new file. This is illustrated by the following example. Note that an asterisk will appear on each line after you press the enter key to terminate the preceding line. This indicates that you are moving the current line up one position as you enter each line of data.

```
A>EDLIN B:LETTER.TXT
New file
*15I
     1:*                                                        June 23, 1982
     2:*
     3:*Mr. Jonathan Held
     4:*Sales Director
     5:*Widgets of America
     6:*Anycity USA
     7:*
     8:*Dear Jonathan:
     9:*
     10:*This short note is to inform you that the eight zillion cases of all
     11:*American widgets will be shipped no latter than July 23, 1999. I hope
     12:*this shipment will arrive prior to your multibillion dollar advertising
     13:*campaign.
     14:*
     15:*                                                        J.T.
     16:*\
*
```

To exit from the insert mode, you can press the Ctrl+Break keys. When this was done on line 16, a backslash (\) was generated and that line will not be included in memory. Thus, the current line will be line 15.

EDIT Command

Now that you have entered your letter, suppose you wish to edit it. You can use the EDIT command to edit a specific line by entering the line number followed by the Enter key. Thus, the format of the EDIT command is

format$_E$: [line]

The use of this command is shown below

```
  *1
          1:*                                              June 23, 1985
          1:*
```

In the preceding example, the number 1 was entered as a request to edit line 1. Thus the format of the EDIT LINE command is simply the line you wish to edit. Each EDIT request will result in a two-line display response. The first line will display the current contents of the line to be edited and the second line will serve as the prompt for changing the information on the line. With the asterisk after the colon on line 1 this indicates that line 1 is now the current line. If you desire, you can use the DOS function keys to facilitate editing. Thus, if you wish to rapidly change the date of the letter, you could move the cursor to the letter J in June by entering F2 followed by the character J. The result of this key sequence will move the cursor on the second line beneath the J in June as shown below.

```
*1
        1:*                                                  June 23, 1985
        1:*
```

To change June to July, you would type July. If you wish, you could change the date to the 15th. Suppose you also desire to retain the rest of the line. You would then press the F3 key and the line would appear as follows:

```
*1
        1:*                                                  June 23, 1985
        1:*                                                  July 15, 1985
```

At this point, you could press the Enter key to save the changed line, extend the changed line by typing more text on the line, press the F5 key to do more editing with the changed line, without changing the original line, or you can use the Esc or the Ctrl + Break keys to cancel the changed line. The latter action would result in the original contents of the line being preserved.

REPLACE TEXT Command

Suppose after typing your letter you realize you repeatedly misspelled a word or misused some term. You can use the REPLACE TEXT command to make the required changes. The format of this command is shown below.

format$_E$: [line][,line][?]Rstring[<F6>string]

All occurrences of the first string that follows the character R in the specified range of lines will be replaced by the second string. If you omit the second string from the preceding format, all occurrences of the first string within the specified range of lines will be deleted. By specifying the optional parameter (?), you can request EDLIN to generate the prompt message (O.K.?) after each modified line is displayed. This is useful when you wish to change a majority of the occurrences of a given string but not every string. If you wish EDLIN to accept the modification, you will press the Y character or the Enter key. To reject the modification, you would enter some other character than Y. At this point, EDLIN will continue to search for further occurrences of the first string within the specified range of lines. You can see the use of the REPLACE TEXT command by the following examples.

```
*1,15 Rwidgets^ZWIDGETS
    11: American WIDGETS will be shipped no latter than July 23, 1999. I hope
*
```

When the F6 key is pressed, it will be displayed as ^Z. If you attempt to replace a string that is not in the file, the message "Not found" will be displayed as shown by the following replacement request to change widgets to midgets.

```
*1,15 Rwidgets^Zmidgets
Not found
*
```

Note that if you do not specify the value of the first line, a default value of 1 will be used. Similarly, by omitting the value of the second line, a default value of the last line in memory will be used. The following example shows the use of the optional parameter (?) that provides you with a mechanism to accept or reject on a line by line basis string replacements as they occur.

```
*1,15 ?Reight zillion^Znine billion
    10: This short note is to inform you that the nine billion cases of all
O.K.? y
*
```

LIST LINES Command

If you wish to take a look at a large part of or perhaps the entire file, you can use the LIST LINES command whose format is shown below.

format$_E$: [line][,line]L

The following examples will illustrate the use of this command to display a specified range of lines onto the screen.

```
*1,5L
    1:                                                    July 15, 1985
    2:
    3: Mr. Jonathan Held
    4: Sales Director
    5: Widgets of America
*
```

In the preceding example, the range of lines, from line 1 through line 5, was displayed. If you omit the first line parameter, up to 11 lines before the current line will be displayed and the display will end with the specified line. In the following format,

,lineL

note that the beginning comma is required to signify that the first line parameter was omitted. If you omit the second line parameter, up to a total of 23 lines will be displayed, starting with the specified line. When the second parameter is omitted, you can use either of the two formats shown below.

lineL

or

line,L

If you omit both line parameters by entering only the character L, a total of up to 23 lines will be displayed to include up to 11 lines before the current line and 11 lines after the current line. If there are less than 11 lines prior to the current line, then extra lines from memory after the current line resulting in a total of 23 lines will be displayed.

SEARCH TEXT Command

Rather than list the contents or a large portion of a file, you can use the SEARCH TEXT command to rapidly locate a specified string. The format of this command is shown below.

format$_E$: [line][,line][?]Sstring

You can use this command as a mechanism to change the location of the current line in the file. Knowing that the first line of text contains the year, you could enter

```
1,15S1985
```

or

```
1,S1985
```

or

```
,15S1985
```

to search for the first occurrence of 1985 in the file. The result for all three operations is shown below.

```
*1,15S1985
     1:                                              July 15, 1985
*1, S1985
     1:*                                             July 15, 1985
*,15 S1985
     1:*                                             July 15, 1985
*
```

Line 1 would now become the current line in the file. If your search does not result in a match, the message "Not found" will be displayed and the current line will remain unchanged. You can use the optional parameter (?) to request a prompt after each display of a line that contains a string that matches the search string. If you press the Y or Enter key, the matching line will become the current line and the search will end. If a different character is entered, the search will continue until another match is found or until all the lines within the specified range have been searched. At that time, the absence of a match will cause a "Not found" message to be displayed. Several examples of the use of this command on your previously entered file are illustrated below.

```
*1,15 ?SWidget
     5: Widgets of America
O.K.? n
Not found
```

```
*1,15 ?SJ
    1:*                                                         July 15, 1985
O.K.? n
     3: Mr. Jonathan Held
O.K.? n
     8: Dear Jonathan:
O.K.? n
    11: American WIDGETS will be shipped no later than July 23, 1999. I hope
O.K.? n
    15:                                                         J.T.
O.K.? y
*15L
    15:*                                                        J.T.
*
```

In the first search example, a prompt is requested in your search through lines 1 through 15 looking for Widget. It is found on line 5, but n is entered in response to the prompt. Since that string does not occur again in the file, the message "Not found" is displayed. In the next example, the letter J is searched for in the file. In response to this search request, lines 1, 3, 8, 11, and 15 are displayed as n is entered in response to the first four prompts. When Y is entered in response to the prompt generated after line 15 was displayed, line 15 then becomes the current line. This is verified by next entering 15L to list line 15. The asterisk on that line indicates it is the current line.

DELETE LINES Command

If you wish to delete one line or a range of lines, you can do so by using the DELETE command, whose format is indicated below.

format$_E$: [line][,line]D

If the first line parameter is omitted,

,line D

will cause line deletion to start with the current line. Deletion will end when the line specified by the second parameter is reached. If you omit the second parameter,

line D

or

line,D

only the single specified line will be deleted. If both line parameters are omitted, only the current line will be deleted by the D command and the line following the deleted line will become the current line.

Suppose you wish to delete Mr. Held's title from the letter. Since you may not be sure of or remember the line number containing the title, you can use the SEARCH TEXT command to locate the appropriate line as shown below.

```
*1,15 SSales Director
      4: Sales Director
```

Now you can delete the current line by entering the character D in response to the prompt*.

```
*D
```

It should be noted that when one or a group of lines are deleted, the line following the deleted line or range of lines will become the current line. This holds true even if the deleted line or the range of deletions includes the last line in memory. After the deletion occurs, the current line and all the following lines will be automatically renumbered. This is illustrated by listing the current file in memory and examining the location of the asterisk and observing that the file now contains 14 lines as shown below.

```
*1,15l
       1:                                                         July 15, 1985
       2:
       3: Mr. Jonathan Held
       4:*Widgets of America
       5: Anycity USA
       6:
       7: Dear Jonathan:
       8:
       9: This short note is to inform you that the nine billion cases of all
      10: American WIDGETS will be shipped no later than July 23, 1999. I hope
      11: this shipment will arrive prior to your multibillion dollar advertising
      12: campaign.
      13:
      14:                                                         J.T.
*
```

END EDIT Command

If you wish to end EDLIN and save your updated file, you must use the END EDIT command. The format of this command is simply the character E as shown below.

format$_E$: E

Once the command is entered, the edited file will be saved by the system writing it to the drive under the file specification established when EDLIN was invoked. In our example, a file named LETTER.TXT will be saved on the diskette in drive B. After saving this file, EDLIN will return you to the DOS command processor level as illustrated by the following example.

```
*E
A>
```

A word of caution is in order concerning file saving. If your diskette does not have enough available space to save the entire file, only a portion of the file will be saved. The remainder of the file in memory will be lost when EDLIN returns you to DOS. Thus, it is a good practice to use the DOS command CHKDSK prior to performing extensive editing of files.

QUIT EDIT Command

In comparison to the END EDIT command, which saves the updated file and returns you to the DOS prompt, the QUIT EDIT command will cause you to exit the editing session without saving changes. The format of this command is the character Q as shown below.

format$_E$: Q

Since the entering of the character Q will cause EDLIN to terminate without saving changes, the editor will issue a prompt message that you must respond to prior to actually exiting EDLIN. This prompt message serves to verify that you really do not wish to save any previous changes to the file. An example of the use of the QUIT EDIT command and the resulting prompt message is shown below.

```
*Q
Abort edit (Y/N)?
```

In response to the EDLIN prompt, you can enter the character Y to quit the editing session. If you do so, no backup file with the file extension .BAK will be created. If you have second thoughts about quitting, you can enter the character N or any other character and continue the present editing session.

APPEND and WRITE LINES Commands

There are two special EDLIN commands that are meaningful only if the file being edited is too large to fit into memory. These are the APPEND LINES and WRITE LINES commands.

The format of the APPEND LINES command is shown below.

format$_E$: [n] A

Invoking the APPEND LINES command will cause n lines from the diskette to be appended to the file in memory that is presently being edited. Since as much of the file as possible was previously read into memory for editing, you must use the WRITE LINES command to remove a portion of the file in memory to diskette prior to appending lines to the file in memory. The format of the WRITE LINES command is shown below.

format$_E$: [n] W

The WRITE LINES command causes n lines in memory, beginning with line number 1, to be written to the diskette. Similar to the APPEND LINES command, this command is only meaningful if the file being edited is too large to fit in memory.

The APPEND LINES command operates until available memory reaches 75% of capacity, while the WRITE LINES command operates until available memory is less than 25% full, that is, if the number of lines is not specified in an APPEND LINES command, lines will be appended until available memory is filled to 75% of capacity. Similarly, if the number of lines in a WRITE LINES command is not specified, lines will be written until available memory is less than 25% of capacity. If available memory is already less than 25% of capacity, the issuance of a WRITE LINES command will not cause any action to be effected.

CHAPTER FIVE

Fixed Disk Organization

Until now we have avoided mentioning one of the key features of DOS—its ability to have a hierarchical directory structure. For a floppy disk based system, you will normally use a single directory, which limits the number of files per diskette to 64 for single-sided diskettes and 112 for dual-sided diskettes. If a fixed disk is installed in your PC AT, your file storage capability can increase over twentyfold and, as a result, present you with several problems that you would normally not encounter when working with a floppy disk storage system. First, access to a specific file on a fixed disk may be exceedingly slow since DOS would have to search a directory that could contain one thousand or more filenames and addresses to enable a specific file to be located. Second, the simple process of initiating a DIR command could result in several minutes of display time as you watch countless files scroll off the screen. To alleviate these problems, DOS permits you to use a hierarchical directory structure where you can customize specific directories to your requirements.

In a hierarchical directory structure, the top of the directory is known as the "root" directory, similar to an inverted tree. Each directory entry in the hierarchical structure can be a DOS file or the name of another directory. In the case of the latter, the entry is more accurately known as a subdirectory. You can access a file or subdirectory by selecting a path through the directory structure until you locate the desired file or subdirectory. Thus, the link between connected directories is known as a path and you move up and down the hierarchical tree structure by specifying a pathname.

Another advantage of a hierarchical directory structure is its ability to permit an increase in the number of files that can be stored on a diskette. Without a hierarchical directory structure, the number of files that can be stored is limited to 64 or 112, even if room remains on the diskette for additional programs or data files. Since directories other than the root directory are actually files, using a hierarchical directory structure removes the limit to the number of entries a diskette can contain, assuming room remains for programs or data files.

To facilitate access to files and directories, DOS contains several commands that can be used to directly move from one directory to another as well as to create and delete directories. We will review the use of these commands by structuring an example that would be more appropriate for a fixed disk system than for use on a floppy diskette.

Suppose you use your AT for budgeting, financial analysis, word processing, and communications. In addition, suppose you wish to store your library of software on the fixed disk in their appropriate categories. To do so, you would have a master directory known as the root directory through which you would access any of the four operating subdirectories under which you wish to place your files. A schematic of your initial directory structure is illustrated in Fig. 5-1. Each subdirectory is given a name and, although all subdirectories are shown as being on the same level with respect to the root directory, you will shortly see that you can have an infinite variety of subdirectory structures.

Suppose Bev and Gil share access to a PC AT that has a fixed disk. If you wish, you could set up a directory structure so each person has his or her own subdirectory in the root directory, with his or her own separate hierarchy of directories under it. Furthermore, suppose that Bev does the word processing and communications, while Gil performs the budgeting and financial analysis, with the latter function including the use of spreadsheets and graphing programs. A directory structure that might satisfy these requirements is illustrated in Fig. 5-2. Note that the subdirectories are not balanced, since Gil in this example has more subdirectories than Bev. If a requirement existed, you could continue to nest directories until you ran out of logical reasons for doing so or reached the maximum path length permitted by DOS (63 characters). Note that three files, two in Gil's directory and one in Bev's directory

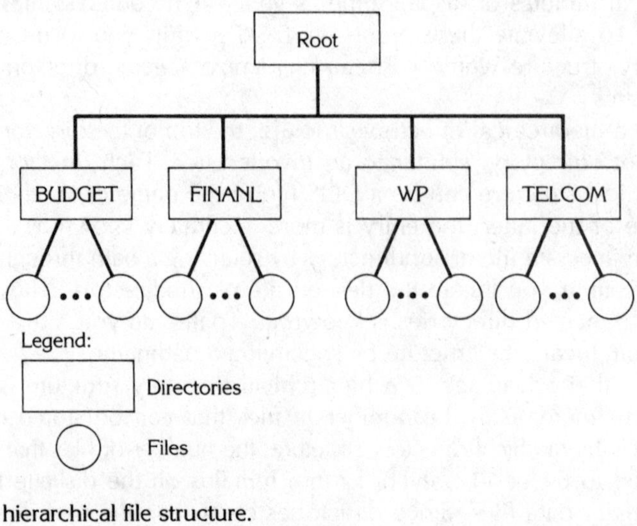

Fig. 5-1. Initial hierarchical file structure.

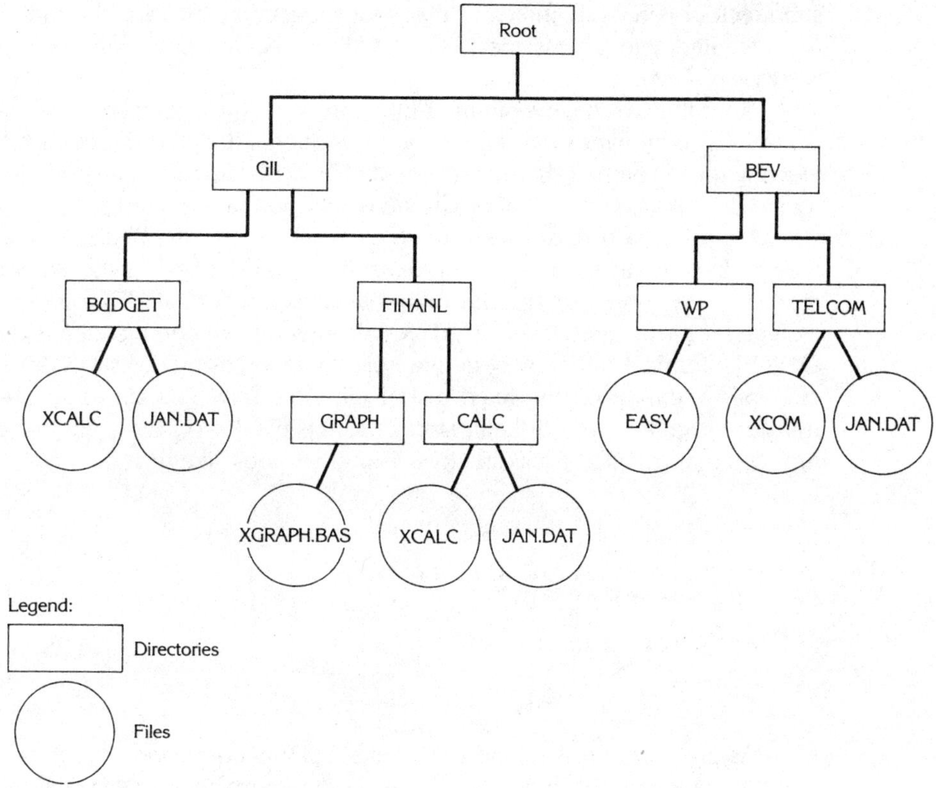

Fig. 5-2. Assigning directories to personnel.

are named JAN.DAT. How does the system distinguish among these three files? The answer lies in the path through the directory structure beginning at the root that is traveled to find the required file.

DIRECTORY AND PATH NAMES

In specifying a path to a file you must consider both directory and path names when you initially design your hierarchical file structure. Subdirectory names follow the same conventions as standard DOS filenames; that is, they can be up to eight characters in length and can optionally contain a three-character extension, with a period (.) used to prefix the extension. Thus, although the subdirectory names illustrated in Fig. 5-2 are perfectly legal, you could add extensions if by doing so, such extensions better reflect the contents of a particular directory or subdirectory.

Path names are the route through a directory structure required to locate a specific directory or file. Path names start at the root and consist of strings of directory names separated by the backslash "\" character. Thus, to access the file XGRAPH.BAS, your route or path name would be \GIL\FINANL\GRAPH\XGRAPH.BAS. Here, the backslash preceding the subdirectory name GIL indicates that your route commences at the root directory. Similarly, to access the TELCOM directory, the path name would be \BEV\TELCOM.

Now that we have examined directory structures, let us review the relevant DOS commands that allow you to use tree-structured directories. In reviewing these commands you will use the DOS hierarchical file structure with a diskette in the A drive. Although one would normally use a hierarchical file structure on a hard disk, DOS also provides you with the ability to use this type of file structure on floppy diskettes if you so desire. For the DOS command review, you will assume that you have just formatted a diskette and assigned it the volume label MASTER. When you have completed a review of DOS hierarchical directory structure commands by using diskette storage, focus your attention on the fixed disk, examining how you can organize and transfer programs from diskette storage to the fixed disk. By using the directory command (DIR), your directory listing will look like this:

```
A>DIR

 Volume in drive A is MASTER
 Directory of A:\

File not found

A>
```

As previously mentioned in Chapter 4, DOS commands can be entered in either lowercase or uppercase letters. For the remainder of this chapter they will be presented both ways.

Now that you have a formatted working diskette, let us examine the DOS commands used for a hierarchical directory structure.

MKDIR Command

The MKDIR command is used to create or make a directory. Its format is:

$$\text{format}_{\text{DOS}}\text{:} \begin{Bmatrix} \text{MD} \\ \text{MKDIR} \end{Bmatrix} \text{path}$$

Like several other directory-related commands, this command has an abbreviation; thus you can enter MD or MKDIR followed by the path name. This command is an internal DOS command, which means it is resident in the AT when DOS is initialized. Thus, you do not have to insert the DOS diskette or prefix the command with the drive designator C: if DOS is on the fixed disk each time you wish to use this command to create a directory on another diskette. Returning to the example illustrated in Fig. 5-2, let us create the directories GIL and BEV.

After you type MKDIR GIL and MKDIR BEV, take a directory listing as shown next.

```
A>MKDIR GIL

A>MKDIR BEV

A>DIR

 Volume in drive A is MASTER
 Directory of A:\

GIL          <DIR>       1-19-84  12:13a
BEV          <DIR>       1-19-84  12:13a
        2 File(s)     178688 bytes free
```

Note that you have created two subdirectories under the root directory—one named GIL and the other named BEV. Now, create the two subdirectories directly under GIL, BUDGET, and FINANL using either of two methods. The first method involves issuing additional MKDIR commands while you are currently at the root directory level. To do so, you will have to issue the full path names of your new subdirectories (\GIL\BUDGET and \GIL\FINANL), or DOS will create these subdirectories under the root at the same level as GIL and BEV.

To create the subdirectory BUDGET under GIL, you would specify the path name as \GIL\BUDGET. Here, the first backslash specifies that your path name commences at the root directory level. Since you are presently at the root directory level this first backslash is optional. Thus, you could issue either of the following commands to create the subdirectory BUDGET under GIL.

```
A>MKDIR\GIL\BUDGET
A>MKDIR GIL\BUDGET
```

To see that you have indeed created a new subdirectory, you should again use the DIR command, whose resulting listing follows.

```
A>DIR

 Volume in drive A is MASTER
 Directory of A:\

GIL          <DIR>       1-19-84  12:13a
BEV          <DIR>       1-19-84  12:13a
        2 File(s)     178176 bytes free
```

Wait a second, you say! I just created a subdirectory named BUDGET but it's not on the directory listing. So where is it?

If you reexamine what you did you will note that you were presently located at the root when you took a directory listing. Therefore, the directory command only listed those subdirectories directly under the root directory—GIL and BEV.

To obtain a listing of subdirectories under the GIL directory, you must either change directories (which is the next topic to be covered) or indicate you want the directory of GIL by specifying the path from the root directory to GIL as follows.

```
A>DIR \GIL

 Volume in drive A is MASTER
 Directory of A:\GIL

.            <DIR>       1-19-84  12:13a
..           <DIR>       1-19-84  12:13a
BUDGET       <DIR>       1-19-84  12:16a
        3 File(s)     178176 bytes  free
```

Well, there BUDGET lies—under the directory GIL where you originally placed it. The other two entries in the directory listing, dot (.) and double dot (..), will be covered shortly. For now, just think of them as two system subdirectories that perform special functions.

Prior to examining an alternate method to create the FINANL directory, let us review the CHDIR command.

CHDIR Command

The change directory command permits you to change the current or working directory level. This internal DOS command provides you with a mechanism to rapidly move around a hierarchical directory structure. The format of this command is:

$$\text{format}_{\text{DOS}}: \left\{\begin{array}{l}\text{CHDIR}\\ \text{CD}\end{array}\right\}\text{path}$$

To move down the hierarchy to GIL you would issue the command:

```
A>CHDIR GIL
```

Once you have moved the current directory to GIL, you can issue the DIR command without the path \GIL and obtain the same result as if you had specified the path when you were located in the root directory. This is illustrated by the following example.

```
A>CD \GIL

A>DIR

 Volume in drive A is MASTER
 Directory of A:\GIL

.            <DIR>       1-19-84  12:13a
..           <DIR>       1-19-84  12:13a
BUDGET       <DIR>       1-19-84  12:16a
        3 File(s)     178176 bytes  free
```

From the preceding, you should note that the DIR command provides a listing only of the current directory, excluding any files in the root or parent directory. Also note that the "Directory of" message shows the path name of the current directory at which you are located, followed by two files designated as dot (.) and double (..). The first file, dot (.), designates the current or working directory and is the directory at which the system is currently logged onto. The second file, double dot (..), indicates the directory immediately above the current directory and is known as the parent directory. This abbreviation is very useful for moving up one level in the hierarchy. Thus, if you issued the command CHDIR.., you would change the current directory up to the parent directory, which is the root directory at this point.

Assuming you have issued the command CHDIR GIL, you have only to enter the command MKDIR FINANL to create the subdirectory FINANL under GIL. To verify this, you should again use the DIR command, whose resulting listing follows.

```
A>MKDIR FINANL

A>DIR

 Volume in drive A is MASTER
 Directory of A:\Gil

.            <DIR>       1-19-84  12:13a
..           <DIR>       1-19-84  12:13a
BUDGET       <DIR>       1-19-84  12:16a
FINANL       <DIR>       1-19-84  12:39a
        4 File(s)      177664 bytes free
```

In the preceding example, note that you can create a subdirectory simply by making the parent directory the current directory and using the MKDIR command with a relative path name. Otherwise, if you start at the root directory or a directory that is not the parent directory, you would have to use the MKDIR command with an absolute path name. To reexamine the latter, move back to the root directory to create the subdirectories GRAPH and CALC.

Since your current directory is GIL, you can issue the command

```
A>CHDIR..or A>CHDIR\
```

to move back to the root directory level. Doing so, you can then issue the command

```
A>MKDIR\GIL\FINANL\GRAPH
```

to create the subdirectory GRAPH, and the command

```
A>MKDIR\GIL\FINANL\CALC
```

to create the subdirectory CALC. At this point, your hierarchical structure is as illustrated in the following.

Directory	Path	Hierarchical level
Root	(\)	root
GIL	(\GIL)	level 1
BEV	(\BEV)	
BUDGET	(\GIL\BUDGET)	level 2
FINANL	(\GIL\FINANL)	
GRAPH	(\GIL \FINANL\GRAPH)	level 3
CALC	(\GIL\FINANL\CALC)	

To verify that GRAPH and CALC are subdirectories of FINANL, change the current directory to FINANL and take a directory listing as shown below.

```
A>CD \GIL\FINANL

A>DIR

 Volume in drive A is MASTER
 Directory of A:\GIL\FINANL

.            <DIR>       1-19-84  12:39a
..           <DIR>       1-19-84  12:39a
GRAPH        <DIR>       1-19-84  12:43a
CALC         <DIR>       1-19-84  12:44a
        4 File(s)     176640 bytes free
```

File References

When you employ a hierarchical file structure, you must include the path to the file in the file specification unless it is the same as the default or current path name, in which case it need not be entered, since all file references without a path name will be assumed by DOS to reference the current directory.

To see how to include path names in a file specification, assume you now wish to copy a program on a diskette where all files are located under the root directory to the GRAPH directory. You would use the DOS command

```
A>COPY A:XGRAPH.BAS B:\GIL\FINANL\GRAPH\XGRAPH.BAS
```

to transfer the file XGRAPH to your hierarchically structured diskette. This copy command would cause the file XGRAPH to be placed under the GRAPH subdirectory with the name XGRAPH and the extension.BAS. In the preceding command, you specified the target diskette to be on drive B, so DOS will prompt you when to change diskettes if you only have one diskette drive.

To verify that the file XGRAPH.BAS has been placed in the GRAPH subdirectory, change your current directory to GRAPH and again use the DIR command as shown below.

```
A>DIR \GIL\FINANL\GRAPH

 Volume in drive A is MASTER
 Directory of A:\GIL\FINANL\GRAPH
```

```
.              <DIR>        1-19-84  12:43a
..             <DIR>        1-19-84  12:43a
XGRAPH    BAS      1920   10-20-83  12:00p
        3 File(s)      174592 bytes free
```

Now that you have established a few subdirectories and transferred one file to your hierarchically structured diskette, it is quite possible that you might take a coffee break and return some time later confused as to where you are in establishing the structure illustrated in Fig. 5-2. At this time you may want to use the DOS TREE command.

TREE Command

The TREE command can be used to obtain a report of the directory structure of a diskette or hard disk. The format of this command is:

format$_{DOS}$: [d:]TREE[d:][/F]

where d represents the physical device and the /F option causes all the files in each directory to be listed. TREE is an external command, which means it must be loaded from the DOS diskette or the fixed disk if DOS resides there by prefixing the command with C:. If you wish to use the DOS diskette in drive A you would enter:

```
A>TREE B:/F
```

If you have only one diskette drive, DOS will prompt you to exchange diskettes. On entering the diskette, whose volume is MASTER, the TREE command would produce the following report.

```
TREE B:/F

DIRECTORY PATH LISTING FOR VOLUME MASTER


Path: \GIL

Sub-directories: BUDGET
                 FINANL

Files:           None


Path: \GIL\BUDGET

Sub-directories: None
Files:           None


Path: \GIL\FINANL
Sub-directories: GRAPH
                 CALC

Files:           None
```

```
Path: \GIL\FINANL\GRAPH

Sub-directories: None
Files:           XGRAPH .BAS

Path: \GIL\FINANL\CALC

Sub-directories: None

Files:           None


Path: \BEV

Sub-directories: None

Files:           None
```

Instead of continuing the subdirectory construction process, we will leave it as an exercise for you to complete. Remember, you can use the CHDIR command to reposition your location in the hierarchical file structure to issue a relative address in the MKDIR command or you can provide an absolute address.

RMDIR Command

You may occasionally wish to delete a directory. To do so requires the prior removal of any entries presently contained in that directory, be they subdirectories or files. Thus, returning to Fig. 5-2, you would have to remove the file XGRAPH.BAS prior to removing the subdirectory GRAPH. Similarly, you would have to remove the files XCALC and JAN.DAT under the CALC subdirectory, as well as the file XGRAPH.BAS and the GRAPH subdirectory before removing the subdirectory FINANL. Therefore, prior to the removal of a directory, you should make certain that it is at the end of a path and does not contain any files.

The format of this internal DOS command is:

$$\text{format}_{\text{DOS}}: \begin{Bmatrix} \text{RMDIR} \\ \text{RD} \end{Bmatrix} \text{path}$$

Like the MKDIR command, you can use either relative or absolute path names in the RMDIR command, and as with the MKDIR command, whose abbreviation is MD, you can use the abbreviation RD for the RMDIR command.

Suppose you wish to remove the subdirectory GRAPH but forgot that the file XGRAPH.BAS is located under that subdirectory. Entering the command

```
A>RMDIR \GIL\FINANL\GRAPH
```

causes DOS to issue the message:

```
A>RMDIR \GIL\FINANL\GRAPH
Invalid path, not directory,
or directory not empty
```

If you do not want the preceding file, you can use the DOS ERASE command to remove it as indicated below.

```
A>ERASE \GIL\FINANL\GRAPH\XGRAPH.BAS
```

The use of this command, which was previously covered in Chapter 4 along with many other DOS commands, illustrates an important principle. That is, if you are working with a hierarchical file structure, you must incorporate a path name in the command in order for the command to conduct the desired operation. If you did not specify a path name, the ERASE command would search the current directory for the file XGRAPH.BAS, which in this case would not be your intention.

Now that you have removed XGRAPH.BAS, you can remove the GRAPH subdirectory as shown below.

```
A>RMDIR \GIL\FINANL\GRAPH

A>
```

Having examined hierarchically related DOS commands, you can now focus your attention on two additional DOS features—pipes and filters.

In DOS, piping provides you with the ability to pass data from one command to another. Filters permit you to change or modify data that are transferred due to a piping activity. Prior to actually examining how to use pipes and filters let us first cover the concept of what is known as standard I/O.

STANDARD I/O

In its normal or default state, the AT's operating system expects to receive input from the keyboard while output is directed to the video display. As these two devices are the standard input and output devices, they are also known as the standard I/O devices.

Unless otherwise specified, DOS commands are written to standard I/O. Thus, a directory listing logically appears on your video display while DOS would scan the keyboard in order to recognize the command DIR. By using the greater than (>) and less than (<) characters you can redirect standard I/O.

Output Redirection

The general format used for output redirection is:

$$\text{format}_{\text{DOS}}\text{: DOS COMMAND} \begin{Bmatrix} > \\ >> \end{Bmatrix} \begin{Bmatrix} \text{reserved name} \\ \text{filespec} \end{Bmatrix}$$

In the preceding format, you use one greater than sign (>) to redirect output. Since you could redirect the results of a particular command onto a file, DOS also provides you with a mechanism to append data to a file that already exists. This is accomplished by using two greater than signs (>>).

The reserved name in the format can include any permissible device name such as CON: for the console keyboard/display, COM1:, LPT1:, and so on. If you wish, you can direct the output resulting from a DOS command onto a file by including a file specification in place of a reserved name. In addition, if you have a hierarchical directory structure, you can include the path in the file specification to send output to a file located in a specific subdirectory. To see how output redirection operates, consider the following example:

```
A>DIR>LPT1:
```

The preceding example results in the directory listing being routed to the first parallel printer instead of being displayed on the console screen. Now, consider the following example:

```
A>BASIC\GIL\BUDGET\XCALC.BAS>>\GIL\BUDGET\JAN.DAT
```

This command runs the BASIC program XCALC.BAS and directs the output to be appended to the file JAN.DAT.

When output is redirected to a file, DOS will first check to see if the file exists. If it exists, DOS will cause the output to overwrite the file unless two greater than signs (>>) are included in the output redirection. This will result in DOS appending the requested output to the end of the file. If the file does not exist, DOS will actually create the requested file. This means you must be careful in a hierarchical file structure or your output could wind up in the wrong subdirectory.

Input Redirection

By using the less than symbol (<) you can specify input redirection. The format for input redirection is:

$$\text{format}_{\text{DOS}}\text{: DOS COMMAND} < \left\{\begin{matrix}\text{reserved name}\\ \text{filespec}\end{matrix}\right\}$$

One use of input redirection is to change the execution requirements of programs. As an example of this, consider a program named STAT that normally requires the AT user to sit at the terminal and type several keyboard entries during the execution of the program. With input redirection, you could type your keyboard entries into a file and direct input to the program from that file. Thus, the command

```
A>BASIC STAT.BAS<JAN.DAT
```

would execute the program STAT.BAS and cause input to the program to occur from the file JAN.DAT. If the program STAT.BAS normally displays results on the screen, you could combine I/O redirection and take a long coffee break. One possibility to satisfy your break requirement might be the following command.

```
A>BASIC STAT.BAS<JAN.DAT>LPT1:
```

This command not only runs the BASIC program STAT.BAS with input to the program from the file JAN.DAT, but, in addition, causes the output from that program to be listed on the printer.

Now that you have a feel for I/O redirection, let us examine piping and filtering.

PIPES AND FILTERS

Piping permits the chaining of commands and programs with the automatic redirection of standard I/O, making it possible for the screen output of one command to be used as the keyboard input to another command or program. A filter is a program or command that reads data from a standard input device, modifies the data, and then outputs the results to a standard output device.

DOS has a special symbol (¦) to indicate piping and three commands that can be used to perform filtering operations. In examining the piping of standard I/O, each of the three DOS filter commands will be discussed.

SORT Command

The DOS SORT command causes data to be read from the standard or a specified input device, sorted, and then written onto the standard or a specified output device. The format of this command is:

format$_{DOS}$: [d:]SORT [/R][/+n]

where the /R option results in a reverse sort being performed, while the /+n option causes the sort field to commence in column n. If the /R option is not specified, an ascending sort is performed and the omission of the /+ option causes the sort to begin in column 1.

The SORT command is an external DOS command. This means that you must place a copy of the DOS diskette into your disk drive or prefix the command with the location of DOS on the fixed disk to load and execute the command. Let us first examine a simple sorting action to see the utility of this filter.

If you do not specify I/O redirection, the standard I/O devices are used when you execute this command. Thus, entering SORT by itself will cause this DOS filter to accept input from the keyboard, sort the input, and output the results to the standard output device that is the screen. This is demonstrated by the following activity.

```
A>SORT
WASHINGTON
JACKSON
KENNEDY
NIXXON
JOHNSON
^Z
JACKSON
JOHNSON
KENNEDY
NIXXON
WASHINGTON

A>
```

In the preceding example, note that you use a control Z (shown as ∧Z) to inform DOS that your input was terminated. The preceding example has omitted one key peculiarity of the SORT command that warrants additional discussion—it sorts data according to the ASCII value of the characters it encounters. This means that any items that start with an uppercase letter will be placed before any items that start with a lowercase letter, which would place WASHINGTON before jackson if you were inconsistent in your usage of upper- and lowercase letters. Thus, as long as you are consistent in your data formats, the SORT filter can be a valuable tool.

Suppose you now wish to sort the directory and output the result on your display. You could do this as follows:

```
A>DIR>TEMP
A>SORT<TEMP
```

The first operation would output the directory to a file labeled TEMP, while the second operation would sort that file and display the results on the screen. You can perform both operations at once without the use of an intermediate file by using the piping feature of DOS. When you employ piping, you can send the output of one command directly to the input of another command as illustrated by the following example:

```
A>DIR¦SORT
```

In this example, the (¦) character denotes to DOS that the output of the DIR command is to be used as input to the SORT command. Although DOS will actually create a temporary file, when it finishes sorting and displaying the directory, it will delete the file automatically and invisibly.

You can also employ piping with I/O redirection as illustrated by the following example:

```
A>DIR¦SORT>LPT1:
```

In this example, the directory is first sorted and then listed on your printer instead of being routed to the screen. Now that you have initially examined the SORT filter, let's take a look at the other DOS filters.

FIND Command

The FIND filter command searches each line in a specified file for the occurrence or non-occurrence of the string indicated in the command. Its format is:

format$_{DOS}$: FIND [/V][/C][/N]"string"[filespec]

where the /V option causes all lines *not* containing the specified string to be displayed. The /C option causes only a count of matches to be displayed, while the /N option causes the relative line number of each matching string to be displayed ahead of the line from the file.

Consider the following example of the use of this filter.

```
A>DIR¦SORT¦FIND "12:00">LPT1:
```

The preceding would cause all files on the diskette in drive A containing 12:00 in the directory to be displayed on the printer in sorted order.

The FIND and SORT filters provide you with a mechanism to perform elementary data base searches of ASCII text files without a data base management system. As an example of this, assume you have a file named INVENT whose record format is as follows:

1 30	31 40	41 50	51 60
VENDOR	PART #	QUANTITY ON HAND	UNIT COST

Suppose you wish a list of all parts produced by the vendor named XYZ Corporation sorted by unit cost.

You can first use the FIND filter to locate all records that contain the string "XYZ Corporation." Since you must later sort the string, instead of directing the output to the screen, you should direct the output of the filter operation to a temporary file, TEMP. This is accomplished by the following command.

```
A>FIND "XYZ Corporation" INVENT>TEMP
```

Next, you will sort the contents of TEMP; however, since unit cost commences in column 51 of each record, you must signify this in the SORT command by using the /+n option, with n assigned the value 51. Thus, you would type:

```
A>SORT/+51<TEMP>LPT1:
```

If you wish to avoid using a temporary file that you would have to later delete manually, you can let DOS create and automatically delete a temporary file (invisible to you) by using the piping feature as shown below.

```
A>FIND "XYZ Corporation" INVENT¦SORT/+51>LPT1:
```

MORE Command

The last DOS filter command to be reviewed is the MORE command. Like SORT and FIND, this is an external command that must be loaded from the DOS diskette. This command causes data from the standard or a specified input file to be displayed one screen at a time. When the screen is filled, the message MORE is displayed and you must then press any key on the keyboard to cause the next screen to appear.

The utilization of this filter is illustrated by the following example:

```
A>MORE<SORT<DIR
```

The preceding causes the directory to be sorted and displayed one screen at a time.

FIXED DISK BASED APPLICATIONS

Now that you have reviewed the DOS commands applicable to heirarchical directory structures, let us focus our attention on placing application programs on the fixed disk and then using those applications.

Let us assume that at the present time you have only transferred DOS to the fixed disk. Thus, entering the directory command would result in the following screen display or a quite similar display if you also transferred the DOS supplemental program files to the fixed disk.

```
C>dir/w

 Volume in drive C has no label
 Directory of C:\

COMMAND  COM  ANSI     SYS  SORT     EXE  SHARE    EXE  FIND     EXE
ATTRIB   EXE  MORE     COM  ASSIGN   COM  PRINT    COM  SYS      COM
CHKDSK   COM  FORMAT   COM  VDISK    SYS  BASIC    COM  BASICA   COM
FDISK    COM  COMP     COM  TREE     COM  BACKUP   COM  RESTORE  COM
LABEL    COM  DISKCOPY COM  DISKCOMP COM  KEYBSP   COM  KEYBIT   COM
KEYBGR   COM  KEYBUK   COM  KEYBFR   COM  MODE     COM  SELECT   COM
GRAPHICS COM  RECOVER  COM  EDLIN    COM  GRAFTABL COM
        34 File(s) 17518592 bytes free

C>
```

Now, suppose you wish to transfer to the fixed disk a word processing program you've purchased. You may put the program in a directory labeled WP, since that is an acronym easily remembered. If you are at the root level, you would enter the following command to create this directory.

```
C>md \wp
```

Now, you should issue another directory command to see how you can distinguish between files and directories. In the following display, note that WP has no extension.

```
C>dir/w

 Volume in drive C has no label
 Directory of C:\

COMMAND  COM    WP                 ANSI      SYS    SORT      EXE    SHARE     EXE
FIND     EXE    ATTRIB    EXE      MORE      COM    ASSIGN    COM    PRINT     COM
SYS      COM    CHKDSK    COM      FORMAT    COM    VDISK     SYS    BASIC     COM
BASICA   COM    FDISK     COM      COMP      COM    TREE      COM    BACKUP    COM
RESTORE  COM    LABEL     COM      DISKCOPY  COM    DISKCOMP  COM    KEYBSP    COM
KEYBIT   COM    KEYBGR    COM      KEYBUK    COM    KEYBFR    COM    MODE      COM
SELECT   COM    GRAPHICS  COM      RECOVER   COM    EDLIN     COM    GRAFTABL  COM
       35 File(s) 17516544 bytes free

C>
```

To transfer the word processing program files from diskette to the fixed disk requires the use of the COPY command. Before doing so, however, you should change the directory to WP or the files will be transfered to the directory you are currently logged onto, which is the root directory. Thus, you should first use the CD command to change directories and then use the COPY command to transfer the program files from the diskette to the fixed disk under the WP directory. This process is illustrated below.

```
C>cd\wp

C>copy a:*.* c:
A:RECONFIG.BAT
A:TRANSFER.EXE
A:EW.COM
A:TARGET.COM
A:IBM88VMI.COM
A:CONFIG.COM
A:CONTARG.COM
A:EZWRITER.OPT
        8 File(s) copied
```

In the preceding example, you first changed the directory to WP and then copied all files from the diskette in drive A to the fixed disk under the WP directory by using the global asterisk character (*). If you carefully read the names of the eight files copied, you may recognize that this is the EasyWriter word processing program that was transferred.

To verify that the EasyWriter program was transferred to the WP directory, you can again use the directory command. The result is illustrated below.

```
C>dir /w

 Volume in drive C has no label
 Directory of C:\WP

.              ..                RECONFIG BAT    TRANSFER EXE    EW         COM
TARGET  COM    IBM88VMI  COM     CONFIG   COM    CONTARG  COM    EZWRITER   OPT
      10 File(s) 17405952 bytes free

C>
```

If you follow the Easy Writer operating instructions and enter the command EW to operate the program, EasyWriter's main menu would appear on your display with the message "Insert storage diskette in drive A, then press ENTER." This means that although you have transferred EasyWriter to the fixed disk, the program continues to operate as it was designed—to use diskette drives A and B. If you wish to store your EasyWriter data files on the fixed disk, you could use the ASSIGN command; however, care must be taken since this is a DOS command and DOS was previously transferred to the root directory. Thus, if you issue the following ASSIGN command, the error message results from the fact that you are in the WP directory that does not contain the DOS ASSIGN program

```
C>assign a=c b=c
Bad command or file name

C>
```

To properly use the ASSIGN command, you must first change your directory to the root directory. Then, you could enter the appropriate ASSIGN commands, change your directory to WP, and then enter the command EW to execute EasyWriter as illustrated by the following sequence.

```
C>cd\

C>assign a=c b=c

C>cd\wp

C>ew
```

If this sequence is not entered each time you wish to use EasyWriter, the program will revert back to its original design of using drives A and B. Since the preceding sequence is laborious, you can automate the process by creating a batch file that will automatically execute the ASSIGN command and switch directories as required. Although we will defer a detailed coverage of batch file processing until a later chapter, we will discuss the construction and use of this type of file to facilitate running an application program in this chapter.

To create a batch file, you can use the COPY command with the console as the source device and a filename with the extension .bat as the target batch file. Into this file enter the DOS commands you wish to be executed and terminate your data entry by pressing the Ctrl+Z keys. Prior to creating the batch file, switch the directory to WP and then enter the file in that directory as illustrated by the following.

```
C>cd\wp

C>copy con: wp.bat
cd\
assign a=c b=c
```

```
cd\wp
ew
^Z
            1 File(s) copied

C>
```

After the batch file is created, you can automatically execute EasyWriter with drives A and B assigned to drive C by simply entering the command WP once you are logged onto the WP directory. This is because you previously created a batch file named wp.bat and only have to enter the filename of a batch file for it to execute.

If you wish, you can place a batch file in the root directory, which allows you to forgo changing directories when you power-up a fixed disk system that has DOS in that directory. Thus, you can enter the following batch file into the root directory.

```
COPY CON:WP.BAT
ASSIGN A=C B=C
CD\WP
EW
CD\
^Z
```

In the preceding example, you first assign drives A and B to C prior to changing directories. Once you change directories to WP, you can run the EasyWriter program. The last command in the batch file (CD) moves you back to the root directory, at which time you use the EasyWriter exit to DOS command instead of having to manually change directories.

Based upon the preceding examples, batch files can be valuable for automating any predefined sequence of DOS commands to fit your requirements.

FILE BACKUP AND RESTORATION

Two of the most important DOS commands for fixed disk operations are BACKUP and RESTORE. Although both commands can be used to back up files from one diskette to another or one fixed disk to another fixed disk, their primary use is for backing up the contents of a fixed disk to a diskette and restoring files from a diskette to a fixed disk.

BACKUP Command

The BACKUP command provides you with the capability to back up one or more files from one type of disk to another. The format of this external DOS command is:

format$_{DOS}$: [d:][path]BACKUP d:[path][filename[.ext]]d:
[/S][/M][/A][/D:mm-dd-yy]

Since BACKUP is an external command, it must be loaded into memory. Thus, [d:][path] before BACKUP is used to specify the drive and path to the BACKUP command file. The d: after BACKUP specifies the drive that contains the files you wish to back up. Thus, if you have one fixed disk and wish to back up files on that disk, you would enter C: in the command. The [path] [filename[.ext]] is used to indicate the name of a specific file or group of files you wish to back up. If you wish, you can use global filename characters in the filename and extension. Thus, you could enter the command

```
BACKUP C:\*.*A:
```

to back up all files in the root directory to the diskette in drive A, assuming you have a formatted diskette in that drive. The /S, /M, /A, and /D parameters permit you to further define the backup process, which becomes important as you fill your fixed disk.

The /S parameter results in the backup of subdirectory files in addition to the files in the specified or current directory, while the /M parameter causes only files that were modified since the last backup operation to be transferred. The /M option can considerably reduce the time required for a backup operation if you have a large number of files and only add or change a few files between backup operations.

The /A parameter causes the specified files in the BACKUP command to be added to the files already present on the backup storage media, while the /D parameter causes only files modified on or after the specified data to be transferred to the backup media. It should be noted that BACKUP is not the same as COPY, since a COPY command results in an exact duplicate of a file or group of files, whereas backup files include control information that is used by the RESTORE command. This means that you should use the COPY command if you wish to use a program on another PC system, since backup files cannot be used as program or data files until they are restored.

Returning to the fixed disk, let us assume you wish to back up your WP directory. Assuming you are in the root directory with the DOS program BACKUP in that directory, you would enter the following command:

```
C>backup c:\wp a:
```

After you enter the preceding command, the prompt "Insert backup diskette 01 in drive A:" and "Strike any key when ready" will be displayed. If existing files are on the diskette in drive A you would receive the following warning:

```
Warning! Files in the target drive
A:\ root directory will be erased
Strike any key when ready
```

The reason for this warning is that BACKUP erases existing files on the target storage media before it starts backing up the source, unless the /A parameter was used in the command.

Once backup is in operation, the name of each file backed up is displayed as it is transferred to the backup media as you continue the backup of your WP directory. The following example illustrates this procedure.

```
*** Backing up files to drive A: ***
Diskette Number: 01

\WP\RECONFIG.BAT
\WP\TRANSFER.EXE
\WP\EW.COM
\WP\TARGET.COM
\WP\IBM88VMI.COM
\WP\CONFIG.COM
\WP\CONTARG.COM
\WP\EZWRITER.OPT
\WP\TEST.EWF
\WP\WP.BAT
```

If you had an extensive number of files to back up you would require multiple diskettes. After the first diskette is filled, BACKUP will prompt you to insert the next backup diskette. Since the RESTORE command requires you to insert the backup diskettes in the order they were created, you should label each backup diskette as it is created.

Now that you are familiar with the capability of BACKUP, let us examine how to restore files.

RESTORE Command

The complement of the BACKUP command, RESTORE provides you with a mechanism to restore one or more files that were previously backed up. The format of this command:

format$_{DOS}$: [d:][path]RESTORE d:
[d:][path]filename[.ext][/S][/P]

The parameters [d:] and [path] that prefix the command function the same as in the previously described BACKUP command, since RESTORE is an external command that must be loaded into memory to operate. The parameter [d:] after the command specifies the drive that contains the file or files to be restored. Thus, if you wish to restore files from a diskette in the high-capacity disk drive, you would enter A:. The parameters [d:][path]filename[.ext] are used to indicate where you wish to place the restored files and what files you wish to restore. As with BACKUP, you can use global characters in the filename and extension.

The /S parameter is required to restore all files in subdirectories in addition to the files in the specified directory. Thus, if you were at the root directory and used the /S parameter, all subdirectories would be restored. If the /P parameter is specified, RESTORE will prompt you prior to restoring files that changed since they were last backed up or are marked read-only. Then, you can indicate whether or not you wish those files to be restored.

Returning to the WP directory example, suppose you inadvertently erased the file test.ewf. You can use the RESTORE command to recover that file as follows:

```
C>restore a: c:\wp\test.ewf

Insert backup diskette 01 in drive A:
Strike any key when ready
```

Note that in the preceding example a: was entered because the diskette produced as a result of the backup operation was placed in drive A. Then you entered c:\wp\test.ewf since you wished to restore the file to the fixed disk in the WP directory, and the file you want to restore is test.ewf. Once you enter the backup diskette into drive A and press a key, RESTORE will display the date the file or files were backed up and list each file as it is restored, as shown below.

```
*** Restoring files from drive A: ***
Diskette: 01
\WP\TEST.EWF

C>
```

CHAPTER SIX

BASIC Overview

Three versions of BASIC can operate on the PC AT. The version or versions operable on your system will depend on the presence or absence of disk storage and whether or not you have a copy of the DOS diskette in drive A or have placed DOS on your fixed disk.

CASSETTE BASIC

Cassette BASIC can be considered as a nucleus BASIC, since it is available on every IBM PC AT. This BASIC is contained in 32K bytes of ROM located in the system board inside the system unit.

If your PC AT has only a diskette drive, you should remove any diskette in the drive. Then, when you switch power on, cassette BASIC will be "brought up" or initialized.

When cassette BASIC is initialized, your screen will display a copyright notice and the words "Version C" followed by the release number and the number of free bytes of memory available for use. In cassette BASIC, the only data and program storage device that is available is a cassette tape recorder. Since the PC AT does not contain a cassette port, you cannot store information using this version of BASIC. Thus, PC AT users should not use cassette BASIC because each AT comes with a minumum of one high-capacity diskette drive installed, which enables the use of two upwardly compatible versions of cassette BASIC—disk BASIC and advanced BASIC.

DISK BASIC

Disk BASIC is supplied as a program file on the IBM DOS diskette and must be loaded into memory in order for you to use it. The method employed to load disk BASIC will depend on where your DOS files reside.

If you have only diskette drives on your AT, you must bring up DOS from drive A prior to loading the BASIC program. If power to your AT was off, you can insert a diskette with DOS on it in drive A and turn power on. Once power is switched on, the self-test diagnostics will be executed and then the initial portion of DOS will be read from drive A. During the DOS initialization process, you will be requested to enter the date and time. Since the AT has a battery-operated clock/calendar, in most situations you will simply press the Enter key if the date and time are correct. If not, you can enter a new date or time, using the same format in which the date and time are displayed. The DOS day and time prompts as well as the IBM DOS initialization message and the command required to load disk BASIC are illustrated below. The DOS initialization message is displayed after the date and time are entered and consists of a copyright notice and information concerning the version of DOS being used.

```
Current date is Tue 11-06-1984
Enter new date (mm-dd-yy):
Current time is 19:51:40.74
Enter new time:

The IBM Personal Computer DOS
Version 3.00 (C)Copyright IBM Corp 1981, 1982, 1983, 1984

A>BASIC
```

After the initialization message is displayed, one line will be skipped and the prompt message A> will be generated. Here, the character A says you are working with diskette drive A, and the > character says you are at the DOS system level of operation. By typing the word BASIC and pressing the Enter key, you will inform DOS that you wish disk BASIC to be loaded from the diskette in drive A. The result of entering the BASIC command is illustrated in Fig. 6-1. The words "Version D" in the disk BASIC initialization display inform you that you are in disk BASIC, while the number following the character D tells you the revision level of the software you are operating with. Normally, a digit is used for major revisions, while a fractional change in the revision number indicates a minor revision. The number of free bytes of memory available for use by disk BASIC will also be displayed, while the 25th line will have the initial values of the soft keys displayed. The prompt "Ok" is issued by BASIC and indicates it is ready for operation.

Disk BASIC is a superset of cassette BASIC in that it can execute all cassette BASIC statements as well as several additional BASIC statements. Key differences between disk and cassette BASIC are disk BASIC's ability to support I/O to the diskette and fixed disk in addition to a cassette, communications support, an internal clock to keep track of the date and time, and the ability to support up to two printers attached to the system unit in place of the one printer cassette BASIC supports.

Note that when disk BASIC is initialized, the values of the soft keys are displayed on line 25. The number preceding each soft key indicates the function key you must press to generate the literal assigned to the key. Later in this chapter you will learn how to use the function keys as a labor saving device to perform predefined functions, such as listing the contents of a pro-

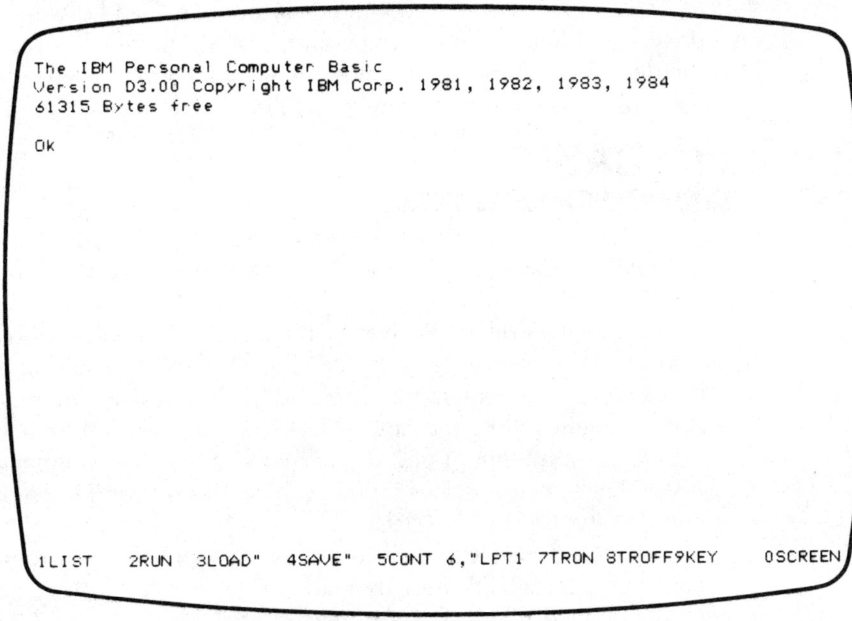

Fig. 6-1. Disk BASIC initialization display.

gram by pressing the F1 key and the Enter key in place of typing the word LIST into your system.

If your AT is powered up and you previously transferred DOS to the root directory of your fixed disk, you can load disk BASIC from that device. If you are at the root directory level of drive C, you can simply enter the command BASIC to initialize disk BASIC. Otherwise, if you were in a different directory and the BASIC program was in the root directory, you would enter the command CD\ to change to the root directory prior to entering the command BASIC.

If your system was powered off but DOS was on the root directory of drive C and no diskette was in drive A, upon applying power to your system, the root directory of drive C would be searched for DOS. This would result in the familiar request to enter the date and time, as well as the display of the DOS copyright notice. Once the prompt C> is displayed, you can bring up disk BASIC by entering the command BASIC as illustrated here.

```
Current date is Mon 11-05-1984
Enter new date (mm-dd-yy):
Current time is 22:08:36.44
Enter new time:

The IBM Personal Computer DOS
Version 3.00 (C)Copyright IBM Corp 1981, 1982, 1983, 1984

C>BASIC
```

Once the command BASIC is entered, disk BASIC will be initialized and your display screen will appear as previously illustrated in Fig. 6-1.

If DOS was on the root directory of drive C and drive A was the default drive, you could enter the command C:BASIC to initialize disk BASIC. Again, the disk BASIC initialization message illustrated in Fig. 6-1 would appear and the "Ok" prompt would signify that disk BASIC was awaiting your action.

ADVANCED BASIC

The most extensive form of BASIC available on the IBM PC AT—advanced BASIC—can be viewed as a superset of both disk and cassette BASIC.

Since the original PC was manufactured with only 16K of RAM memory, IBM offered three versions of BASIC, each version requiring a larger amount of memory to operate. Cassette BASIC requires a minimum of 16K, disk BASIC requires 48K, and advanced BASIC requires 64K of RAM. Since every PC AT has a minimum of 256K of memory, you will normally use advanced BASIC because it operates on every AT and is upwardly compatible with disk and cassette BASIC.

Like disk BASIC, advanced BASIC is supplied as a program on the IBM DOS diskette, which must be loaded into memory to use. Advanced BASIC can be loaded like disk BASIC, except that the command BASICA is entered in response to the DOS prompt character instead of the BASIC command. The following three examples illustrate three command entries that can be used to bring up or initialize advanced BASIC.

```
A>BASICA      DOS on drive A, default drive is A
A>C:BASICA    DOS on drive C, default drive is A
C>BASICA      DOS on drive C, default drive is C
```

For the last two examples, it was assumed that DOS was in the root directory of drive C.

Once advanced BASIC is loaded, the words "Version A," followed by a number indicating the revision level of the software will be displayed, along with the number of bytes of memory available for use. Figure 6-2 illustrates the screen display initialization message once advanced BASIC is loaded. Like disk BASIC, advanced BASIC can be initialized in many ways, depending on where DOS is located and whether or not your AT is powered on.

The preceding examples for the initialization of disk BASIC are applicable to advanced BASIC; simply replace the command BASIC with the command BASICA.

RETURNING TO DOS

To return from disk or advanced BASIC to DOS, you must have a DOS diskette in drive A or a copy of DOS on your fixed disk. Once the BASIC prompt (Ok) appears on your display you can type the command SYSTEM and press the Enter key. This command will cause you to exit BASIC and return to DOS, causing the DOS prompt (A> or C>) to appear, which indicates that DOS is ready for you to give it a command. In the following example, you will return to DOS from advanced BASIC.

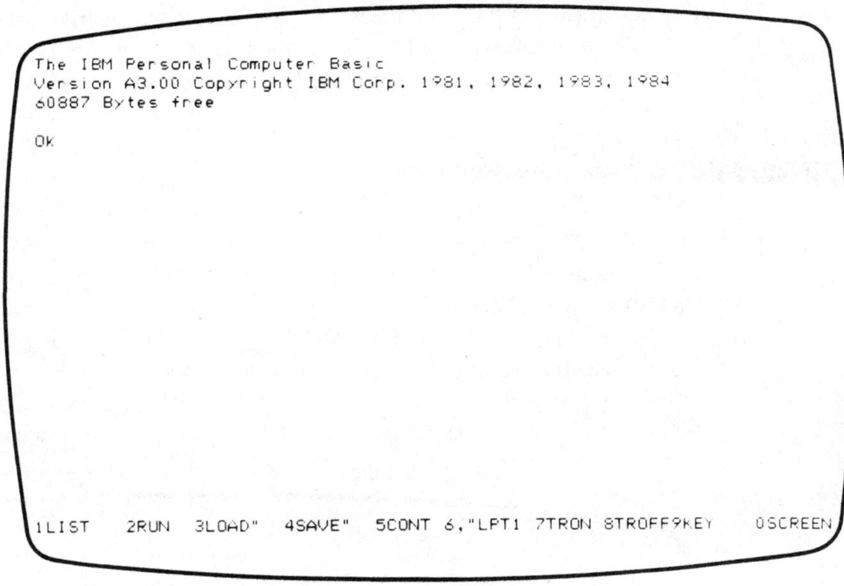

Fig. 6-2. Advanced BASIC initialization display.

```
The IBM Personal Computer Basic
Version A3.00 Copyright IBM Corp. 1981, 1982, 1983, 1984
60887 Bytes free

Ok
SYSTEM

A>
```

Note that if the soft keys were displayed, upon entering the command SYSTEM, those keys would disappear from view since you have gone from BASIC back to DOS.

BASIC MODES OF OPERATION

Once any version of BASIC becomes operational, the prompt "Ok" will be displayed on your television or monitor. This prompt message means that BASIC is ready for you to tell it what to do. This state of readiness is also known as the BASIC command level because BASIC is awaiting your command. At this point, BASIC can be used in either of two modes of operation—direct or indirect mode.

The direct mode of operation is used to tell BASIC to immediately perform your request after you terminate an input line with the Enter key. BASIC automatically differentiates between direct and indirect modes by examining the input line for the presence or absence of a line number. If no line number is at the beginning of the input line, BASIC will immediately execute the statement or command entered. If a line number is encountered, BASIC will treat the line input as part of the program to be stored in memory. This is known as the indirect mode, and the resulting program can be executed by entering the RUN command or by pressing the F2 key.

Direct Mode

The direct mode provides you with the capability of a calculator to solve computations that do not require the use of a complete BASIC program. In addition, direct mode operations can be employed to debug a program by interspacing program execution and direct mode computations. Since direct mode computations occur immediately after the Enter key is pressed, this mode is also referred to as the immediate program mode.

The top part of Fig. 6-3 illustrates the entry and execution of several direct program mode operations. In each example, the PRINT statement is a BASIC

DIRECT

```
Ok
PRINT 317.5+4.106                              'ADDITION
 321.606
Ok
PRINT 350-105                                  'SUBTRACTION
 245
Ok
PRINT 27.5*10                                  'MULTIPLICATION
 275
Ok
PRINT 14.515/3.14159                           'DIVISION
 4.620272
Ok
PRINT 2^5                                      'EXPONENTIATION
 32
Ok
PRINT 2^5-12+1.7*5/3                           'COMBINED
 22.83334
Ok
PRINT "PUFF"+"NTOOT"                           'CONCATENATION
PUFFNTOOT
Ok
```

INDIRECT

```
Ok
1 PRINT 50/2
RUN
 25
Ok
2 PRINT 2^4
RUN
 25
 16
Ok
```

Fig. 6-3. Direct and indirect program modes.

language statement that causes the display of the resulting operation to appear on the screen. In the first direct mode operation, the numerical quantity 317.5 is added to the quantity 4.106. Here, the plus sign (+) is the BASIC operator employed to conduct addition. After the line is entered, the results of the computation are displayed on the next line. In the following five examples, numerical data is operated on using the subtraction (−), multiplication (*), division (/), and exponentiation (/\) BASIC operators. The apostrophe (') to the left of the comment on each line concerning the type of operation performed serves as an indicator to BASIC that all of the following characters on the line should be treated as comments. This comment indicator character (') can be used in both direct and indirect modes. The last direct mode example illustrates how BASIC can operate on data strings. In this example, concatenation or the combining of two strings into one is shown. The wide range of BASIC operators available for use in both direct and indirect modes will be covered in detail later in this chapter.

Indirect Mode

The indirect mode of operation is the more powerful of the two available BASIC modes. This is because many statements can be entered as part of a program and executed with one command. The first example in the lower portion of Fig. 6-3 shows a one-line program entered into memory. With the program in memory, the RUN command must be entered to execute the program or you can simply press F2. The example in the lower portion of Fig. 6-3 shows what happens after a second line is added to the program and the two-line program in memory is then executed by entering the RUN command. Note that the program prints two lines of output, one for each program line that contained a PRINT statement.

LINES, STATEMENTS, AND ELEMENTARY COMMANDS

Although you may not recognize the fact at this time, you have already entered and executed your first BASIC program. Every BASIC program consists of one or more line numbers. In turn, each line number contains one or more BASIC statements, such as the PRINT statements shown in Fig. 6-3.

A BASIC program line always begins with a line number and is terminated by the Enter key. Valid line numbers range between 0 and 65,529 and may contain a maximum of 255 characters, including the enter character. When this logical line exceeds 80 characters in length, it will "wrap" itself onto the next physical line as you continue to enter data as shown below.

```
Ok
NEW
Ok
10PRINT"DUE TO THE POSITIONS REQUIRED ON A LINE FOR A LINE NUMBER AND THE PRINT
STATEMENT AN 80 CHARACTER MESSAGE WOULD REQUIRE MORE THAN ONE PHYSICAL LINE"
RUN
```

```
DUE TO THE POSITIONS REQUIRED ON A LINE FOR A LINE NUMBER AND THE PRINT STATEMEN
T AN 80 CHARACTER MESSAGE WOULD REQUIRE MORE THAN ONE PHYSICAL LINE
Ok
```

If the logical line exceeds 255 characters in length, the extra characters will be truncated when the Enter key is pressed. Although the extra characters will appear on your display, they will not be processed by BASIC.

To determine what the contents of memory are at a particular point in time, you can use the LIST command. In its elementary form, this command will cause the program currently in memory to be listed on the display. Later when you cover this command in detail, you will see how you can list single lines or segments of a program. Returning to the two-line indirect program illustrated in the lower part of Fig. 6-3, suppose that program is currently in memory. The effect of the LIST command results in the complete two-line program being displayed as shown.

```
Ok
LIST
1 PRINT 50/2
2 PRINT 2^4
Ok
```

Now suppose you wish to modify the program currently residing in memory. If you wish to add one or more new lines to the program, you can do so by entering a valid line number followed by at least one nonblank character and then press the Enter key. Each line so entered will be added to the BASIC program in memory. If a line already exists with the same line number as the line entered, then the old line number will be erased and replaced by the newly entered one. If line numbers are entered out of sequence, BASIC will internally sort the program lines into sequence as shown below. Here, we added line 0 into memory after the listing of the file displayed its contents, showing it combined two lines, numbered 1 and 2. After entering line 0 the program was again listed and, as shown, the program has been placed in numerical line number sequence by BASIC.

```
Ok
LIST
1 PRINT 50/2
2 PRINT 2^4
Ok
0 PRINT "ANSWERS FOLLOW"
LIST
0 PRINT "ANSWERS FOLLOW"
1 PRINT 50/2
2 PRINT 2^4
Ok
```

Line Format

Each BASIC program line entered will follow the following format:

nnnnn BASIC statement [:BASIC statement . . .]['comment]

The characters "nnnnn" indicate the line number, which can be from one to five digits, ranging in magnitude from 0 to 65,529. The line number is in essence, the address of a program statement or series of statements. The latter occurs when multiple statements are contained on one line. Normally, program execution is in sequential line number order, beginning with the first statement in the program and continuing until the physical end of the program is reached. An example of this is shown in the following:

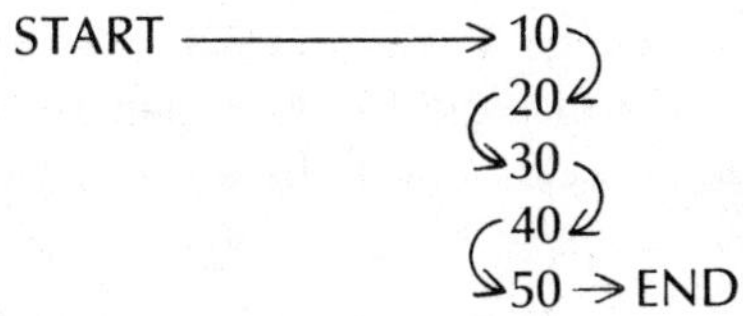

Since BASIC contains many statements that can be used to alter the sequence in which operations are performed, you can develop programs that execute lines or groups of lines nonsequentially as shown below.

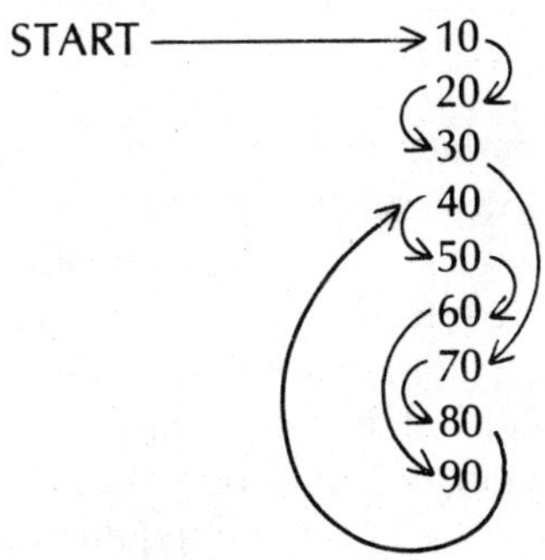

Since line numbers are the address of one or more statements contained on a program line, they are a necessity if you wish to have a mechanism to identify changes in the sequence of the execution of statements within a program.

The line number is followed by one or more BASIC statements where the brackets in the format indicate optional items that can be contained within the format. If you desire to have multiple BASIC statements on a line, each statement must be separated from the preceding statement by a colon (:). Although multiple statements on a line sometimes reduce the clarity of a program for debugging purposes or the visual comprehension of a program's actions, it results in less memory being required for program storage and execution. This fact is illustrated by the simple three-line program shown below. Lines 1 and 2 print the results of two computations, while line 3 prints the number of bytes in memory not being used by BASIC. This is accomplished by the use of the FRE function. The FRE function uses what is known as a dummy argument and returns the number of available or free bytes of memory not used by BASIC. In this example, 60,854 bytes are shown to be available.

```
OK
LIST
1 PRINT 50/2
2 PRINT 2^4
3 PRINT FRE(0)
OK
RUN
 25
 16
 60854
OK
```

Now, modify line 1 to incorporate the BASIC statement contained in line 2 and delete line 2 from memory. LIST and RUN this program as shown below.

```
OK
LIST
1 PRINT 50/2 :PRINT 2^4
3 PRINT FRE(0)
OK
RUN
 25
 16
 60857
OK
```

Note that available memory has increased by three bytes from the previous program where the first two BASIC statements were on individual lines. By combining line 2 with line 1, you are able to eliminate one line number as well as the carriage return and line feed characters associated with each line.

If you have previously programmed other computers, you may be aware that some BASIC languages allow statements with no separations between keywords as well as between keywords and operators. With each version of AT BASIC, separators in the form of a space are required or a syntax error will occur when you RUN your program. An example of a syntax error due to the improper separation between the BASIC keyword PRINT and the operand is shown below.

```
OK
LIST
1 PRINT50/2
3 PRINT FRE(0)
OK
RUN
Syntax error in 1
OK
1 PRINT50/2
```

When a syntax error is discovered while a program is running, BASIC will automatically display the line that caused the error so you can correct it. In the above example, line 1 is displayed and the cursor will be positioned under the digit 1. You can move the cursor right to the 5 in 50 and press in the Ins key to put you in the insert mode. Doing so will change the cursor from a line to a square. You can then press the space bar to insert the required space between the keyword PRINT and the operand. By pressing the

Enter key, you will store the corrected line back into memory and can now return the program as shown.

```
OK
LIST
1 PRINT50/2
3 PRINT FRE(0)
OK
RUN
Syntax error in 1
OK
1 PRINT 50/2
RUN
 25
 60864
OK
```

In the preceding example, the second statement on the first line was purposely omitted. Note that available memory increased by ten bytes, from 60,854 to 60,864. This shows us that we can easily determine the amount of memory required for one or more BASIC statements. This can be a valuable tool if you have limited memory in your system unit or if you are developing a very large program and have to examine various ways to economize on the use of memory.

One useful feature of AT BASIC is the ability to document what a particular statement or group of statements is designed to perform. This can be accomplished by adding comments to the end of a line by using the single quotation mark (') to separate the comment from the rest of the line. Thus, if you were computing and printing the circumference of a circle whose radius is 24 feet, you might add the appropriate comment to the BASIC statement as shown below.

```
OK
LIST
10 PRINT 3.14159*24^2 'CIRCUMFRENCE IN FEET
OK
RUN
 1809.556
OK
```

Note that when the one-line program is executed the comment is ignored. This part of the line is referred to as being nonexecutable. Later, when BASIC is covered in detail, you will see that there is a REM statement (for remarks) that permits you to add nonexecutable comments to a program.

Comments can be valuable for interpreting what is occurring in a program. However, while comments are nonexecutable, they require memory for storage that would otherwise be available for program execution.

BASIC CHARACTER SET

The BASIC character set consists of alphabetic characters, numeric characters, and special characters that have specific meanings in BASIC. The character set that BASIC recognizes is a subset of the 256 characters that can be printed or displayed by using BASIC. While we can use the additional characters for printing or display purposes, they have no particular meaning to BASIC.

The alphabetic characters in BASIC are the 26 uppercase and 26 lowercase letters of the alphabet. Although BASIC keywords can be entered in any combination of upper- and lowercase alphabetic characters, BASIC will automatically convert keywords to uppercase characters after they are entered. In this book, all BASIC keywords are shown as uppercase characters, although you could enter them as mixed upper- and lowercase characters.

Similar to the conventional alphabet, the numeric characters recognized by BASIC are the 10 digits, 0 through 9. Table 6-1 contains a listing of the special characters that have a specific meaning in BASIC.

Table 6-1. Special Characters Recognized by BASIC

CHARACTER	MEANING
	Blank
=	Equal sign or assignment symbol
+	Plus sign or concatenation symbol
–	Minus sign
*	Asterisk or multiplication symbol
/	Slash or division symbol
\	Backslash or integer division symbol
^	Up arrow, circumflex, or exponentiation symbol
(	Left parenthesis
)	Right parenthesis
%	Percent
#	Number (or pound) sign
$	Dollar sign
!	Exclamation point
&	Ampersand
,	Comma
.	Period or decimal point
'	Single quotation mark (apostrophe)
;	Semicolon
:	Colon
?	Question mark
<	Less than
>	Greater than
"	Double quotation mark
_	Underline

RESERVED WORDS

When programming in BASIC, certain words are interpreted as a request to perform predefined operations. As an example, the word PRINT tells BASIC to display data on the screen. Such words are known as reserved words and include all BASIC commands, statements, function names, and operator names.

If you are using variable names to represent values that are used in a BASIC program, you may not use any reserved word as a variable name. Otherwise, BASIC would attempt to perform the predefined operation associated with the reserved word and, most likely, some type of syntax error would result. Thus, instead of using the reserved word PRINT in the following assignment statement, you could change PRINT to APRINT to avoid obtaining an error.

```
OK
10 PRINT=4.5              incorrect (reserved word)
RUN
Syntax error in 10
OK
10 PRINT=4.5
10 APRINT=4.5             changing reserved word
RUN
OK
```

In the top portion of the preceding example, you were trying to assign the value 4.5 to the variable named PRINT. PRINT is a reserved word that operates on a given syntax that differs from the equality sign in which you are attempting to associate the value 4.5 with the variable name. The result of this attempted operation will be a syntax error. By changing PRINT to APRINT, the word is no longer reserved for a predefined operation, and you can now associate a value to the variable name.

When you wish to use a reserved word, you should insure that it is appropriately delimited. This will permit BASIC to recognize the word. You delimit reserved words by using spaces or other special characters that may be permissible according to the syntax of the command, statement, function name, or operator name. A list of all the reserved words in BASIC is contained in Table 6-2.

Table 6-2. BASIC Reserved Words

ABS	BSAVE	CIRCLE	CONT	DATA
AND	CALL	CLEAR	COS	DATE$
ASC	CDBL	CLOSE	CSNG	DEF
ATN	CHAIN	CLS	CSRLIN	DEFDBL
AUTO	CHDIR	COLOR	CVD	DEFINT
BEEP	CHR$	COM	CVI	DEFSNG
BLOAD	CINT	COMMON	CVS	DEFSTR

Table 6-2. BASIC Reserved Words (cont.)

DELETE	IMP	MID$	PRINT	STOP
DIM	INKEY$	MKDIR	PRINT#	STR$
DRAW	INP	MKD$	PSET	STRIG
EDIT	INPUT	MKI$	PUT	STRINGS$
ELSE	INPUT#	MKS$	RANDOMIZE	SWAP
END	INPUT$	MOD	READ	SYSTEM
ENVIRON	INSTR	MOTOR	REM	TAB(
ENVIRON$	INT	NAME	RENUM	TAN
EOF	INTER$	NEW	RESET	THEN
EQV	IOCTL	NEXT	RESTORE	TIME$
ERASE	IOCTL$	NOISE	RESUME	TIMER
ERDEV	KEY	NOT	RETURN	TO
ERDEV$	KILL	OCT$	RIGHT$	TROFF
ERL	LEFT$	OFF	RMDIR	TRON
ERR	LEN	ON	RND	USING
ERROR	LET	OPEN	RSET	USR
EXP	LINE	OPTION	RUN	VAL
FIELD	LIST	OR	SAVE	VALPTR$
FILES	LLIST	OUT	SCREEN	VALPTR
FIX	LOAD	PAINT	SGN	WAIT
FN*xxxxxxxx*	LOC	PEEK	SHELL	WEND
FOR	LOCATE	PEN	SIN	WHILE
FRE	LOF	PLAY	SOUND	WIDTH
GET	LOG	PMAP	SPACE$	WINDOW
GOSUB	LPOS	POINT	SPC(	WRITE
GOTO	LPRINT	POKE	SQR	WRITE#
HEX$	LSET	POS	STEP	XOR
IF	MERGE	PRESET	STICK	

CONSTANTS AND VARIABLES

Numerical quantities are referred to in BASIC as numbers or constants. There are five ways to indicate numeric constants to include integer, fixed point, floating point, hexadecimal, and octal. In addition, BASIC permits a second type of constant, which is called a string constant. Here, a string constant is a sequence of up to 255 characters that is enclosed in double quotation marks.

Numeric Constants

Numeric constants are positive or negative numbers that may be preceded by a plus or minus sign. If the sign does not appear, the number is considered positive. Numeric constants cannot contain commas and can be expressed in one of five ways as indicated in Table 6-3.

Examples of valid integer numeric constants include the following:

```
  0
  1
+10
-4
-0
```

Note that the positive sign is optional, since the number is taken to be positive if the sign is not included. Since two 8-bit bytes of storage are used for storing integer variables, their range of values must lie between −32768 and +32767.

Examples of valid fixed point numeric constants include the following:

```
  5
-14.75
 14.75
+14.75
  0
 146
```

Floating point numbers are similar to scientific notation except that the base 10 is replaced by the letter E for single-precision or D for double-precision data representation. A floating point constant consists of an option-

Table 6-3. Types of Numeric Constants

TYPES OF NUMERIC CONSTANTS	WAYS TO INDICATE NUMERIC CONSTANTS
Integer	Whole numbers between −32768 and +32767; integer constants do not contain a decimal point
Fixed point	Positive or negative real numbers that can contain a decimal point
Floating point	Positive or negative numbers represented in exponential form
Hexadecimal	Hexadecimal numbers with up to four digits can be expressed by using the prefix &H
Octal	Octal numbers with up to six digits can be expressed by using the prefix &O or the prefix &

ally signed integer or a fixed point number known as the mantissa, which is followed by the character E and an optionally signed integer known as the exponent. The two formats for numbers represented in floating point notation are as follows:

number E± ee
number D ± ee

where number is an integer, whole number with a decimal fraction, or just a decimal fraction—the number portion of the notation contains its significant digits and is called the mantissa, and if an integer is employed that contains no decimal point, the decimal point is considered to be to the right of the mantissa; E stands for single-precision exponential notation; D signifies double-precision exponential notation; ± is an optional plus sign or a minus sign; and ee is a one- or two-digit exponent. The exponent specifies the magnitude of the number, which is the number of places to the right (positive exponent) or left (negative exponent) that the decimal point must be moved to obtain its true decimal point location. The maximum exponent value in all versions of BASIC is 38.

Some examples of floating point constants include:

−4.76E+3
.1E−4
5E+10

In the first example, −4.76 is the mantissa and +3 is the exponent. This number could be read as −4.76 times 10 to the third power and could be written as −.00476 in regular fixed point notation. The second example is equivalent to expressing the number as .00001 in fixed point notation, while the third number is equivalent to 50000000000. Double-precision floating point constants permit numbers to be stored with 17 digits of precision and printed with up to 16 digits of accuracy. In comparison, with single precision, up to 7 digits can be stored and printed, although only 6 digits will be accurate. Any number from 10E−38 to 10E+38 can be represented as a floating point constant; however, greater mantissa accuracy is obtained when a double-precision floating point constant is used, since the mantissa can be expanded from 7 to 17 digits. Various examples of numeric constant precision will be covered later in this chapter.

Hexadecimal numbers with up to four digits can be expressed by using the prefix &H. Hexadecimal digits are the numbers 0 through 9 and the letters A through F, which represent the decimal digits 10 through 15. Thus, decimal 255 can be represented in a hexadecimal as &HFF. Other examples of hexadecimal numbers include the following:

&H1234
&HAB7
&H5F

Octal numbers with up to six digits can be expressed in BASIC by using the prefix &O or just & before the number. Octal digits include the numbers 0 through 7. Some examples of octal numbers include the following:

```
&O1717
&O147676
&77
```

String Constants

A string constant is a sequence of characters bounded by quotation marks. The sequence of characters can include most characters from the ASCII character set to include blanks, letters, numbers, and special characters such as $, +, −, /, and so on. The string cannot include quotation marks because this terminates the string, nor can it include certain characters that have special meanings such as the backspace character. The maximum number of characters that can be included in a string is 255, which is the maximum size of one logical line of information. We will typically use strings to represent such nonnumeric information as names and addresses as well as to label numeric output data and to print messages. Some examples of string constants include the following:

```
"TRY AGAIN"
"THE ANSWER IS"
"$2,5000,000"
```

Numeric Constant Precision

Numeric constants can be stored internally in memory as either integer, single precision, or double precision. When constants are entered in integer, hexadecimal, or octal format, two bytes of memory are used and the numbers are interpreted as integers, which are whole numbers without a decimal point.

A single-precision constant is any numeric constant that is not an integer constant and is written with seven or fewer digits, uses the character E in exponential form, or has a trailing exclamation point (!). By using the exclamation point, you can declare a numeric constant to be single precision.

When expressed in double precision, numeric constants will be stored with up to 17 digits of precision and are printed with up to 16 digits. A double-precision constant is any numeric constant that contains eight or more digits or the character D when expressed in exponential format or contains a trailing number sign (#). By using the number sign, we can declare a numeric constant to be double precision. Examples of single- and double-precision numeric constants are listed in Table 6-4.

Table 6-4. Examples of Numeric Constants

SINGLE PRECISION	DOUBLE PRECISION
27.44	27.44143207
27.44!	27.44143207#
1.76E+12	1.76304159D+12

Roundoff

As we mentioned earlier in this section, BASIC stores up to 7 digits in single precision and up to 17 digits in double precision. If you have more than 7 digits in single precision or 17 digits in double precision, the AT will round off the excess digits. This is illustrated by the following example.

```
K
10 A=12345678:PRINT A
RUN
1234568E+07
OK
```

Scalar Variables

Variables are names that are used to represent numbers or strings in a BASIC program. Similar to constants, there are two types of variables—numeric and string.

Within each type of variable are two classes—scalar variables and array variables. A scalar variable has only one value associated with it at any particular point in time, while an array variable can have one or more values associated with it at any particular point in time. An example of the latter would be an array containing five elements, where each element is initialized to a unique value different from the values of each of the other elements. In the following discussion, attention will be focused on scalar variables, and array variables will be examined as a separate topic later in this chapter.

A numeric variable always has a value that is a number. If you use a numeric variable prior to assigning a value to it, BASIC will assume its value is zero without generating an error message. Therefore, it is important to insure that your variables are assigned values prior to their usage.

One method to assign the value of an expression to a variable is through the use of the LET statement. The following examples illustrate the assignment of values to numeric variables.

```
OK
10 LET A=347.16
20 LET PIE=3.14159
30 RATIO =PIE/A
40 PRINT A,PIE,RATIO
RUN
 347.16        3.14159        9.049401E-03
OK
```

In line 10, the variable A is assigned the value 347.16, while in line 20, the variable PIE is assigned the value 3.14159. In line 30, an optional form of the assignment statement excluding the word LET is shown. Here, the variable RATIO is assigned the value of PIE divided by A. In line 40, the values of the three variables are printed through the use of the PRINT statement.

A string variable can range anywhere from 0 to 255 characters in length. String variables are initially assumed to have a null value and a length of zero prior to your assigning a value to it. String variables can have a constant value, in which case they are string constants, or you can set the value of the string based on the result of some computation or the value of data input from the keyboard or from a data file. In this case, the string will be variable.

Some examples of the assignment of values to string variables are shown below. Note that the name of each string variable terminates with a dollar sign, which indicates to BASIC that it is a string variable. We will discuss variable naming conventions shortly.

```
OK
10 NAME$="JOHN DOE"
20 ADDRESS$="6750 PROGRAMMERS ROW"
30 CITY$="COMPUTERVILLE"
40 PRINT NAME$,ADDRESS$,CITY$
RUN
JOHN DOE        6750 PROGRAMMERS ROW        COMPUTERVILLE
OK
```

The type of variable used, string or numeric, must match the type of data assigned to it or a "Type mismatch" error will occur. Thus, string variables must be assigned string values and numeric variables must be assigned numeric values.

In the following example, a "Type mismatch" in line 10 occurred, since assigning a numeric value to a string variable was attempted.

```
OK
LIST
10 NAME$=3.14159
20 PRINT NAME$
OK
RUN
Type mismatch in 10
OK
```

We could either change NAME$ to NAME or 3.14159 to "3.14159" to remove the mismatch. In the first case, NAME would be a numeric variable name. In the second case, we would be converting the number to a string.

Variable Names

BASIC variable names can be any length up to 255 characters; however, only the first 40 characters are used.

Numeric variable names can consist of letters, numbers, and the decimal point. The first character in a variable name must be a letter and a special character that identifies the type of variable permitted as the last character of the variable name. If the last character in the variable name is the dollar sign ($), the variable is considered to be a string variable. The format for variable names can be expressed as follows:

format: Numeric variable name = LC . . . CT

where L is a letter; C is letters, numbers, or decimal point, of which up to 39 characters are significant, and a maximum of 254 characters permitted; and T represents the type—% for integer, ! for single precision, # for double precision, and $ for string variable. If type is not specified, single precision is assumed by BASIC.

Although a variable name cannot be a reserved word as explained earlier in this chapter, it may contain embedded reserved words as long as it is not a reserved word with one of the type declaration characters such as $, !, #, or $ appended to the end of the word. Thus,

```
10 FRE = 50
```

is illegal, because FRE is a reserved word. If we change the preceding statement to

```
10 FREE = 50
```

the statement is legal, since FRE is only part of the variable name. Table 6-5 lists some examples of legal and illegal BASIC variable names. Can you as-

Table 6-5. Examples of Variable Names

NAMES	TYPE/REASON
Valid	
A$	String
ADDRESS$	String
AMOUNT	Numeric
AMOUNT%	Numeric integer
SSN$	String
SSN#	Numeric double precision
TAX!	Numeric single precision
TAX5	Numeric
TAX.SALES#	Numeric double precision
Invalid	
ADDRESS > STREET	Only letters, numbers, and decimal point permitted
AMOUNT!#	Only one type declarator permitted
CLEAR	Reserved word
$TAX	First character must be a letter

certain why the illegal examples are invalid? In addition, can you differentiate between numeric and string variables and understand the type of numeric variable listed? If not, you may want to read this section a second time.

Variable Storage and Operation Considerations

Numeric variable names can be declared as integer, single-precision, or double-precision values by appending, respectively, the characters %, !, #, or $ to the variable name. Although you may obtain less accuracy by performing computations with integer and single-precision variables, there are several storage and program operational considerations that may favor declaring a variable to be a particular precision.

In Table 6-6, the storage requirements for numeric variables of different precision are listed. Since variables of a higher precision require more storage than lower-precision variables, it may become important to sacrifice precision if memory space is insufficient for your program's operation. If you try to add a line to a program when there is no more room in memory, you will receive an "Out of memory" error message, and the line will not be added to the program. If this should occur, you may want to consider changing the precision of some variables to obtain additional storage or you could subdivide your program into two or more logical programs that could be "chained" together.

Table 6-6. Numeric Variable Storage Requirements

VARIABLE TYPE	STORAGE REQUIREMENT
Integer	2 bytes
Single precision	4 bytes
Double precision	8 bytes

Another reason to change the precision of variables is because you require program speed optimization. Whenever possible, you should use integer counters in loops, since only two bytes are acted on when integers are used. This can be extremely important if you are writing a communications program where you must perform a repetitive computation and then quickly sample the communications buffer to process the next group of received data. Here, if we cannot sample the buffer quickly enough we could lose data as incoming characters could overlay data previously sent to the AT.

In addition to declaring the precision of a numeric variable or defining a string variable with a trailing declaration character, BASIC has four type declaration statements that perform similar operations. These declaration statements can be used to declare variables as integer (DEFINT), single precision (DEFSNG), double precision (DEFDBL), or string (DEFSTR). If used, they should be placed at the beginning of your program and must be executed prior to using any variables that they declare. A few examples of the use of type declaration are illustrated by the following programs:

```
Ok
LIST
10 DEFINT I,J,K
20 DEFSNG X,Y,G
30 I=26/5
40 X=2/3
50 X#=2/3
60 PRINT "I=",I
70 PRINT "X=",X
80 PRINT "X#=",X#
Ok
RUN
I=             5
X=             .6666667
X#=            .6666666865348816
Ok
```

In the above example, the DEFINT statement in line 10 declares that the variable names beginning with the letters I, J, and K will be integer, while the DEFSNG statement declares variable names beginning with X, Y, and G to be single precision. In line 30, the division of 26 by 5 is rounded to an integer and will be printed with the value 5 as a result of the PRINT statement in line 60. In line 50, a type declaration character is used to denote that the variable X is a double-precision variable even though it was defined as a single-precision variable by the DEFSNG statement. When a type declaration character such as $, !, #, or $ occurs in a program, it takes precedence over a DEF type statement in the typing of a variable. Thus, when 2 is divided by 3 and converted to double precision, the result is .6666666865348816. The reason that this value is not accurately expressed as .6666666666666667 is that the computation was performed in single precision and then rounded upward when the results of the operation were converted to double precision. Note that in line 40 the assignment of the computation of 2 divided by 3 is printed in line 70 as .6666667, since all operators are in single precision. In the following example, line 50 was changed so that the numerator is in double precision prior to its being divided. As shown, this results in an accurate 16-digit fraction.

```
Ok
LIST
10 DEFINT I,J,K
20 DEFSNG X,Y,G
30 I=26/5
40 X=2/3
50 X#=2#/3
60 PRINT "I=",I
70 PRINT "X=",X
80 PRINT "X#=",X#
Ok
RUN
I=             5
X=             .6666667
X#=            .6666666666666667
Ok
```

Array Variables

When you are writing a computer program, it is often convenient to refer to an entire collection of items at one time. Such a collection is normally referred to as an array. In BASIC, an array can be considered as a group or table of values that is referenced by the same name. Each individual value in the array is known as an element. The elements in the array can be either numerical quantities or string values; however, all of the elements in a given array must be of the same type, either all numerical quantities or all string values.

In mathematical notation, you might write A_0, A_1, A_2 . . . A_N to denote the N elements of a one-dimensional array named A. Since there are no subscripts in BASIC, you are forced to find an alternate method to denote the elements of an array. This alternate method is obtained by using parentheses to define the elements of an array. In BASIC, you will use the left and right parentheses after the name of an array as delimiters in which the specific element of the array you wish to examine or operate on will be defined. Thus, the preceding mathematical notation of N elements of the array A would be referenced as A(0), A(1), A(2) . . . A(N) in BASIC, and the fifth element of the array A would be referenced as A(4) if your base element were zero (0).

To better visualize the usefulness of arrays, consider the following problem. Suppose you know the daily sales of a store during a 31-day period and wish to perform a statistical analysis on those sales. Without arrays, you would have to assign a unique variable name to each of the daily sales figures. Just to obtain the sum of the sales might require a laborious statement such as the following:

```
10 LET TOTAL=SALES1+SALES2+ . . . SALES 31
```

Using the array variable named SALES, you could give the entire monthly table of sales one name and identify daily sales activity by their position within the table. You could view the array named SALES as the table shown below, filled in with some arbitrary daily sales values.

SALES ARRAY

127.14	215.13	419.87	......	310.54
SALES(1)	SALES(2)	SALES(3)	......	SALES(31)

If you wished to sum the value of sales within the month, you could build a counter in BASIC that would add the value of each element in the SALES array to a counter as shown below.

```
OK
10 TOTAL=0
```

```
20 FOR I=1 TO 31
30 TOTAL=TOTAL+SALES(I)
40 NEXT I.
```

In the preceding example, line 10 initializes the value of the TOTAL counter to zero. The FOR and NEXT statements form a boundary in which all statements in between are executed as the I counter loops in value from its initial value of 1 to a final value of 31. Thus, each time the loop occurs, line 30 is executed, and the value of TOTAL is incremented by the value of SALES(I). When I is 1, the value of the first elements of SALES, SALES(I), which is 127.14, is added to TOTAL and so on. Note that in this example your array base is one (1). In BASIC, your array base is always zero, but you can reset it with the OPTION BASE statement. Suppose you had a requirement to add 365 daily sales figures. You would then change the end loop parameters in line 10 from 31 to 365. As you can see, arrays can provide a convenient mechanism for manipulating data.

In addition to one-dimensional arrays, BASIC permits you to have two-dimensional arrays. In fact, you can have up to 255 dimensions in an array with a maximum of 32767 elements per dimension, although doing so could rapidly use up large segments of program memory. A two-dimensional array can be thought of as being composed of horizontal and vertical columns. The first of two subscripts then refers to the row number while the second subscript refers to the column number. An array of three rows and three columns would be expressed in mathematical notation as:

$$A_{0,1}\ A_{0,2}\ A_{0,3}$$
$$A_{1,1}\ A_{1,2}\ A_{1,3}$$
$$A_{2,1}\ A_{2,2}\ A_{2,3}$$

In BASIC, the element of the second row, second column, would be expressed as A(1,2). As shown, each array element will be named or referenced by the name subscripted with a number of sequence of numbers separated by commas. A three-dimensional array could be used to define a particular object and a point on that object might be expressed as A(5,20,15).

Numeric variable array names are similar to numeric variable names; however, no type declaration character is permitted. Thus, all numeric variable array names will consist of single-precision values. In addition, numeric variable array names are followed by a pair of left and right parentheses that define the specific size of or an element of the array.

When we operate with arrays, we must first inform the computer how much memory to set aside for the array. This process is known as defining or dimensioning the array. You can do this through the use of the BASIC DIM statement, which is used to specify the maximum values for array variable subscripts and allocate storage accordingly. Since 0 (zero) is the lowest position of an element in an array unless changed by the BASIC OPTION BASE statement, you can dimension a 10-element array named TAXRATE as follows:

```
100 DIM TAXRATE(9)
```

Once TAXRATE is dimensioned, you could initialize the various elements of the array to 10 specific tax rates and perform tax computations using the index of the array to retrieve a specific tax rate.

String variable arrays are named similar to numeric variable arrays with the only exception being that a trailing dollar sign is appended to the name. This signifies to the BASIC interpreter that the values of the elements of the array are strings. Thus, if we wished to dimension space for 100 names and addresses, we could use the following DIM statement.

```
10 DIM NAME$(99), ADDRESS$(99)
```

BASIC has an automatic dimensioning feature that you can use to your advantage if the number of elements in an array does not exceed 11. If you use an array element prior to defining the array, BASIC will automatically assume that it is to be dimensioned with a maximum subscript of 10, permitting you to have up to 11 elements in an array without dimensioning it.

In programming, you should reserve caution in the mechanism you employ to dimension variables. Although the maximum dimension for an array is 255, a four-dimension array of 10 by 10 by 10 by 10 would require 10,000 locations to be set aside. If the array were numeric and thus consisted of single-precision values, four bytes would be required to store each value, resulting in a total of 40,000 bytes of memory being reserved for the array.

OPERATORS AND NUMERIC EXPRESSIONS

In BASIC you must use special symbols, called operators, to indicate the operation you wish to perform. BASIC operators can be divided into four categories: arithmetic, relational, logical, and functional. The operators are used to connect numbers, numeric variables, or string variables, thus forming formulas or expressions. Thus, a formula can be composed of a single number or a single numeric variable as well as some combination of numbers, numeric variables, and operators. A numeric variable must be assigned some numerical quantity prior to its appearing in a formula, or it will be used in the formula with a 0 (zero) value.

The failure to assign values to numeric variables may cause expressions to be evaluated incorrectly, resulting in an erroneous computation that, if embedded in a lengthy program, may be hidden from casual observation. In some cases, the failure to assign values to numeric variables can result in the unintentional generation of an error message by the program in addition to obtaining a nondesired value. Both situations are illustrated by the following program.

```
OK
10 LET X=A*42.5
20 PRINT "X=",X
30 LET V=23.5/A
40 PRINT "V=",V
RUN
```

```
X=             0
Division by zero

V=             1.701412E+38
Ok
```

In line 10, the multiplication operator (*) is used to multiply the value of the variable A by 42.5. Since A has not been assigned a value in the program prior to its use in line 10, it is used in the formula computation with a 0 value. This results in X being assigned the value 0, which may not be what you really wanted to occur. In line 30, the slash (/) character is used as a division operator to divide 23.5 by the value of A and assign that value to V. Since A has not been assigned a value, division by zero is attempted. This results in a division-by-zero error message, since machine infinity with the sign of the numerator is supplied as the result of the division. Note that the value assigned to the variable V is the largest value that the PC AT can store.

Arithmetic Operators

Table 6-7 lists the BASIC arithmetic operators according to their hierarchy of operations. The hierarchy of operation is important, since, together with the order of execution, it defines how a formula is evaluated. BASIC formulas are evaluated equivalent to mathematical expressions, in that operations are conducted from left to right with a given hierarchical group. As an example, consider the following formula expressed using BASIC operators.

```
A+B/C+D^2
```

Proceeding from left to right, the value of the variable A is added to the value of the variable B divided by the value of variable C. Next, the previously computed value is added to D squared. Suppose the mathematical formula

Table 6-7. Arithmetic Operators

OPERATOR SYMBOL IN BASIC	OPERATION	HIERARCHY	SAMPLE EXPRESSION USING OPERATOR
^	Exponentiation	1	A^B
−	Negation	2	−A
*, /	Multiplication, floating point division	3	A*B A/B
\	Integer division	4	A\B
MOD	Modulo arithmetic	5	A MOD B
+, −	Addition, subtraction	6	A+B A−B

you wished to evaluate was $A+B/C + D^2$. Then, the initial formula you expressed using the preceding BASIC operators would be incorrect. You can alter the way operations are conducted in BASIC through the insertion of pairs of parentheses into formulas. When parentheses are inserted into formulas, the operations within the parentheses are performed as separate entities. If several pairs of parentheses are nested within a formula, the operators within the innermost pairs of parentheses are performed first, followed by the operations within the second innermost pair and so on. Within each pair of parentheses, the hierarchy of operations as shown in Table 6-7 will apply unless they are altered by other pairs of parentheses that are embedded inside the outer pair. To properly express the required mathematical formula in BASIC, you could use parentheses to modify the initial BASIC expression as follows:

```
(A+B)/C+D∧2
```

Now, the value of variable A will be added to the value of variable B and the sum will then be divided by the value of variable C.

Table 6-8 illustrates the conversion of 10 mathematical expressions to their BASIC language equivalents.

Although most of the operators listed in Table 6-7 should be familiar to you, two of them may appear unfamiliar due to their limited use in day to day computations. These are the integer division and modulo arithmetic operators.

Table 6-8. BASIC Equivalents of Mathematical Expressions

MATHEMATICAL EXPRESSION	BASIC LANGUAGE EQUIVALENT
$A + \frac{B}{C}$	A+B/C
$\frac{A}{B+C}$	A/(B+C)
$\frac{A \cdot B}{C \cdot D}$	(A*B)/(C*D) or A*B/(C*D) or (A/C)*(B/D)
$A-(B-C)$	A−(B−C) or A−B+C
$A_x^5+D^E$	A(X)∧5+D∧E
$A \cdot X^3+B \cdot X^2+C$	A*X∧3+B*X∧2+C
$-X$	−X
$A_1+A_2^2+A_3^3$	A(1)+A(2)∧2+A(3)∧3
$\frac{(A+B)\cdot(A-C)}{D+E}$	((A+B)*(A−C))/(D+E)
$3.14159 \cdot R^2$	3.4159*R∧2

Integer Division

An integer division operation is denoted by the backslash (\) character. When integer division is specified, the operands are first rounded to integers if they are not integer values and then integer division is performed. The operators must lie in the valid range of numbers between −32768 and 32767, and, after division is performed, the quotient is truncated to an integer. Several examples of the results obtained from the use of integer division are illustrated by the program shown below.

```
Ok
10 LET A=10\4
20 LET B=11\4
30 LET C=12\4
40 LET D=13\4
50 PRINT A,B,C,D
60 LET E=40.25\5
70 LET F=36.49\6
80 LET G=36.51\6
90 PRINT E,F,G
RUN
 2             2             3             3
 8             6             6
Ok
```

Note that in integer division no rounding occurs. Only the "whole" or integer portion of the division is assigned to the appropriate variable and the remainder is discarded.

Modulo Arithmetic

In BASIC, modulo arithmetic is denoted by the operator symbol MOD. Whereas integer division results in a quotient truncated to an integer while the remainder is discarded, modulo arithmetic gives the integer value that is the remainder of an integer division. The following program shows several results of modulo arithmetic operations.

```
Ok
LIST
10 A=14 MOD 3
20 B=16.8 MOD 4
30 C=25.49 MOD 5
40 D=25.51 MOD 5
50 PRINT A,B,C,D
Ok
RUN
 2             1             0             1
Ok
```

If the results of some of the computations appear to be off by one from what you may have hand calculated, you probably forgot that BASIC rounds when converting numbers to integers. Thus, 25.49 is rounded to 25 while 25.51 is rounded to 26. Then, 25 MOD 5 is 0, since 25/5 has a remainder of zero. Likewise, 26/5 is 5 with a remainder of 1.

Mixed Precision within Statements

When variables or constants of mixed precision occur within a statement, BASIC will perform variable assignment values or computations based on a series of predefined rules.

If a numeric value in one precision is assigned to a numeric variable typed to a different precision, the number will be stored with the precision of the target variable as illustrated by the following example.

```
OK
LIST
10 A%=100/3 :PRINT A%                    'INTEGER
20 B!=100/3 :PRINT B!                    'SINGLE PRECISION
30 C#=100/3 :PRINT C#                    'DOUBLE PRECISION
OK
RUN
 33
 33.33333
 33.33333206176758
OK
```

In the preceding examples, we converted from a lower-precision number to a higher-precision number. Note that the resulting higher-precision number can only be as accurate as the lower-precision number. If you wish to increase the precision, you must use arithmetic operations instead of an assignment statement. This is because in an assignment statement, if you would assign a single-precision value to a double-precision variable, only the first six digits of the double-precision variable will be accurate, since only six digits of accuracy are supplied by a single-precision value. If you use arithmetic operations in a statement, all of the operands in the arithmetic operation will be converted to the most precise operand. This is illustrated by the following example.

```
OK
LIST
10 A%=100!/3 :PRINT A%                   'INTEGER
20 B!=100!/3 :PRINT B!                   'SINGLE PRECISION
30 C#=100#/3 :PRINT C#                   'DOUBLE PRECISION
OK
RUN
 33
 33.33333
 33.33333333333333
OK
```

Note that by typing the value 100 in line 30 as double precision, the resulting division became accurate to 16 places.

In the preceding examples, lower-precision values were assigned to higher-precision variables. What happens if you wish to assign a higher-precision value to a lower-precision variable? The answer to this question is provided by the following program.

```
Ok
10 A%=33.33333!:PRINT A%
20 B!=33.33333333333333# :PRINT B!
RUN
 33
 33.33333
Ok
```

In the preceding examples, the result of the assignment of a higher-precision value to a lower-precision value causes the assigned number to be rounded.

Relational Operators

In order to carry out what are known as conditional branching operations in BASIC, a mechanism is required to express conditions of equality and inequality. This mechanism is provided by the use of relational operators. When relational operators are used to compare two values expressed as numerics or strings, you must take care to insure that similar type operands are used on both sides of the relational operator sign. That is, you cannot mix numeric and string constants or variables. Doing so would violate the grammatical construction of the language and result in a Syntax error. Table 6-9 lists the relational operators available in BASIC.

Relational operators can be used to control program execution flow by initiating branching based on certain conditions. In addition, they can be employed to cause a BASIC statement or sequences of BASIC statements to be executed when certain conditions occur.

The results of relational comparisons are bistable. They are either "true" (−1) or "false" (0). The result of the relational comparison is normally used to determine where a program statement will branch to or what sequence of program statements will be executed.

While a detailed description of the use of relational operators will be deferred until later in this book, some elementary examples are in order. In the short program segment that follows, a numeric value is read from the keyboard through the use of the BASIC INPUT statement and assigned to the variable X. Next, three conditional tests are conducted to see if the value entered is equal to, less than, or greater than 5. If the result of a comparison operation

Table 6-9. Relational Operators

OPERATOR SYMBOL	RELATION TESTED
=	Equality
<> or ><	Inequality
<	Less than
>	Greater than
<= or =<	Less than or equal to
>= or =>	Greater than or equal to

is "true," then the appropriate branch to the indicated line number in the program occurs. If the results of the comparison are "false," then the next program line number is executed.

```
Ok
LIST
10 INPUT;X
20 IF X=5 THEN 500
30 IF X<5 THEN 1000
40 IF X>5 THEN 1500
500 PRINT " EQUAL":STOP
1000 PRINT " LESS THAN":STOP
1500 PRINT " GREATER THAN":STOP
Ok
RUN
? 5 EQUAL
Break in 500
Ok
```

When the program was executed with the RUN command, the value 5 was entered. This resulted in a branch to line 500 in the program where the string "EQUAL" was printed. The STOP statement on that line caused the message "Break in 500" to be generated, and the program terminated its execution. In the following example, the value of X is used as a decision variable regarding the value of the variable P in the program. If X is equal to 2, then P will be set equal to 7, otherwise P will be assigned the value 3.

```
Ok
LIST
10 INPUT;X
20 PRINT
110 IF X=2 THEN P=7:ELSE P=3
120 PRINT "FOR X= ";X;"P= ";P
Ok
RUN
? 1
FOR X= 1 P= 3
Ok
RUN
? 2
FOR X= 2 P= 7
Ok
RUN
? 3
FOR X= 3 P= 3
Ok
```

When arithmetic and relational operators are combined in one expression, the arthimetic operations are performed prior to the relational test. As an example, consider the following BASIC statement:

```
10 IF (A+B)^2<=C THEN 50
```

First, the values of A and B are added and the combined value is then squared. The result of the arithmetic operations is then compared to the value of C. If the square of A plus B is less than or equal to C, the branch to program line 50 occurs. Thus, if the expression is true (−1), the branch occurs. If the expression is false (0), then the next sequential program statement is executed. For the expression to be false, the value of A plus B squared must be greater than C in this example.

When strings are compared, the comparison is based on the ASCII value of the characters in the string. The ASCII codes of the character set used by the AT are listed in Appendix A. If you turn to Appendix A, you will note that the first 32 characters in order of their ASCII value are control characters that are used for video display or communications. These characters are followed by a series of punctuation characters to include the space character, exclamation point, quotation symbol, and so on. Next, the 10 decimal digits occur, followed by a few additional punctuation characters and all the uppercase letters of the alphabet. After a few more punctuation characters, the 26 lowercase alphabetic characters are encountered, followed by a series of special characters to include graphics, language, and mathematical symbols.

For string comparisons consisting of digits and alphabetic characters, we can think of the comparison being conducted in alphabetical order. This is because the ASCII value of the digits appears first, followed by the uppercase alphabet, which is then followed by the lowercase alphabet. Thus, numbers are "less than" letters and uppercase alphabetic letters are "less than" lowercase alphabetic letters.

When two strings are compared, the AT actually takes one character at a time from each string and compares their ASCII values. If the ASCII values are the same, the computer will continue comparing, examining the next character in each string. If all the characters in each string are in the same order, the strings are equal. If the ASCII values of the strings differ, the string with the lower ASCII value is less than the string with the higher value. If two strings of different lengths are compared, if the end of the shorter string is reached during the comparison, then the shorter string is considered to be smaller. Both leading and trailing blanks are significant, since each such blank has the ASCII value of 32 for string comparison purposes. Table 6-10 lists several true and false string comparisons. If you cannot easily determine why these comparisons are true or false, you may wish to review the preceding material concerning relational operators.

In addition to individual string comparisons, strings can be joined together and pairs of strings can be compared. The joining together of strings is called concatenation, and several examples of string concatenation are shown below.

Table 6-10. String Comparisons

TRUE COMPARISONS	FALSE COMPARISONS
"1AX" < "2AA"	"4UIPROGRAM" < "1HECKOFAJOB"
"TEST" > "ZETA"	"PAYROLL.1" < "PAYROLL"
"four" > "FOUR"	"GILBERT" > "GILBERT HELD"
"TIMEOUT" > "TIME"	

"SALES" + "REPORT"	becomes "SALESREPORT"
"STATE" + "ZIP"	becomes "STATEZIP"
N$ + Z$	becomes the value of N$ followed by the value of Z$

In the preceding examples, the plus sign (+) is used as concatenation operator.

By concatenating strings, you can perform many important sorting functions expediently. As an example, you could concatenate state and zip code strings to sort addresses by zip code within a state.

Boolean Operators

Boolean operators provide us with the ability to make logical decisions on numeric data under program control. Hence, Boolean operators are often referred to as logical operators. There are six Boolean operators: NOT, AND, OR, XOR, IMP, and EQV.

Each of the Boolean operators takes a combination of true/false values and returns a true or false result. The operand of a Boolean operator is considered to be true if it is not equal to zero or false if it is equal to zero. This is similar to the −1 and 0 results obtained from relational operators. The result of a Boolean operation is a number that is considered to be true if it is not equal to zero or false if it is equal to zero. The number is computed by performing the Boolean operation on the operand or operands bit by bit. We can obtain a firm understanding of Boolean operators by examining each of the operators in detail through the use of what is known as truth tables as well as looking at some examples of their use in BASIC statements. Each of these Boolean operators will be discussed in order of their precedence of operation. That is, the NOT operator will have its operands evaluated prior to the operands of an AND operator, if those two Boolean operators appear in one expression.

NOT

The NOT operator is also known as the logical complement operator. The truth table showing the results of this Boolean operator appears below.

A	NOT A
T	F
F	T

An example of the NOT operator used in a BASIC statement is shown below.

```
10 IF NOT A THEN 500
```

In the above example, the program will branch to line 500 if A is not true. This is because NOT A is true only if A is false, since NOT A would be false only if A is true.

AND

Also known as a conjunction operator, the AND operator can be employed to join two operands together as shown in the following truth table.

A	B	A AND B
T	T	T
T	F	F
F	T	F
F	F	F

In examining the preceding truth table, the conjunction of the two operands has the value true only if both operands are true. It has the value false if either or both operands are false. The AND operator is a valuable mechanism for testing for ranges of values as shown by the following BASIC statement.

```
10 IF AGE>=20 AND AGE <=40 THEN 500
```

In the preceding statement, you will always branch to line 500 if a person's age is found to be between 20 and 40.

OR

The OR or disjunction operator performs an inclusive operation on two operands as shown in the following truth table.

A	B	A OR B
T	T	T
T	F	T
F	T	T
F	F	F

The result of the OR operation has the value true if either or both operands are true. The result of the operation has the value false only if both operands are false. Suppose age requirements were immaterial if a person's height were under 5 feet. Maybe you have a secret mission for short people! You could modify the BASIC statement used to explain the AND operator as follows.

```
10 IF AGE>=20 AND AGE <=40 OR HEIGHT <5 THEN 500
```

You would now always branch to line 500 if a person's age were between 20 and 40 or if their height were less than 5 feet.

XOR

The results of the XOR operation on two operands are illustrated by the following truth table.

A	B	A XOR B
T	T	F

T	F	T
F	T	T
F	F	F

If both operands are true or if both operands are false the result has the value false. If either operand differs in value from the other, the result has the value true. The following program statement illustrates the use of the XOR operator in BASIC.

```
10 IF HEIGHT <5 AND AGE XOR TESTAGE THEN 500
```

For the branch to line 500 to occur, HEIGHT has to be less than 5 AND AGE must be different from TESTAGE.

IMP

The IMP or implication operator has the value false only if the value of the first operand is true and the value of the second operand is false. Otherwise, the value of the implication operation is true. This is shown by the following truth table.

A	B	A IMP B
T	T	T
T	F	F
F	T	T
F	F	T

EQV

The results of the EQV or equivalence operation are true if both operands are true or both operands are false. Otherwise, the value of the equivalence operation is false. This is shown by the following truth table.

A	B	A EQV B
T	T	T
T	F	F
F	T	F
F	F	T

Binary Manipulation

The use of Boolean operators provides us with the means to perform binary manipulation of data. Boolean operands are converted to integers in the range −32768 to 32767 and two 8-bit bytes are used to store the resulting binary number. This is illustrated below with the decimal value of each binary position indicated as well as the sign bit of the two-byte integer.

S	16384	8192	4096	2048	1024	512	256	128	64	32	16	8	4	2	1

A sign bit of 0 indicates the number is positive. Negative numbers are expressed in what is known as twos complement form. First, the complement of the binary number is obtained and then a binary one is added to obtain its twos complement. As an example of twos complement notation, consider the decimal number 15. It would be stored as:

0	0	0	0	0	0	0	0	0	0	0	0	1	1	1	1

Its ones complement would be:

1	1	1	1	1	1	1	1	1	1	1	1	0	0	0	0

To obtain its twos complement, a binary one is added to the ones complement, resulting in the storing of minus decimal 15 in twos complement notation as shown below:

1	1	1	1	1	1	1	1	1	1	1	1	0	0	0	1

If the Boolean operands fall outside the range −32768 to +32767, an "Overflow" error will occur. When a Boolean operation occurs, the operation is performed on a sequence or sequences of 16 bits. Each bit position in the result is determined by the corresponding bits in the operand or two operands, according to the previously defined truth tables. For binary manipulation, a 1 bit is considered to be "true" while a 0 bit is considered to be "false." We can see how Boolean operators manipulate binary information by examining several sample program statements.

```
10 LET A=15 AND B
```

Suppose when line 10 is executed the value of B is decimal 10. Since 15 = binary 1111 and 10 = binary 1010, then 15 AND 10 will be 1010 in binary, which is 10 decimal.

Now consider the following program statement.

```
10 IF A AND B=12 THEN 1000
```

In this example, only if the result of the conjunction operation is binary 1100 will the branch to line 1000 occur. By using Boolean operators you obtain the ability to "mask" bit positions. This provides you with the ability to test the status of the contents of program registers, machine I/O ports, and unique portions of memory bytes. If you wanted to perform a certain operation only if bit position 2 were set, you could "mask" all the other bits by ANDing by 2. The following statement would then cause a branch to line 1000 only if bit 2 in the variable named A were set.

```
10 IF A AND 2=2 THEN 1000
```

Precedence of Operators in Expressions

Although the precedence of operators within a given category has been discussed, what happens if you have a program statement that requires the execution of different types of operators? The different categories of numeric operations have their own order of precedence. In an expression, all function calls will be evaluated first. Although a detailed discussion of function calls will be deferred for the time being, you can view them being used in an expression similar to a variable; however, their use results in a predefined operation being performed. As an example, the SQR(X) function results in the square root of X being returned.

After function calls are performed, arithmetic operations will be conducted. These operations are followed in sequence by relational operations while Boolean operators are conducted last. Table 6-11 summarizes the operator precedence for arithmetic, relational, and Boolean operations.

Table 6-11. Operator Precedence

OPERATOR	OPERATION
Arithmetic	
^	Exponentiation
−	Negation
*, /	Multiplication, floating point division
\	Integer division
MOD	Modulo arithmetic
+, −	Addition, subtraction
Relational	
=	Equality
<> or ><	Inequality
<	Less than
>	Greater than
<= or =<	Less than or equal to
>= or =>	Greater than or equal to
Boolean	
NOT	Complement
AND	Conjunction
OR	Disjunction
XOR	Exclusive or
IMP	Implication
EQV	Equivalence

Loading and Running Programs

If a program is stored on the fixed disk or diskette, you can easily load and execute it. This can be accomplished by using the LOAD command whose format is illustrated below.

format: LOAD"filespec[,R]

The file specification, or filespec for short, describes the physical file in the form of the device where it resides, the path to the file, and the filename. The device name tells BASIC where to look for a file, the path tells BASIC which directory contains the file, and the filename informs BASIC which file you are looking for on a particular device in a particular directory.

The file specification is a string expression of the form:

[device][path]filename[.ext]

Note that the device, path, and file extension are optional. If the device is omitted, the default drive is assumed. Omitting the path causes the current directory to be used as the directory to be searched for loading the indicated file when a LOAD command is entered.

Device Names

The device name consists of one to four characters and is terminated by a colon(:). Table 6-12 contains a list of currently available device names, their association with a physical device, and their BASIC language version appli-

Table 6-12. Device Names

NAME	PHYSICAL DEVICE ADDRESSED	BASIC VERSION(S)
KYBD:	Keyboard (input only)	All
SCRN:	Display (output only)	All
LPT1:	First printer (output only)	All
LPT2:	Second printer (output only)	Disk and advanced
LPT3:	Third printer (output only)	Disk and advanced
COM1:	First asynchronous communications adapter	Disk and advanced
COM2:	Second asynchronous communications adapter	Disk and advanced
CAS1:	Cassette tape player (input and output)	*All
A:	First diskette drive (input and output)	Disk and advanced
B:	Second diskette drive (input and output)	Disk and advanced
C:	First fixed disk (input and output)	Disk and advanced
D:	Second fixed disk (input and output)	Disk and advanced

*Although this device is supported by DOS there is no cassette port on the AT.

cability. Once the device name is specified, you must provide BASIC with the path and the filename you are looking for on a particular device, since storage devices can contain more than one directory and the same filenames may exist in different directories.

Path

A path is a list of directory names separated by backslashes (\). If you have a directory named FINANCE under the root directory on drive C, the device and path specifiers in the LOAD command to load a file named INCOME in that directory can be:

```
A>LOAD"C:\FINANCE\INCOME"     if default drive is A
C>LOAD"\FINANCE\INCOME"       if default drive is C
```

When naming files, a series of file naming conventions must be adhered to.

Filename Conventions

For both disk and diskette files, hereafter referred to as disk files, the filename may consist of two parts separated by a period (.). If so specified, the part to the left of the period is the name of the file, while the part to the right of the period is known as the file extension. Thus, disk files are of the form: name.extension.

The name of the disk file must be eight or less characters in length. If you have more than eight characters in the name of the file, BASIC will insert a period after eight characters and use up to the first three extra characters as the extension. Thus, a disk filename specified as PAYROLLDATA would be stored as PAYROLLD.ATA. Only the characters A through Z, digits 0 through 9, and the ( ), { }, @, $, %, /\, &, !, –, —, '', /, and ~ characters can be used for a filename or extension. If you use a filename longer than eight characters and have specified an extension, an error message will be displayed. Normally, you will use the extension to define the type of the file for reference purposes as illustrated below.

```
PAYROLL.BAS
EMPLOYEE.DAT
STAT105.FTN
```

In the above example, PAYROLL could be a program file written in BASIC, and you will use the abbreviation BAS in the file extension to indicate this. The EMPLOYEE file might contain data to be used by the PAYROLL program, and you indicate that it is a data file by adding DAT as its extension. The STAT105 could be a statistical program for course number 105 you are taking, and if you wrote the program in FORTRAN, you could so indicate by adding FTN as its file extension. DOS reserves certain predefined functions for files with the extensions: .COM (command), .BAK (backup), and .BAT (batch). Unless you specifically intend to use a file with one of those three extensions for a specific system function, you should normally attempt to use some other extension in your file extension naming process.

R Option

If the R option is specified in the LOAD command, the program will commence execution immediately after it is loaded. Program execution will then commence at the first program statement in the file.

Keyboard Program Entry

Before typing a program into your AT, you may want to enter the NEW command into the system. The NEW command is used to delete the program residing in memory from the system and clears all variables. If you just powered on the system, there would be no current program in memory, and you could load a program from disk or enter a program from the keyboard without having to use the NEW command. If you previously entered a program, loading a new program will clear memory automatically unless you use the MERGE command. This command could result in a mixture of two programs in storage. This is illustrated by the following example. Assume line numbers 5, 15, and 25 represent a three-line program in memory. If you merge another three-line program from disk that consists of line numbers 10, 20, and 30, what do you wind up with in memory? As shown below, you would wind up with a six-line program that is a mixture of the old program previously entered into the system and the new program.

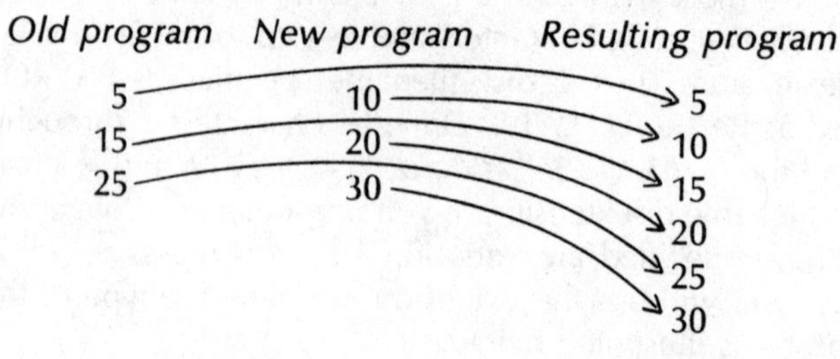

If you do not require the old program to be merged with the new program, you can eliminate it from memory by using the NEW command as shown below.

```
OK
NEW
OK
```

The effect of the NEW command can be shown by the following example.

```
OK
10 REM TRIAL PROGRAM
20 PRINT "HI THERE"
```

```
NEW
LIST
Ok
```

In the preceding example, your short two-line program is erased from memory when you enter NEW. This is verified by the use of the LIST command, which does not list the previously entered program because it has been erased from memory.

Program Execution

If you did not use the R option when loading your BASIC program, you can either press the F2 key or enter the keyword RUN to execute your program. Pressing the F2 key generates the keyword RUN followed by a return, causing any BASIC program in memory to be executed. Similarly, if you entered a program from the keyboard after BASIC was initialized, pressing the F2 key or entering the keyword RUN will cause your program to execute.

CHAPTER SEVEN Basic BASIC

In this chapter, attention will be focused on a variety of processing, branching, and I/O statements. These statements can be viewed as forming the nucleus of the BASIC language common to all versions BASIC that can operate on the AT. Prior to examining one or more examples of each statement, the format that must be followed to obtain the correct construction of the statement will be defined. In this and succeeding chapters, the following notations will be used for BASIC format specifications:

format: Common to all versions of BASIC
$format_{D/A}$: Applicable to both disk and advanced BASIC
$format_{A}$: Applicable only to advanced BASIC.

Each of the formats presented for BASIC commands, statements, and functions will be constructed based on the following syntax construction rules:

- Words in capital letters are keywords and must be entered as shown. Keywords may be entered in any combination of upper- and lowercase characters; however, BASIC will convert keywords to upper case.
- Items shown in lowercase are to be supplied by you when creating a command, statement, or function.
- Items in brackets ([ ]) are optional and may or may not be included in the format based on a particular circumstance.
- Braces ({ }) indicate that a choice of one of the enclosed items is to be made. Braces do not appear in the actual statements.
- Ellipses (. . .) are used to indicate an item that may be repeated as many times as you wish.
- All punctuation characters with the exception of square brackets must be included as shown in the format.

In developing format conventions, several generic terms and abbreviations have been employed to develop a standard scheme for presenting each BASIC language statement. The terms and abbreviations that will be used throughout this book are listed in Table 7-1.

Table 7-1. Generic Terms and Abbreviations

GENERIC TERMS AND ABBREVIATIONS

A—Option added to a *filespec* to denote an ASCII file

address—Memory location

arg—Argument

arrayname—String or numeric array name

aspect—Ratio of X-radius to the Y-radius

background—Background color of screen

boundary—Edge of screen or of a figure to be filled with color

col—Screen column number between 1 and 40 or 1 and 80, depending on screen width

color—Numeric value that indicates color selection

constant—Actual value BASIC uses during program execution; can be string or numeric

constant$—String constant

dummy—Dummy argument

dummy$—Dummy string argument

errorcode—Numeric number associated with an error message

exp1, exp2—Expressions that are evaluated

expr$—Any valid string constant, variable, or expression

exprnm—Any numeric constant, variable, or expression

exprnm%—Any integer numeric constant variable or expression

exprnm#—Any double-precision numeric constant variable, or expression

exprnm!—Any single-precision numeric constant, variable, or expression

filenum—File number assigned to a file that was opened

filespec—File specification of a program to be loaded or a data file

foreground—Foreground color of screen

length—Numeric expression with a value between 1 and 65535 that specifies a range

letter—Any letter in BASIC character set, A through Z

line$_I$—The Ith line number of a BASIC program

memadr—Memory address

n—References the communications adapter (0 or 1) when referring to communications statements or a microprocessor hardware port

newnum—New BASIC program line number

numvar—Numeric variable name

Table 7-1. Generic Terms and Abbreviations (cont.)

offset—Numeric expression with a value between 1 and 65535 that specifies a starting point
oldnum—Previous or old BASIC program line number
P—Option added to *filespec* to denote encoded binary files
palette—Color mix selection
promptmsg—Prompt message displayed on screen
R—Option added to *filespec* to denote execution from first line in program after program loading
range—Group of line numbers affected by a command
recnum—Record number
remark—Nonexecutable comment
row—Screen row number between 1 and 25
statement(s)—One or more BASIC language statements
sub—Subscript
var—Numeric or string variable
varnm—Numeric variable
var$—String variable
xctr—x-axis center point of drawing
yctr—y-axis center point of drawing
&—Current line number
&H—Hexadecimal number prefix
&O—Octal number prefix
;—Continue printing or display on same line
.—Current line

PROCESSING

REM Statement

The REM statement is an abbreviation for REMark. This statement permits the insertion of explanatory remarks into a program. The format of this statement is illustrated below:

format: REM – remark

The REM statement provides you with a mechanism to internally document a program by adding information concerning calculations, variable assignments, and the like to a program. While the REM statement is nonexecutable, it is output exactly as entered when the program is listed and provides you with a mechanism to "internally document" a program.

In addition to the REM statement, you can also use a single quotation mark followed by your comments. This allows you to add comments to a line containing a BASIC statement or to put comments on a separate line. If you have a program line containing multiple statements, any REM statement on that line must be the last statement on the line. Some examples of the use of REM statements and remarks preceded by a single quotation mark are shown in the following example:

```
100 REM Initialization Section
110 REM Variable Naming Assignments
120 REM SALES(X) Array containing daily sales receipts
.
.
.
500 'Lines 500 through 600 compute regression analysis
.
.
1000 X=X+1 'increment counter
.
.
1500 Flag=1 : REM Reset flag
```

The addition of comments to a program can be extremely helpful if you desire to modify the program at a later date; however, a word of caution is in order. Comments take up space in memory and will slow program execution time. For these reasons, it is advisable to use comments selectively and supplement "internal documentation" with external documentation in the form of notes concerning the intricacies of your program.

Although REM statements are nonexecutable, like all BASIC statements they are preceded by a line number. This means that you can have a branch to a REM statement within a program. When a branch to a REM statement occurs, program execution will continue with the first executable statement that follows the REM statement. Thus, REM statements can be used to both document looping activities as well as to provide entry and exit points to loops.

Assignment Statements

In BASIC, there are several methods to assign a numerical or a sting value to a variable. One of the most popular methods employed is through the use of the assignment statement whose format is shown below:

format: [LET] var=expression

In some versions of BASIC on other computers, this statement is known as the LET statement due to the keyword being required for the statement to be operable. In all versions of BASIC on the AT, the word LET is optional. Here, the equal sign is sufficient when assigning an expression, numeric, or a string value to a variable. Some examples of the use of the assignment statement are shown below.

```
10 LET X=1
20 LET NAME$="GIL"
30 A=B+C+D
40 PRODUCT=A*B*C*D
```

In line 10, the numeric variable X is assigned the value 1. Since the keyword LET is optional, this statement could have been written as:

```
10 X=1
```

In line 20, the string variable NAME$ is assigned the string value "GIL". In line 30, the sum of the values associated with the variables B, C, and D are assigned to the variable named A. If, at the point of assignment, the variables in a statement are undefined, BASIC will assign a value of zero to such variables. While forgetting to assign values to variables prior to their use can cause incorrect results, it can also cause an overflow error if the unassigned variable is used as a divisor in an equation. In such instances, this will cause a "Division by zero" error message to occur.

From the preceding examples, note that the variable to the left of the equal sign and the term to the right must be of the same type, numeric or string. If you attempt to assign a numeric value to a string variable or a string value to a numeric variable, you will obtain a "Type mismatch" error as shown below.

```
OK
100 REM BET WE GET AN ERROR
110 NAME$=105
RUN
Type mismatch in 110
OK
```

Although there are many assignment terms that look like algebraic equations, there are certain assignment terms that make little sense if you view them as an algebraic equation. One example of this is

```
100 LET X=X+1
```

The assignment term X=X+1 does not correspond to an algebraic equation, since the equation X=X+1 has no meaning from an algebraic equation standpoint. When written in BASIC, you are increasing the value of the numeric variable X by one unit. Here, the assignment term becomes logical when you interpret it to mean you wish to add 1 to the value represented by the variable X and then assign this new value to X. This new value of X will then replace the old value. Later, you will see that this type of assignment statement is frequently used as a counter in BASIC.

Although some BASICs allow multiple assignments of the form,

```
100 A=B=C=0
```

such assignments are not permitted in any version of AT BASIC. Instead, you must use several assignment statements, although you can include multiple assignment statements on a single line as long as each statement is separated from the preceding statement by a colon (:). An example of this is:

```
100 A=0:B=0:C=0
```

READ and DATA Statements

Many BASIC programs require that a large number of variables be initialized or changed to certain values within a program. While you can use many assignment statements to accomplish this, it may be cumbersome to do so. Instead, you may use one or more pairs of READ and DATA statements. When used in BASIC, a READ statement must always be used in conjunction with one or more DATA statements. DATA statements contain the values of constants that READ statements will assign to the variables in the READ statement. READ statement variables may be numeric or string; however, the values read from the DATA statement must correspond to the types of constants in the DATA statements. That is, a string variable in a READ statement must correspond with a string constant in a DATA statement, and a numeric variable in a READ statement must correspond to a numeric constant in a DATA statement. The formats of the READ and DATA statements are:

format: READ var[,var . . .]
format: DATA constant[,constant . . .]

An example of the use of a pair of READ, DATA statements is shown below:

```
100 READ A,B,C,X$,E
110 DATA 5,10,15,"GIL",20
```

In the preceding example, the statement in line 100 specifies that you should read the values for five variables from one or more DATA statements. The first three variables are numeric and must be expressed as numeric constants in the associated DATA statement or statements. The fourth variable is a string variable and the value in the associated DATA statement must be a string. The fifth variable in the READ statement is a numeric variable, and the value of the associated DATA statement must be a numeric constant. In the above example, the execution of line 100 results in the assignment of the value 5 to A, 10 to B, 15 to C, "GIL" to X$, and 20 to E. Since a single READ statement can access the constant values from a number of DATA statements, you could rewrite the preceding example in a number of ways to include using two DATA statements as shown below.

```
100 READ A,B,C,X$,E
110 DATA 5,10,15
120 DATA "GIL",20
```

While two DATA statements are shown following the READ statement, they can be placed anywhere within a program. All DATA statements are nonexecutable and merely reserve space in memory for the values of the constants associated with each DATA statement. Then, each variable in a READ statement will have a sequential value taken from memory and assigned to the variable. We can visualize the effect of the DATA statement as generating a pool of values in sequential order. As more DATA statements occur in a program, the values associated with each statement are appended to the end of the pool in the sequence of occurrence. Thus the two DATA statements from the previous example can be visualized as creating the following data pool.

```
100 DATA 5,10,15
110 DATA "GIL",20
```

When a READ statement is encountered in a program, you can visualize that it causes a pointer to move from one value to the next value for each variable in the statement. In effect, a value is obtained from the data pool and assigned to a variable in the READ statement, and the pointer will then move to the right one position, ready to assign the next value in the data pool to the next variable in the READ statement.

If there are more variables in the READ statement or statements than there are constants in one or more DATA statements, when the pointer is shifted to the right and encounters no data, the error message "Out of DATA" will occur and the program will terminate. This is shown by the following example where you attempt to read three elements from a data pool that only contains two data items.

```
50 READ A,B,C
75 DATA 1,2
RUN
Out of DATA in 50
OK
```

You can have multiple READ statements within a program. When this occurs, the second and subsequent READ statements will continue to take values from the data pool in sequence, with each value assigned to the variable in each READ statement in their order of occurrence. This is shown by the following example.

```
100 DATA 1,3,5,9,"MIGHTY","FINE"
500 READ A,B,C
750 READ D,XRAY$
1000 READ OHMY$,X$
1500 DATA "SUNSET","STRIP"
```

The two DATA statements generate the values assigned to the data pool as follows:

With the pointer at the beginning of the data pool, the READ statement in line 500 can be thought of as causing the following pointer actions to occur.

When A was READ, the pointer moved to the first value and assigned the contents of the first position in the data pool to that variable. Thus, A was given the value 1. Next, B was assigned the value 3 and C was assigned the value 5. Note that the pointer is now at the position where the value 5 was held in the pool. Upon encountering the READ statement in line 750, the pointer would again move to the right one position for each variable in the READ statement. Here, the variable D would be assigned the value 9 and the string variable XRAY$ would be assigned the string value MIGHTY. The movement of the pointer in response to the second read statement is shown below.

Since there are two variable names contained as part of the READ statement in line 1000, the execution of this statement will cause the pointer to move two positions to the right through the data pool. As the pointer moves over the string "FINE", this string will be assigned to the string variable OHMY$, while the string "SUNSET" will be assigned to the string variable X$. Note that in this short program example, the number of data constants in the data pool exceeds the number of string variables in READ statements. This is perfectly valid as sometimes you may branch around one or more READ statements and forgo assigning constants to variables based on certain program conditions. In such cases, the extra data will be ignored. The opposite of this situation, however, is not permitted. That is, you cannot read more variables in READ statements than there are constants in data statements, unless you reread the constants. The mechanism to reread constants is obtained through the RESTORE statement, which will be covered shortly.

Two final notes on READ and DATA statements. You can obtain an idea of the rationale for using these statements instead of multiple assignment statements by comparing the previous example using READ and DATA statements to a program segment performing the same variable assignments using assignment statements as shown below.

```
100 A=1
110 B=3
120 C=5
130 D=9
140 XRAY$="MIGHTY"
150 OHMY$="FINE"
160 X$="SUNSET"
```

From the above, it is apparent that READ and DATA statements are labor-saving devices for the assignment of constant values to variables.

Although the preceding examples showed quotation marks around string constants contained in DATA statements, there are occasions where we can safely do without such string specifiers. If a string does not have commas, semicolons, or significant leading or trailing blanks, you can place that string in a DATA statement without surrounding quotation marks. This is illustrated by the following example.

```
10 PRINT "LAST NAME","FIRST NAME","SSN"
20 READ LAST$,FIRST$,SSN$
30 DATA Held,Gilbert,000000000
40 PRINT LAST$,FIRST$,SSN$
RUN
LAST NAME     FIRST NAME    SSN
Held          Gilbert       000000000
OK
```

RESTORE Statement

There are many programming situations in which you would like to read the data more than once. To do this requires a mechanism to move the position of the pointer in the data pool back to its initial position at the beginning of the first data element. This repositioning of the data pool pointer is accomplished by the RESTORE statement whose format is:

format: RESTORE [line]

When a RESTORE statement is executed, the first variable in the next READ statement in the program will be assigned the value of the first item in the first DATA statement in the program. If a line number is specified in the RESTORE statement, the first variable in the next READ statement will be assigned the value of the first item in the DATA statement specified by the line number of the RESTORE statement. Thus, specifying a line number within a RESTORE statement permits us to selectively move the data pool pointer through the data pool. This is shown by the following example.

```
OK
LIST
10 READ A,B,C,D
20 DATA 1,3,5,9,11,13
30 PRINT A,B,C,D
40 DATA 15,17,19,21
50 RESTORE
60 READ X,Y,Z
70 PRINT X,Y,Z
80 RESTORE 40
90 READ X,Y,Z
100 PRINT X,Y,Z

RUN
 1             3             5             9
 1             3             5
 15            17            19
OK
```

In the preceding example, the data pool contains 10 constants, formed by the data in lines 20 and 40. The READ statement in line 10 results in the assignment of 1 to A, 3 to B, 5 to C, and 9 to D. The PRINT statement in line 30 outputs the values of the four variables. Here, the comma (,) between each variable is a print control mechanism that permits data to be placed in fixed positions on a line when used as a separator in the PRINT statement. The use of print separators will be covered in detail later in this chapter when the PRINT statement is examined.

The RESTORE statement in line 50 moves the pointer back to the beginning of the data pool, since no line number was specified. The execution of line 60 will cause the values of 1, 3, and 5 to be assigned to the variables X, Y, and Z. The result of the PRINT statement in line 70 confirms the assignment of these values. In line 80, the line number appended to the RESTORE statement causes the pointer in the data pool to be repositioned to the first element in the referenced DATA statement. Now, the READ statement in line 90 will result in the assignment of the values 15, 17, and 19 to the variables X, Y, and Z. This is confirmed by the execution of the PRINT statement in line 100.

In the preceding example, we have seen how the RESTORE statement permits you to assign the same or a different sequence of values to different variables. Although specifying a line number in a RESTORE statement permits you to move the data pool pointer, its movement is controlled by the number of constants contained in a particular DATA statement. If you wish to selectively move the pointer to the right, you can do so by introducing dummy variables into your READ statements. In such cases, the dummy variable will be assigned a value; however, since you will not use the variable in the program, its assignment is immaterial. To see the use of dummy variables, assume that a pointer was positioned in a data pool as shown in the following.

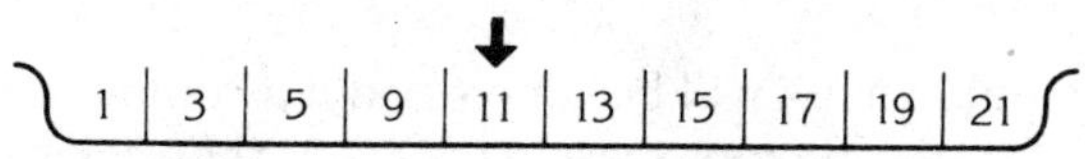

If you wanted to assign the values 15 to X, 17 to Y, and 19 to Z, you would have to first skip over the number 13. If all the data elements were contained in one DATA statement, you would have no such mechanism. You would have a similar problem if you had several DATA statements but the number 15 in the data pool was not at the beginning of a DATA statement that you could reference the line number of in a RESTORE statement. The solution to such problems is the use of one or more dummy variables in a READ statement. One example of the use of a dummy variable follows.

```
100 READ DUM,X,Y,Z
```

In line 100, the variable DUM will be assigned the value 13 as a mechanism to move the pointer so variables X, Y, and Z can be assigned the required values of 15, 17, and 19. Although DUM is assigned the value 13, since you have no intention of using it within the program with that value, it is known as a dummy variable. Although the variable name DUM was used for this dummy variable, you could use any valid name as long as you insulate it from use within the program.

INPUT Statement

Until now, the only methods that have been covered to assign values to variables were internally within a program. What happens if you wish to control the value of variables during program execution? One method might be to include every possible variable value in numerous assignment or READ and DATA statements and branch to the appropriate point in the program based on certain predefined criteria. Obviously, this would be an extremely difficult if not impossible task. A far easier and more effective mechanism would result from allowing input from the keyboard during program execution. This is accomplished by the use of the INPUT statement whose format is as follows.

format: INPUT["prompt msg"]{;/,}var[,var . . .]

format$_{D/A}$: INPUT[;]["prompt msg"]{;/,}var[,var . . .]

When an INPUT statement is encountered, program execution will be temporarily suspended and a question mark will be displayed. The question mark is a BASIC program level prompt character that serves as an indicator to the computer operator that the program is awaiting data input. If a "prompt message" is included in the statement, the string contained in quotation marks will be printed prior to the question mark as shown by the following example.

```
Ok
100 INPUT "Enter the radius of the circle";R
RUN
Enter the radius of the circle?
```

The question mark will be suppressed if a comma is used in place of the semicolon after the prompt message. This is shown by replacing the semicolon in the previous example with a comma and reexecuting the one-line program.

```
100 INPUT "Enter the radius of the circle",R
RUN
Enter the radius of the circle
```

When you respond to an INPUT statement, you must enter the same number of data items as there are variables in the variable list of the INPUT statement. Data items must be separated from one another by commas and the type of data, string or numeric, must agree with the type specified by the variable name in the variable list. An example of the use of an INPUT statement for multiple assignment of values to variables is shown below.

```
100 INPUT "ENTER WIDGETS SOLD AND COMMISSION RATE"SOLD,RATE
110 LET COM=500*SOLD*RATE/100
```

```
120 PRINT "COMMISSION=",COM
RUN
ENTER WIDGETS SOLD AND COMMISSION RATE? 100,5
COMMISSION=     2500
OK
```

If you should make a mistake and respond to an INPUT statement with too many or too few data items or with the wrong type of data such as entering a string value for a numeric variable, the error message "?Redo from start" will be displayed. At this point, you must re-input all values.

When entering strings in response to an INPUT statement, the use of quotation marks is optional as illustrated by the following example.

```
OK
100 INPUT "Enter your name,rank and serial number,",N$,R$,S
110 print N$,R$,S
RUN
Enter your name,rank and serial numberMarval,CPT,007
Marval         CPT          7
OK
```

If you examine the preceding example, you will notice that there was no space between the printout of the prompt message contained in the INPUT statement and the first character entered in response to the prompt. If you wish to make the response to such prompt messages more legible, you can insert a blank character after the last character of the prompt message. This is shown in the following example where a blank was appended to the end of the word "number" in line 100. Note that the response was now positioned to the right one character, separating the prompt message from the response.

```
100 INPUT "Enter your name,rank and serial number ",N$,R$,S
110 PRINT N$,R$,S
OK
RUN
Enter your name,rank and serial number Wonder,Boy,0
Wonder         Boy          0
OK
```

If you are familiar with other versions of BASIC or are developing programs on the AT for use on other computers, you may wish to retain quotation marks to delimit strings. This will make your program easier to convert to a different computer if the requirement should arise.

The second format of the INPUT statement is only relevant for disk and advanced BASIC. Here, the use of the optional semicolon immediately following the keyword INPUT is designed to suppress the generation of a carriage return and line feed sequence once you press the enter key. The use of the semicolon is intended to have the cursor remain on the same line as the user's response and will be a valuable tool for permitting multiple input responses on a single line.

INKEY$ Variable

A secondary method to enter data from the keyboard during program execution is obtained by the use of the INKEY$ variable. The use of this variable permits the program to read data on a character-by-character basis and is similar to the GET statement found in other, non-IBM versions of BASIC. The format of the INKEY$ variable is:

format: var$ = INKEY$

When a BASIC statement containing an INKEY$ variable is executed, a single character string will be input to the program from the keyboard. No characters will be displayed on the screen unless the program was written to echo input characters onto the display through the use of a PRINT statement. A null string will be returned if a key is not pressed when the INKEY$ variable is executed. We can force a program to wait for a certain character or group of characters by repeatedly looping back to the statement containing the INKEY$ variable as illustrated by the execution of the following program segment.

```
Ok
100 PRINT "Enter C to continue"
110 A$=INKEY$
120 IF A$="C" GO TO 140
130 GOTO 110
140 REM program continues

RUN
Enter C to continue
Ok
```

After the "Enter C to continue" message is displayed, the INKEY$ variable in line 110 will return a character string from the keyboard whose value will be assigned to the string variable A$. In line 120, the value of A$ will be compared to the character C by the use of the BASIC IF statement. If A$ equals C, the program will branch to line 140. If A$ does not equal C, then line 130 will be executed, which will cause the program to branch back to line 110. This will cause the keyboard to be scanned again, and this looping will continue until the character C is pressed.

Note that since you are testing for an uppercase C, entering a lowercase c or any character other than the uppercase C will cause the program to cycle between lines 110 and 130. If you wish to test for either uppercase or lowercase, you would change line 120 as follows.

```
120 IF A$="C" OR A$="c"GOTO 140
```

You can also force a program to wait for the input of one or more characters by the use of multiple statements on a single line. In the following example, line 110 performs the exact functions of lines 110 through 130 in the previous example.

```
110 A$=INKEY$:IF A$="C"GOTO 140:GOTO 110
```

Since INKEY$ returns a string, if you wish to input a digit and compare it to one or more digits in the program, you must convert the input string to a numerical value or compare the input string to a string consisting of one or more digits in the program. You can obtain the numerical value of a string by the use of the VAL function whose use is illustrated by the following program segment.

```
100 PRINT "Remove single part paper, insert multipart paper"
110 PRINT "Enter 1 when ready to resume"
120 X$=INKEY$
130 X=VAL(X$)
140 IF X=1 GOTO 160
150 GOTO 120
160 REM program continues
RUN
Remove single part paper, insert multipart paper
Enter 1 when ready to resume
Ok
```

In the preceding example, the VAL function will return the numerical value of the specified string. A word of caution is in order since VAL(X$) will return 0 (zero) if X$ is not numeric. Thus, if you were testing for 0, pressing any nonnumeric key would cause you to continue, which may not be what you intended to do. An easier method when testing for numeric characters is to perform the test against the numeric value employed as a string as shown by line 130 in the following example.

```
100 PRINT "Remove single part paper, insert multipart paper"
110 PRINT "Enter 1 when ready to resume"
120 X$=INKEY$
130 IF X$="1" GOTO 150
140 GOTO 120
150 REM program continues
```

When the INKEY$ variable is used a zero-, one-, or two-character string can be returned. If a null (zero-length string) is returned, this indicates that no character was pressed at the keyboard when it was scanned. You can continuously cycle in a loop awaiting the entry of a character by the use of the following or a similar statement to that shown below.

```
100 X$=INKEY$:IF X$="" GOTO 100
```

Note that the double quotation marks follow one another in line 100 because we wish to continuously cycle back to line 100 if no character has been entered.

In the preceding example, the first statement in line 100, X$=INKEY$, causes a character to be read from the keyboard and assigned to the variable X$. The second statement on that line, IF X$="''GOTO 100, causes the program to branch back to line 100 if no key has been pressed. If a key was pressed, then X$ would not equal a null string of length zero, and the next sequential statement in the program will be executed.

If a one-character string is entered when the INKEY$ variable is encountered in a program, the string will contain the actual character that was pressed at the keyboard. This will be the primary result of the use of the INKEY$ variable. In certain instances, however, a two-character string will result from the use of the INKEY$ variable. This two-character string is generated to differentiate certain characters from the characters in the ASCII character set. Since the AT can only have 256 distinct characters by using the different combinations of an 8-bit byte, adding a prefix character permits an extension of the character set. When this occurs, a null character (ASCII code 000) is returned as the first character of a two-character string. The second character in the string will then have a different meaning from its normal ASCII representation. A list of extended two-character codes and their meanings is contained in Appendix B. For an example of comparing these codes with standard ASCII codes, consider the character in Appendix A that has an ASCII value of 71. In the normal ASCII character set, the character G has the ASCII value of 71. In Appendix B, a two-character string with the first character being an ASCII 000 (null character) and the second character being an ASCII 71 is considered to be the cursor "Home" control character.

Since the first character in an extended code is ASCII 000, a logical question at this point is how can you differentiate a 00071 from a 71? To differentiate between the two characters numerically is impossible, since 00071 is the same as 71. Since one character is actually a two-character string, you must differentiate between the two characters based on their string length. You can use the LEN function for this purpose, since it can be employed to obtain the number of characters in a string. The format of this function is:

format: LEN(var$)

If you wish to test the character or characters entered when an INKEY$ variable is executed, you can do so with a program using logic similar to that shown by the execution of the following program.

```
LIST
100 X$=INKEY$:IF X$=""THEN 100
110 IF LEN(X$)=2 THEN 140
120 PRINT "One character code",X$
130 GOTO 100
140 PRINT "Two character code",X$
150 GOTO 100
RUN
One character code          1
One character code          a
Two character code           G
Two character code           H
Two character code           I
```

Enter the above program into your AT, then press the F2 key to run the program. As you press different keys, look in Appendices A and B and note which keys are returned as one-character strings and which are returned as two-character strings. Note that no characters are displayed on the screen when you press a key. This means that the INKEY$ variable would be appropriate for controlling the movement of a spaceship or some other type of game movement where predetermined characters could be entered to move an object in a different direction, or for controlling the screen display that you wish to obtain a printout of and you do not wish to clutter the screen with the characters entered. Also, note that all two-character code strings are printed shifted one position to the right. This is because the first part of the string is a nonprintable null. To exit this endless loop program, press Ctrl + Break.

Another example where the INKEY$ variable would be valuable is in a program that displays mathematical problems and after each problem awaits the entry of the operator's response. Here, you might construct a loop to read one digit at a time from the terminal. You could test each character obtained from the use of the INKEY$ variable for the ASCII value 13. When a 13 is encountered, it would indicate that a carriage return was entered. Upon the detection of an ASCII value of 13, you would then exit from the loop. Since you might wish to echo each character entered onto the display, you could use a PRINT statement to perform this function. In the following example, the ASC function is used to return the ASCII code for the first character of the string indicated within the function. The format of this function is:

format: ASC(expr$)

The result of the ASC function is a numerical value that is the ASCII code of the first character of the string specified in the parentheses. In the following example, the ASC function to test for the entry of a carriage return character will be used.

```
Ok
10 B$=""
20 PRINT "15 X 24 ="
30 A$=INKEY$:IF A$="" THEN 30 'wait for character
40 PRINT A$;                  'echo to screen
50 IF ASC(A$)= 13 THEN 80     'concatenate
60 B$=B$+A$
70 GOTO 30
80 REM program continues
```

In the preceding example, all numeric responses are concatenated into the string B$ until a carriage return is entered. Then the program branches to line 80. Later you could use the VAL function to obtain the numeric value of B$ to test it to the correct answer.

Since you wish to retain control of certain operational functions, there are four characters or character combinations that will not be passed through to the program by the use of the INKEY$ variable. These multikey combinations and their meanings are:

Key combination	Meaning
Ctrl + Break	Stop program execution
Ctrl + NumLock	Put system into a pause state
Alt + Ctrl + Del	System reset
Shift + PrtSc	Print the screen

PRINT Statement

Just as there are a number of statements that can be used to input data values into a program, a variety of methods exists to transmit numerical or string output data from the computer. Two of the most commonly used statements are in PRINT and LPRINT statements. The LPRINT statement will be covered later.

The PRINT statement provides you with the mechanism to display data on your screen. The LPRINT statement functions very similar to the PRINT statement, with the exception that data will be printed on the attached printer instead of the display.

The PRINT statement consists of a line number, the keyword PRINT, and an optional list of expressions that can consist of numbers, formulas, or strings. The two formats of this statement are shown below:

$$\text{format:}\left\{\begin{array}{l}\text{PRINT[list of expressions]}\left\{\begin{array}{l}[,]\\ [;]\end{array}\right\}\\[2ex] \text{?[list of expressions]}\left\{\begin{array}{l}[,]\\ [;]\end{array}\right\}\end{array}\right\}$$

By themselves, the keyword PRINT or the question mark character will cause a blank line to be displayed. This is equivalent to generating a carriage return and line feed character. Thus, you can use the PRINT statement to control horizontal spacing when you desire to display a heading and skip one or more lines prior to printing the body of a report.

Concerning vertical spacing within a PRINT statement, the position of each printed item will be determined by the punctuation character employed to separate the items in the list of expressions. Successive items in the list of expressions must be separated by either a comma (,) or a semicolon (;).

IBM BASIC is similar to most BASICs in that a print line is divided into print zones that contain 10 or 14 character positions as illustrated in Fig. 7-1. When a comma is used as a separator between items in the list of expres-

	Zone 1	Zone 2	Zone 3	Zone 4	Zone 5
First line	1 14	15 28	29 42	43 56	57 70	71 80
succeeding lines	5 14	15 28	29 42	43 56	57 70	71 80

Fig. 7-1. BASIC print zones. Each print zone contains 10 or 14 print positions. A logical line containing more than one physical line will have the second and subsequent print lines contain a contracted first zone.

sions, the next value in the list will be printed at the beginning of the next zone.

If more than six items are in the list of expressions and you are using commas as separators, the seventh through twelfth items will be printed on a second line with their positions on that line corresponding to the positions of the zones shown in Fig. 7-1 for succeeding lines. Similarly, items 13 through 18 would be printed on a third line and so on. An example of a printout being "wrapped" around from line to line is shown by the following example. Note that BASIC always prints positive numbers preceded by a space if you wish to verify the zone positions in this example.

```
10 PRINT 1,2,3,4,5,6,7,8,9,10,11,12,13,14,15
RUN
 1             2             3             4             5             6
       7             8             9             10            11            12
       13            14            15
Ok
1234567890123456789012345678901234567890123456789012345678901234567890123456789012345678901234567890
```

Expressions listed in a PRINT statement may be numeric or string; however, string constants must be enclosed in quotation marks or they will be considered to be variables. If they are unassigned a value, then they will be shown as having a zero value. When a semicolon is used as an item separator, the value of the next item will be printed immediately after the previous value. This permits you to display more data items on one line than using commas as separators. In the following example, 10 items are printed on one line by using semicolons as separators. You could also use one or more spaces between items, since BASIC will treat the spaces similarly to the use of semicolons; however, this feature is not common on many BASICs available on other machines.

```
Ok
10 PRINT 1;"TWO";3;"FOUR";5;"SIX";7;"EIGHT";9;"TEN"
RUN
 1 TWO 3 FOUR 5 SIX 7 EIGHT 9 TEN
Ok
```

Since the use of a comma permits the placement of data items into predetermined positions, it provides you with an elementary mechanism for formatting data output. This is shown by the following program segment.

```
Ok
100 PRINT "COLUMN ONE","COLUMN TWO"
110 X=123.33
120 PRINT X,X/2
RUN
COLUMN ONE    COLUMN TWO
 123.33        61.665
Ok
```

A carriage return will be generated at the end of the print line when you terminate a PRINT statement without a comma or semicolon. Then, the next

PRINT statement will cause a new line of information to be displayed. If a comma or semicolon is used at the end of the PRINT statement, the carriage return will be suppressed and the next PRINT statement will cause information to be displayed on the same line. This function is shown by modifying the previous example as illustrated below.

```
LIST
100 PRINT "COLUMN ONE","COLUMN TWO"
110 X=123.33
120 PRINT X,X/2,
130 PRINT X/3,X/4
RUN
COLUMN ONE     COLUMN TWO
 123.33         61.665        41.11      30.8325
Ok
```

While either a comma or semicolon can be used at the end of a PRINT statement to signify that the next PRINT statement should display data on the same line, the semicolon will also serve to compress the next printed item out of its zone. This is shown by changing the terminator in line 120 to a semicolon in the following example.

```
LIST
100 PRINT "COLUMN ONE","COLUMN TWO"
110 X=123.33
120 PRINT X,X/2;
130 PRINT X/3,X/4
RUN
COLUMN ONE     COLUMN TWO
 123.33         61.665        41.11      30.8325
Ok
```

Since many types of displays and monitors can be attached to the AT there is a WIDTH statement that can be used to set the number of characters that will appear on one line of the display.

WIDTH Statement

When used to set the output line width, the format of this statement is:

format: WIDTH size

Here, the size is the number of characters you wish to set the output line width to. As an alternate format, you can include the device name in the WIDTH statement as shown below:

format: WIDTH device, size

Valid devices are SCRN:, LPT1:, LPT2:, LPT3:, COM1:, or COM2:. To set the width of the display, you could use either:

WIDTH size

or

WIDTH "SCRN:", size

A screen of 40 or 80 columns is permitted; however, WIDTH 40 is not valid if you are using the IBM monochrome display. If the line to be printed exceeds the length defined by a WIDTH statement, BASIC will cause the following data to be printed on the next physical line. This is demonstrated by the execution of the previous program where line 10 has been added that includes a WIDTH 40 statement.

```
OK
LIST
10 WIDTH 40
100 PRINT "COLUMN ONE","COLUMN TWO"
110 X=123.33
120 PRINT X,X/2;
130 PRINT X/3,X/4
OK
RUN
COLUMN ONE    COLUMN TWO
 123.33        61.665  41.11
 30.8325
OK
```

When you print exactly 80 characters when the screen width is set to 80, an additional line feed will be generated by BASIC.

Numerical Treatment of Output

BASIC will always print positive numbers preceded by a space. This means that if you are using commas as listed separators, positive numbers will be printed in columns 2, 16, and so on. No matter what separator is used, BASIC will automatically append a space to the end of a number. This eliminates the possibility of two numbers being interpreted as one.

When the value of a variable is to be printed, its significance will depend on the type of the variable as explained in Chapter 6.

Prior to concluding this initial discussion of the PRINT statement, the review of two additional BASIC functions is warranted—the SPC function and the TAB function.

SPC Function

The SPC function can be used to space the cursor to the right a given number of spaces. Its format is shown below.

format: SPC (exprnm)

In addition to being used with the PRINT statement, the SPC function can be used with the LPRINT and PRINT # statements, to be discussed later.

When used with the PRINT statement, it will print the number of spaces specified by the numeric expression, in effect, moving the cursor exprnm positions to the right on the screen. Since a logical line can be up to 256 character positions, the numeric expression must be in the range of 0 to 255. The use of this function in a PRINT statement is illustrated by the following program segment.

```
OK
200 PRINT "DEBITS" SPC(30)"CREDITS"
RUN
DEBITS                              CREDITS
OK
```

In the preceding example, the SPC function results in 30 spaces or column positions between the words DEBITS and CREDITS.

In the following example, note that if a floating point number is used, it will be rounded to an integer. Thus, X=14.51 results in 15 spaces, while Z=14.49 results in 14 spaces prior to printing the appropriate string.

```
OK
LIST
10 X=14.51
20 PRINT SPC(X)"BASIC"
30 Y=15
40 PRINT SPC(Y)"OVERVIEW"
50 Z=14.49
60 PRINT SPC(Z)"OF SPC FUNCTION"
OK
RUN
               BASIC
               OVERVIEW
              OF SPC FUNCTION
OK
```

If the specified value in the SPC function is greater than the width of the device, the value used will be exprnm MOD width.

TAB Function

Another function that can be used to control the cursor location on a line is the TAB function. This function is used in a PRINT statement, and its format follows:

format: TAB (exprnm)

Instead of spacing over the number of positions specified by the numeric expression, the TAB function causes the cursor to move to the right to the position specified by the numeric expression. When this function is used, exprnm must be between 1 and 255 in value. The leftmost position on the display is position 1, while the rightmost position is the defined WIDTH. Like the SPC function, the TAB function can only be used in PRINT, LPRINT, and

PRINT # statements. The following program segment illustrates the use of the TAB function in several PRINT statements.

```
OK
10 PRINT TAB(32)"INVENTORY REPORT"
20 PRINT
30 PRINT TAB(5)"PRODUCT" TAB(20)"UNITS ON HAND" TAB(40)"UNIT COST";
40 PRINT TAB(60)"PRODUCT COST"
RUN
                                INVENTORY REPORT

    PRODUCT        UNITS ON HAND       UNIT COST           PRODUCT COST
OK
```

In the preceding example, the TAB function in line 10 causes the string INVENTORY REPORT to be printed starting in column 32. Line 20 causes one blank line to be printed, while lines 30 and 40 cause four strings to be printed starting at columns 5, 20, 40, and 60, respectively. Note that the semicolon at the end of line 30 serves as a print continuation identifier to BASIC, informing the interpreter that the output of the next PRINT statement should follow on the same line.

LPRINT Statement

While the PRINT statement causes data to be displayed on the screen, the LPRINT statement provides you with a mechanism to print information on the printer under program control. While you could output data to the screen and use the Shift+PrtSc keys to obtain a printed copy of the display, many times you will prefer to use the BASIC LPRINT statement to automatically generate printed information. While the distinction between using Shift+PrtSc keys and the LPRINT statement may not appear too meaningful when you are printing a few lines of data, consider the case in which you have to output a report consisting of hundreds of lines of data. Obviously, you would prefer not to hit the Shift+PrtSc keys every time 24 lines of data are displayed. Thus, you will have a tendency to use the LPRINT statement to generate reports or substantial data output, whereas you may prefer to use the PRINT statement when you need the results of some computation and hard copy may not be necessary or can be easily obtained by the Shift+PrtSc keys. The format of the LPRINT statement is:

$$\text{format: LPRINT[list of expressions]}\left\{\begin{matrix}[;]\\ [,]\end{matrix}\right\}$$

In comparison to the PRINT statement, the only difference in formats is the prefix of L in the keyword. This L indicates that the expressions in the list will be printed. This statement functions similar to the PRINT statement, including the use of the SPC and TAB functions within the statement. The key difference between statements is that the PRINT statement causes data to be displayed on the screen, while the LPRINT statement causes the output to be listed on the printer.

The LPRINT statement assumes a default value of an 80-character width printer. This width can be changed if your printer is capable of recognizing special control characters to perform condensed printing, has switches for changing print width, or has a platen greater than 80 characters in width. We can also change the printer width through the use of the WIDTH statement. When BASIC is initialized, the value of the printer width is set to 80 characters. Some printers, like the IBM 80 cps graphics printer, are capable of printing up to 132 characters per line in a condensed print operating mode. Other printers have extended carriages and can normally print up to 132 characters per line in their normal print mode.

If your printer is capable of changing its settings by receiving special codes, you can change its operation under program control. Table 7-2 contains a list of special print functions and their control codes for the IBM 80 cps graphics printer. Although many, if not all, of the functions of the IBM printers can be obtained on printers manufactured by other vendors, the control codes may differ. Therefore, it is recommended that you consult your printer manual to ascertain the appropriate control codes to perform the printing functions available if you have a non-IBM printer attached to your system.

In addition to sending data to the printer, you can send "special" codes that will cause the printer to perform such functions as printing narrow or wide letters, double printing, and printing the actual graphic characters shown on your screen. To perform these functions requires the use of one or more CHR$ functions in an LPRINT statement.

Table 7-2. IBM 80 cps Graphics Printer Control Codes

FUNCTION	CODE	ASCII VALUES
Bell	BEL	7
Cancel	CAN	24
Cancel ignore paper end	ESC 9	27 57
Cancel skip perforation	ESC O	27 79
Carriage return	CR	13
Compressed character	SI	15
Compressed character Off	DC 2	18
Double strike	ESC G	27 71
Double strike Off	ESC H	27 72
Double width (one line)	SO	14
Double width	ESC W1	27 87 1
Double width (SO only)	DC 4	20
Emphasized	ESC E	27 69
Emphasized Off	ESC F	27 70
Escape	ESC	27
Form feed	FF	140

Table 7-2. IBM 80 cps Graphics Printer Control Codes (cont.)

FUNCTION	CODE	ASCII VALUES
Home head	ESC<	27 60
Horizontal tab	HT	9
Ignore paper end	ESC 8	27 56
Line feed	LF	10
Null	NUL	0
Select character set 1	ESC 7	27 55
Select character set 2	ESC 6	27 54
Set horizontal tab stops	ESC D	27 68
Set length of page	ESC C	27 67
Set lines per page	ESC C	27 67
Set skip perforation	ESC N	27 78
Set variable line feed 0.12 mm (1/216 in.)	ESC 3	27 51
Set variable line feed 0.35 mm (1/72 in.)	ESC A	27 65
Start variable line feed 0.35 mm (1/72 in.)	ESC 2	27 50
Subscript-superscript On	ESC S	27 83
Subscript-superscript Off	ESC T	27 84
Underline	ESC_	27 45
Unidirectional printing	ESC U	27 85
Variable line feed 0.12 mm (1/216 in.)	ESC J	27 74
3.18 mm (1/8 in.) line feed	ESC 0	27 48
2.47 mm (7/72 in.) line feed	ESC 1	27 49
480-bit-image graphics mode	ESC K	27 75
960-bit-image graphics mode	ESC L	27 76
960-bit-image graphics mode normal speed	ESC Y	27 89
1920-bit-image graphics mode	ESC Z	27 90

CHR$ Function

The CHR$ function converts an ASCII code to its character equivalent and can be used to send special characters to the screen or a printer. For the former, you would use the CHR$ function in a PRINT statement, while the latter would require its use in an LPRINT statement. The format of this function is:

format: X$=CHR$(exprnm)

Since there are 256 characters in the ASCII character set, the numeric expression can range in value from 0 to 255. You can use this function in an

LPRINT statement to send special characters to the printer, or you can use it in a PRINT statement to display special characters. In either situation, the numeric expression represents the ASCII code of the character you wish to send to the screen or printer. The ASCII character set showing each of the 256 characters and their ASCII code values is contained in Appendix A.

Now that you know how to send special characters to the printer, let's actually operate some of the printer's functions under program control. Suppose you wish to produce the title of a report in double-width characters. According to Table 7-2, you must transmit an ASCII 14 to the printer to enable double-width printing. You can use the CHR$ function in an LPRINT statement as follows:

```
OK
100 LPRINT CHR$(14)"REPORT TITLE"
```

This results in the following action on your printer.

```
REPORT TITLE
```

If you wish to center the report title on the page in double width, you could use the TAB function as shown by the following LPRINT statement.

```
200 LPRINT TAB ((40-12)/2) CHR$(14)"REPORT TITLE"
```

Since you are operating in double width, you only have 40 character positions per line. Thus, you will tab out to position 14 when the expression in the TAB function is evaluated. Although you could have simply put TAB(14) in the statement, you purposely put the expression in its place so you can see how you can compute where to center a string for output. Since "report title" contains 12 character positions to include the space between report and title, subtract 12 from 40. Then divide the difference by 2 to obtain the position where the string will be centered.

The two-line program and its execution result on the printer is shown below. Note that the second line that was printed has the output centered on the page.

```
100 LPRINT CHR$(14)"REPORT TITLE"
200 LPRINT TAB((40-12)/2) CHR$(14)"REPORT TITLE"
REPORT TITLE

                            REPORT TITLE
```

Double-width printing operates on a line-by-line basis on the IBM printer when an ASCII 14 is transmitted to that device. That is, once turned on by an ASCII 14 on one line, it will terminate at the end of that line. Unless you use an ASCII 14 in the next line to be printed, that line will be printed in single width. Thus, the double-width feature can be viewed as having an automatic shutoff feature. If you transmit an ESC W followed by a 1, this double width mode is not canceled by a line feed and will remain in effect until it is canceled by an ESC W followed by a 0 (zero). On other printers, like the C.ITOH 8510, this feature will remain on until turned off by sending another special character to the printer to signify double-width inhibit. If you are using the 8510 printer, a "shift-in" character (ASCII 15) can be used to turn off the double-width feature on that printer. If you wish to print both double width and single width on the same line, you can turn double width off by using ASCII 20 in a CHR$ function. An example of normal and double-width printing on a single line is shown in the following example.

```
LIST
100 LPRINT "NORMAL" CHR$(14) TAB(10)"DOUBLE" CHR$(20)TAB(20)"NORMAL"
RUN
OK
```

The result of this execution of this statement is shown below.

```
NORMAL    DOUBLE    NORMAL
```

What happens if your report is chock full of columns of data, so much data that you require more than 80 columns to be printed? In such a situation, you will want to place the printer in the compressed-character print mode, which will permit up to 132 characters to be printed on one line. To place your printer in the compressed-character print mode, you must send an ASCII 15 to the printer. Once sent, the printer will remain in the compressed-character print mode until an ASCII 18 is transmitted. Again, these control characters are listed in Table 7-2. The use of compressed-character printing is shown in the following.

```
THIS IS AN EXAMPLE OF COMPRESSED PRINTING
```

You can mix both double-width and compressed-mode printing on one line. When you do so, double-width printing results in 66 characters per line instead of 40 characters per line. In Table 7-3, a comparison of line printing capacity by mode is tabulated.

Now, let's focus our attention on the double-strike printing feature available on the IBM 80 cps graphics printer. From Table 7-2, you see that to enable this option requires you to issue an ESCAPE code plus an ASCII G. The ESCAPE code should not be confused with the Esc key. The Esc key causes an entire logical line to be erased from the screen when pressed. An ESCAPE

Table 7-3. Line Print Capacity

MODE	CHARACTERS PER INCH
Normal width	80
Normal width/compressed	132
Double width	40
Double width/compressed	66

code is the ASCII value 27, which is normally used as part of a two-character sequence to perform some predefined function. Here, an ESCAPE character followed by an ASCII G will place the printer in a double-strike operational mode. When this occurs, everything on a program line will be printed twice. Since the paper is rolled up just 1/216th of an inch before the second printing, this helps to fill in the spaces resulting from the dot matrix print head and results in a bold and solid output that makes the print quality appear similar to typewriter quality. Once the printer is placed in the double-strike mode, it will remain in that mode until an ESCAPE H character sequence is sent to the printer. This will return printing to the normal print mode of operation. On some printers, the double-strike mode is called bold printing, and different character sequences are used to enable and inhibit this feature. The following example illustrates one possible use of the double-strike print capability on the C.ITOH 8510 printer where the ESCAPE! turns on bold printing and ESCAPE" turns off that print mode. If you were using the IBM graphics printer, you would use the ESCAPE G and ESCAPE H character sequences to perform the same function.

```
LIST
100 LPRINT
110 LPRINT "Mr. George Deadbeat"
120 LPRINT "Anycity , USA"
130 LPRINT
140 LPRINT "Dear George:"
150 LPRINT
160 LPRINT "Reference our invoice dated July 16, 1776. It has come to our"
170 LPRINT "attention that " CHR$(27)CHR$(33)"PAYMENT IS LONG OVERDUE"
180 LPRINT CHR$(27)CHR$(34) "Hope your check is in the mail."
190 LPRINT
200 LPRINT "With much thanks"
```

```
Mr. George Deadbeat
Anycity , USA

Dear George:

Reference our invoice dated July 16, 1776. It has come to our
attention that PAYMENT IS LONG OVERDUE
Hope your check is in the mail.

With much thanks
```

STRING$ Function

Now that you know how to place into operation many of your printer's features, let's examine one additional control mechanism prior to moving on. This control mechanism provides you with the ability to easily print a string containing characters that all have the same ASCII code. This capability is obtained through the use of the STRING$ function whose two formats are:

format: $\left\{ \begin{array}{l} \text{var\$} = \text{STRING\$}(\text{exprnm}_1\ \text{exprnm}_2) \\ \\ \text{var\$} = \text{STRING\$}(\text{exprnm,expr\$}) \end{array} \right\}$

The STRING$ function returns a string of length exprnm in which all characters will have the ASCII code specified by $exprnm_2$ or by the first character of expr$. The use of this function in an LPRINT statement is shown below.

```
OK
100 LPRINT TAB(30)"VERY LONG REPORT TITLE"
110 LPRINT TAB(30)STRING$(22,42)
RUN
                             VERY LONG REPORT TITLE
                             **********************
```

In the preceding example, the function STRING$(22,42) results in 22 asterisks being printed (ASCII code 42 is the asterisk character), commencing at column 30.

Alternatively, you would have to place a string of 22 asterisks in line 110 or use a loop to control the printing of the asterisks if you did not use the STRING$ function. You can also use this function in a PRINT statement to display a string of similar characters or use it in a program to initialize a string to a particular character setting of a certain length.

WRITE Statement

The operational result of the execution of the WRITE statement is very similar to the PRINT statement. The difference between these two statements is that the WRITE statement inserts commas automatically between items to be displayed and delimits strings with quotation marks. The format of this statement is:

format: WRITE[list of expressions]

Like the PRINT statement, if the list of expressions is omitted, a blank line will be generated by the WRITE statement. Although you will normally display data without commas between items and quotation marks surrounding strings, on occasion you may wish to use this statement to facilitate displaying examples of how data should be entered into a program. The following example illustrates one possible use of this statement:

```
200 PRINT "USE THE FOLLOWING EXAMPLE FOR DATA ENTRY"
210 X=14:Y$="NEW YORK,NY":Z=31221
220 WRITE X,Y$,Z
RUN
USE THE FOLLOWING EXAMPLE FOR DATA ENTRY
14,"NEW YORK,NY",31221
OK
```

BRANCHING

Normally, the statements in a BASIC program will be executed in a sequential order. On occasion, you may wish to change the flow of program execution by jumping to another part of the program. You can accomplish this change of program execution flow by the use of a number of branching statements. These statements will alter the sequence of execution of the statements in a program. Several branching statements will be discussed starting with what is commonly known as the unconditional branching statement.

GOTO Statement

The GOTO statement is known as an unconditional branching statement. The execution of this statement always results in a branch out of the normal program sequence to a specified line number. The format of this statement is:

format: GOTO line

Note that the keyword GOTO is one word and must be entered as such.

The execution of a GOTO statement causes the program to branch to the referenced line number. If the referenced line number contains a REM or a DATA statement, program execution will resume at the first executable statement after the REM or DATA statement. If the line number references an executable statement, then the program will immediately branch to the referenced line and execute the referenced statement. The listing of a program segment illustrating the use of a GOTO statement and its execution with sample data is shown below. Note that as constructed, this program contains an infinite loop by repeatedly branching back to line number 100.

```
100 INPUT "ENTER A NUMBER ",N
110 S=N*N
120 PRINT "THE SQUARE OF ";N;" IS ";S
130 GOTO 100
OK
RUN
ENTER A NUMBER 5
THE SQUARE OF  5  IS  25
ENTER A NUMBER 7
THE SQUARE OF  7  IS  49
ENTER A NUMBER 99
THE SQUARE OF  99  IS  9801
ENTER A NUMBER
```

To terminate the execution of this program, you could enter the multikey combination Ctrl + Break. Later, you will examine a conditional branch that can be used to automatically terminate a program under predefined conditions.

In addition to using the GOTO statement within a program, you can also use it in direct mode without a line number. In this manner, you can directly jump to a desired line within a program. This can be extremely useful for diagnostic purposes. An example of the use of the GOTO statement in this manner is illustrated below.

```
OK
100 PRINT "DEMONSTRATION PROGRAM"
110 PRINT "TO SHOW THE USE OF A DIRECT MODE GOTO STATEMENT"
```

```
120 PRINT "LETS SEE IF WE CAN SKIP THE FIRST TWO"
130 PRINT "LINES OF THIS PROGRAM"
GOTO 120
LETS SEE IF WE CAN SKIP THE FIRST TWO
LINES OF THIS PROGRAM
Ok
```

In the preceding example, the direct mode GOTO 120 statement causes the program in memory to begin execution at line 120. This is equivalent to entering the BASIC command RUN 120.

Computed GOTO Statement

The computed GOTO statement causes the branch to one of several specified line numbers, with the precise branch taken dependent on the value resulting from the evaluation of an expression contained in the statement. The format of the computed GOTO statement is shown below.

format: ON exprnm GOTO line[,line] . . .

The value of the numeric expression (exprnm) can be a constant, variable, or expression. This value will determine which line number in the list the program will branch to. If exprnm is not an integer, it will be rounded. The following program segment illustrates the use of this program statement.

```
Ok
100 PRINT "ENTER COMPUTATION DESIRED"
110 PRINT TAB(5)"(1) REGRESSION"
120 PRINT TAB(5)"(2) CORRELATION"
130 PRINT TAB(5)"(3) NON-LINEAR REGRESSION"
140 INPUT "ENTER CHOICE (1,2 OR 3) ",CHOICE
150 ON CHOICE GOTO 300,500,750
300 REM REGRESSION MODULE
500 REM CORRELATION MODULE
750 REM NON-LINEAR REGRESSION MODULE
```

In the preceding example, the statements in lines 100 through 130 cause a heading and three program choices to be displayed. The display of program choice is normally called a menu, since the computer operator is provided with a number of items to select his or her action from. The INPUT statement in line 140 will first cause the prompt message "ENTER CHOICE (1,2 or 3)" to be displayed. Then the program will halt execution, awaiting a response from the keyboard. When a number is entered, it will be assigned to the variable named CHOICE. The computed GOTO statement in line 150 will cause a branch to one of the line numbers in the list depending on the value of the variable named CHOICE. If CHOICE is 1, the program will branch to line number 300. If CHOICE is 2, the program will branch to line number 500, while a value of 3 will cause the program to branch to line 750.

The menu displayed by the execution of this program segment is shown next.

```
RUN
ENTER COMPUTATION DESIRED
     (1) REGRESSION
     (2) CORRELATION
     (3) NON-LINEAR REGRESSION
ENTER CHOICE (1,2 OR 3)
```

Suppose the keyboard character entered does not correspond to one of the selection numbers in the menu. What will occur when the program gets to line 150 and the number of the variable differs from the number of lines in the list? If the number of the variable is zero or it is greater than the number of items in the list but less than 256, BASIC will continue program execution at the program line following the computed GOTO statement. If the value of the variable is negative or greater than 255 an "Illegal function call" error will occur. This will cause program execution to terminate.

You can trap potential errors prior to their occurrence by sampling data before it is used in a statement. In the following example, several lines of coding have been added to the previous computed GOTO example. Lines 142 through 146 check the value entered in response to the INPUT statement. If the value entered is not 1, 2, or 3, an error message will be displayed, and the program will branch back to line 140 to accept the operator's next choice.

```
Ok
LIST
100 PRINT "ENTER COMPUTATION DESIRED"
110 PRINT TAB(5)"(1) REGRESSION"
120 PRINT TAB(5)"(2) CORRELATION"
130 PRINT TAB(5)"(3) NON-LINEAR REGRESSION"
140 INPUT "ENTER CHOICE (1,2 OR 3) ",CHOICE
142 IF CHOICE =1 OR CHOICE=2 OR CHOICE=3 THEN 150
144 PRINT "NUMBER MUST BE 1,2, OR 3"
146 GOTO 140
150 ON CHOICE GOTO 300,500,750
300 REM REGRESSION MODULE
500 REM CORRELATION MODULE
750 REM NON-LINEAR REGRESSION MODULE
Ok
```

The comparison in line 142 tests to see if the value of the variable CHOICE is equal to 1 or 2 or 3. If the value of CHOICE is 1, 2, or 3, the program will branch to line 150. If the value of CHOICE does not equal 1, 2, or 3, the next program statement will be executed. Thus, line 144 would cause the message "NUMBER MUST BE 1, 2 OR 3" to be displayed and the program would then branch back to line 140 as a result of the GOTO statement in line 146. At line 140, the INPUT statement would again cause the prompt message "ENTER CHOICE (1, 2 OR 3)" to be displayed. Then, the program will halt, awaiting keyboard input of data. Let's run the program and purposely enter an invalid choice to see the response generated by the addition of lines 142 through 146.

```
RUN
ENTER COMPUTATION DESIRED
     (1) REGRESSION
     (2) CORRELATION
     (3) NON-LINEAR REGRESSION
```

```
ENTER CHOICE (1,2 OR 3) 4
NUMBER MUST BE 1,2 OR 3
ENTER CHOICE (1,2 OR 3)
```

Now that you have explored one use of what is commonly called the IF-THEN statement, let's examine this statement in detail.

IF-THEN-ELSE Statement

The IF-THEN statement on the AT differs from those on many other microcomputers using BASIC, since an optional ELSE clause can be contained as part of the statement. The format of this statement is:

format: IF expr $\left\{\begin{array}{l}\text{THEN clause}\\ \text{GOTO line}\end{array}\right\}$ [[,]ELSE clause]

Any expression (expr) in the statement is evaluated. If the expression is determined to be true (not zero), the THEN or GOTO portion of the statement is executed. The clause following THEN can be either a line number that will serve as a reference for branching, or it can consist of one or more statements to be executed based on the evaluation of the expression. The GOTO portion of the statement is always followed by a line number. If the evaluation of the expression is determined to be false (zero), the THEN or GOTO portion of the statement will be ignored, and program execution will continue with the next executable program statement. Ignoring the optional ELSE portion of the statement for the time being, let's examine a few examples of the use of the IF-THEN statement by looking at the following program segment.

```
OK
200 INPUT "ENTER AGE",AGE
210 IF AGE >30 THEN 500
220 IF AGE >10 AND AGE <30 GOTO 800
```

After the prompt message "ENTER AGE" is printed as a result of the INPUT statement, the program will halt execution, awaiting data input. When you enter a numeric variable representing an age, that number will be assigned to the variable labeled AGE. In line 210, the value assigned to AGE will be compared to 30. If AGE is greater than 30, a branch to line number 500 will occur. Suppose the number 29 is entered in response to the "ENTER AGE" prompt. Since AGE is not greater than 30, no branch will be taken and the THEN portion of the statement will be ignored. With execution continuing at the next executable program statement, line 220 will be executed. In line 220, another comparison occurs. This time, we are comparing AGE to the range of values exceeding 10 and less than 30. Mathematically, this can be denoted as:

$$10<AGE<30$$

Since AGE lies within this range, the branch to line 800 in the program will occur. Now, let's examine how you can use a clause in an IF-THEN statement to change the value of a variable automatically within a program based on the results of the evaluation of an expression. Consider the following statement.

```
500 IF(A+B-C)^2<(D/E)^3 THEN P=4
```

When line 500 is executed, the values of the variables A and B will be added, and the value of the variable C will be subtracted from the previously computed sum. Next, the resulting quantity will be squared. This value will then be compared to the cube of the values of variables D divided by E. If the left-hand expression is determined to be less than the right-hand expression, the variable P will be assigned the value 4. If the left-hand expression is not less than the right-hand expression, the clause will be ignored.

Now, let's expand the IF-THEN statement to investigate the utilization of the ELSE portion of the statement. When included in an IF-THEN statement, the ELSE clause will be executed when the results of the evaluation of the expression are false (zero). This is illustrated by modifying our previous example as follows:

```
500 IF(A+B-C)^2<(D/E)^3 THEN P=4 ELSE P=2
```

In this example, when the left-hand expression is less than the expression to the right of the less-than sign, P will be set to 4; otherwise P will be set to a value of 2.

Let's look at several more examples of the IF-THEN-ELSE statement. First, consider the following statement.

```
100 IF DISPLAY THEN PRINT"ANSWER IS" ELSE LPRINT "ANSWER IS"
```

In the preceding example, the IF-THEN-ELSE statement provides you with a mechanism to print your output either on the display or on the printer. If the variable named DISPLAY has a non-zero value, output from that statement will be directed to the screen; otherwise program output from this statement will go to the printer. Note that the IF-THEN-ELSE statement must be used as an entity. That is, the ELSE clause must not be separated by a colon or contained on a line separate from the rest of the statement. As an example, consider the execution of the following program segment.

```
OK
LIST
110 INPUT "ENTER VALUE ",A
120 IF A=4 THEN B=1 ELSE B=3
130 PRINT A,B
OK
RUN
ENTER VALUE 1
 1            3
OK
RUN
ENTER VALUE 4
 4            1
OK
```

In the first execution of the program segment, the value 1 was entered. Since A did not equal 4, then B was set equal to 3. In the second execution of the program segment, the value 4 was entered. Since line 120 sets B equal to 1 when A is 4, the PRINT statement in line 130 verifies this assignment.

Now consider what happens if you separate the ELSE clause from the rest of the IF statement.

```
LIST
110 INPUT "ENTER VALUE ",A
120 IF A=4 THEN B=1
125 ELSE B=3
130 PRINT A,B
OK
RUN
ENTER VALUE 1
 1             0
OK
RUN
ENTER VALUE 4
 4             1
OK
```

When the ELSE clause is separated from the IF-THEN statement it is ignored by BASIC. Thus, entering the value 1 for A does not assign 3 to B, and since B is undefined, its value is 0. When you execute the program segment a second time with the value 4 assigned to A, B is assigned the value 1. Thus, you should be extremely careful to insure the ELSE clause is contained in the IF-THEN statement when used.

Prior to moving on to a new group of statements, a discussion of data precision is warranted. As you have seen previously in this book, the internal representation of numerical values may not be exact in many situations, since single- and double-precision values are stored internally in floating point binary representation. In addition, when you convert a lower-precision type to a higher-precision type, you retain the accuracy of the lower-precision type. This is demonstrated by the following program segment.

```
OK
100 A=2/3:PRINT A
110 B#=A:PRINT B#
120 C#=2#/3:PRINT C#
RUN
 .6666667
 .6666666865348816
 .6666666666666667
OK
```

Based on the preceding, you may wish to test the result of a single- or double-precision computation against the range on which the accuracy of the value may vary. Since a single-precision computation is accurate to ±.000001, suppose you wished to compare a computed variable named X with the value 27.4. Consider X to be equal to 27.4 if X is 27.4−.000001 or 27.4+.000001. Thus, you wish to test the absolute value of X−27.4 to .000001. In BASIC, you can use the ABS function to obtain the absolute value of an expression. The format of this function is:

format: ABS(exprnm)

where exprnm is the numeric expression you wish to obtain the absolute value of. You can then write your comparison as follows:

```
IF ABS(X-27)<.000001 THEN . . .
```

Since .000001 is 1.0E–6 in exponential notation, the test comparison can be rewritten as follows:

```
IF ABS(X-27)<1.0E-6 THEN . . .
```

SCREEN CONTROL

There are numerous programming techniques that can be used to control the display of information. As previously noted, the INPUT and PRINT statements can be used to display information on the screen. In this section, several statements and functions that can be used to clear the display, position the cursor to a specific location, read the contents of a specific display location, or obtain the current cursor column position will be examined. Discussion will be limited to the text mode of operation; in later chapters some of these statements will be reexamined to ascertain their use when you are in a graphics-operating mode.

CLS Statement

You can clear the screen through the use of the CLS statement. The format of this statement is indicated below:

format: CLS

When used in the direct mode without a line number, this statement will immediately clear the screen and return the cursor to the home position in the upper left-hand corner of the screen. This provides you with a handy mechanism to immediately clear the display and reposition the cursor if you have previously filled the screen with data you no longer wish to reference. Note that the use of this statement does not clear the contents of memory of a previously entered program. If you wish to delete the program memory and clear all variables you would enter the NEW command. Since that command does not clear the screen, you might wish to follow it with the CLS statement entered in direct mode. Alternatively, you can press the Ctrl+Home keys to clear the screen.

When used within a BASIC program, the execution of a CLS statement clears the screen under program control. Since screen clearing will occur automatically many times, you may wish to insert a status prompt to enable the user of a program to acknowledge that he or she is ready to continue prior to clearing the screen. This is particularly important if your program is displaying the results of some computation that cannot fit on one screen and you wish to clear the screen and continue the display of output. Without some control mechanism, the output would be displayed at the AT's operating speed and the execution of the CLS statement would then clear the display. This could conceivably make it difficult if not impossible for the user to determine the results of the computation. When used after the data input process is completed, no such prompt may be necessary. In this type of situation, you may wish to clear the screen prior to displaying the results of some computation based on previously entered data. The use of prompt messages prior to a CLS statement is illustrated by the following segment.

```
100 PRINT "ENTER C TO CONTINUE"
110 A$=INKEY$:IF A$<>"C"THEN 110
120 CLS
```

In the preceding program segment, after the message "ENTER C TO CONTINUE" is displayed, the program will constantly loop in line 110 until the appropriate character is entered. Once the character C is entered, line 120 will be executed and the screen will be cleared. This type of control mechanism is important if you wish to provide time for the user to print the contents of the display with the Shift+PrtSc keys prior to the program continuing with a new screen of information.

LOCATE Statement

You can position the cursor to a specific row and column on the screen through the use of the LOCATE statement. Prior to examining the use of this statement, let's first examine in some detail the screen positions resulting from text mode operation.

The format of the screen in text mode is illustrated in Fig. 7-2. As illustrated, characters can be displayed on 25 lines across the screen. These lines are numbered 1 through 25, from top to bottom. The number of character positions per line will be 40 or 80, depending on the use of the BASIC WIDTH statement. The character positions on a line are numbered 1 to 40 or 1 to 80 from left to right. Although line 25 is used for the soft key display, you can use this line on the screen if you turn the soft key display off. This can be accomplished in direct mode or under program control by using one version of the KEY statement where the word OFF follows key as shown below.

100 KEY OFF	Turns off soft key in indirect program mode
KEY OFF	Turns off soft key in direct mode method

Having completed the initial examination of the text mode screen format, let's focus our attention back on the LOCATE statement. In addition to positioning the cursor on the screen, optional parts of this statement will permit you to turn the cursor on or off and to define its size. The format of this statement is shown below.

format: LOCATE[row][,[col][,[cursor][,[start][,stop]]]]

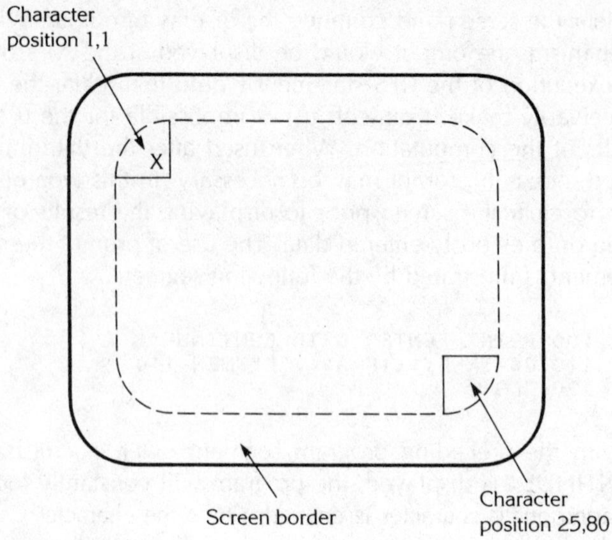

Fig. 7-2. Text mode screen format.

where row is the screen line number and is a numeric expression in the range 1 and 25; col is the screen column number (this must be a numeric expression between 1 and 40 or 1 and 80, based on the screen width); cursor is a value that will define whether or not the cursor is visible (a value of zero turns the cursor off, 1 turns the cursor on); start is the cursor starting scan line and must be a numeric expression between 0 and 31; and stop is the cursor stop scan line and must be a numeric expression between zero and 31. Figure 7-3 shows the 8 bars that define the cursor on the AT when the color/graphics monitor adapter is used. These lines are numbered from 0 at the top of the character position to 7 at the bottom. Note that by defining the appropriate start and stop scan lines you can vary the size of the cursor. If the IBM monochrome display adapter is used, the bottom scan line is 13, resulting in 14 bars that can be used to define the cursor.

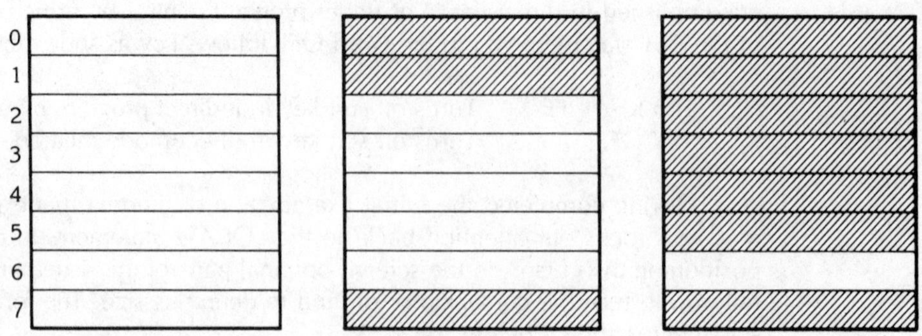

Fig. 7-3. Bars that form the cursor using color/graphics monitor adapter.

If any format parameter is entered that is outside the specified range of values, an "illegal function call" error will result. Any parameter can be omitted, in which case the omitted parameter will assume the current value. Let's take a look at some examples of the use of this statement to obtain a feel for its utilization within a program.

Since the default value of the cursor is off when a program runs, suppose you wish to turn it in. You can do so by the following statement.

```
100 LOCATE,,1
```

Note that by using two commas prior to turning the cursor on you have omitted the row and column positions from the specification. This means they will assume the current value and the cursor will become visible where the program first places it on the screen. Now, suppose you wish to print the message "SPACEMAN" on line 12, starting at column position 36. You can first position the cursor to that location, since subsequent I/O statements to the screen will place characters beginning at the specified location. Thus, you can satisfy your requirement through the use of the following two statements.

```
100 LOCATE 12,36
110 PRINT"SPACEMAN"
```

Line 100 causes the cursor to be positioned on row 12 at column 36. The PRINT statement on line 110 causes the string SPACEMAN to be displayed on line 12, starting at column 36. Suppose you wish to display a screen of questions and position the cursor to an appropriate location to receive the response to each question. This can be accomplished by multiple LOCATE statements as indicated by the following program segment.

```
LIST
100 CLS
110 LOCATE 5,15,1
120 PRINT "PART NUMBER"
130 LOCATE 7,15
140 PRINT "QUANTITY ON HAND"
150 LOCATE 9,15
160 PRINT "UNIT COST"
170 LOCATE 5,40
180 INPUT "",PN
190 LOCATE 7,40
200 INPUT "",QTY
210 LOCATE 9,40
220 INPUT "",COST
```

In the preceding program segment, the LOCATE statement in line 110 positions the cursor at row 5, column 15, and turns it on. The PRINT statement in line 120 causes the string "PART NUMBER" to be displayed on line 5, commencing at column 15. The LOCATE and PRINT statements in lines 130 through 150 cause the strings "QUANTITY ON HAND" and "UNIT COST" to be displayed on lines 7 and 9, each left justified in column 15. Now that you finished displaying the items you wish values to be entered for, you can reposition the cursor to appropriate locations to receive data input. Assuming you wish data to be entered at column 40 on each line where the string was displayed, you can use the LOCATE statements in lines 170, 190, and 210 for that purpose. After you move the cursor to the appropriate position, the following INPUT statement will be used to assign the data to a variable. Note that the word INPUT is followed by a null character signified by double quotes. This null character was used to suppress the generation of a question mark (?) by the INPUT statement. The execution of this program segment with sample data input is shown below. Note that you are able to align responses to questions on a line-by-line basis and space and position questions and responses through the use of the LOCATE statement.

```
PART NUMBER                 3433

QUANTITY ON HAND            122

UNIT COST                   14.75
```

You can use the start and stop parameters in the LOCATE statement format to vary the size of the cursor. This is accomplished by indicating the starting and ending scan lines. Scan lines are numbered from 0 at the top of the character position to 7 or 13, depending on whether you are using the color/graphics or the monochrome adapter. By using the LOCATE statement with appropriate start and stop values you can change the cursor from a dash to a square or into a rectangular shape. In addition, you can split the cursor into equal or non-equal segments, as illustrated in the right-hand portion of Fig. 7-3. Once set, the cursor will retain that shape until it is altered by a subsequent LOCATE statement. The following examples illustrate the use of the LOCATE statement by changing the size of the cursor.

```
100 LOCATE ,,,0,13
```

Here, the position and cursor visibility remain unchanged. The cursor will cover the entire character cell on the display, starting at scan line 0 and ending on scan line 13.

```
100 LOCATE 1,1,1,0,6
```

Here, the cursor will move to the home position in the upper left-hand corner, the cursor will become visible and cover one-half of the character cell, starting at scan line 0 and ending at scan line 6.

When specifying scan lines, you can omit either or both values. If start is given and stop is omitted, stop will take on the value of start. If you specify a start value greater than stop, you will obtain a two-part cursor. In this event, the cursor will "wrap" itself from the bottom line back to the top.

AT BASIC contains a function for locating the current cursor column position and a variable that can be used to obtain the cursor's row location.

POS Function

The POS function can be used to obtain the current column position of the cursor. The format of this function is:

format: X=POS(dummy)

Here, a dummy argument is used in the function call. The returned value of the function call will be between 1 and 40 or 1 and 80, depending on the current WIDTH setting. The use of this function is demonstrated in the following program segment.

```
100 IF POS(X)>50 THEN 130
110 PRINT A$
120 GOTO 150
130 LOCATE 10,1
140 PRINT A$
150 REM Program continues
```

In the preceding example, you assumed you would display variable length information. If so, you may wish to see where the cursor is located prior to continuing output to the screen. In line 100, you compared the cursor's column position to 50. If it is less than or equal to 50, the program will display the string contained in A$ and then branch to line 150. If the cursor's column position is greater than 50, the program will branch to line 130 where the cursor will be relocated to line 10, column 1, and the string A$ will be displayed starting at that position.

CSRLIN Variable

The CSRLIN variable can be used to obtain the vertical coordinate (row) of the cursor. The format of the use of this variable is:

format: varnm=CSRLIN

If you are developing a program that has the number of output lines displayed based on user response, you could use the CSRLIN variable to test the row cursor position prior to generating a CLS statement that would clear the display and home the cursor back to position 1,1. Another use of this variable is in conjunction with the POS function to obtain the current row and column positions of the cursor prior to generating a message at a location on the screen. Once the message is generated, you could then restore your cursor to its previous location as indicated by the following program segment.

```
OK
100 KEY OFF          'Turn off soft keys
.
.
.
```

```
500 X=CSRLIN           'Get current line
510 Y=POS(0)           'Get current column
520 LOCATE 25,10
530 PRINT "WRONG ANSWER-ENTER C TO CONTINUE"
540 A$=INKEY$:IF A$<>"C"THEN 540
550 LOCATE 25,10       'Clear error message from screen
560 PRINT "                                 "
570 LOCATE Y,X         'Restore cursor position
```

In the preceding example, the statement in line 100 causes the "soft key" display to be turned off. The statements in lines 500 and 510 assign the column and row positions of the cursor to the variables X and Y. In line 520, the cursor is repositioned to column 10 in line 25 and the message "WRONG ANSWER—ENTER C TO CONTINUE" is displayed. The statements in line 540 cause the program to await the entry of the upper-case character C from the keyboard prior to resuming program execution. Once C is entered, the error message is cleared from the screen and the cursor is relocated to its previous location by the statement in line 570. In line 570, the position of the cursor is restored to what was the current line and current column positions to generating and clearing the indicated error message.

PROGRAM EXECUTION CONTROL

You can terminate program execution and return to command level through the use of an END or a STOP statement. The format of each statement is:

format: END
format: STOP

END Statement

The END statement may be placed anywhere in a program. Once executed, the program will terminate. Unlike many other versions of BASIC, the use of an END statement at the end of a program written for the AT is optional. In addition to terminating program execution and returning to command level, the END statement will automatically close any open files. The use of this statement is illustrated by the following program line.

```
100 IF X<Y THEN END ELSE 500
```

In the preceding example, if the value of X is less than Y the program will terminate. Since the only message displayed will be the "Ok" command level prompt, you might consider revising the previous example as follows.

```
100 IF X>=Y THEN 120
110 PRINT "X<Y CAUSED PROGRAM TERMINATION":END
120 REM Program continues
```

Now, when X is less than Y the message "X<Y CAUSED PROGRAM TERMINATION" will be displayed prior to the command level prompt "Ok" appearing on the screen.

STOP Statement

When a STOP statement is encountered, the program will terminate execution and return to command level. Prior to generating the command level prompt "Ok", this statement will display the message:

```
Break in nnnnn
```

Here, nnnnn is the line number where the STOP statement was executed. Unlike the END statement, this statement will not close any open files. The use of this statement is illustrated by the following program segment.

```
Ok
100 INPUT "ENTER LENGTH AND WIDTH ";L,W
110 A=L*W
120 IF A>0 THEN 140
130 STOP
140 PRINT "AREA= ";A
150 END
RUN
ENTER LENGTH AND WIDTH ? -2,4
Break in 130
Ok
```

In the preceding example, the STOP statement was used to halt program execution when an apparent illogical computation had occurred.

CONT Command

You can resume program execution after a break by the use of the CONT command. Although BASIC commands will be discussed as an entity in the next chapter, it is worthwhile to point out the use of this command at the present time. The format of this command is:

format: CONT

This command can be used to resume program execution after a STOP or END statement has been executed, after a "Ctrl + Break" has been pressed, or after an error has occurred. The CONT command causes program execution to continue at the point where the break occurred.

The use of this command to resume execution of the prior program whose execution was halted by a STOP statement follows.

```
Ok
100 INPUT "ENTER LENGTH AND WIDTH ";L,W
110 A=L*W
120 IF A>0 THEN 140
```

```
130 STOP
140 PRINT "AREA= ";A
150 END
RUN
ENTER LENGTH AND WIDTH ? -2,4
Break in 130
Ok
CONT
AREA= -8
Ok
```

Normally, you will use this command in conjunction with a STOP statement for program debugging purposes as illustrated by the following example.

```
Ok
100 X=47.5
110 Y=32.5
120 Q=X*Y
130 PRINT "Q= ";Q
140 STOP
150 LET V=Q+250:PRINT V
RUN
Q= 1543.75
Break in 140
Ok
Q=1500
Ok
CONT
 1750
Ok
```

In this example, after program execution terminated as a result of the STOP statement, a direct mode statement (Q=1500) was used to change the value of a variable prior to resuming execution with the CONT command. Alternatively, you could use a direct mode GOTO statement, which would also cause program execution to resume at the referenced line number.

Before leaving this topic, it should be noted that the CONT command will be invalid if you edit the program during the break. In comparison, the use of a direct mode GOTO statement will always cause the program to resume execution at the referenced line number.

LOOP CONTROL

A computer loop can be defined as a repeating sequence of program statements. Using the GOTO and IF-THEN statements, you can construct a program loop as illustrated by the following example, which results in a table of squares for the numbers 1 to 5.

```
Ok
LIST
5 PRINT"NUMBER","SQUARE"
10 I=1
20 IF I>5 THEN 60
30 PRINT I,I^2
```

```
40 I=I+1
50 GOTO 20
60 END
OK
RUN
NUMBER          SQUARE
 1              1
 2              4
 3              9
 4              16
 5              25
OK
```

In this example, a loop control variable was initialized to 1 in line 10. In line 20, the value of the loop control variable was tested against the value you wanted to exit from the loop when reached. In this example, you wished to exit the loop and branch to line 60 when the value of 1 exceeded 5. In line 30, the PRINT statement will cause the value of 1 and its square to be displayed. While this loop shows only the repeated use of a PRINT statement, you could construct a loop to repeatedly obtain a set number of input data items or to perform a series of computations a desired number of times. In line 40, your loop control variable is incremented by 1 and line 50 causes the program to unconditionally branch back to line 20 where the program again tests the value of the loop control variable against 5. Once you cycle through the loop 5 times, you will have the value 6 and the statement in line 20 will cause the program to branch to line 60, terminating the loop. Note that this method of constructing a loop requires you to set the initial value of the loop control parameter, test for the loop exit value, increment the loop control parameter, and have a branching mechanism to return you to the loop parameter comparison once the loop variable has been incremented. By the way, you can also have loops that decrement by initializing the loop parameter to the end value and testing for the lowest permissible loop value. This can be accomplished by decrementing the value of the loop variable each time you pass through the loop as illustrated by the execution of the next program segment.

```
OK
LIST
5 PRINT"NUMBER","SQUARE"
10 I=50
20 IF I<10 THEN 60
30 PRINT I,I^2
40 I=I-10
50 GOTO 20
60 END
OK
RUN
NUMBER          SQUARE
 50              2500
 40              1600
 30              900
 20              400
 10              100
OK
```

FOR and NEXT Statements

Loops are used so routinely in programming that BASIC provides you with a built-in set of loop control statements known as the FOR and NEXT statements. The format of each statement is:

format: FOR varnm = $exprnm_1$ TO $exprnm_2$[STEP $exprnm_3$]
format: NEXT[varnm][,varnm]..

The NEXT statement specifies the boundary in which a series of instructions will be executed a given number of times. The beginning of the loop is specified by the FOR statement whose parameters will control the number of times the loop is executed. The initial value of the counter that controls the loop is specified by $exprnm_1$, while the value of $exprnm_2$ specifies the final value of the counter. The program lines bounded by the FOR and NEXT statements will be executed until the NEXT statement is reached. At this time, BASIC will increment or decrement the counter by the amount specified by the STEP value ($exprnm_3$). If $exprnm_3$ is positive, the counter will be incremented while a negative value will result in the counter being decremented. If $exprnm_3$ is not specified, an increment of 1 will be assumed. After the increment or decrement operation is performed, a comparison of the value of the counter against the final value $exprnm_2$ will occur. If incrementing was specified and the value of the counter is less than or equal to the final value, BASIC will branch back to the statement following the FOR statement and the process will be repeated. If the counter exceeds the final value, execution will continue with the statement that follows the NEXT statement.

If $exprnm_3$ is negative and the counter is decremented, the test will be reversed. Here, the counter will be decremented each time through the loop and the process will be repeated until the counter is less than the final value $exprnm_2$. Some examples of the use of a single FOR-NEXT loop follow.

```
OK
LIST
5 PRINT"NUMBER","SQUARE"
10 FOR I=I TO 5
20 PRINT I,I^2
30 NEXT I
OK
RUN
NUMBER         SQUARE
 1              1
 2              4
 3              9
 4              16
 5              25
OK
```

Note that the preceding example provides the same loop control mechanism as obtained through the use of IF-THEN and GOTO statements combined to generate a looping mechanism. You can generate a loop by decrementing the counter as illustrated by executing the following program segment.

```
OK
LIST
5 PRINT"NUMBER","SQUARE"
10 FOR I=100 TO 50 STEP -10
20 PRINT I,I^2
30 NEXT I
OK
RUN
NUMBER         SQUARE
 100            10000
 90             8100
 80             6400
 70             4900
 60             3600
 50             2500
OK
```

You can specify a zero increment if you wish to perform some operation a number of times but do not know how many times are required. The use of a zero increment will cause an infinite loop to be created; however, you can construct your program to terminate the loop by setting the counter greater than the final value or by branching out of the loop when your goal is reached. An example of the use of zero increment in a FOR statement is illustrated by the following program segment.

```
OK
LIST
100 K=1:X=0
110 FOR I=1 TO 2 STEP 0
120 K=K+1/K^2
130 X=X+1
140 IF K>=3 THEN 160
150 NEXT I
160 PRINT X;"ITERATIONS FOR K= ";K
RUN
 7 ITERATIONS FOR K=  3.011531
OK
```

In this example, you wish to determine the number of iterations of the sequence $1 + 1/1^2 + 1/2^2 + 1/3^2 + \ldots 1/N^2$ that is required for the sum of the sequence to equal or exceed 3. Initialize K to 1 and a counter labeled X to 0 in line 100. The FOR statement has a zero STEP, which will keep you in the loop until K equals or exceeds 3. Once this occurs, the program will branch out of the loop due to the statement in line 140. Here, seven iterations were required until K exceeded 3.

If the initial value of the counter is greater than the final value when the STEP value is positive, the body of the loop will be skipped. This is indicated by the following program segment.

```
OK
10 A=10:B=20
20 FOR X=B TO A STEP 5
30 PRINT X
40 NEXT X
RUN
OK
```

If the STEP value is negative and the initial value of the counter is less than the final value, the body of the loop will also be skipped over.

The FOR and NEXT statements become invaluable as a mechanism for easily performing many computations. As an example, consider factorial numbers when $n! = n \cdot (n-1) \cdot (n-2) \ldots 2 \cdot 1$. The following program can be used to compute any factorial number between 1 and 33. The reason the upper limit is 33 is that factorials beyond this number exceed the largest number the AT can operate on.

```
Ok
LIST
10 INPUT "ENTER FACTORIAL DESIRED 0 TO EXIT ",F
20 IF F=0 THEN 90
30 X=1
40 FOR I=F TO 1 STEP-1
50 X=X*I
60 NEXT I
70 PRINT  F;" FACTORIAL = ";X
80 GOTO 10
90 END
Ok
RUN
ENTER FACTORIAL DESIRED 0 TO EXIT 4
 4  FACTORIAL =  24
ENTER FACTORIAL DESIRED 0 TO EXIT 33
 33  FACTORIAL =  8.683316E+36
ENTER FACTORIAL DESIRED 0 TO EXIT 34
Overflow

 34  FACTORIAL =  1.701412E+38
ENTER FACTORIAL DESIRED 0 TO EXIT
```

Another valuable use of FOR and NEXT statements is to provide an easy mechanism for the manipulation of array elements. Suppose you have an array containing 50 data elements and you wish to obtain the average value of all elements. You can accomplish this task easily as shown by the following program segment.

```
100 FOR I=1 TO 50
110 X=X+A(I)
120 NEXT I
130 PRINT "AVERAGE= ";X/50
```

Here, the Ith element of array A will be added to the counter labeled X each time the FOR-NEXT loop is executed. When all 50 elements have been added to X, the loop will terminate, and the line following the NEXT statement, line 130, will be executed. The PRINT statement on this line will cause the string "AVERAGE=" to be displayed, and the value of X will be divided by 50 prior to being displayed on the screen.

Suppose you have a two-dimensional array. How could you use a FOR-NEXT loop to add the elements of that type of array? Since FOR-NEXT loops can be nested, you can use several such loops to perform the required loop control mechanism. By nested loops we mean that one FOR-NEXT loop can be placed inside another FOR-NEXT loop. An example of the use of nested FOR-NEXT loops follows.

```
100 FOR I=1 TO 10
110 FOR J=1 TO 5
120 X=X+A(I,J)
130 NEXT J
140 NEXT I
```

Here, the FOR J loop is known as the inner and the FOR I loop is known as the outer loop. When loops are nested, each loop must be assigned a unique variable name as its counter. The NEXT statement for the inner loop must appear prior to the occurrence of a NEXT statement for the outer loop or an error will occur. To examine the use of nested FOR-NEXT statements, execute this short program segment.

```
LIST
100 FOR I=1 TO 6 STEP 2
110 FOR J=10 TO 30 STEP 10
120 PRINT I,J
130 NEXT J
140 NEXT I
RUN
 1            10
 1            20
 1            30
 3            10
 3            20
 3            30
 5            10
 5            20
 5            30
OK
```

In this example, the I counter is initialized to 1 in line 100. The J counter is initialized to 10 in line 110. Since the execution of the complete inner loop will occur for each loop cycle, J will vary from 10 to 30 in increments of 10 when I is 1. Once the inner loop is completed, the program continues and initializes another outer loop cycle when the following NEXT statement is encountered. Thus, I is incremented by 2 to a value of 3 in the outer loop. This causes the inner loop to be repeated a second time and the process will be repeated a third time with I having a value of 5 as J varies from 10 to 30. Note that in AT BASIC you can replace lines 130 and 140 with the common NEXT statement.

```
130 NEXT I,J
```

The error message "FOR without NEXT" will be generated if a FOR statement is encountered without a matching NEXT. This can result from a loop being initialized and a cycle being in progress when an END, STOP, or a RETURN statement is encountered in the program. The error message "NEXT without FOR" will occur if a NEXT statement is encountered prior to its corresponding FOR statement. A good technique for checking the validity of FOR-NEXT loops is to draw a line on the left-hand side of your program listing to connect each FOR statement with its corresponding NEXT statement. This will ensure a 1 to 1 correspondence. In addition, if the lines form concentric brackets that do not intersect, the FOR-NEXT statements are used in their appropriate order. If the lines drawn between statements cross, the FOR-NEXT statements will not operate and the variable assignments must be changed. The following examples illustrate the use of lines to connect FOR-NEXT statements.

```
100 FOR I=1 TO 5
110 FOR J=6 TO 12
120 PRINT I,J
130 NEXT I
140 NEXT J
```

Since the lines connecting each FOR statement with its corresponding NEXT statement intersect, the statement sequence is illegal.

```
100 FOR I=1 TO 5
110 FOR J=6 TO 12
120 PRINT I,J
130 NEXT I
140 NEXT J
```

The concentric lines connecting each FOR statement with its corresponding NEXT statement indicate the statement sequence is legal.

WHILE-WEND Statements

The WHILE and WEND statements provide another mechanism for executing a series of statements in a loop. Unlike the FOR and NEXT statements that directly control the number of times the statements within a loop will be executed, the WHILE and WEND statements cause the statements bounded by those two statements to be executed as long as a given condition is true. The format of these two statements is shown below:

format: WHILE expression
format: WEND

As long as the expression in the WHILE statement is true (not zero), the statements bounded by the WHILE and WEND statements will be executed. Each time the WEND statement is encountered, BASIC will pass control back to the WHILE statement and check the value of the expression in that statement. If the expression is still true, another pass through the loop will occur. If the expression is false, BASIC will cause the program to resume execution with the statement following the WEND statement. The following program segment illustrates the use of these two statements.

```
OK
100 REM ACCEPT INPUT UNTIL COMPUTED VALUE EXCEEDS TOTAL
110 X=0:COUNT=0:TOTAL=132.65
120 TEST=1
130 WHILE TEST
140 INPUT "ENTER VALUE ",VALUE
150 X=X+VALUE/3.14159
160 COUNT=COUNT+1
170 IF X>TOTAL THEN TEST=0
180 WEND
190 PRINT "NUMBER OF ENTRIES= ";COUNT
```

```
RUN
ENTER VALUE 13.212
ENTER VALUE 32
ENTER VALUE 543
NUMBER OF ENTRIES=  3
OK
```

In this example, two counters, X and COUNT, were initialized to zero, in line 110, and the value tested for, TOTAL, was initialized to 132.65. The expression used to control the WHILE-WEND loop execution, TEST, is initialized to 1 in line 120. In line 140, the INPUT statement will cause the prompt "ENTER VALUE" to be displayed, and the program will temporarily halt execution awaiting a numeric quantity to be entered. This quantity will be assigned to the variable VALUE. In line 150, the counter X will be incremented by the quantity VALUE divided by 3.14159. In line 160, the counter, COUNT, which is used to keep track of the number of items entered is incremented by one. When the value of X exceeds the predefined value contained in the variable TOTAL, TEST will be reset to zero in line 170. This will cause the program to resume execution at the statement after the WEND statement, and the number of entries will then be printed as a result of the BASIC statement in line 190. As shown, three entries were required until the WHILE-WEND loop was exited.

Like FOR-NEXT loops, WHILE-WEND loops can be nested. Each WEND statement will match the most recent WHILE statement as illustrated below.

```
┌── WHILE expression1
│   .
│   .
│ ┌ WHILE expression2
│ │ .
│ │ .
│ └ WEND
│   .
│   .
└── WEND
```

Error messages resulting from the improper usage of WHILE and WEND statements are similar to the error messages from the improper use of FOR and NEXT statements. An unmatched WHILE statement will cause a "WHILE without WEND" error message while an unmatched WEND statement will result in a "WEND without WHILE" error message.

SUBROUTINES

Many times in programming you recognize that a sequence of statements that performs one or more functions requires repeated usage. You can construct these statements as a subroutine and easily invoke their usage by branching to the statement where the subroutine starts. In addition, BASIC provides you with a mechanism to conveniently return program execution to the statement after the statement that invoked the subroutine or to any other program statement you may desire to resume program execution.

GOSUB Statement

The most common method to reference a subroutine is by means of the GOSUB statement whose format is:

format: GOSUB line

The execution of the GOSUB statement causes the program to branch to the line number indicated in the statement. Program execution will continue at the indicated line number until a RETURN statement is encountered.

RETURN Statement

The RETURN statement defines the physical end of the subroutine. The format of this statement is:

format: RETURN
format$_A$: RETURN[line]

In all versions of BASIC, the RETURN statement will cause BASIC to branch back to the statement following the most recently executed GOSUB statement. In advanced BASIC, the optional line number in the RETURN statement allows you to resume program execution at any line in the program, although the use of this feature must be carefully considered as any other GOSUB, FOR, or WHILE statement that was active will remain active.

The subroutine itself does not require any special statement at its beginning. Thus, a subroutine can begin with a REM statement, a FOR statement, a CLS statement, and so on. The last statement, however, must be a RETURN statement. As an example of the use of subroutines, suppose you are developing a program that requires many screens of information to be displayed, each screen requesting the entry of several items of data. Furthermore, suppose that, after the last item of data is entered on each screen, you wish to provide a mechanism for the operator to either reenter the data elements in case one or more items were previously entered incorrectly or to clear the display prior to generating the next screen display and requesting the entry of new data elements. Our main program with the appropriate subroutine branches might be constructed as follows:

```
100 REM Display first screen section
.
.
.
200 GOSUB 4000
210 IF X=1 THEN 100
.
.
```

```
300 REM Display second screen section
.
400 GOSUB 4000
410 IF X=1 THEN 300
.
.
4000 REM Beginning of subroutine
4010 X=0                          'Reset X
4020 LOCATE 25,10
4030 PRINT"ENTER C TO CONTINUE R TO REENTER DATA"
4040 A$=INKEY$:IFA$<>"C" OR A$<>"R" THEN 4040
4050 IF A$="R" THEN X=1
4060 CLS
4070 RETURN                       'End of subroutine
```

In this example, each GOSUB 4000 statement causes the program to transfer control to the subroutine that begins at line 4000. Here, the first statement in the subroutine is a nonexecutable REM statement. The second statement in the subroutine sets the variable labeled X to zero. This variable will be used for control purposes when you return to the main program. Line 4020 positions the cursor at row 25, column 10, where the message "ENTER C TO CONTINUE R TO REENTER DATA" will be printed, starting at row 25, column 10. Line 4040 uses the INKEY$ variable to read a character from the keyboard and causes a branch back to this line if neither the uppercase C nor R is entered. Line 4050 compares the value of A$ to the character R. If A$ equals R, then X will be reset to 1. If A$ does not equal R, the X will retain its initialized value of 0. The CLS statement in line 4060 causes the screen to be cleared, and the RETURN statement in line 4070 causes the program to transfer control to the statement following the most recent GOSUB statement. Thus, if lines 100 through 200 of the program display the first screen and obtain the values for the appropriate data elements, if one enters the character R when the subroutine prompt message is displayed, the RETURN from the subroutine to line 210 will cause the program to branch back to line 100 and redisplay the screen. This is because the variable X was set to 1 in the subroutine. This will permit all previous entries to be changed and provides an easy mechanism for reentering previously entered data elements within a program.

Prior to examining what is commonly known as a computed subroutine statement, a word of caution concerning the usage of subroutines is in order. While subroutines can be physically located anywhere within a program, good programming practice is to place them at the end of a program for ease of visual reference in program debugging. This can simplify program debugging considerably, since in AT BASIC a subroutine may be called from within another subroutine and the only limit to such nesting of subroutines is available memory.

If you place subroutines at the end of your program, their physical structure would appear as illustrated in Fig. 7-4.

When the last line in the main program is executed, what occurs next? If the last statement is not a STOP, END, or a GOTO statement that branches to a STOP or END statement, the first subroutine will be executed again. Since this is obviously not your intention, you should always place a STOP, END,

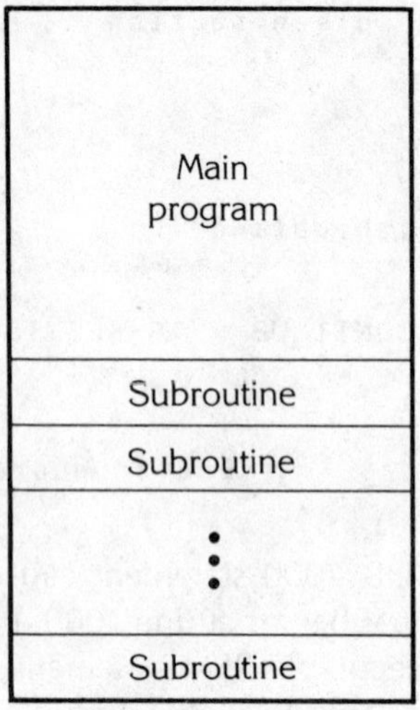

Fig. 7-4. Recommended program structure.

or GOTO statement that will branch to a STOP or END statement at the end of the main program when you physically locate subroutines at the end of a program. This fact is illustrated by the execution of the following program segment.

```
Ok
LIST
100 REM Main program
110 INPUT "NAME ",N$
120 GOSUB 500
130 INPUT "ADDRESS ",A$
500 PRINT "I LIKE ";N$
510 RETURN
Ok
RUN
NAME GIL
I LIKE GIL
ADDRESS 4736 OXFORD ROAD
I LIKE GIL
RETURN without GOSUB in 510
Ok
```

In this example, after line 130 is executed, the program falls back into the subroutine. This results in the unintentional printing of the "I LIKE" message in the subroutine a second time and causes the "RETURN without GOSUB in 510" error message to be displayed. By placing a STOP or END statement in line 140 as shown below, this extra and unwanted fall into the subroutine is prevented.

```
100 REM Main program
110 INPUT "NAME ",N$
120 GOSUB 500
130 INPUT "ADDRESS ",A$
140 END
```

```
500 PRINT "I LIKE ";N$
510 RETURN
Ok
RUN
NAME GIL
I LIKE GIL
ADDRESS 4736 OXFORD ROAD
Ok
```

ON-GOSUB Statement

BASIC contains a computed GOSUB statement whose format and functional operation is very similar to the computed GOTO statement. The computed GOSUB statement provides you with the capability to branch to one of two or more subroutines based on the value of a numeric expression. The format of this statement is:

format: ON exprnm GOSUB line[,line] . . .

The value of the numeric expression, exprnm, will determine which line number in the list the program will branch to when the statement is executed. If the value of the expression is not an integer, it will be rounded to one. If the value of the numeric expression is zero or greater than the number of items in the list but less than or equal to 255, BASIC will ignore the statement and resume execution with the next executable statement following the ON-GOSUB statement. When the value of the numeric expression used for branch control is negative or greater than 256, an "Illegal function call" error will result, and program execution will be halted.

The use of this statement is most beneficial if you wish to divide your program into segments and control the branch to the appropriate segment by the user. This can be accomplished by providing an initial menu and associating a value with the response to branch to the desired program segment that was written as a subroutine. Once the subroutine is completed, the RETURN statement will provide you with a mechanism to branch back to the line following the computed ON-GOSUB statement where you can provide the program operator with another segment by branching back to the menu. This concept is demonstrated by the following program segment.

```
100 CLS
110 LOCATE 10,15
120 PRINT "PROGRAM SECTION SELECTION"
130 PRINT
140 PRINT TAB(15)"(1) CONVERTIBLE BOND ANALYSIS"
150 PRINT TAB(15)"(2) INTEREST RATE ANALYSIS"
160 PRINT TAB(15)"(3) HOME MORTGAGE ANALYSIS"
170 PRINT TAB(15)"(4) RETIREMENT FUNDING ANALYSIS"
180 PRINT TAB(15)"(5) EXIT PROGRAM"
190 PRINT
200 LOCATE 18,15
210 INPUT "ENTER SECTION DESIRED",X
220 ON X GOSUB 1000,2000,3000,4000,5000
230 GOTO 100
```

```
1000 REM Convertible bond analysis subroutine
.
.
1990 RETURN
.
.
.
5000 END
```

In this example, the section number desired is used as the mechanism to control which subroutine the program will branch to. Note that the entry of a number greater than 5 will cause line 230 to be executed, which will result in the initial menu being displayed again. In addition, each RETURN statement in the program will also cause line 230 to be executed, also causing the menu to be displayed again and allowing the operator to select another program section. If 5 is entered, a branch to line 5000 will occur. Here, an END statement is used to terminate the program. The initial menu displayed on the screen is indicated below.

```
PROGRAM SECTION SELECTION

(1) CONVERTIBLE BOND ANALYSIS
(2) INTEREST RATE ANALYSIS
(3) HOME MORTGAGE ANALYSIS
(4) RETIREMENT FUNDING ANALYSIS
(5) EXIT PROGRAM

ENTER SECTION DESIRED
```

ERROR HANDLING

Several variables and error-handling statements are contained in BASIC. These statements and variables provide you with the capability to enable error trapping, obtain an error code and line number associated with an error, simulate the occurrence of an error, or define an error code that will be used for error trapping by your program.

ERR and ERL Variables

BASIC contains two predefined variables that will return the error code and line number in which an error was detected. The variable labeled ERR contains the error code for the last error encountered within a program, while the variable labeled ERL will contain the line number in the program where the error was detected. The format illustrating the use of these two variables is indicated below:

format: varnm=ERL
format: varnm=ERR

You can use the ERL and ERR variables in IF-THEN statements to control program execution within an error-handling routine you may wish to include in a program. Since a logical question is how do you develop an error-handling routine, let's examine this aspect of BASIC and then see how you can use the ERR and ERL variables within such a routine.

ON ERROR GOTO Statement

The BASIC statement that enables trapping is the ON ERROR GOTO statement whose format is:

format: ON ERROR GOTO line

Once this statement is executed, error trapping will be enabled and any detected error will cause the flow of program control to branch to the line number indicated in the statement. While all errors to include syntax errors resulting from improper grammatical construction of statements within a program will cause a branch to the indicated line, normally you will insert the ON ERROR GOTO statement into your program after it has been completely tested with the exception of your error-handling routine. You should follow this procedure, since the ON ERROR GOTO statement can result in an infinite program loop if you have an error that is not trapped in your error-handling routine and use a RESUME statement at the end of the routine to return to the line where the error originated.

Your error-handling routine will typically check for recoverable errors such as a device timeout or a printer-out-of-paper error. In these situations, you can test for those error codes that signify these errors and display predefined messages to alert the operator to take appropriate action and then resume program execution after such action is completed.

RESUME Statement

To continue program execution after the completion of an error recovery procedure requires the use of the RESUME statement whose format is:

```
         ⎧ RESUME [0]   ⎫
format:  ⎨ RESUME NEXT  ⎬
         ⎩ RESUME line  ⎭
```

Any of the preceding formats of the RESUME statement can be used, with the precise format based on where you want program execution to resume after your error-recovery procedure is completed. The RESUME or RESUME 0 statement will cause program execution to resume at the statement that caused the error. A RESUME NEXT statement will result in program execution being resumed at the statement following the one that caused the error. A RESUME LINE statement will cause program execution to resume at the specified line number. Now that you have an overview of how to enable error trapping and resume program execution, let's develop the appropriate BASIC coding to perform a predefined error-handling routine.

Suppose you are developing a program that prints a report. Normally, if you are running a program and the printer runs out of paper the AT will sense this fact, generate an "Out of paper" message on the display and terminate program execution. This could result in untold hardship if your program was updating files at the same time it was printing the report. Here you might not be able to simply rerun the program, since it would update a portion of the files a second time, which is not what you would normally want to occur. You would either have to develop a mechanism to reenter the program at the point where the updating stopped or add an error-handling procedure to suspend execution while you add paper and then resume program execution once your printer is ready to continue printing the report. Since we are discussing error control, let's examine how you can accomplish the latter. Appendix C lists all of the BASIC error messages and their associated error codes. Note that error code 27 results from the printer being "Out of paper." This error condition will result if the printer is out of paper or if the printer is not powered on. Our error-handling routine and the enabling of error trapping is indicated by the following program segment.

```
100 ON ERROR GOTO 5000
.
.
5000 REM Error handling routine
5010 IF ERR<> 27 THEN 5070
5020 CLS
5030 LOCATE 12,20
5040 PRINT "PRINTER NOT READY - CHECK PAPER AND POWER"
5050 PRINT TAB(20);"ENTER R WHEN READY TO RESUME"
5060 A$=INKEY$:IF A$<>"R"THEN 5060
5070 RESUME
```

In this example, line 100 enables error trapping and will cause the program to branch to line 5000 if an error should occur. In line 5010, the program tests for error code 27. If error code 27 did not occur, the program will branch to line 5070 where the RESUME statement causes the program to RESUME execution at the line that enabled error trapping. If you wish to check for several errors you might branch to line 5080 where you would add another comparison of the ERR variable with the next error code you wish to develop a procedure to process. If error code 27 occurred, the program will clear the screen and generate the messages "PRINTER NOT READY—CHECK PAPER AND POWER" and "ENTER R WHEN READY TO RESUME". Once the character R is entered, the RESUME statement in line 5070 will cause the program to resume execution at the statement that caused the error. From the preceding, error trapping can be viewed similar to constructing a subroutine, the key difference being that the program will branch from any line to the beginning of the error recovery routine on the detection of an error, whereas you have to specify each branch to a subroutine with a GOSUB statement. While a RETURN statement causes the program to pass control to the statement following the last GOSUB, an error recovery routine will use a RESUME statement to continue program execution after an error-recovery procedure has been performed.

Once you enable error trapping, it will remain on until disabled. You can disable error trapping by having the program execute an ON ERROR GOTO 0 statement. Once error trapping is disabled, subsequent errors will cause the appropriate error message to be printed and program execution will halt. Returning to the previous example, if you only wish to take corrective action on the occurrence of error code 27, you could change line 5070 in the program to:

```
5070 ON ERROR GOTO 0
```

The above statement will cause an error message to be printed, and the program will terminate execution if any error other than error code 27 should occur. It is good programming practice to include an ON ERROR GOTO 0 statement in your error-trapping routine to identify all errors for which no recovery procedure has been implemented. Otherwise, the use of a RESUME statement at the end of the error-handling routine could cause the program to loop continuously between the line causing the error and the recovery procedure as indicated by the execution of the following program segment.

```
OK
10 ON ERROR GOTO 5000
20 INPUT "ENTER WIDGETS SOLD ",W
30 C=365/W
.
.
5000 REM Error recovery routine
5010 IF ERR<>27 THEN 5070
5020 CLS
5030 LOCATE 12,20
5040 PRINT "PRINTER NOT READY - CHECK PAPER AND POWER"
5050 PRINT TAB(20)"ENTER R WHEN READY TO RESUME"
5060 A$=INKEY$:IF A$<>"R"THEN 5060
5070 RESUME
RUN
ENTER WIDGETS SOLD 0
Division by zero

^C
Break in 5010
OK
```

In this example, the entry of a zero (0) value in response to the "WIDGETS SOLD" prompt message will cause a "Division by zero" error and the program will branch to the error-trapping routine starting in line 5000. Since the routine ends with a RESUME statement in line 5070, the program will automatically go into a loop, executing lines 110, 5000, 5010, 5070, and back to 110. The poor terminal operator will think something productive is taking place; however, unknown to him or her the program is in a loop. While it is obvious that line 110 will cause a "Division by zero" error, other errors may not be as obvious, and you should account for their possible occurrence by placing an ON ERROR GOTO 0 statement at the end of your error-trapping routine. In the example, a Ctrl + Break key combination was used to terminate the infinite program loop.

Based on our discussion of error control, a logical question that should arise is how can you test the error-trapping routine you program? While it is easy to remove the paper from the printer, there are other error conditions you may wish to check for that are difficult to establish, especially in the area of device and file errors. Fortunately, BASIC has an ERROR statement by which you can simulate the occurrence of a BASIC error.

ERROR Statement

The format of the BASIC ERROR statement is:

format: ERROR varnm

Here, the numeric variable, varnm, is an integer expression between 0 and 255. This variable is used to define an error code. If the defined error code is the same as an error code used by BASIC, this statement will simulate the occurrence of that error. If you previously developed an error-handling routine and enabled that routine by the use of an ON ERROR GOTO statement, the ERROR statement will cause the program to pass control to the error-handling routine. Thus, the ERROR statement provides you with a mechanism to test the programming logic of your error-handling routine.

Let's add the statement

```
15 ERROR 27
```

to the previous program segment. Now when you execute the program, error code 27 will be simulated. This results in the screen being cleared and the error trap message being displayed. Note that if you entered the ERROR statement in a line prior to the ON ERROR GOTO statement, your program would terminate when it is executed as the error trap would not be enabled when the error was simulated. This is illustrated by the next printout, where the statement previously entered in line 15 was erased and placed in line 5 of the program.

```
Ok
15
5 ERROR 27
RUN
Out of Paper in 5
Ok
```

If no error-handling routine is in your program, the ERROR statement will cause the error message that corresponds to the number associated with the ERROR statement to be printed and the program will then halt execution. This is indicated by the following example.

```
Ok
10 X=27
20 ERROR X
RUN
```

```
Out of Paper in 20
OK
```

You can also use the ERROR statement to define your own error codes. Since the highest error number presently used by BASIC is 76, it is good practice to use values greater than that number. This user-defined error code can then be tested in your error-handling routine similar to testing any other error. The utilization of user-defined error codes is illustrated by the following program segment.

```
100 ON ERROR GOTO 5000
110 INPUT"ENTER CITY ",C$
120 IF LEN(C$)>15 THEN ERROR 100
.
.
5000 IF ERR=100 THEN PRINT"ONLY 15 CHARACTERS ALLOWED - REENTER DATA"
ELSE GOTO 5030
5020 RESUME 110
5030 REM program continues
RUN
ENTER CITY MAXWELLSMARTSVILLE
ONLY 15 CHARACTERS ALLOWED - REENTER DATA
ENTER CITY
```

In this example, error code 100 was associated with the occurrence of a string representing the name of a city that exceeds 15 characters in length. When the operator enters the name of a city that exceeds 15 characters, the program will automatically transfer control to the error-handling routine beginning at line 5000. At this line number, an error code of 100 is tested for by use of the ERR variable. If the error code is equal to 100, the message "ONLY 15 CHARACTERS ALLOWED—REENTER DATA" will be displayed.

LIBRARY AND USER-DEFINED FUNCTIONS

Prior to concluding this initial examination of AT BASIC, a group of frequently used internal BASIC routines that form an integral part of the language will be presented. These routines are known as functions. They include the BASIC library functions, which are prewritten routines that can be accessed by invoking their names followed by the appropriate information you must supply to the function, or you can use the capability of BASIC to develop your own functions.

AT BASIC contains over 50 library functions in the areas of numeric functions, string-related functions, string functions, and I/O and miscellaneous functions. While some of the more commonly employed functions have already been covered, such as the TAB and SPC functions, in this section the use and operation of several commonly used BASIC functions will be discussed as an entity. Each of these functions, unless noted otherwise, is accessed by stating its name followed by whatever information must be supplied to the function, enclosing the information supplied in parentheses. The numeric quantity or string value passed to the function for use by its prewritten routine is known as its argument. Once you access the function and specify an argument, the desired operation will be conducted automatically.

Numeric Functions

Table 7-4 lists the BASIC numeric functions and their operations. One of the simplest ways to show the use of a function is by examining its use in a program. Suppose you wanted to obtain the square root of a number. Without the SQR function you would have to develop your own routine to perform this function. To do this, you might first divide the number you wish the square root of by 2. You could then multiply that number by itself and test it against the original number. If it is greater than the original number, your derived number is too large. You can make it smaller by subtracting some small amount from it and repeat the process. When the derived number times itself is less than the original number, your number is too small and you can now add a small increment to the number and again repeat the process. Eventually, the derived number times itself will equal the number you wish to obtain the square root of or be very close to that number. Once you fall within a certain range, you can stop the repetitive process and consider the derived number to be the square root of the number you seek. Wow! All this just to obtain the square root of a number. By now you can begin to appreciate functions that automatically perform the desired operations for you once you specify

Table 7-4. Numeric Functions

FUNCTION	OPERATIONAL RESULT
ABS(exprnm)	Returns the absolute value
ATN(exprnm)	Returns the arctangent in radians
CDBL(exprnm)	Converts the expression to a double-precision number
CINT(exprnm)	Converts the expression to an integer by rounding
COS(exprnm)	Returns the cosine of an angle expressed in radians
CSNG(exprnm)	Converts the expression to a single-precision number
EXP(exprnm)	Returns the base of the natural logarithm (e) raised to the specified power
FIX(exprnm)	Truncates the specified expression to an integer
INT(exprnm)	Returns the largest integer that is less than or equal to exprnm
LOG(exprnm)	Returns the natural logarithm of the specified number
RND(exprnm)	Returns a random number
SGN(exprnm)	Returns +1 if exprnm is positive, −1 if negative, and 0 if its value is zero
SIN(exprnm)	Returns the sine of an angle expressed in radians
SQR(exprnm)	Returns the square root
TAN(exprnm)	Returns the tangent of an angle expressed in radians

the argument. Now let's see how easy it is to use functions. Suppose you want the square root of 2,4,6, and 8. The arguments to be passed to the SQR functions are 2, 4, 6, and 8. You can use a FOR-NEXT loop to control the passing of the arguments as follows.

```
OK
LIST
10 PRINT "NUMBER","SQUARE ROOT"
20 FOR I=2 TO 8 STEP 2
30 PRINT I,SQR(I)
40 NEXT I
OK
RUN
NUMBER              SQUARE ROOT
 2                   1.414214
 4                   2
 6                   2.44949
 8                   2.828427
OK
```

If you require the square root of a variable within a program, your program statement might be:

```
100 X=SQR(Y)
```

Here, the variable X is set equal to the square root of the variable Y.

The ABS function returns the absolute value of a numeric expression. That is, the absolute value of a number is its value with its sign discarded; hence, the ABS function will first evaluate an expression and then discard its sign. The following example shows the use of this function operating on an expression.

```
10 X=3.14159
20 B=-12.5
30 PRINT ABS(X*B)
RUN
 39.26988
OK
```

The INT function returns the largest integer part of a numeric expression used as the argument in the function call. In the following example, note that the integer of both 12.51 and 12.49 is 12. Since -3 is less than -2.49, the integer of -2.49 is -3.

```
10 X=12.51:PRINT INT(X)
20 Y=12.49:PRINT INT(Y)
30 Z=-2.49:PRINT INT(Z)
RUN
 12
 12
-3
OK
```

While the use of most of the functions listed in Table 7-4 should be apparent, some notes concerning the use of the trigonometric functions and a description of the exponential and logarithm functions may be in order for those not familiar with their utilization. Each trigonometric function, such as the SIN, COS, TAN, and ATN functions, is used to calculate the trigonometric value when the argument is expressed in radians. You can do this by multiplying degrees by pi/180, where pi = 3.141593. Since each trigonometric function is calculated in single precision, it is irrelevant to carry the value of pi to any further degree of precision. The following example shows how you can generate a table of values of the sine and cosine of an angle as the angle varies from 0 to 360° in increments of 45°.

```
LIST
100 PRINT "ANGLE","SINE(ANGLE)","COSINE(ANGLE)"
110 FOR I=0 TO 360 STEP 45
120 PRINT I, SIN(I*3.141593/180),COS(I*3.141593/180)
130 NEXT I
RUN
ANGLE              SINE(ANGLE)    COSINE(ANGLE)
 0                  0              1
 45                 .7071068       .7071068
 90                 1             -3.74507E-07
 135                .7071066      -.7071068
 180               -3.74507E-07   -1
 225               -.7071068      -.7071065
 270               -1              6.516827E-07
 315               -.7071063       .7071075
 360                6.516827E-07                1
Ok
```

Several items in the preceding example require some elaboration. Those familiar with trigonometry know that the sine function starts at a zero value at 0°, peaks at a value of 1 at 90°, and decreases to a value of zero at 180°. In the preceding example a value of −3.74507E-07 is given for 180°. This and other slight variances are due to the fact that pi was entered rounded to six significant positions. The small magnitude of the error, while insignificant, does not do justice to any type of tabular output you may desire. You can avoid this problem by using a formatted PRINT statement and specifying the precision of accuracy you desire. Thus, specifying values of say five significant positions would result in a zero value being printed.

The EXP function calculates the exponential function that can be expressed mathematically as e^x, where e represents the base of the natural (Naperian) logarithm whose value is approximately 2.718282. In AT BASIC, the power must be less than 88.02969 or an overflow will occur. If the power exceeds this value, an "Overflow" message will be displayed, and program execution will continue with positive machine infinity used as the result of the function call.

The LOG function calculates the natural logarithm of a numeric variable. If X represents the numeric variable, the use of the function represents the mathematical expression logeX, where e is the base of the natural system of logarithms previously discussed.

One of the most interesting numeric functions has been saved for the end of this short discussion—the RND function. This function permits you to easily generate random numbers. The use of this function returns a seven-digit decimal fraction greater than zero but less than one. The numeric variable in the argument is optional. If it is positive or omitted, the next RND function call will generate the next random number in the sequence of random numbers generated each time the program is executed. Since a fixed computational procedure is used by the RND function to generate random numbers, the numbers obtained from the RND function are not actually random. Thus, every time a program containing the RND function is executed, the same sequence of numbers will be generated. This is illustrated by running the following program two times.

```
OK
10 FOR I=1 TO 5
20 PRINT RND;
30 NEXT I
RUN
 .6291626  .1948297  .6305799  .8625749  .736353
OK
RUN
 .6291626  .1948297  .6305799  .8625749  .736353
OK
```

Although the ability to regenerate a random number sequence may be very helpful for program-debugging purposes, many times it is desirable to be able to generate a different sequence of random numbers each time a program is executed. This can be accomplished by reseeding the random number generator. The random number generator can be reseeded by using a negative numeric variable in the function call. Since this will generate a particular sequence of random numbers for the numeric variable used, you can generate a different sequence each time the program is executed by using a different starting value each time the program runs. One way to accomplish this is to use the value of the system clock as the mechanism for entry into the random number generator. If you use the elapsed time in seconds and hundreds of seconds as your starting place in the random number generator, it becomes highly unlikely that anyone can turn on the system and execute the program twice at exactly the precise time in hundreds of seconds.

A second method to reseed the random number generator is through the use of the RANDOMIZE statement whose format is:

format: RANDOMIZE[exprnm]
format$_A$: RANDOMIZE TIMER

The use of the RANDOMIZE statement provides you with the ability to specify a different starting point for the random number generator. If the numeric expression is omitted, the program's execution will be suspended when the RANDOMIZE statement is executed and the message

```
Random Number Seed(-32768 to 32767)?
```

will be displayed. On entering the value of the seed, program execution will resume. Since the RANDOMIZE statement reseeds the random number generator, this statement must precede the first reference to the RND function in a program. The use of this statement is illustrated by the execution of the following program segment.

```
OK
10 RANDOMIZE
20 FOR I=1 TO 5
30 PRINT RND;
40 NEXT
RUN
Random number seed (-32768 to 32767)? 1
 .9527948  1.293463E-02  .7467608  .9900456  .3634014
OK
RUN
Random number seed (-32768 to 32767)? 2
 .3591821  .1843976  6.049669E-02  .5644628  9.327507E-02
OK
RUN
Random number seed (-32768 to 32767)? 1
 .9527948  1.293463E-02  .7467608  .9900456  .3634014
OK
```

In this example, note that the use of the same seed (first and third program RUNs) results in the same sequence of random numbers. If you are familiar with tables of random numbers, you can view the seed as a page of random numbers and the numeric expression in the RND function as a particular random number on the page.

In advanced BASIC, you can obtain a different starting point for the random number generator without being prompted to enter a new random number. This is accomplished by using the RANDOMIZE TIMER statement.

One of the tricks associated with using random numbers is to convert the decimal functions obtained from the use of the RND function into an appropriate range of numeric values you wish to associate with some activity to be simulated. As an example, suppose you desire to simulate the roll of a die. Since a die is six-sided with one to six dots on a side, you must use the RND function to generate a random number having a value between 1 and 6. The statement listed below can be used to obtain this range of values.

```
10 D=1+INT(6*RND)
```

In analyzing the above statement, it should be noted that the RND function's maximum value is .9999999, while its minimum value would be .0000001. Thus, the minimum value assigned to the variable labeled D would be 1+INT(.0000001), which results in a value of 1, while the maximum value that could be assigned to that variable would be 1+INT(5.9999999), which results in a value of 6. Using the preceding information, you can use the following program segment to simulate 20 rolls of the die.

```
LIST
5 FOR I=1 TO 20
10 D=1+INT(6*RND):PRINT D;
15 NEXT I
OK
```

```
RUN
 4  2  4  6  5  6  1  6  1  1  5  3  5  1  1  4  6  1  4  2
OK
```

User-Defined Functions

BASIC provides you with the capability to avoid repeated programming steps to conduct the same computation. This is accomplished by the use of the DEF FN statement. This statement permits you to DEFine your own FunctioNs. The format of this statement is:

format: DEF FN name[(arg[,arg] . . .)] = expression

The function name can be any valid variable name. When preceded by the keyword FN, this name becomes the name of the function. The arguments in the function are variable name(s) that will be replaced with a value when the function is called in a program. The expression performs the operation of the function with the values assigned to the argument(s) when the function is called.

The function name may be numeric or string and the expression defined must match the type of the name. That is, if the function name is a numeric variable, then the expression associated with the function must perform operations on numeric variables. Similarly, your expression must operate on strings if your function name is a string variable. If the expression does not match the function type, a "Type mismatch" error will result.

In comparison to other BASICs that limit a program to 26 separate functions labeled A through Z, AT BASIC permits you to have virtually an unlimited number of functions, since any variable name can be used as the function name. Similar to the functions defined with other BASICs, each DEF FN statement is limited to a single line.

The following program segments illustrate the use of the DEF FN statement.

```
10 DEF FNEQUATION(A,B,C)=A^3+3*B^2+2*C+27.5
20 LET X=FNEQUATION(1,2,3):PRINT X
30 LET Y=FNEQUATION(4,5,6):PRINT Y
RUN
 46.5
 178.5
OK
```

In this example, line 10 defines the function FNEQUATION, which computes the expression $A^3+3\cdot B^2+2\cdot C+27\cdot 5$. The function is called in line 20 with argument values 1, 2, and 3 that will replace the variables named A, B, and C in the expression when it is evaluated. Similarly, line 30 calls the function for evaluation with 4, 5, and 6 used to replace the variables named A, B, and C. From this example, you see that the DEF FN statement only defines a function. To evaluate the function, you must refer to the function name elsewhere in the program by specifying the name of the function and providing the values of the arguments within a BASIC statement.

You can include one or more library functions within a DEF FN statement as illustrated by the next program segment.

```
10 DEF FNROOT(A,B,C)=SQR(A^3+B^2+C)
20 PRINT FNROOT(1,2,3)
RUN
 2.828427
Ok
```

You can also define string operations as indicated by the next program segment.

```
10 N$="NAME "
20 A$="ADDRESS"
30 DEF FNONE$(X$,Y$)=N$+A$
40 PRINT FNONE$(N$,A$)
RUN
NAME ADDRESS
Ok
```

From the preceding examples, you may have noticed that the DEF FN statement precedes the reference of the function within a program. This is because you must define the function prior to calling it. You can see this by reversing lines 30 and 40 in the previous example and then attempting to execute that program statement. Note in this example, the error message "Undefined user function in 30" tells you that at the time of the function call the function was undefined.

```
Ok
LIST
10 N$="NAME "
20 A$="ADDRESS"
30 PRINT FNONE$(N$,A$)
40 DEF FNONE$(X$,Y$)=N$+A$
Ok
RUN
Undefined user function in 30
Ok
```

When using user-defined functions, it is good programming practice to group together all DEF FN statements and place them in one area of the program prior to the first function call. This not only improves the legibility of the program, but can simplify program modifications and reduce any program debugging time that may be required.

STRING AND STRING-RELATED FUNCTIONS

BASIC includes many string and string-related functions that provide us with the capability to easily manipulate data. These functions and the operations they perform are listed in Table 7-5.

Although some of these, including the ASC, VAL, CHR$, and STRING$ functions, have been discussed previously in the context of their use within

Table 7-5. String and String-Related Functions

FUNCTION FORMAT	OPERATIONAL RESULT
String Functions	
CHR$(exprnm)	Converts an ASCII code to its character equivalent
LEFT$(expr$,exprnm)	Returns the left-most exprnm characters of expr$
MID$(expr$,$exprnm_1$[,$exprnm_2$])	Returns $exprnm_2$ characters from expr$, beginning with character $exprnm_1$
RIGHT$(expr$,exprnm)	Returns the right-most character specified by exprnm in string expr$
SPACE$(exprnm)	Returns a string consisting of exprnm spaces
STRING$(exprnm,expr$)	Returns a string of length exprnm in which all characters have the ASCII code of the first character in expr$
STRING$($exprnm_1$,$exprnm_2$)	Returns a string of length $exprnm_1$ in which all characters have the ASCII code specified by $exprnm_2$
String-related Functions	
ASC(expr$)	Returns the ASCII code of the first character of a string
CVD(expr$)	Converts an 8-byte string to a numeric variable
CVI(expr$)	Converts a 4-byte string to a numeric variable
CVS(expr$)	Converts a 2-byte string to a numeric variable
INSTR([exprnm,]$string_1$,$string_2$)	Searches for $string_1$ in $string_2$ starting at position exprnm
LEN(expr$)	Returns the length of the specified string
MKI$(exprnm%)	Converts the specified integer expression to a string
MKS$(exprnm!)	Converts the specified single-precision expression to a string
MKD$(exprnm#)	Converts the specified double-precision expression to a string
STR$(exprnm)	Returns the string value of the numeric expression
VAL(expr$)	Returns the numeric value of a string

certain statements, the use of each of these functions will be reviewed in more detail in this section. These functions provide you with the ability to perform special computer-related operations through the BASIC language, including communications processing, forms control, symbol generation, and so on.

You can examine the use of the functions listed in Table 7-5 by constructing several program segments that can demonstrate their operational result.

Suppose you wish to output a string on a character-by-character basis, one character on each line of the display. Since you may not know the length of the string, you can employ the LEN function to determine its length and use the length in a FOR-NEXT statement to control its output. If you wish to obtain the characters in the string in sequence from left to right, you can use the MID$ function as shown in the following program segment.

```
100 INPUT"ENTER STRING ",X$
110 X=LEN(X$)
120 FOR I=1 TO X
130 PRINT MID$(X$,I,1)
140 NEXT I
RUN
ENTER STRING GIL
G
I
L
OK
```

The LEN function in line 110 will return the number of characters in the string argument to include blanks and any unprintable characters such as control characters. The variable X is assigned the length of the string and is used in line 120 as the loop control mechanism, since you wish to print each character of the string on a character-by-character basis. The MID$ function in line 130 is used to obtain one character beginning at the Ith character in the string. Note that as I increases in value due to the FOR-NEXT loop counter being incremented, each character in the string will be obtained in sequence. If you added a semicolon to the end of line 130, each character in the string would be printed on the same line. Normally, a group of BASIC statements similar to the previous example but with a semicolon as the print line terminator will be used for communications processing. This will provide you with the ability to read a string of unknown length from the communications buffer and output that string to the display, to the line printer, or to another device.

In addition to being used as a function, you can use MID$ as a statement. When used in this manner, its format is:

format: MID$(expr$$_1$,exprnm$_1$[,exprnm$_2$])=expr$$_2$

When used as a statement, the characters in expr$$_1$, beginning at position exprnm$_1$, are replaced by the characters in expr$$_2$. The optional exprnm$_2$ can be used to specify the number of characters from expr$$_2$ that will be used by the replacement. If exprnm$_2$ is omitted, all of expr$$_2$ will be used in the replacement; however, the length of the original string, expr$$_1$, will not change. The following program segment illustrates one possible use of the MID$ statement.

```
OK

100 X$="CHICAGO,ILL. 22045"
110 MID$(X$,14)="33111"
120 PRINT X$
```

```
RUN
CHICAGO,ILL. 33111
OK
```

The LEFT$ and RIGHT$ functions can be used to extract a portion of the specified string beginning at the left or right end of the string. The utilization of these two functions is illustrated by the next program segment.

```
LIST
50 X$="JANFEBMARAPRMAYJUNJLYAUGSPTOCTNOVDEC"
60 PRINT RIGHT$(X$,3)
70 PRINT LEFT$(X$,3)
80 PRINT LEFT$(X$,88)
OK
RUN
DEC
JAN
JANFEBMARAPRMAYJUNJLYAUGSPTOCTNOVDEC
OK
```

The RIGHT$ function in line 60 results in the rightmost three characters of the specified string being printed. The LEFT$ function in line 70 provides the leftmost three characters of the specified string. For both functions, if the number of characters requested exceeds the length of the string, the entire string will be returned by the function call. This is shown by the execution of line 80 in the program segment. If the second argument is specified as zero, a null string of length zero will be returned by the function call.

The CHR$ function provides you with the ability to convert an ASCII code to its character equivalent. The value of the argument used in the function call must be between 0 and 255, which represents the ASCII values of the character set used by the AT. You can use this function to send special characters to the communications buffer, printer, the screen, or another device. For example, if you wish to display the square root symbol on the screen, you could do so by the following statement.

```
100 PRINT CHR$(251)
```

In the above statement, 251 is the ASCII value that represents the square root symbol (see Appendix A). If you wish to alert the operator to special conditions or perhaps preface an error message with sound, you can do so by the use of CHR$(7). Here, the ASCII7 represents the BEL character, which, when encountered in a PRINT statement, will beep the speaker in the system unit. An example of the use of this function to alert the operator to an error is illustrated by the next program segment.

```
100 INPUT"ENTER VALUE BETWEEN 1 AND 30 ",X
110 IF X>=1 AND X<=30 THEN 140
120 PRINT CHR$(7) "FOLLOW INSTRUCTIONS"
130 GOTO 100
140 REM Program continues
```

The STRING$ function can be used to obtain a string of specified length whose characters all have a specified ASCII code or are set to the first character of a specified string. This function is valuable for generating runs of similar characters that can be used for such purposes as report title or column heading highlighting. Several examples of the use of this function are illustrated by the following program segment.

```
100 PRINT TAB(30)"HEADING GOES HERE"
110 X$=STRING$(17,42)
120 PRINT TAB(30) X$
RUN
                                    HEADING GOES HERE
                                    *****************
OK
```

In the above example, the STRING$ function assigns a string of 17 asterisks (ASCII code 42) to the string vairable X$. While the following example shows two other methods to produce the same result, note that each of these methods is slightly more complex than using the STRING$ function.

```
OK
LIST
100 PRINT TAB(30)"HEADING GOES HERE"
110 LOCATE ,30
120 FOR I=1 TO 17
130 PRINT "*";
140 NEXT I
OK
RUN
                                    HEADING GOES HERE
                                    *****************

LIST
100 PRINT TAB(30)"HEADING GOES HERE"
110 PRINT TAB(30)"*****************"
OK
RUN
                                    HEADING GOES HERE
                                    *****************
OK
```

The use of the second format of the STRING$ function is illustrated by the next program segment. Here, a string of specified length will consist of the first character of the string used in the argument call.

```
100 XRAY$="DONALD"
100 Q$=STRING$(10,XRAY$)
120 PRINT Q$
RUN
DDDDDDDDDD
OK
```

The last string function to be examined is the SPACE$ function. This function returns a string of spaces, the number of spaces returned based on the value of the argument in the function call. The utilization of this function is illustrated by the following program segment.

```
OK
10 X$="GIL"
20 Y$=SPACE$(20)
30 Z$="HELD"
40 PRINT X$+Y$+Z$
RUN
GIL                     HELD
OK
```

Note that, since a string can be up to 256 characters in length, the argument in the function call must be in the range of 0 to 255.

String-Related Functions

The ASC function is the inverse of the previously discussed CHR$ function, returning the ASCII code for the first character of the string specified in the function call. This is illustrated by the following example.

```
10 X$="*XYZ"
20 PRINT ASC(X$)
RUN
 42
OK
```

In the above example, 42 is the ASCII value of the asterisk character as indicated in Appendix A. If the string used in the function call is a null string, an "Illegal function call" will result. You can alleviate this potential error from occurring in a program by checking the length of a string with the LEN function and taking appropriate action if it is a null string.

Three functions are available in advanced BASIC to convert string variables to numeric variables. The CVI function converts a two-byte string to an integer while the CVS function results in the conversion of a four-byte string to a single-precision number. The third string conversion function, CVD, results in the conversion of an eight-byte string to a double-precision number. The primary use of these functions is in random file operations. This is because numeric values that are read from such files are stored as strings and must be converted from strings into numbers.

Advanced BASIC also contains three other functions that can be used to convert numeric number values to string values. The MKI$ function can be used to convert an integer to a two-byte string, while the MKS$ function converts a single-precision number to a string. The third function in this category, MKD$, converts a double-precision number into an eight-byte string. These three functions will be typically used when programming random files, since numeric values placed in such files through the use of certain BASIC statements must be first converted into strings. The utilization of these six statements will be covered when we examine data file manipulation techniques later in this book.

The last two functions that will conclude this discussion of string and string-related functions are the STR$ and VAL functions. These functions in effect are the inverse of each other.

The STR$ function results in the return of a string representation of the numeric expression appearing in the calling argument. The VAL function returns the numerical value of the string used in the calling argument.

If you wish to enter one or more data elements numerically and convert them to a string, you can do so through the use of the STR$ function. This conversion of numeric values to string representation is illustrated by the following program segment.

```
100 INPUT"ZIP CODE ",ZIP
110 IF ZIP <99999 THEN 140
120 PRINT "ZIP CODE CANNOT EXCEED 5 DIGITS"
130 GOTO 100
140 ZIP$=STR$(ZIP)
150 X$=NAME$+ADDRESS$+CITY$+STATE$+ZIP$
```

In this example, the program reads the value of ZIP as a numeric variable to facilitate its comparison to a numeric quantity for error-checking purposes. In line 140, the numeric value of ZIP is converted to a string and assigned to the variable ZIP$. In line 150, ZIP$ is concatenated with strings representing the name, address, city, and state to form one record of information labeled X$.

I/O and Miscellaneous Functions

Sixteen I/O and miscellaneous functions have been grouped together to conclude this preliminary discussion concerning functions. The operational result from the use of these functions is indicated in Table 7-6.

Table 7-6. I/O and Miscellaneous Functions

FUNCTION	OPERATIONAL RESULT
EOF(filenum)	Returns (−1) true if end of file reached, 0 if the end of file has not been reached
FRE(dummy)	Returns the number of bytes in memory not being used by BASIC
INP(exprnm)	Returns the byte read from port n
LOC(filenum)	Returns the number of characters in the communications buffer waiting to be read, the number of records read or written to a sequential file since it was opened, or the record number of the last record read or written to a random file
LOF(filenum)	Returns the length of a file in multiples of 128 bytes or the amount of free space in the communications input buffer
LPOS(exprnm)	Returns the current position of the print head

Table 7-6. I/O and Miscellaneous Functions (cont.)

FUNCTION	OPERATIONAL RESULT
PEEK(memadr)	Returns an integer value between 0 and 255 that represents the byte read from the designated memory position
PEN(exprnm)	Returns the value of the light pen coordinates according to the supplied numeric argument.
POINT($exprnm_1$, $exprnm_2$)	Returns the color of the specified point on the screen for graphics operation
POS(exprnm)	Returns the current cursor column position
SCREEN(row,col[,exprnm])	In text mode returns the ASCII code for the character (if exprnm zero) at the specified location or the character's attribute (if exprnm non-zero)
STICK(exprnm)	Returns the X and Y coordinates of the two joysticks based on the value of exprnm
STRIG(exprnm) {ON / OFF}	Enables and disables the trapping of the joystick buttons in advanced BASIC
USR[digit](exprnm)	Causes a branch to a machine language subroutine with the argument specified by exprnm
VARPTR(exprnm)	Returns the address in memory of the specified variable

CHAPTER EIGHT

BASIC Commands

A BASIC command is commonly referred to as a system command, since it is recognized by BASIC as a request to perform a predefined operation built into that system on the entire program. Thus, commands are normally entered in direct mode without a line number; however, in AT BASIC, most commands can be entered in either direct or indirect mode. In comparison, a BASIC language statement is an instruction within a BASIC program that will be interpreted by that BASIC language interpreter to perform an operation within the program. Thus, commands can be thought of as initiating operations at the system level, while statements initiate operations at the program language level.

COMMAND OVERVIEW

Table 8-1 lists each BASIC command, its format, and an operational description of its usage. A format indicated as $\text{format}_{D/A}$ means that the particular command is applicable to disk and advanced BASIC. From reviewing the operational description of the commands in Table 8-1, you will note that many BASIC commands have DOS counterparts. Those commands and their DOS counterparts are listed in Table 8-2.

BASIC commands can be divided into six logical areas—directory reference commands, line reference commands, file reference commands, program reference commands, program tracing commands, and system reference commands—and will be covered according to their logical area of use. In this chapter any reference to disk will refer to both the fixed disk and diskette storage, while references to a diskette will be denoted as such.

Table 8-1. BASIC Commands

COMMAND	FORMAT	OPERATIONAL DESCRIPTION
AUTO	format: AUTO[.][number][,[increment]]	Generates line numbers automatically after the Enter key pressed
BLOAD*	format: BLOAD filespec[,address]	Loads a memory image file into the computer's memory at the specified address
BSAVE*	format: BSAVE filespec,offset,length	Saves portions of memory on the specified device starting at the specified address for the specified length
CHDIR*	format$_{D/A}$:CHDIR path	Changes the current directory on the disk
CLEAR	format: CLEAR[,[exp_1][,exp_2]][,int]]	Initializes numeric variables to zero and string variables to null; optionally sets the end of memory (exp_1) and the amount of stack space (exp_2) and the number of bytes to be set aside for video memory
CONT	format: CONT	Causes program execution to resume after a break
DELETE	format: DELETE[.][$line_1$][-$line_2$][;]	Erases the specified range of lines from the program
EDIT	format: [.][line]	Displays a program line for editing
FILES*	format$_{D/A}$: FILES[filespec]	Displays the names of all files or a specified file stored on a disk
KILL*	format$_{D/A}$: KILL filespec	Deletes a file from the disk
LIST	format: LIST[$line_1$[.][-$line_2$[.]]][,filespec]	Causes the program in memory or on the device specified by filespec to be listed on the display
LLIST	format: LLIST[$line_1$[-[$line_2$]]]	Prints all or a specified part of the program currently in memory
LOAD*	format: LOAD filespec[,R]	Loads a program from the device specified by filespec into memory and optionally (R) commences its execution
MERGE*	format: MERGE filespec	Merges the specified ASCII program with the program currently in memory
MKDIR*	format$_{D/A}$: MKDIR path	Creates a directory on the disk

Table 8-1. BASIC Commands (cont.)

COMMAND	FORMAT	OPERATIONAL DESCRIPTION
NAME*	$format_{D/A}$: NAME filespec AS filename	Renames the file specified by filespec to filename
NEW	format: NEW	Deletes the program currently in memory
RENUM	format: RENUM[new#][,[old#][,incr]]	Renumbers a program beginning with old line number; assigning new numbers starting at new one, with increments incr
RESET	$format_{D/A}$: RESET	Closes all disk files and clears the system buffer
RMDIR*	$format_{D/A}$: RMDIR path	Removes a directory from the specified disk
RUN*	format: RUN {[line] / filespec[,R]}	Begins execution of the program currently in memory or loads and executes a program specified by filespec
SAVE*	format: SAVE filespec {[A] / [P]}	Saves a BASIC program in compressed binary format, ASCII (A) or protected encoded binary (P) format
SYSTEM	$format_{D/A}$: SYSTEM	Causes an exit from BASIC and a return to DOS
TRON	format: TRON	Enables program tracing
TROFF	format: TROFF	Disables program tracing

*Commands that allow the specification of a path in the filespec.

Table 8-2. BASIC Commands and Their DOS Counterparts

BASIC COMMAND	DOS COMMAND
CHDIR	CHDIR
FILES	DIR
LIST	TYPE
KILL	ERASE
MKDIR	MKDIR
NAME	RENAME
RMDIR	RMDIR

DIRECTORY REFERENCE COMMANDS

CHDIR Command

The CHDIR command functions like its DOS counterpart previously described in Chapter 6, providing you with a mechanism to move through a tree structured directory. You can use this command in both direct and indirect modes; however, the path must be enclosed in quotes. The following examples illustrate the use of this command.

Command Structure	**Operational Result**
CHDIR"\"	Changes to the root directory from any directory
CHDIR"C:\SALES"	Makes SALES on drive C to current directory
CHDIR"A:\SALES\EAST"	Makes EAST under the directory SALES on the diskette in drive A the current directory

MKDIR Command

The MKDIR command also functions like its DOS counterpart previously described in Chapter 6, providing you with the capability to create a directory on a disk from BASIC. Like the CHDIR command, the path in the MKDIR command must be enclosed in quotes.

To see how this command works, assume you are on the root directory of drive C and want to create a directory named SALES under the root directory on that drive. Thus, you would enter:

```
MKDIR"\SALES"
```

If you were logged onto drive A, you would enter:

```
MKDIR"C:\SALES"
```

Note that you can specify a path in the MKDIR command or you can use the CHDIR command in combination with the MKDIR command. Thus, you could enter

```
CHDIR"C:\SALES"
MKDIR"\EAST"
```

to create the directory named EAST under the directory named SALES on drive C or you could just enter the command:

```
MKDIR"C:\SALES\EAST"
```

RMDIR Command

The RMDIR command provides you with a mechanism to remove a directory from a specified disk or the default disk through BASIC. When you use this command, the directory must first be empty of all files and subdirectories before it can be removed, with the exception of the dot (.) and double dot (..) entries (like its DOS counterpart). In addition, you must be located in a different directory prior to removing the specified directory. To see how this command operates, assume you are in the directory EAST and wish to delete that directory. You could first enter the KILL command (to be covered later in this chapter) with global specifiers to delete all files in that directory. This would be accomplished by entering the following command:

```
KILL"C:*.*"
```

Next, you would change directories by using the CHDIR command. Here, you could change to the root directory, back up to the directory names SALES, or change to any other directory as long as it is not the directory to be deleted. Thus, you might enter:

```
CHDIR"\SALES"
```

Now, since the directory named EAST is directly under the current directory, you would enter the following command to remove it from the disk.

```
RMDIR"\EAST"
```

Note that the three directory reference commands can be used in both direct and indirect modes. When used in an indirect mode by including a line number with the command in a BASIC program, these commands provide you with a mechanism to manipulate program and data files in tree structured directories under program control. Thus, as an example, you could keep your sales analysis program in one directory, while your monthly sales are kept in a second directory. Then your program could be written to read the required data from the directory in which the sales data files are stored.

LINE REFERENCE COMMANDS

AUTO Command

The AUTO command can be a very valuable mechanism for speeding the entry of BASIC program statements into the AT. This command automatically generates a line number each time the Enter key is pressed, permitting you to avoid the necessity of manually entering program line numbers. Since line numbers will increment by some specified value, you should write your program prior to entering it with the AUTO command. This will permit you to correctly reference statements you wish to branch to and permit you to fully utilize the capability of the command.

The AUTO command will result in line numbering beginning at the number you specify in the command, and each subsequent line number will be incremented by the specified increment. When both values are omitted, the default values of 10,10 will be used. If the beginning line number is followed by a comma but the increment is not specified, the increment previously specified by a previous AUTO command will be used. If the beginning line number is omitted, but the increment is included, line numbering will commence with line 0.

Let's look at some examples of the use of the AUTO command prior to continuing this discussion of various options available with this command.

To generate a sequence of line numbers beginning at 10 and incrementing by 10, you can use the AUTO command as follows:

```
AUTO
```

or

```
AUTO 10,10
```

Suppose you wish to begin your program line numbering at 1000 and increment each line by 25. This can be accomplished by using the AUTO command with the parameters 1000 and 25 as shown.

```
AUTO 1000,25
```

The execution of the preceding command will generate line numbers 1000, 1025, 1050, and so on. By now your curiosity should be aroused to how you exit from automatic line numbering. You can exit AUTO by pressing Ctrl + Break. When you exit the AUTO command, the line in which Ctrl + Break is entered will not be saved. Thus, once you have completed the entry of the program lines you wish to place in memory you should press the Enter key to terminate that line and generate one additional line number. Then you can use the Ctrl + Break keys to terminate the AUTO command without losing any information.

If after entering a program segment you wish to use the AUTO command again, you can omit the increment and the command will use the increment specified in the previous AUTO command. Thus,

```
AUTO 2000,
```

will generate line numbers 2000, 2025, 2050, and so on, since 25 was the increment used in the previous AUTO command.

If you already have a program in memory when you initiate the AUTO command, an asterisk (*) will be printed as a warning that any input will replace the current line in memory. By pressing Enter immediately after the asterisk is generated, the line in memory will not be replaced and the AUTO command will generate the next line number as illustrated by the following example.

```
10 READ X,Y,Z
20 DATA 1,3,5,9,11
30 PRINT X,Y,Z
AUTO 30,10
30*
40 READ Q,R
50 PRINT Q,R
60
Ok
RUN
 1          3          5
 9          11
Ok
```

There are two other features of the AUTO command that deserve mention. As indicated in Table 8-1, a period (.) may be used in place of the line number to specify the current line. Since the AUTO command permits you to make changes only to the current line, if you wish to change another line in an existing program or a line previously entered with this command, you must first exit AUTO by the Ctrl+Break keys. Then you can use normal editing procedures to change another line.

DELETE Command

The DELETE command provides you with an easy mechanism to delete a range of program lines from a program in memory. In addition, you can use this command to delete a specific program line. For the latter, this is equivalent to entering a specific line number followed by the Enter key, which also serves to delete the specified line from memory. The following examples illustrate the use of this command and alternate means to accomplish the same function.

Command structure	Operational result
DELETE 30 or 30	Deletes line 30
DELETE 20-50	Deletes lines 20 to 50
DELETE -80	Deletes all line numbers up to and including line 80
DELETE .-50	Deletes all line numbers from the current line up to and including line 50
DELETE 80-.	Deletes all line numbers from 80 up to and including current line

In the last two examples, a period was used to indicate the current line. If the DELETE command is invoked with a line number that does not exist, an "illegal function call" error will result.

EDIT Command

The EDIT command enables you to display a line from a program in memory for editing. Once the line is displayed, you can then use any of the editing keys on the keyboard to modify the line. This command is similar to the LIST command that will be covered next; however, note that the EDIT command only displays one line, while the LIST command displays one or a range of program lines.

As indicated in Table 8-1, a period can be used in the command to indicate that you wish to edit the current line. This is a handy mechanism to redisplay the last line entered for editing. The following examples indicate the utilization of this command.

Command structure	Operational result
EDIT 10	Displays line 10 for editing
EDIT .	Displays the current line for editing

If the line specified in the EDIT command does not exist, an "Undefined line number" error message will be displayed.

LIST Command

The LIST command allows you to list a portion of or an entire program in memory on the screen or onto a specified device. When the file specification indicated in the command format in Table 8-1 is omitted, the specified line or lines will be listed on the screen. You can explore the utility of this command by examining several versions of the use of this command.

Note that pressing the F1 key automatically generates the word LIST on our screen. This permits you to generate the keyword of the command with one keystroke.

Command structure	Operational result
LIST	Lists the entire program in memory on the screen
LIST 10	Lists line 10 in memory on the screen
LIST 10-50	Lists line 10 through line 50 on the screen
LIST 10-	Lists line 10 through the last line in memory on the screen
LIST -50	Lists all lines from the beginning of the program through line 50 on the screen
LIST .-100	Lists all lines from the current line through line 100 on the screen
LIST 500-.	Lists all lines from line 500 through the current line on the screen

Command structure	Operational result
LIST 50,"LPT1:"	Lists line 50 on the printer
LIST 50-500,"LPT1:"	Lists lines 50 through 500 on the printer
LIST -500,"LPT1:"	Lists all lines from the beginning of the program in memory through line 500 on the printer
LIST 10-300,"A:JOB1.BAS"	Lists lines 10 through 300 from the program in memory to a file named JOB1 with the extension BAS on the diskette in the A drive

When you list all or a portion of a program in memory to a file on disk, the specified lines will be saved in ASCII format. Such files may then be used with the MERGE command. The MERGE command can be used to merge lines from an ASCII program file into a program currently in memory. In comparison, a SAVE command will save a file in a compressed binary (tokenized) format unless an optional parameter is added to save the program in ASCII format. Since programs saved in ASCII can be read as data files, if you wish to transmit such files through the communications adapter you must normally save them in ASCII format.

Once you invoke a LIST command, it will continue until it reaches its specified range if the listing is directed to a specified device such as a printer. Since you may conceivably change your mind about listing a 3000 line program on the printer, you can turn off the printer and obtain an "Out of paper" error message, which will terminate the execution of the LIST command. You can suspend or terminate a listing directed to the screen or to the printer by pressing Ctrl+Num Lock and Ctrl+Break, respectively; however, data in the printer's buffer will continue to be printed until the buffer is emptied. You can also stop printing immediately by turning the printer off.

LLIST Command

The LLIST command has the capability of listing all of or a specified range of lines of a program in memory on the printer with device address "LPT1:".

The ways in which you can specify line numbers for the LLIST command are the same as previously indicated for the LIST command. Similar to using the LIST command with the filespec "LPT1:", LLIST can be interrupted by a Ctrl+Break key sequence, or you can immediately stop the listing on the printer by turning it off. This will result in an "Out of paper" error message and return you to the BASIC command level. Examples of the use of this command are shown below.

Command structure	Operational result
LLIST	Prints the entire program
LLIST 30	Prints line 30
LLIST 10-50	Prints lines 10 through 50

Command structure	Operational result
LLIST 200-	Prints all lines from line 200 through the end of the program in memory
LLIST -200	Prints the first line through line 200
LLIST 10-.	Prints lines 10 through the current line
LLIST .-100	Prints the current line through line 100

Since the F1 key generates the keyword LIST, you can reduce the LLIST keyword to a two-keystroke operation. This is accomplished by typing L followed by the F1 key.

RENUM Command

The RENUM command provides you with the ability to renumber the lines of a program currently in memory. When this command is used, all line references following GOTO, GOSUB, THEN, ELSE, ON-GOTO, ON-GOSUB, RESTORE, RESUME, and ERL test statements will be changed automatically to reflect the new line numbers. As illustrated by the format in Table 8-1, up to three line numbers can be specified in this command. The new number is the first line number to be used in the renumbering process. If not specified, a default value of 10 will be used by the command. Old number specifies the line in the current program where the renumbering will begin. If not specified, line renumbering will begin at the first line of the program. The third line number that can be specified in the command defines the increment to be used in the renumbering process. If omitted, a default value of 10 will be used.

The RENUM command not only permits you to renumber lines in a program but also provides you with a mechanism to verify that all line number references reference an existing program line. If you use the RENUM command and a statement references a nonexistent line number, the following error message will be displayed.

```
Undefined line number xxxxx in yyyyy
```

While the incorrect line number reference (xxxxx) will not be changed by RENUM, line number yyyyy, which indicates the location where the undefined line number reference occurred in the program, may be changed from the original program. If your program has the sequence of line numbers 10,20,30 . . . and you use the RENUM command with default values, the new line numbers will match the old line numbers. Thus, you can use the RENUM command to check your program for nonexistent line number references. This is illustrated by the following example, which has an undefined line number reference that was added purposely.

```
Ok
10 INPUT"ENTER QUANTITY ",Q
20 IF Q>30 THEN 50
30 COM=Q*.07
40 GOTO 70
```

```
50 COM=Q*.09
60 PRINT "COMMISSION= ",COM
RENUM
Undefined line 70 in 40
Ok
```

PROGRAM REFERENCE COMMANDS

In this section, the utilization of four BASIC commands will be examined. These commands can be grouped into the category of program reference commands.

CLEAR Command

The CLEAR command has the capability of setting all numeric variables to zero and all string variables to null. Optionally, you can use this command to set the end of memory and the amount of stack space that is used by the PC AT for controlling FOR-NEXT loops and GOSUB references and the total number of bytes to be set aside for video memory. The last option is only applicable to disk and advanced BASIC and is used to control the number of video pages available within video memory. The use of this option will be covered when we examine PC AT graphics later in this book.

The BASIC stack can be thought of as a data structure like a stack of books. New items can be added to the top of the stack, which results in the position of all the previous books becoming one less in reference to the top of the stack. An item previously entered into a BASIC stack can only be removed when the items above it are removed. This type of stack can be considered as a push-down, pop-up stack where items are popped off the stack in the reverse of the order in which they were pushed on. It is this stack space that is a physical area of memory set aside for branching references that can be increased by the use of the CLEAR command.

An example of the use of the CLEAR command in direct mode follows.

```
Ok
A$="NEXT"
Ok
PRINT A$
NEXT
Ok
CLEAR
Ok
PRINT A$

Ok
```

In the indirect mode, you can use the CLEAR command to reset the pointer in your data pool similar to the RESTORE statement. This is shown below.

```
Ok
100 READ X,Y,Z
110 DATA 1,2,3,4,5
```

```
120 PRINT X,Y,Z
130 A$="HOHOHO"
140 PRINT A$
150 CLEAR
160 READ A,B
170 PRINT A,B
RUN
 1             2             3
HOHOHO
 1             2
Ok
```

When the first optional parameter listed in Table 8-1 is added to the CLEAR command you can set the maximum number of bytes that will be available in memory to store your program and data. Thus,

```
CLEAR,32768
```

would permit a maximum of 32,768 bytes in memory to be used by our BASIC program and data. Normally, you would incorporate this optional parameter if you wish to reserve space in memory for one or more machine language programs that you will link to your BASIC program.

If you have a BASIC program with numerous nested GOSUBs or FOR-NEXT loops, you will probably have to increase the stack space size above the default value, which is the smaller of 512 bytes or one-eighth of available memory. You can increase the size of the BASIC stack space by using the second optional parameter in the CLEAR command as indicated below.

```
CLEAR ,,2000
```

The above command would set the stack space to 2000 bytes.

CONT Command

The CONT command has the ability to resume program execution after a Ctrl+Break key combination, when a STOP or END statement is executed in a program, or after an error is encountered that causes a program to terminate. The following examples illustrate the use of this command.

```
LIST
10 INPUT"SALES ",S
20 XOM=.045*S
30 PRINT "COMMISSION= ";XOM:END
40 PRINT "NOW WE RESUME"
Ok
RUN
SALES 12
COMMISSION=  .54
Ok
CONT
NOW WE RESUME
Ok
```

Note that even the END statement in a program may not be the final termination if you use the CONT command.

```
10 X=47
20 Y=2
30 PRINT X+Y
40 STOP
50 PRINT X+Y
RUN
 49
Break in 40
OK
Y=3
OK
CONT
 50
OK
```

In the second example, once execution is stopped you can change the value of any variables by using one or more direct mode statements and then resume execution by using the CONT command. Now, consider the following example where an error has been deliberately introduced into a program. The error will be corrected after the program terminates execution, and then the CONT command will be used to try to resume program execution.

```
10 INPUT "FACTORIAL ",F
20 N=1
30 FOR I=F TO 1
40 N=N*F
50 NEXT N
RUN
FACTORIAL 5
NEXT without FOR in 50
OK
LIST 50
50 NEXT F
CONT
Can't continue
OK
```

Note that the use of CONT is invalid, since the program was edited during the break.

NEW Command

The NEW command can be used to delete the program currently in memory. This command should be used to free memory if you have previously entered a program and then wish to enter a new program. Otherwise, there will be the potential of one or more of the lines of the previous program becoming part of the newly entered program. Once this command is entered, any open files will be closed, and BASIC will return you to its command level signified by the prompt OK. This is illustrated by the following example.

```
10 X=5
20 PRINT X
```

```
RUN
 5
OK
NEW
OK
RUN
OK
```

RUN Command

The first format of the RUN command listed in Table 8-1 can be considered a program reference command. Although the second format does reference a program, since it requires a file specification it will be covered under the file reference commands later in this chapter.

The RUN command is used to initiate the execution of a program. In its first format

RUN[line]

this command begins the execution of a program currently in memory. If the optional line parameter is specified, program execution will begin with the specified line number. The use of this command and its optional line parameter is shown in the following example.

```
OK
100 PRINT "SEGMENT ONE"
500 PRINT "SEGMENT TWO"
750 PRINT "SEGMENT THREE"
RUN 500
SEGMENT TWO
SEGMENT THREE
OK
RUN 750
SEGMENT THREE
OK
RUN
SEGMENT ONE
SEGMENT TWO
SEGMENT THREE
OK
```

Note that you can only use the F2 key if you wish to execute a program in memory beginning at its first program line. This is because the F2 key generates the characters RUN followed automatically by an enter character.

You can also use the RUN command to execute a program located on a different directory by including a path to the program in the command. Thus, you could enter the following command to execute the program named ANALYSIS under the SALES directory on drive A, assuming the SALES directory is under the root directory.

```
RUN "A:\SALES\ANALYSIS"
```

FILE REFERENCE COMMANDS

In this section, nine BASIC commands with the common function of performing operations on defined file specifications will be reviewed. Although up to now commands have been discussed in alphabetical order in each section, discussion of the BLOAD and BSAVE commands will be deferred to the end of this section, since their usage is best explained by first covering the LOAD and SAVE commands.

Explaining Drive B

Although the original hardware configuration of the entry level AT includes only one diskette drive, you can use any of the BASIC commands presented in this chapter to reference drive B. When a command referencing drive B is executed, DOS will prompt you to "insert the diskette for drive B: and strike any key when ready." This prompt message, in effect, tells you to remove a diskette in your disk drive A if you do not want the command to operate on that diskette. Then, you can insert another diskette into drive A and press any key to have the BASIC command operate on the diskette placed into drive A. If you have a second diskette drive, issuing a BASIC command that references drive B will cause the command to take effect immediately without requiring you to remove and insert diskettes in drive A. Of course, if you have a fixed disk containing DOS, issuing a BASIC command without a drive specifier will cause the command to take effect immediately on drive C.

FILES Command

The FILES command is the counterpart of the DOS DIR command. This command has the capability to display the names of the files residing on the current directory of a disk. Unlike the DIR command, you cannot obtain information about the file size nor the date the file was created. Similar to the DIR command, you can use the question mark (?) and asterisk (*) as global characters in your file specification. The question mark will serve as a replacement for any character in the file name or extension. When used as the first character in the file name or extension, the asterisk will cause a match of any name or extension on a diskette. If the file specification is omitted, all the files on the default or specified disk will be listed. The following examples illustrate the use and resulting operation of this command.

Command structure	Operational result
FILES	Displays all files on the current directory of the DOS default drive
FILES "B:*.BAS"	Displays all files with an extension of BAS on the current directory on drive B

Command structure	Operational result
FILES "STAT???.BAS"	Displays all files on the current directory of the DOS default drive that begin with STAT followed by three or less other characters and having an extension of BAS
FILES "C:\SALES"	Displays all files on drive C under the directory SALES

The use of this command in the direct mode is illustrated by the following example.

```
OK
FILES
C:\SALES
        .      <DIR>             . .   <DIR> ANALYSIS.BAS
 45056 Bytes free
```

As a result of the preceding FILES command you can tell that drive C is the DOS default drive and that the current directory on that drive is SALES, which contains the file ANALYSIS.BAS.

KILL Command

The KILL command is the counterpart of the DOS ERASE command, providing you with the capability to delete a file from a disk at the BASIC operating level. When invoked, you must specify the file extension, if one exists. The following examples illustrate the different structures of this command and their operational result. Again note that you can specify a path to the file in the file specification.

Command structure	Operational result
KILL "STAT.BAS"	Deletes file STAT with extension BAS from disk in default drive
KILL "A:STAT.BAS"	Deletes file STAT with extension BAS from diskette in drive A
KILL "C:\SALES\EAST"	Deletes file EAST from the SALES directory on the fixed disk

Like all diskette file specification references, if you omit the device name you will default to the current diskette drive. If the file does not exist or a referenced file is currently open, an appropriate error message will be displayed.

The KILL command can be used in both direct and indirect modes. The following shows a direct mode use of this command.

```
KILL "A:SPACE.BAS
```

You can write a BASIC program that will automatically delete a file from a diskette by using this command within the program. This is shown by the following program segment. Note that in this example the diskette was write protected and the program terminated after the appropriate error message was displayed.

```
LIST
100 REM AFTER A FILE MANIPULATION PROCESS YOU MAY
110 REM WISH TO DELETE A FILE THAT YOU NO LONGER REQUIRE
120 REM BY USING THE KILL COMMAND IN INDIRECT MODE
130 KILL "SPACE.BAS
135 PRINT
140 PRINT "PROGRAM CONTINUES"
OK
RUN
Disk Write Protected in 130
OK
```

If the diskette had not been write protected, the file SPACE.BAS would have been deleted from the diskette under program control if the file existed on the diskette in the default drive.

LOAD Command

The LOAD command provides you with the capability to load a program from a specified device into memory. When the R option indicated in the command format in Table 8-1 is specified, the program will begin execution at the first statement after loading is completed.

When you load a file from the fixed disk or diskette, you must include a device specifier or the default drive is assumed. In addition, if you have a tree structured directory, you must specify the path to the file or the file is assumed to be in the current directory.

Loading from diskette can be conducted in either direct or indirect modes. The following examples indicate the command structure and operational results of the use of the LOAD command in the direct mode.

Command structure	**Operational result**
LOAD "STAT"	Loads the program file named STAT from the default drive
LOAD "C:\SALES\ANALYSIS"	Loads the program file named ANALYSIS in the SALES directory on drive C
LOAD "A: SALES.BAS"	Loads the program file named SALES with extension BAS from the diskette in drive A
LOAD "B:SALES.BAS,R	Loads and runs the program file named SALES with extension BAS on the diskette in drive B

If you wish to automatically load a program file from within a program, you can do so by the use of an indirect mode LOAD command. Several examples of the command structure and operational result of this mode follow.

Command structure	**Operational result**
100 LOAD "A: SALES.BAS,R	Loads and runs the program file named SALES with extension BAS from the diskette in drive A
200 LOAD "C:\SALES\DATA"	Loads but does not run the program file named DATA on the fixed disk under the directory named SALES

A word of caution is in order concerning the use of the R option. The indirect statement

```
100 LOAD"SPACE
```

will load the file SPACE from the disk into memory. However, the statement

```
100 LOAD"SPACE,R
```

will cause a "File not found in 100" error message, since you must use the appropriate file extension when the R option is used or BASIC will use the R as the extension in its search for the file. This is shown by the following two indirect mode operations.

```
LIST
100 LOAD"A:SPACE,R"
RUN
File not found in 100
Ok

LIST
100 LOAD"SPACE.BAS,R
RUN
Ok
```

From the preceding examples, note that the only difference between the direct and indirect mode formats of the LOAD command is the inclusion of a program line number for the latter. When using a LOAD command in the indirect mode, a "File not found" error message will be displayed if the requested file does not exist on the disk in the specified drive or in the directory you are currently logged onto. Thus, if you are writing a program that uses program files on multiple diskettes, you should prompt the operator to insert the appropriate diskettes before executing the LOAD command in the program. Otherwise, the wrong diskette will cause the "File not found" error message to be displayed and the program will terminate.

It should be noted that under DOS you can assign labels to diskettes and under program control check to ensure that the correct diskette is inserted into the appropriate drive.

MERGE Command

The MERGE command provides the capability to merge the lines from an ASCII program file on disk with the program currently in memory. Whereas the LOAD command clears memory automatically, this command loads the specified ASCII file into memory without clearing existing memory. Any lines loaded from the specified file will replace the corresponding lines in memory, while any lines in memory that do not have a corresponding line number in the specified file will remain in memory. After the merge operation is completed, BASIC will return to the command level, and you will have one merged program representing the prior contents of memory and the specified file that was merged with those contents.

The MERGE command is very useful if you previously developed a comprehensive program as a series of modules saved as individual files and then wish to merge them together into one program. If you did not use a distinct range of line numbers for each module, you should use the RENUM command to do so prior to merging the modules. Otherwise, when you merge each file, one or more line numbers in one module in effect could erase the line number of a previous program module. To use the RENUM command you will first have to load each module, renumber the lines in the module, and then save the module. Then, you could merge each module into memory to obtain one program.

The following examples illustrate the command structure and operational result from the use of the MERGE command. Note that you must specify a path to the file if it is not in the directory you are currently logged onto.

Command structure	**Operational result**
MERGE "A:STAT.BAS	Merges the ASCII program file named STAT with extension BAS on the diskette in drive A into the program in memory
MERGE "C:\SALES\DATA"	Merges the ASCII program file named DATA on the fixed disk under the SALES directory into the program in memory

A "Bad file mode" error will result if the program you attempted to merge was not saved in ASCII format using the A option parameter in the SAVE command. You can then save the program in memory and if the program you wish to merge is unprotected, you can LOAD it into memory and resave it using the A option parameter. Then, you can reload the original contents of memory and merge the newly formed ASCII file.

NAME Command

The BASIC NAME command is the counterpart of the DOS RENAME command. This command provides you with the ability to change the name of a disk file.

Similar to most BASIC commands, the NAME command can be used in both direct and indirect modes. If the file to be renamed is not in the current directory a path to the file must be included in the file specification. The following example illustrates the command structure and operational result of this command.

Command structure	**Operational result**
NAME "A:STAT" AS"DATA"	Renames the file STAT on the diskette in drive A to DATA

If the file you wish to rename does not exist or the name you wish to change it to already exists on the diskette an error will result. If the file you wish to rename is not on the current directory you must include a path in the file specification. This is illustrated by the following use of the NAME command to change the name of the program file ANALYSIS.BAS located in the SALES directory on the DOS default drive to DATA.BAS.

```
OK
NAME "\SALES\ANALYSIS.BAS" AS "\SALES\DATA.BAS"
OK
```

In the indirect mode the NAME command allows you to change the name of a disk file within a program. In developing a program that updates sequential files, this provides you with the ability to construct a continuous update cycle in a program. This can be seen from the flowchart in Fig. 8-1. In the file

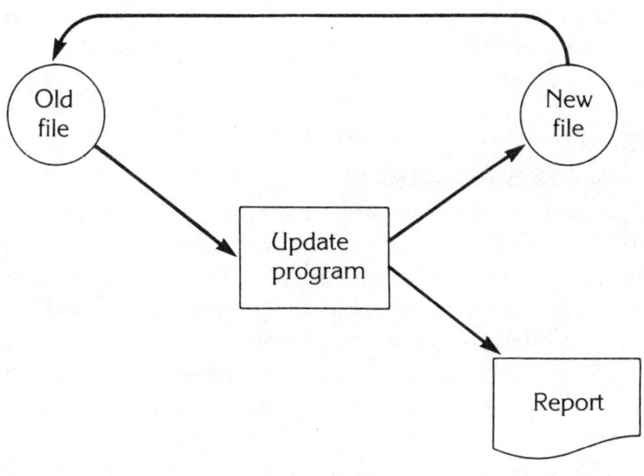

Fig. 8-1. Cyclic file update and report generator program.

update and report generation program process in Fig. 8-1, the update program will read the data on the file named OLD. After updating the data, the program will output it to a file named NEW and print a report. Once the updating is complete, the NEW file will become the OLD file for the next update process. To perform the file manipulation required within your update program will require the following operations.

1. Save the file named NEW.
2. Delete the file named OLD.
3. Rename OLD as NEW.

The preceding operations can be performed in the indirect mode as indicated by the following program segment.

```
500 SAVE "NEW
510 DELETE "OLD
520 NAME "NEW AS "OLD
```

Prior to writing a program using file reference commands, it is recommended that Chapter 10 be read. This chapter covers the use of BASIC file statements that are necessary to read and write data items to and from sequential and random files.

RESET Command

The RESET command closes all diskette files and clears any data in file buffer areas. It can be used in both direct and indirect modes.

In the indirect mode, you can use it in a program to close all open files if you have previously opened the maximum number of files permitted and wish to manipulate data on other files. When file operations are covered in Chapter 10, you will see that this command is the same as a CLOSE statement with no file number assigned to the statement. In direct mode, this command is invoked by entering the keyword RESET. In indirect mode, this command will be executed in a program when the line number that prefixes the keyword is reached.

RUN Command

As previously discussed under program reference commands in this chapter, the RUN command is both a program reference and a file reference command, depending on the format of the command. In this section, the second format indicated in Table 8-1 will be examined. Since this format requires a file specification, it falls into the file reference command category. Note that if the program to be executed is on a different drive or directory from the default drive or directory, you must then specify the drive and a path to the file.

The RUN command clears memory and loads and runs a file from disk. If the R option is included, all open data files will remain open. Since you must specify the file, you cannot use the F2 key because that key results in the generation of the keyword RUN followed by an enter character and is effective only for executing a program currently in memory.

The following examples illustrate the command structure and operational results from the use of various RUN commands that reference files. Note that the default file extension BAS will be automatically supplied when such files are referenced.

Command structure	**Operational result**
RUN "ANALYSIS"	Loads and runs the file named ANALYSIS from the diskette in the default drive
RUN "ANALYSIS.BAS,R	Loads and runs the file named ANALYSIS from the diskette in the default drive; keeps all open files open
RUN "C:\SALES\EST"	Loads and runs the file named EST located under the directory SALES on drive C

Similar to the R option in the LOAD command, you must enter the complete extension of the file when you use the R option, or BASIC will confuse the R as part of the file extension and return the message "File not found." We can also place the end quotation mark after the file specification to insure that BASIC recognizes that the R option is not part of the file extension.

The ability to keep all open files open with the R option allows you to have one program automatically continue using a file accessed by a previous program.

Similar to most commands, the RUN command can be used in both direct and indirect modes. To obtain a feel for the effectiveness of the RUN command in the indirect program mode, assume you wish to construct a program that permits the operator to select one of five programs from a menu in a main program. After the menu is displayed and the program number requested is entered, your program segment might be as shown below.

```
100 ON X GOTO 110,120,130,140,150
110 RUN "STAT1.BAS
120 RUN "STAT2.BAS
130 RUN "STAT3.BAS
140 RUN "STAT4.BAS
150 RUN "STAT5.BAS
```

Since the execution of the RUN command deletes the contents of memory before loading and running the specified file, you do not have to worry about a second RUN statement in a following line in the main program being executed after the command in the line number you branched to is executed. At the appropriate point in each of the five programs, you can automatically load and rerun the main program containing the menu by using a statement similar to the following in each STAT program.

```
500 RUN "MAIN.BAS
```

To see how you can employ a path in the RUN command, consider the following example. In this example, you will list the program named FIRST located in the root directory. Then you will use the CHDIR command in direct mode to change the current directory to SALES (CHDIR"C:\SALES") and load and list the program named ANALYSIS located in the SALES directory. After this is accomplished, you will again use the CHDIR command in direct mode, this time to change the current directory to the root directory (CHDIR"\"). Now you can load and run the program file named FIRST located in the root directory. Notice that the program FIRST automatically executes the program named ANALYSIS, even though it is not in the same directory, since the appropriate path was specified in line 40 of the first program.

```
OK
LIST
10 REM lets execute one program from another
20 PRINT "first program here"
30 PRINT "lets get next one"
40 RUN "C:\SALES\ANALYSIS"
OK
CHDIR "C:\SALES"
OK
LOAD"ANALYSIS"
OK
LIST
10 PRINT "test"
OK
CHDIR "\"
OK
LOAD"FIRST"
OK
RUN
first program here
lets get next one
test
OK
```

SAVE Command

The SAVE command provides you with the ability to save a BASIC program file on disk. If you are saving a file on disk and do not specify a file extension, BAS will be automatically added to the file directory as the file extension.

In the format of this command listed in Table 8-1, the A option results in saving the program in ASCII format. If you wish to read such files as data files for transmission to another computer or for other purposes, you should save it using this option. The P option results in the program being saved in an encoded binary format that protects its contents from being listed or edited. This option should be used with care, since no way is provided to "unprotect" such files. Normally, you will want to use this option to create a duplicate copy of a program you wish to give to someone but do not desire to provide them with the ability to modify or list the contents of the program. If no option is specified, the program will be saved in a compressed (tokenized) format. In this format, the ASCII code resulting from the Alt key combined with one of the alphabetic keys is used to replace certain BASIC keywords

Table 8-3. BASIC Keyword Tokens

ALT KEY PLUS	KEYWORD	ALT KEY PLUS	KEYWORD
A	AUTO	N	NEXT
B	BSAVE	O	OPEN
C	COLOR	P	PRINT
D	DELETE	Q	(No word)
E	ELSE	R	RUN
F	FOR	S	SCREEN
G	GOTO	T	THEN
H	HEX$	U	USING
I	INPUT	V	VAL
J	(No word)	W	WIDTH
K	KEY	X	XOR
L	LOCATE	Y	(No word)
M	MOTOR	Z	(No word)

as indicated in Table 8-3. Since the indicated key combination replaces a keyword, tokenized files take up less storage space on disk. If you wanted to read such files as data files, you would first have to write a program to detokenize them. Thus, it is simpler to save such files using the A option if you wish to use them as data files. If you wish to save the program in memory on a device other than the DOS default drive or in a different directory, you must include a drive specifier and/or a path in your file specification.

The following examples illustrate the command structure and operational result from the use of the SAVE command. Note that you can use the F4 key to generate the keyword SAVE followed by a quote sign.

Command structure	**Operational result**
SAVE "A:STAT	Saves program under name STAT in tokenized format on diskette in drive A
SAVE "A:STAT,A	Saves program under name STAT in ASCII format on diskette in drive A
SAVE "A:STAT,P	Saves program under name STAT in protected format on diskette in drive A
SAVE "C:\SALES\EST"	Saves program under name EST in the directory named SALES on the fixed disk drive C

The SAVE command can be used in both direct and indirect program modes. In the indirect mode, you can use the SAVE command to automatically save a data file without operator intervention.

BSAVE Command

The BSAVE command (along with the BLOAD command) provides the capability to load a memory image (binary) file into memory and to save a specified portion of the AT's binary memory on a specified device. After reviewing how a specified portion of memory can be saved with the BSAVE command, the BLOAD command will be examined.

As indicated in Table 8-1, you must include a file specification and offset and length parameters in the BSAVE command. In addition, if you wish to save the memory image onto a file located on a directory different from the current directory, you must include a path in your file specification. The offset parameter is a numerical expression that specifies where in the currently defined segment of memory saving will commence. The length parameter specifies the number of bytes of storage from the offset position that will be saved. To understand how you use the offset parameter to specify where in a segment of memory saving commences requires you to examine the DEF SEG statement as the offset parameter points into the segment of memory declared by the last use of the segment.

DEF SEG Statement

Since a 20-bit physical address is used internally to address memory while the PC AT operates on 16-bit words, a technique known as segmented addressing is used to reference memory. In this technique, two 16-bit numbers are used to reference memory. The first number is known as the segment address and is multiplied by 16, which is equivalent to adding 4 binary zeros to it, making it 20 bits long. The second 16-bit number is used as is and is known as the relative portion of the address. By adding both numbers, a 20-bit address is formed that can be used to reference any memory address up to 1024K. Thus, the segment can be viewed as a base address, while the relative address provides an offset relative to that base address.

The DEF SEG statement defines the memory segment address portion of the address. The format of this statement is:

format: DEF SEG= [address]

Here, the address is a numerical expression between 0 and 65535. If the address is omitted the beginning of user work space in memory will be used as the default value. When an address is specified, its value should be based on a 16-byte boundary and should be one-sixteenth of the desired address. This is because the specified value is shifted 4 bit positions to the left, which is equivalent to multiplication by 16 to form the segment address for subsequent operations. As an example, suppose you wish to define your memory segment to be the address where the buffer for the color screen begins. This address in hexadecimal is B8000. Dividing by 16 results in B800. Thus, the DEF SEG statement that would set the memory segment to the beginning location of the color screen buffer would become:

```
100 DEF SEG=&HB800
```

Let's digress from our coverage of the BSAVE and BLOAD commands for a moment to see how the DEF SEG segment can be employed. Suppose you wish to write a program to "dump" the contents of the screen to the printer. Knowing where the buffer that holds the contents of information displayed on the screen is located solves part of the programming problem. Now let's introduce the PEEK function that will provide us with the capability to read a byte of information from a specified memory location.

PEEK Function

The format of this function is:

format: varnm = PEEK(exprnm)

Each value returned will be an integer between 0 and 255, which will be the ASCII value of the location in memory PEEKed. The numeric expression used in the function call will be offset from a current segment if you used a DEF SEG statement in your program. Thus, you can write the following short subroutine to dump the contents of the screen to the printer.

```
100 DEF SEG=&HB800
110 FOR I=0 TO 3838 STEP 2
120 X=PEEK(I)
130 LPRINT CHR$(X);
140 NEXT I
150 DEF SEG
160 RETURN
```

If you are puzzled as to why the FOR-NEXT loop goes from 0 to 3838 in increments of 2, an explanation is in order. First, your display is assumed to be 25 lines of 80 characters, or a total of 2000 characters. Then, why do you vary I from 0 to 3838? This is because each 16-bit location that specifies a character on the display consists of two parts. The first 8 bits define the character (ASCII 0 to 255), while the second 8 bits specify its attribute. The use of attributes will be discussed in Chapter 12. Now you can see the rationale for incrementing the variable I by 2 to skip over the attribute, since you wish only to dump the contents of the screen to the printer.

Since the screen can be represented by character positions as indicated in Fig. 8-2 in decimal notation, why does your incremental value stop at 3838? This is because that is the last character position of the 24th line. Thus, this subroutine allows you to dump the entire screen with the exception of the 25th line which you could then use as a program continuation or print request area. If you wish to dump the entire screen, changing the final value to 3998 would accomplish this task. The DEF SEG statement in line 150 resets your segment to the initial value. Otherwise, any additional PEEK statements in your program would reference memory using an offset of hexadecimal B800. if in doubt, try the preceding program. You may wish to vary the starting and ending parameters of the loop to dump a specified portion of the screen to the printer. If you wish to try the preceding screen dump for the screen buffer on the IBM monochrome display and parallel printer adapter, change line 100

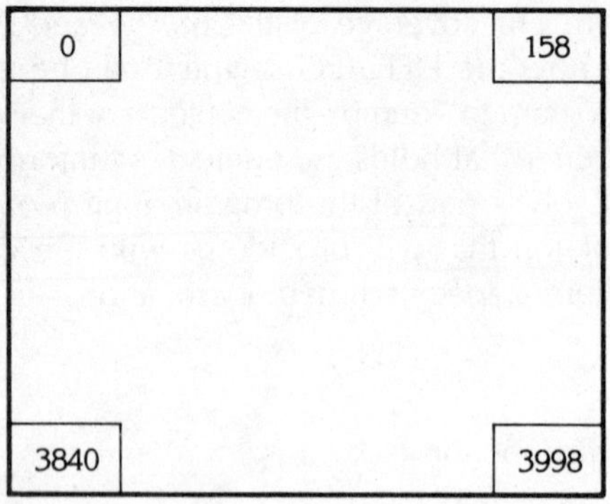

Fig. 8-2. Character positions on display when WIDTH is 80.

in the program to read DEF SEG=&HB000, which is the address of that display.

Suppose you wish to save the screen image on the color screen buffer at a particular point in your program. Since the color screen buffer is 16K bytes in length, your program segment to perform this function would appear as follows:

```
100 DEF SEG=&HB800
110 BSAVE "C:\GRAPH\PIX",0,&H4000
```

In the preceding example, the DEF SEG statement sets the segment address to the start of the color screen buffer. Address B800 is used, since you must divide the actual address of B8000 by 16. In line 110, you use the BSAVE command with a zero (0) offset and length of Hex 4000 to specify that the entire 16K screen buffer is to be saved. The file named PIX will be created on the disk and will then contain the image of the screen.

In addition to saving memory images, the BSAVE command can be used to save machine language programs. One example of the command structure and operational result of the BSAVE command is listed below.

Command structure	**Operational result**
BSAVE "WAR,100,&100	Saves 256 bytes from the buffer starting at offset position 100; memory image is saved on the diskette in the current drive on the file named WAR

The BSAVE command can be used in both direct and indirect modes of operation. In the indirect program mode, this command is very useful to store graphic images after they have been developed on the screen. Then the BLOAD command can be used to load those images previously saved on a file into memory to automatically recreate the screen image. Thus, these commands provide you with the ability to save the results of many complex programs that generate one or more screen displays and simply reference those displays through a BLOAD command.

BLOAD Command

The BLOAD command has the capability to load a memory image (binary) file into memory. The use of this command requires a file specification parameter while the offset parameter is optional. As indicated in the format listed in Table 8-1, the offset parameter is a numeric expression between 0 and 65535 that specifies where in the segment declared by the last DEF SEG statement loading will occur. Thus, the offset parameter can be viewed as a pointer into the currently defined memory segment.

The BLOAD command can be used in both direct and indirect modes. Examples of the command structure and resulting operation from the use of the BLOAD command follow.

Command structure	**Operational result**
BLOAD "A:XRAY.MEM,0	Loads the memory image file named XRAY with extension MEM from the diskette in drive A; a zero offset will be used
BLOAD "C:\GRAPH\PIX.MEM",0	Loads the memory image file named PIX with extension MEM from the directory GRAPH on the fixed disk drive C into memory; a zero offset will be used

In the previous examples, it should be noted that the omission of an offset parameter informs BASIC to use the offset value used in the BSAVE command that previously saved the file. This will insure that the file will be loaded into the same location from where it was saved. If you specify an offset parameter, you should include a DEF SEG statement prior to the BLOAD command. This will inform BASIC that you wish to load the memory image file at a location other than from which it was saved.

PROGRAM TRACING COMMANDS

BASIC contains two program tracing commands that can be employed to assist you in ascertaining the flow of program execution.

TRON Command

The TRON command enables a trace flag in the system that will cause each line number of the program to be displayed as it is executed. To distinguish the line number from any data output to the screen, the line numbers are enclosed in square brackets. The TRON command can be entered in direct or indirect mode. Function key F7 can be used to generate this command in direct mode.

TROFF Command

The TROFF command or the NEW command can be used to disable the tracing of program statements. You should use the former in the indirect mode, since the NEW command would not only disable program tracing but would also delete the program currently in memory, which would probably not be your intention when you wish to terminate tracing the execution of a program. The TROFF command can be generated by the F8 function key. The following examples illustrate the use of these commands in both direct and indirect modes.

In the direct mode, you can press the F7 key to enable program tracing. In the following example after tracing was enabled, the F2 key was pressed to RUN the program in trace mode. After execution was completed, the F8 key was pressed to disable program tracing.

```
OK
LIST
100 INPUT"ENTER VALUE ",R
110 FOR X=1 TO R
120 PRINT X^3,X
130 NEXT X
OK
TRON
OK
RUN
[100]ENTER VALUE 3
[110][120] 1    1
[130][120] 8    2
[130][120] 27                   3
[130]
OK
TROFF
OK
```

Using the TRON and TROFF commands in indirect mode provides you with the ability to selectively trace a portion or portions of a program. This capability is illustrated by the following program segment.

```
LIST
100 INPUT"ENTER VALUE ",R
110 FOR X=1 TO R
115 TRON
120 PRINT X^3,X
130 NEXT X
140 TROFF
150 FOR J=1 TO 5
160 PRINT J;
170 NEXT J
OK
RUN
[100]ENTER VALUE 3
[110][115][120] 1               1
[130][115][120] 8               2
[130][115][120] 27              3
[130][140] 1  2  3  4  5
OK
```

Note that in both examples the tracing of program execution statements does not inform you as to what the values of variables are internally within the program. To obtain this information, which at times can be more valuable than obtaining the sequence of the execution of program statements, you can insert "Dummy PRINT" statements into your program. These statements are called dummy statements, since once you diagnose what is wrong with your program, if anything, you will remove these statements from the program. Thus, these statements serve to provide you with information about what is happening to the variables internally and will not be used in the final version of your program. In the following example, line 115 has been added to a program as a "dummy PRINT" statement. As a result of the execution of this statement, the value assigned to the variable K will be displayed. Without this statement, you would not know the internal value assigned to this variable when the program is run.

```
LIST
100 INPUT"ENTER VALUE ",X
110 K=X^2+X^4
115 PRINT "K= ";K;" WHEN X= ";X
120 TRON
130 FOR I=2 TO X
140 PRINT I ,I*K
150 NEXT I
160 TROFF
Ok
RUN
ENTER VALUE 4
K= 272 WHEN X= 4
[130][140] 2  544
[150][140] 3  816
[150][140] 4  1088
[150][160]
Ok
```

SYSTEM REFERENCE COMMAND

The only system reference command in BASIC is SYSTEM. This command provides you with the capability to exit BASIC and return to DOS. Since this command causes a return to DOS, it requires the use of DOS. The use of this command results in the closing of all open files prior to returning to DOS. As indicated in Table 8-1, no parameters are specified in the command and it is invoked by entering the keyword SYSTEM. The default drive prompt will be displayed in response to this command as shown below.

```
SYSTEM

A>
```

CHAPTER NINE Advanced BASIC

ARRAY PROCESSING

An array or matrix is a set of variables of the same type that is known and referenced by one name. The individual elements of an array are specified by the addition of a subscript to the array name. Thus, A(5) would be the fifth element of the numeric array A, while A$(15) would be the 15th element of the string array A$. Since there is no type declarator permitted for numeric arrays, such arrays will consist of single-precision values.

While many BASICs use 1 as the lowest position of an element in an array, the default value in AT BASIC is 0 (zero). This lowest position can be changed by the OPTION BASE statement, which will be examined later in this section.

Although most BASICs permit a maximum of two dimensions, AT BASIC permits up to 255 dimensions for an array. The maximum number of elements per dimension is 32,767.

A one-dimensional array can be thought of as a single column of many rows. The elements are specified by a single subscript, indicating the row desired as shown in the left portion of Fig 9-1. A two-dimensional array consists of a specified number of rows and columns that can be visualized as organized into a table. This is illustrated in the right portion of Fig. 9-1. In a two-dimensional array, each element is specified by a pair of subscripts separated by a comma. The first subscript indicates the row, while the second subscript indicates the column position within the table.

Unlike many other BASICs, AT BASIC permits two-dimensional string arrays. In fact, up to 255 dimensions can be used for both string and numeric arrays.

ONE DIMENSION

Row	Column
0	A(0)
1	A(1)
2	A(2)
3	A(3)
4	A(4)
5	A(5)

TWO DIMENSION

Row	Column 0	1	2
0	A(0,0)	A(0,1)	A(0,2)
1	A(1,1)	A(1,1)	A(1,2)
2	A(2,1)	A(2,1)	A(2,2)
3	A(3,1)	A(3,1)	A(3,2)
4	A(4,1)	A(4,1)	A(4,2)
5	A(5,1)	A(5,1)	A(5,2)

Fig. 9-1. One- and two-dimensional arrays.

Arrays in a BASIC program are defined in one of two ways. If you use an array element prior to defining the array, it will be assumed to be dimensioned with a maximum subscript of 10, providing 11 elements. This implicit declaration is only valid for one-dimensional arrays having a maximum subscript of 10. Thus, if BASIC encounters the statement

```
200 X(4)=37
```

and the array X was not previously defined, then BASIC will set X to a one-dimensional array of 11 elements and assign the value 37 to the fourth element of array X. The second way to define an array is through the use of a DIM statement.

DIM Statement

The DIM statement provides the mechanism to reserve storage for arrays and to set the upper bounds on the number of elements permitted in each array. The format of this statement is indicated below.

format: DIM var(subscripts)[,var(subscripts)] . . .

Here, the variable names the array and the subscripts specify the amount of storage to be reserved and set the upper bounds on the number of elements in the array.

The DIM statement can appear anywhere in a program, as long as it precedes the first reference to the array. As shown by the following example, the placement of a DIM statement after the reference to the array will result in a "Subscript out of range" message. Note that moving the DIM statement to a location before the reference to the array eliminates this error condition.

```
OK
LIST
80 FOR I=1 TO 50
90 X(I)=0
95 NEXT I
100 DIM X(50)
```

```
OK
RUN
Subscript out of range in 90
OK

LIST
70 DIM X(50)
80 FOR I=1 TO 50
90 X(I)=0
95 NEXT I
OK
RUN
OK
```

The DIM statement is nonexecutable and, if you branch to that statement in a program, execution will resume at the next executable statement following the DIM statement. Several examples of the use of this statement follow.

```
100 DIM A(5),B(3,3)
110 REM A has 6 rows, 1 column
120 REM B has 4 rows, 4 columns
130 REM A has 6 elements - 0 to 5
140 REM B has 16 elements 0,0 to 3,3

LIST
10 X=0
20 PRINT "STOCK","PRICE","SHARES"
30 DIM STOCK$(2),PRICE(2),SHARES(2)
40 FOR I=0 TO 2
50 READ STOCK$(I),PRICE(I),SHARES(I)
60 X=X+PRICE(I)*SHARES(I)
70 PRINT STOCK$(I),PRICE(I),SHARES(I)
80 NEXT I
90 DATA AMERICAN ICE,4.50,110
100 DATA BASIC BARGINS,1.875,50
110 DATA OHVEY INC,.125,5000
120 PRINT "TOTAL VALUE =",X
OK
RUN
STOCK          PRICE          SHARES
AMERICAN ICE    4.5            110
BASIC BARGINS  1.875           50
OHVEY INC       .125           5000
TOTAL VALUE=   1213.75
OK
```

In the second example, one of several methods that can be used to assign values to arrays was used. Here, a READ statement contained within a FOR-NEXT loop assigned the appropriate values to each element of the arrays STOCK$, PRICE, and SHARES. You could also use the assignment statement or use individual elements in an INPUT statement. Note that after the counter that stores the value of each stock (price times number of shares) is incremented in line 60, the PRINT statement in line 70 is used to print data from the arrays. This shows you that printing data from arrays is parallel to the mechanism used for filling arrays. You can print individual elements by using a PRINT statement or you can use that statement within a FOR-NEXT loop to print all or a portion of the elements within an array. This concept will be illustrated by several examples where you will initialize each element of an array to a value and then print out individual elements and selected portions of elements on the display.

```
10 DIM Q(100)
20 FOR I=0 TO 100  'set value of each element
30 Q(I)=I*I        'to its square
40 NEXT I
50 PRINT "SQUARE OF TEN IS ";Q(10)
60 FOR I=18 TO 22
70 PRINT "SQUARE OF ";I;" IS ";Q(I)
80 NEXT I
RUN
SQUARE OF TEN IS 100
SQUARE OF  18  IS 324
SQUARE OF  19  IS 361
SQUARE OF  20  IS 400
SQUARE OF  21  IS 441
SQUARE OF  22  IS 484
OK
```

To obtain an understanding of some of the potential problems that can occur in array processing, several program segments that are designed to be nonoperable will be created and executed.

```
LIST
50 DIM X(20)
60 Z=12
70 FOR I=Z TO Z+15
80 X(I)=I
85 PRINT X(I)
90 NEXT I
OK
RUN
 12
 13
 14
 15
 16
 17
 18
 19
 20
Subscript out of range in 80
OK
```

When using variables to define the elements of arrays you wish to operate on, you should be careful to ensure such variables are used correctly. In the previous example, the subscript became greater than that specified in the DIM statement and caused a "Subscript out of range" error to occur.

In the next example, the type of the arrays used in line 120 purposely does not match the type of the items in the DATA statements. Note that a syntax error occurred, even though it is really a type mismatch. The error was corrected by reversing the array items in line 120 to correspond to the appearance of the type of data in the DATA statements in lines 140 and 150. Line 140 could have been changed, but the items in line 150 would also need to be changed, so changing the sequence of the arrays in the READ statement is easier to correct this error.

```
LIST
100 DIM P$(20),Q(20)
110 FOR I=0 TO 1
120 READ P$(I),Q(I)
125 PRINT P$(I),Q(I)
130 NEXT I
140 DATA 1,WASHINGTON
150 DATA 2,ADAMS
Ok
RUN
Syntax error in 140
Ok

120 READ Q(I),P$(I)
RUN
WASHINGTON     1
ADAMS          2
Ok
```

The next example results in another "Type mismatch" error; however, this results in the display of the correct error message. Here, a numeric value was associated with an element in a string array, which resulted in the type mismatch error occurring.

```
100 DIM P$(20),Q(20)
110 LET P$(1)=87.50
RUN
Type mismatch in 110
Ok
```

Since numeric array elements are stored as single-precision variables, each element will occupy four memory locations. The following example illustrates how easy it is to run out of memory from the dimensioning of just a few large arrays.

```
Ok
LIST
5 PRINT FRE(X)
10 DIM A(2,2,2,2)    '81 elements
15 PRINT FRE(X)
20 DIM B(5.5)        '36 elements
25 PRINT FRE(X)
30 DIM X(49,49)      '2500 elements
35 PRINT FRE(X)
40 DIM Q(19,19,19)   '8000 elements
45 PRINT FRE(X)
50 DIM R(9,9,9,9)    '10000 elements
Ok
RUN
 60650
 60311
 60156
 50145
 18132
Out of memory in 50
Ok
```

As indicated, arrays can rapidly reduce the amount of memory available for program computations. If you require the use of several large arrays in a program, you may wish to use the ERASE statement to eliminate from the program those arrays you have completed your operations on.

ERASE Statement

The ERASE statement allows you to eliminate previously DIMensioned arrays from a program. In addition, it allows you to redimension arrays within a program, since without the prior erasing of an array, you would obtain a "Duplicate definition error". The format of this statement is indicated below.

format: ERASE arrayname[,arrayname] . . .

Suppose you had an array of 1001 elements in your program and only required the data contained in elements 0 through 200. If you wish to make available additional space for your program, you could first dimension a new array of 201 elements, transfer the values of the elements from the old array to the new and smaller array, and then erase the original array.

A program segment that illustrates this concept is listed below. Note that you merely have to list the array name in the ERASE statement.

```
100 DIM X(1000)
.
.
200 DIM Y(200)
210 FOR I=0 TO 200
220 Y(I)=X(I)
230 NEXT I
240 ERASE X
.
.
```

Another use for the ERASE statement is in a program that uses INPUT statements to enter data into one or more elements of arrays. Also, at the end of the program, it provides the operator with the option of requesting another program cycle. Here, instead of constructing one or more loops to zero the array elements, you could ERASE the arrays and then branch back to the beginning of the program where your DIM statement could be located. This concept is illustrated by the following program segment.

```
10 DIM X(30),Y(40),Z(800)
.
.
.
5000 PRINT "ANOTHER (C)YCLE OR (E)XIT"
5010 A$=INKEY$:IF A$="E"THEN 5050
5020 IF A$<>"C" THEN 5010
5030 ERASE X,Y,Z,
5040 GOTO 10
5050 END
```

OPTION BASE Statement

An OPTION BASE statement is provided so that AT BASIC can become compatible with other versions of BASIC that use a minimum value of 1 for array subscripts. The format of this statement is shown below.

format: OPTION BASE value

Here, the default base is 0 and can be specified as such by the statement, or we can use the OPTION BASE statement to change the minimum value of array subscripts to 1. This statement must precede any DIM or array reference statement within a program. Since you may have a natural tendency to operate with subscript elements starting at 1, using the OPTION BASE statement accordingly could eliminate storage allocation for array elements you do not intend to use in your program.

```
10 OPTION BASE 1
20 DIM X(30),Y(30),Z(30)
```

Thus, the preceding example would result in 12 storage locations being freed, since each element requires four memory locations. Without the OPTION BASE statement, one extra element requiring four memory locations of storage would have been reserved for each array.

Processing Examples

Let's examine some additional examples of how you can use arrays in BASIC.

Multiple Report Headings

Suppose you wish to print a financial report that will be 12 pages in length, each page projecting a cash flow analysis for a different month of the year. If the title on each page remains the same and only the month changes, you could use the following program segment that calls a subroutine to print the appropriate heading on each page.

```
100 DIM M$(12)
110 FOR I=1 TO 12
120 READ M$ (I)
130 NEXT I
140 DATA JANUARY,FEBRUARY,MARCH,APRIL,MAY,JUNE
150 DATA JULY,AUGUST,SEPTEMBER,OCTOBER,NOVEMBER,DECEMBER
.
.
500 FOR I=1 TO 12
510 GOSUB 5000
. 'report computations
. 'and data output generator
1000 NEXT I
1010 END
.
.
```

```
5000 LPRINT TAB(30) "CASH FLOW FOR ";M$(I)
5010 RETURN
```

In this example, lines 100 through 150 set aside 12 locations in storage for the array M$ and then initialize each element of the array to the appropriate month. The FOR-NEXT loop bounding lines 500 to 1000 first call a subroutine that prints the heading of the report for the appropriate month and then calculates and prints the computations to be displayed for that particular month. An END statement was placed in line 1010 to prevent an unintentional fall through the main program into the subroutine. Note that in this example, the subroutine merely prints the string "CASH FLOW FOR" followed by the month. A space was purposely left between the R in FOR and the double quote sign in line 5000 to separate the word FOR from the appropriate month that will be printed.

Data Entry Error Processing

Now, let's examine how you can use arrays to allow data to be entered from the terminal and correct incorrectly entered data without rerunning the program.

Suppose you wish to construct a program to compute the mean, standard deviation, variance, and coefficient of variation on data elements obtained from a survey of the number of persons living in homes located in several geographical areas. Further suppose you have 20 people surveying different neighborhoods and you wish to construct one program that can be used to obtain the necessary computations for each geographical area. Since each geographical area most likely has a different number of households, you may wish to construct the program so that it will have an array dimensioned in size based on the number of households surveyed. This can be accomplished by the following two statements that illustrate how you can automatically dimension arrays during program execution.

```
100 INPUT "NUMBER OF HOMES SURVEYED ",X
110 DIM H(X)
```

After you enter the number of homes surveyed, the program should then request the number of occupants of each home to be entered and read this information into the appropriate elements of the H array. This can be accomplished by the following program statements.

```
120 PRINT"ENTER NUMBER OF OCCUPANTS"
130 FOR I=1 TO X
140 PRINT"HOUSEHOLD #";I;"=";
150 LOCATE ,18
160 INPUT "  ",H(I)
170 NEXT I
```

The FOR-NEXT loop results in the prompt "HOUSEHOLD #" and the number 1 to X being printed on the display. The LOCATE statement in line 150 repositions the cursor to column 18 on the current line, while the INPUT statement in line 160 will assign the data value entered to the appropriate element of the H array.

The space between the pair of double quotation marks in line 160 forces a space between the displayed equal sign resulting from the execution of line 140 and the terminal operator's data entry in response to the INPUT statement in line 160. The execution of lines 100 to 170 of the program segment we have developed at this time is shown.

```
RUN
NUMBER OF HOMES SURVEYED 3
ENTER NUMBER OF OCCUPANTS
HOUSEHOLD # 1 =   3
HOUSEHOLD # 2 =   2
HOUSEHOLD # 3 =   4
OK
```

Once all values have been entered into the program, the following statements can be used to correct any data element previously entered incorrectly. These statements permit such changes to occur prior to the program performing the required computations.

```
180 PRINT "ANY DATA ELEMENT ENTERED INCORRECTLY -Y/N "
190 A$=INKEY$:IF A$="N" THEN 250
200 IF A$<> "Y" THEN 190
210 INPUT "WHICH HOUSEHOLD DO YOU WISH TO CHANGE ",C
220 INPUT "ENTER NEW VALUE ",H(C)
230 PRINT "MORE CORRECTIONS -Y/N "
240 GOTO 190
250 REM start computations
```

If data was previously entered incorrectly, the operator will specify which household he wishes to change. The household number (variable C) will be used as a pointer to the element in the H array for entering the new value into the appropriate element of that array. Note that the operator can enter no corrections or correct as many previously entered data elements as he wishes as a result of the preceding code.

This facet of the program is shown by executing the statements in lines 100 to 250. In the following example, the operator first entered the values of 4, 8, 9, and 6 as the number of occupants in homes 1, 2, 3, and 4. Then, he indicated he wished to change household 3 to a new value of 4 and the program automatically changed the value of H(3) to 4.

```
RUN
NUMBER OF HOMES SURVEYED 4
ENTER NUMBER OF OCCUPANTS
HOUSEHOLD # 1 =   4
HOUSEHOLD # 2 =   8
HOUSEHOLD # 3 =   9
HOUSEHOLD # 4 =   6
ANY DATA ELEMENT ENTERED INCORRECTLY -Y/N
WHICH HOUSEHOLD DO YOU WISH TO CHANGE 3
ENTER NEW VALUE 4
MORE CORRECTIONS -Y/N
OK
```

Digressing for a moment, let's review some elementary statistics. The arithmetic average or mean is defined as the sum of the values of the items divided by the number of items. Mathematically, this is noted as follows:

$$\bar{X} = \frac{\sum_{i=1}^{n} X_i}{n}$$

where $\bar{X}$ is the arithmetic average or mean, X_i is the ith element of X, and n is the number of items.

The standard deviation is a measurement of the extent of variation or dispersion of a distribution. The more spread out the distribution, the larger the standard deviation. The more concentrated the distribution, the smaller the resulting standard deviation. Hence, the standard deviation is a more meaningful measure than the average and is expressed mathematically as:

$$Sx = \sqrt{\frac{X^2 - \frac{(\Sigma X)^2}{n}}{n-1}} = \sqrt{\frac{\Sigma(X-\bar{X})^2}{n-1}}$$

The square of the standard deviation, S_x^2, is called the variance. The larger the variability among the items, the larger the standard deviation and consequently the larger the variance.

The coefficient of variation, CV(X), gives you a measure of relative variation, since

$$CV\ (X) = \frac{Sx}{X} \cdot 100$$

Returning to the program, the number of persons in each household can be summed by the following code.

```
260 S=0
270 FOR I=1 TO X
280 S=S+H(I)
290 NEXT I
```

In line 260, S is initialized to zero because it will serve as a counter as you cycle through all elements of the H array, adding the value of each element to S in line 280. While AT BASIC automatically sets all unused variables to zero, it is good programming practice to set counters to zero prior to their use. Otherwise, you may forget that you previously used a variable elsewhere in a program and if you see it later as a counter, this will result in an inaccurate computation. The arithmetic average or mean is simply the sum of the items divided by the number of items. Line 300 performs this calculation.

```
300 M=S/X        'mean
```

Lines 310 through 350 compute the standard deviation, while line 360 computes the variance and line 370 computes the coefficient of variation.

```
310 S=0
320 FOR I=1 TO X
330 S=S+(H(I)=M)^2
340 NEXT I
350 D=SQR(S/(X-1))  'standard deviation
360 V=D*D           'variance
370 CV=(D/M)*100    'coefficient of variation
```

The complete program to include the statements necessary to output the desired computations is shown.

```
100 INPUT "NUMBER OF HOMES SURVEYED ",X
110 DIM H(X)
120 PRINT"ENTER NUMBER OF OCCUPANTS"
130 FOR I=1 TO X
140 PRINT"HOUSEHOLD #";I;"=";
150 LOCATE ,18
160 INPUT " ",H(I)
170 NEXT I
180 PRINT "ANY DATA ELEMENT ENTERED INCORRECTLY -Y/N "
190 A$=INKEY$:IF A$="N" THEN 250
200 IF A$<> "Y" THEN 190
210 INPUT "WHICH HOUSEHOLD DO YOU WISH TO CHANGE ",C
220 INPUT "ENTER NEW VALUE ",H(C)
230 PRINT "MORE CORRECTIONS -Y/N "
240 GOTO 190
250 REM start computations
260 S=0
270 FOR I=1 TO X
280 S=S+H(I)
290 NEXT I
300 M=S/X        'mean
310 S=0
320 FOR I=1 TO X
330 S=S+(H(I)-M)^2
340 NEXT I
350 D=SQR(S/(X-1))  'standard deviation
360 V=D*D           'variance
370 CV=(D/M)*100    'coefficient of variation
380 CLS
390 PRINT "RESULTS BASED UPON SURVEY OF ";X;" HOUSEHOLDS"
400 PRINT
410 PRINT "MEAN= ";M
420 PRINT "STANDARD DEVIATION = ";D
430 PRINT "VARIANCE= ";V
440 PRINT "COEFFICIENT OF VARIATION= ";CV
```

The result from the execution of the previously developed program follows. Here, 10 households were surveyed and the data elements 3, 2, 7, 1, 4, 6, 2, 1, 4, and 2 were entered into the program to obtain the noted results.

```
RESULTS BASED UPON SURVEY OF 10 HOUSEHOLDS

MEAN= 3.2
STANDARD DEVIATION = 2.043961
```

```
VARIANCE=  4.177778
COEFFICIENT OF VARIATION=  63.87379
OK
```

Table Lookup

Another common use of arrays is in the construction of a table lookup procedure. Such procedures are commonly employed in payroll processing where you have to computerize tables of federal, state and local withholding rates. Suppose you pay employees on a monthly basis and the appropriate federal income tax withholding rates are as indicated in Table 9-11 for single persons and heads of households.

You can develop a table lookup process to compute the federal tax as follows. You can assign the first set of numbers in the left-hand column of the tax table that determines the lower limit of the income bracket to the elements of an array labeled L. In a similar manner, you can assign the amount of income tax to be withheld and the prercent of the excess over the lower limit to arrays A and E. This is accomplished by the following statements.

```
100 FOR I=1 To 6
110 READ L(I),A(I),E(I)
120 NEXT I
130 DATA 88,0,.14,133,6.3,.17
140 DATA 217,20.58,.18,433,63.78,.20
150 DATA 583,90.78,.21,917,160.92,.24
```

Once you obtain the amount of the wage, you can test that amount against each lower limit of the income bracket contained in the array L.

If the amount earned does not exceed the first element of the value in array L, the resulting tax will be zero. If the amount earned exceeds the value of one element of array L but is less than the next element of array L, the resulting tax will be the amount in the appropriate element of array A plus the percentage in the element of array E times the excess over the income bracket.

Table 9-1. Federal Income Tax Withholding Rates (Single Person and Head of Household)

AMOUNT OF WAGES		AMOUNT OF INCOME TAX	
Under $88	—	$0	Of excess
Over:	But not over:		over:
$ 88	$133	14%	$ 88
$133	$217	6.30 plus 17%	$133
$217	$433	20.58 plus 18%	$217
$433	$583	63.78 plus 20%	$433
$583	$917	90.78 plus 21%	$583
$917	—	160.92 plus 24%	$917

The following program statements can be used to input the wage of the person and compute the appropriate tax that should be withheld.

```
160 INPUT "WAGE= ",WAGE
170 TAX=0
180 FOR I=1 TO 6
190 IF WAGE > L(I) THEN 230
200 IF I=1 THEN 250
210 TAX=A(I-1)+E(I-1)*(WAGE-L(I-1))
220 GOTO 250
230 NEXT I
240 TAX=A(I)+E(I)*(WAGE-L(I))
250 PRINT "TAX= ";TAX
```

The repeated execution of this program for several different wage rates is indicated below. Note that you could use the statements in lines 170 to 240 in a subroutine to compute and return the tax to a main program. You could also use other subroutines to compute state and local withholding amounts using a similar table lookup procedure.

```
RUN
WAGE = 87
TAX=  0
Ok
RUN
WAGE = 99
TAX=  1.54
Ok
RUN
WAGE = 777
TAX=  131.52
Ok
RUN
WAGE = 917
TAX=  160.92
Ok
```

Let's look at another example of using arrays for table lookup. Suppose you wish to automate a procedure to obtain the zip code of a city. You can use two arrays, C$ to hold the name of each city and Z to hold its associated zip code. Once you enter the name of a city, you will then search the C$ array to see if the city is found. If you encounter the city in the array, its element value will point to the appropriate location in the Z array that contains its associated zip code. The listing and execution of the program that performs this table lookup operation follows.

```
LIST
100 DIM C$(12),Z(12)
110 FOR I=1 TO 12
120 READ C$(I),Z(I)
130 NEXT I
140 DATA AUSTIN, 31204,BALSON, 31215,CLIFTON,31208
150 DATA DOVER,31201,ELSON,31217,FRANKLIN,31815
160 DATA HERPES,31299,IVERSON,31267,LANGLY,31237
170 DATA MC RAY,31219,NUTLEY,31272,TIFTON,31282
180 INPUT "ENTER NAME OF CITY YOU REQUIRE ZIP CODE OF ";CITY$
```

```
190 FOR I=1 TO 12
200 IF CITY$=C$(I) THEN 240
210 NEXT I
220 PRINT "CITY NOT IN DIRECTORY"
230 GOTO 250
240 PRINT "THE ZIP CODE FOR ";C$(I);" IS ";Z(I)
250 INPUT "ANOTHER SEARCH -YES OR NO ";A$
260 IF A$="YES" THEN 180
270 IF A$<>"NO" THEN 250
280 END
OK
```

The execution of the preceding program with both a city not contained and contained in the directory follows.

```
RUN
ENTER NAME OF CITY YOU REQUIRE ZIP CODE OF ? BALSTON
CITY NOT IN DIRECTORY
ANOTHER SEARCH -YES OR NO ? YES
ENTER NAME OF CITY YOU REQUIRE ZIP CODE OF ? BALSON
THE ZIP CODE FOR BALSON IS 31215
ANOTHER SEARCH -YES OR NO ? NO
OK
```

Sorting

To conclude our discussion of arrays, let's look at how you can sort data items by using a very simple and easy to implement technique known as the bubble sort. This is an exchange type of sort, where you can bring items into an ordered sequence by exchanging the positions of items that are out of order. To see how this sort works, examine a list of numbers, such as:

27 18 71 43 22

Begin the sort by first looking at the initial two data elements, 27 and 18. Since they are out of order, you must transpose them so the list of numbers will become:

18 27 71 43 22

Next, compare the second and third numbers. Since they are not out of order, you do not need to transpose them. The next pair of data elements, 71 and 43, are out of order, so you will have to transpose them, resulting in the list:

18 27 43 71 22

When the last two data elements are transposed, the list becomes:

18 27 43 22 71

Note that the largest value in the list was moved to the end of the list. After one compare and exchange pass the list order has improved, but it is not completely in order. You will need to use two more compare and exchange passes, first switching 43 and 22 and then switching 27 and 22, to get the list in order sequence. You can write a program segment using arrays to perform this type of sorting procedure by using the following program statements.

```
LIST
100 INPUT "DATA ELEMENTS TO BE SORTED ";N
110 DIM A(N)
120 PRINT "ENTER THE VALUE OF EACH ELEMENT IN ANY ORDER"
130 FOR I=1 TO N
140 INPUT "";A(I)
150 NEXT I
160 FLAG=0
170 FOR I=1 TO N-1
180 IF A(I)<=A(I+1) THEN 230
190 TEMP=A(I)
200 A(I)=A(I+1)
210 A(I+1)=TEMP
220 FLAG=1
230 NEXT I
240 IF FLAG=1 THEN 160
250 FOR I=1 TO N
260 PRINT A(I);
270 NEXT I
Ok
```

After the data elements are entered, the variable FLAG is set to zero in line 160. This variable will be used to determine whether or not any exchanges resulted from a compare and exchange pass. When an exchange occurred, the FLAG variable will be set to 1 in line 220. At the completion of the pass, the value of FLAG will be 1 if an exchange occurred and the program will continue its compare and exchange passes until it does not make an exchange during a pass. This will signify that the data items are in sequence. Line 180 compares the Ith and I+1 data elements. If they are out of order, lines 190 and 210 will exchange them. The variable TEMP used in lines 190 and 210 is a dummy variable that is used when A(I) is exchanged with A(I+1). The use of this variable permits the program to set the value of A(I+1) to the previous value of A(I). Although a dummy variable was used to permit the interchange of values, you could simplify programming by using the SWAP statement whose format is shown below.

format: SWAP var_1,var_2

This statement provides you with a convenient mechanism to exchange the values of two variables. If you anticipate converting your program to run on a machine whose BASIC interpreter does not contain a SWAP statement, you should use a dummy variable for data exchange. Otherwise, the SWAP statement will allow you to replace three statements by that statement. Thus, the statement:

```
190 SWAP A(I),A(I+1)
```

would replace lines 190 through 210 in the previous example. The execution of this bubble sort program with 15 data values follows.

```
RUN
DATA ELEMENTS TO BE SORTED ? 15
ENTER THE VALUE OF EACH ELEMENT IN ANY ORDER
? 165
? 231
? 2
? 12
? 43
? 198
? 321
? 777
? 317
? 1
? 128
? 587
? 912
? 326
? 876
 1  2  12  43  128  165  198  231  317  321  326  587  777  876  912
OK
```

To sort in descending sequence instead of ascending sequence can be accomplished by changing line 180 as follows:

```
180 IF (I)>=A(I+1) THEN 230
```

The result of executing this one character change to he preceding program with five sample data elements follows. If you wish, it would be a simple matter to incorporate both ascending and descending sorting into a routine, selecting the sorting method to perform based on user input or the status of a variable within the program.

```
RUN
DATA ELEMENTS TO BE SORTED ? 5
ENTER THE VALUE OF EACH ELEMENT IN ANY ORDER
? 21
? 1
? 43
? 12
? 37
 43  37  21  12  1
OK
```

FORMATTED DISPLAY AND PRINTING

BASIC contains two statements that permit you to output a list of items to the printer or to the display according to a predefined format. The LPRINT USING statement provides you with the capability to print strings or numbers in a specified format on the printer while the PRINT USING statement provides you with the same capability for output on the display.

PRINT USING Statement

The format of the PRINT USING statement is illustrated below.

format: PRINT USING var$;list of expressions[;]

Here, the string variable, var$, contains the formatting characters that define the fields and formats of strings or numbers in the list of expressions to be printed on the screen. When this statement is executed, each specification in the format string (var$) is extracted and examined. If the specification calls for a string or a numeric value, the list of expressions will be examined for a corresponding expression. If the specification calls for the display of a string constant embedded in the format string, that string constant will be printed. Each expression in the list of expressions will be printed on the display according to its corresponding specification in the format string; however, if the expression and specification are not of the same type, an error will result and the program will terminate. Thus, string specifications in the format must be used to print string expressions while numeric specifications must be used to print numeric expressions.

Table 9-2 lists the numeric and string formatting characters that can be used to format string and numeric fields. Let's examine the use of these special characters by creating and executing several program segments. Several simple examples will be presented first, and additional formatting characters will gradually be incorporated to illustrate the numerous formatting variations you can develop.

By using the pound (#) and decimal point (.) characters, you can specify integer or floating point formats for the display of numeric information. Suppose you wish to print the values of the variables A and B, allocating six positions to the left of the decimal point and two positions to the right of the decimal point for A and five integer positions for the variable B. Further suppose you wish to separate the printing of the value of each variable by two character positions. The print image you then wish to use would be:

```
####.##  #####
```

Your PRINT USING statement would then become:

```
PRINT USING "####.##  #####";A,B
```

The execution of the following two program lines illustrates the result obtained from incorporating the image within the string variable to represent the format to be followed.

```
100 A=1473.12:B=1056
110 PRINT USING "####.##  #####";A,B
RUN
1473.12  1056
Ok
```

Table 9-2. Numeric and String Formatting Characters

CHARACTER	UTILIZATION
Numeric	
#	Represents each digit position
.	Represents the decimal point location
+	Causes the sign of the number to be displayed
−	Causes negative numbers to be printed with a trailing minus sign
**	Causes leading spaces to be asterisk filled
$$	Causes a dollar sign to be floated to the left of the formatted number
**$	Causes leading spaces to be asterisk filled and the dollar sign to float to the left of the formatted number
,	Causes a comma to be printed to the left of every third digit to the left of the decimal point
^^^^	When placed after the digit position characters, it specifies exponential format
_	Underscore causes the next character to be output as a literal character
String fields !	Causes the first character in the given string to be printed
\n spaces\	Causes 2+n characters from the string to be printed
&	Causes the string to be output exactly as input

Note that the execution of line 110 causes the display of the value of the variable labeled A to occur in columns 1 through 7. Suppose you wish the value of A to be displayed starting at column 11. You could change line 110 as follows.

```
110 PRINT USING "          ####.##  #####";A,B
```

Here, you simply changed the image to reflect your desire to have 10 spaces prior to printing the value of the first variable in the list. Although you could continue to add blanks into the image to shift the beginning of the display of the value of variable A further to the right, it is very easy to make a mistake in entering a large number of blank characters. A far easier method is to use a LOCATE statement prior to the PRINT USING statement to position the cursor to the location where you want the first image to occur. Thus, the pair of statements:

```
105 LOCATE 10,11
110 PRINT USING "####.##  #####";A,B
```

would first locate the cursor at row 10, column 11, and then commence displaying the values of A and B according to the format contained in the string. Now suppose you wish to display the value of A commencing in column 11 and B in column 41. You could insert an appropriate number of blanks in the format between the two variables or you could use two PRINT USING statements linked together by a semicolon (;) at the end of the first statement. Here, the semicolon signifies that printing should occur on the same line. Thus, consider the execution results of the following program segment.

```
LIST
10 A=1234.56
20 B=9876
30 LOCATE 10,11
40 PRINT USING "####.##";A;
50 LOCATE 10,41
60 PRINT USING "#####";B
OK
RUN
          1234.56                              9876
OK
```

Here, the LOCATE statement in line 30 positions the cursor to row 10, column 11. The PRINT USING statement in line 40 displays the value of A according to the format in the string of that statement. The LOCATE statement in line 50 moves the cursor to column 41 of row 10 where the following PRINT USING statement will display the value of B according to the format in the string of this statement.

The format in the formatting string will be repeated if additional variables are in the list of expressions that you wish to display in the same format. This is illustrated by the following example.

```
LIST
110 PRINT USING "####.##";-555,111,9222,-777
RUN
-555.00 111.009222.00-777.00
OK
```

When using one format string for multiple displays of a sequence of values, you should insert spaces at the end of the format string. This will separate the printed values on the line as illustrated by the next example.

```
LIST
110 PRINT USING "####.##     ";-555,111,9222,-777
RUN
-555.00     111.00   9222.00   -777.00
OK
```

Now that you have some idea concerning how you can position formatted data, let's return to your initial formatting example to ascertain what happens if the value of the variable to be displayed exceeds the specified field size. Let's change the values of A and B as follows.

```
100 A=12345.6789:B=-987654321
110 PRINT USING "####.##  #####";A,B
RUN
%12345.68  %-987654400
OK
```

Note that a percent sigh (%) was printed in front of each number. This serves to indicate that the value of a variable overflowed or underflowed the format.

For the variable labeled A, note that five positions to the left of the decimal point were printed even though only four positions were in the field image. Unlike other BASICs, AT BASIC will automatically extend the print image; however, it will also print the percent sign (%) to indicate an overflow or underflow occurred. Also note that the decimal portion of A was rounded from .6789 to .68 upon printout.

Since the largest stored integer value is seven digits, considerable rounding will occur when the value of B is displayed; however, note that the integer image is also automatically expanded by BASIC. When you work with extremely large or small numbers, you should convert those numbers to double precision prior to their output.

While the next example shows how this can increase the accuracy of the integer part of the number to be displayed, note that unless you add additional positions to the fractional part of an image, the fractional accuracy will not improve.

```
100 A#=12345.6789:B#=-987654321
110 PRINT USING "####.##  #####";A#,B#
RUN
%12345.68  %-987654321
OK
```

Plus and Minus Format Characters

You can use a plus sign at either the beginning or the end of a format string. The use of this sign will result in the sign of the number (plus or minus) to be displayed before or after the number. The next two examples illustrate the use of this format character.

```
LIST
100 A=106.42:B=73
110 PRINT USING "+####.##  #####+";A,B
OK
RUN
 +106.42      73+
OK

LIST
100 A=-51.81:B=-77.77:C=8.7:D=-.1
110 PRINT USING "+####.##     ";A,B,C,D
OK
RUN
  -51.81      -77.77      +8.70`      -0.10
OK
```

In the second example, it should be noted that if the format string specifies that a digit is to precede the decimal point, the digit will always be printed, even if zero in value. Thus, although D was assigned the value −.1 it was displayed as −0.10 due to the format image used.

You can use a minus sign at the end of a format field to cause negative numbers to be displayed with a trailing minus sign. This is shown by the next two examples.

```
LIST
100 A=-51.81:B=-77.77:C=8.7:D=-.1
110 PRINT USING "####.##-     ";A,B,C,D
OK
RUN
  51.81-       77.77-       8.70        0.10-
OK
```

```
LIST
100 A=-51.81:B=-77.77:C=8.7:D=-.1
110 PRINT USING "A= ####.## B= ####.## C= ####.## D= ####.##";A,B,C,D
RUN
A=   -51.81 B=  -77.77 C=      8.70 D=   -0.10
```

Note that the second example included four strings (A=, B=, C=, and D=). These strings were placed within the string variable used to define the formats used in displaying the variables in the list of expressions. You can incorporate strings within any string variable used to define formatted output. The concept provides you with a mechanism to label formatted output. The execution of the following program segment illustrates how you can use this capability more fully.

```
LIST
100 INPUT "ENTER FEDERAL STATE AND LOCAL TAX RATES ";F,S,L
110 INPUT "ENTER YIELD OF TAX FREE SECURITY ";Y
120 CTAX=F+(1-F)*(S+L)
125 TEY=Y/(1-CTAX)
130 PRINT
140 PRINT USING "TAX EQUIVALENT YIELD = ##.#### ";TEY
150 PRINT "BASED UPON"
160 PRINT USING "TAX RATES OF .## FEDERAL .## STATE AND .## LOCAL";F,S,L,
OK
RUN
ENTER FEDERAL STATE AND LOCAL TAX RATES ? .50,.06,.02
ENTER YIELD OF TAX FREE SECURITY ? .12

TAX EQUIVALENT YIELD = 0.2609
BASED UPON
TAX RATES OF .50 FEDERAL .06 STATE AND .02 LOCAL
OK
```

Double Asterisk Format Characters

You can use a double asterisk at the beginning of a formatted numeric field to fill all leading spaces in that field with asterisks. When you use a double asterisk, the double stars (**) also specify two additional digit positions. Thus, **###.## defines a numeric field of eight character positions, which will display a number between −9999.99 and 99999.99 without an overflow or underflow notation and fill any leading spaces in the field with asterisks. The next example illustrates the use of this pair of formatting characters.

```
100 A=12345.67 :B=999: C=-.51 :D=-5.1
110 PRINT USING "******.## ";A,B,C,D
RUN
*12345.67 ***999.00 ****-0.51 ****-5.10
OK
```

Double Dollar Sign Format Characters

Another pair of characters you can use at the beginning of a numeric field is the double dollar sign ($$). The double dollar sign causes a dollar sign to be floated to the left of the formatted number. Like the double asterisk, the double dollar sign specifies two additional digit positions; however, one of the positions will be used to print the dollar sign. Thus, the format $$###.## can be used to display a maximum value of 9999.99 without an overflow occurring. If you have negative numbers in a field prefixed by the double dollar sign, the negative sign will appear before the floated dollar sign. You can also use a trailing minus sign to print negative values to the right of the displayed number. The following examples illustrate several uses of the double dollar sign in numeric fields.

```
100 A=12345.67 :B=999: C=-.51 :D=-5.1
110 PRINT USING "$$####.## ";A,B,C,D
RUN
$12345.67   $999.00     -$0.51     -$5.10
OK

LIST
100 A=12345.67 :B=999: C=-.51 :D=-5.1
110 PRINT USING "$$####.##-";A,B,C,D
RUN
$12345.67   $999.00      $0.51-    $5.10-
OK

LIST
10 X$="GILBERT HELD"
20 PAY=87.75
30 LOCATE 15,5
40 PRINT "PAY TO THE ORDER OF ";X$;
50 X=LEN(X$)+5
60 LOCATE 15,X+20
70 PRINT USING " EXACTLY $$#########.##";PAY
OK
RUN

PAY TO THE ORDER OF GILBERT HELD EXACTLY $87.75
OK
```

Double Asterisk Single Dollar Sign Format Characters

You can combine the effect of the double asterisk and double dollar sign by using the three character combination **$ at the beginning of a numeric format field. This three-character sequence fills leading spaces with asterisks and prints the dollar sign to the left of the number. When used in a numeric field format, this three-character sequence specifies three digit positions, one of which will be used to display the dollar sign. The following example illustrates the use of this three-character sequence within numeric format fields.

```
100 A=10.53 :B=987.65 :C=-102.45
110 PRINT USING "**$########.## ";A,B,C
RUN
********$10.53 *******$987.65 ******-$102.45
OK

100 A=10.53 :B=987.6499 :C=-102.45
110 PRINT USING "**$########.##-";A,B,C
RUN
********10.53 *******$987.65 *******$102.45-
OK
```

Note that the largest numeric value that can be displayed without an overflow by the previous examples is 99999999.99, since one position will always be used to display the dollar sign.

Comma Format Character

You can use a comma to the left of the decimal point in numeric format fields to automatically generate a comma to the left of every third digit to the left of the decimal point. The comma itself signifies an additional digit position within the numeric format field. Thus, the format #####,.## could be used to display a variable with a maximum value of 999999.99 without an overflow occurring. This format would result in the number being displayed as 999,999.99. One example of the use of the comma in numeric field format is shown below.

```
LIST
100 NATDEBT#=1234567890987б5.4#
110 PRINT USING "NATIONAL DEBT ###################,.##";NATDEBT#
OK
RUN
NATIONAL DEBT 123,456,789,098,765.40
OK
```

You can combine the three character sequence **$ with the comma preceding the decimal point in a numeric field format. This combination allows you to obtain the display of variables in financial notation used most commonly in printing checks. The following example shows the use of this combination of formatting characters.

```
LIST
100 NETPAY=1873.42
110 PRINT USING "PAY EXACTLY **$#######,.##";NETPAY
OK
RUN
PAY EXACTLY *****$1,873.42
OK
```

Underscore Format Character

The underscore character can also be used in a numeric field format. When used, it will result in the following character being displayed as a literal character. The following examples illustrate the use of the underscore in numeric field formats as well as the use of some conventional characters in the print image.

```
LIST
100 A=37.5:B=9.8:C=-153.14
110 PRINT USING " _!####.## ";A,B,C
120 PRINT USING "  A####.## ";A,B,C
130 PRINT USING "  %####.## ";A,B,C
140 PRINT USING "  !####.## ";A,B,C
OK
RUN
 !   37.50  !    9.80  !-153.14
   A  37.50   A    9.80   A-153.14
   %  37.50   %    9.80   %-153.14

Type mismatch in 140
OK
```

Note that the underscore character in line 110 resulted in the exclamation point being printed at the beginning of each of the print fields resulting from the execution of that line. In lines 120 and 130, the characters A and percent (%) were used without an underscore prefix and they were displayed in the beginning of each field. This shows that you can avoid using the underscore character many times when you desire to print a literal.

There are, however, some characters such as the exclamation point that must be prefixed by a literal or a type mismatch error will occur. This is because such characters are themselves format specifier characters. This is shown by the execution of line 140. Thus, when in doubt use the underscore character to prefix the literal you wish to display.

Caret Format Characters

The last special character to be covered in formatted numeric field utilization is the caret (^). In formatted numeric field you can use four carets (^^^^) after the digit position to specify exponential notation. The four carets provide a display image for the exponent E±nn or D±nn to be printed. When four carets are used, the significant digits (mantissa) of the number will be displayed left justified and the exponent will be adjusted accordingly.

Several examples of the use of this format specifier are shown below.

```
LIST
100 A=14325467#: B=-98765432#
110 PRINT USING "A= ##.###^^^^";A
120 PRINT USING "B=###.#######^^^^";B
OK
RUN
A= 1.433E+07
B=-98.7654300E+06
OK
```

Note that one digit position will be used to the left of the decimal point to print a space or minus sign unless a leading or trailing + or − is specified.

Unlike the diversity of numeric formatting characters, there are only three string formatting characters you must concern yourself with.

Exclamation Format Character

The exclamation character (!) in a string field format specifies that only the first character in a given string should be displayed. The use of this formatting character is illustrated in the following examples.

```
100 A$="GILBERT"
110 B$="HELD"
120 PRINT USING "INITIALS !.!.";A$,B$
RUN
INITIALS G.H.
OK
```

Backslash Format Character

The backslash character, which specifies integer division in arithmetic operations, can be employed as a pair of formatting characters to specify the display of a number of characters from a string. If typed without a space between the pair of characters, two characters will be displayed from the string starting at the left. If n spaces are enclosed by the backslashes, 2 + n characters will be displayed from the string. The use of this string format specifier is shown in the following examples.

```
LIST
100 A$="GILBERT"
110 B$="BEVERLY"
120 PRINT USING "\ \+\  \ ";A$,B$
140 PRINT USING "\ \ ";A$
OK
RUN
GIL+BEVE
GIL
OK
```

Ampersand Sign Format Character

The last string format specifier is the ampersand sign (&) character. The use of this character in a string field format specifies that the field will be of variable length. That is, the string to be displayed will be output exactly as it is stored in memory. This is shown by the following examples.

```
LIST
100 A$="GILBERT"
110 B$="BEVERLY"
120 PRINT USING "PLEASE PAY YOR DUES &";A$
140 PRINT USING "OR WE WILL RUB OUT YOUR &";B$
OK
RUN
PLEASE PAY YOUR DUES GILBERT
OR WE WILL RUB OUT YOUR BEVERLY
OK
```

A portion of a program previously developed for a lease versus purchase analysis will be used to show the effectiveness of combining the LOCATE and PRINT USING statements to obtain a professional display of computational results that is suitable for a report. In this example, lines 20 and 30 were used to generate values so the program segment could be executed with data for illustrative purposes. The statements used to generate the display follow.

```
10 CLS
20 C2=150000!:EX=10000:T=.5:FYE=5000:B=150000!:T1=.1:C3=15000:S=30000
30 TADJ=50000!:NCOST=100000!
40 LOCATE 2,27
50 PRINT"NET COST OF OWNERSHIP"
60 LOCATE 4,10
70 PRINT USING"PURCHASE PRICE                                        ##########.##";
C2
80 LOCATE 6,10
90 PRINT"LESS ADJUSTMENTS"
100 LOCATE 8,10
110 PRINT USING"FIRST YEAR EXPENSING  ########.##";EX
120 LOCATE 9,10
130 PRINT USING"TIMES TAX RATE                  .##   = ########.##";T,FYE
140 LOCATE 11,10
150 PRINT"INVESTMENT TAX CREDIT"
160 LOCATE 12,10
170 PRINT USING"BASE                  #########.##";B
180 LOCATE 13,10
190 PRINT USING"TIMES ITC RATE                  #.### = ########.##";T1,C3
200 LOCATE 15,10
210 PRINT USING"PRESENT VALUE OF CASH FLOWS     ############.##";S
220 LOCATE 17,10
230 PRINT USING"TOTAL ADJUSTMENTS               ############.##";TADJ
240 LOCATE 19,10
250 PRINT USING"NET PRESENT VALUE COST OF OWNERSHIP           ###############"
;NCOST
```

Note that the PRINT USING statements in the program segment contained many strings that were used to label the resulting output and specify how computation results occurred. This is illustrated by the execution of the program segment.

```
                          NET COST OF OWNERSHIP

         PURCHASE PRICE                                        150000.00

         LESS ADJUSTMENTS

         FIRST YEAR EXPENSING      10000.00
         TIMES TAX RATE                0.50   =      5000.00

         INVESTMENT TAX CREDIT
         BASE                     150000.00
         TIMES ITC RATE                0.100 =     15000.00

         PRESENT VALUE OF CASH FLOWS              30000.00

         TOTAL ADJUSTMENTS                        50000.00

         NET PRESENT VALUE COST OF OWNERSHIP                   100000.00
Ok
```

LPRINT USING Statement

The LPRINT USING statement provides you with the capability to print formatted data on the printer. The format of this statement is format: LPRINT USING var$;list of expressions[;]

The LPRINT USING statement functions similarly to the PRINT USING statement, with the exception that formatted output is directed to the printer instead of the display. All formatting characters applicable to the PRINT USING statement can be used in exactly the same manner with this statement.

DATE AND TIME PROCESSING

Included in disk and advanced BASIC are date and time statements and variables. As statements, they permit you to set the date and time internally from within a program or in a direct mode operation. When used as a variable, they provide you with a mechanism to retrieve the current date or time.

DATE$ Statement and Variable

When used as a statement, you can set the date in the PC AT to the value indicated. The format of this statement is:

format$_{D/A}$: DATE$ = var$

Here, the string variable may be in any one of the following forms:

mm-dd-yy
mm/dd/yy
mm-dd-yyyy
mm/dd/yyyy

The year (yy or yyyy) must be in the range 1980 to 2099. If only two digits are used, then the year is assumed to be 19yy. If only one digit is used for the year, a zero will be automatically appended to make it into two digits. If only one digit is used for the month or day a leading zero (0) will be assigned in front of the digit.

When used as a variable, you can retrieve the current date. Here, the format is:

format$_{D/A}$: var$ = DATE$

where the string variable will retrieve a 10-character string, since the year will always be stored internally as yyyy regardless of the method used to set the date. The following example illustrates how you can set and retrieve the date under program control.

```
OK
LIST
100 DATE$="10/20/85"
```

```
110 X$=DATE$:PRINT X$
120 DATE$="6-18-1985"
130 PRINT DATE$
140 DATE$="4-4-85"
150 PRINT DATE$
OK
RUN
10-20-1985
06-18-1985
04-04-1985
OK
```

Since DATE$ is a string variable you must develop a string manipulation and numeric conversion routine if you wish to use the numeric value of the date in a program. With the date stored internally as:

m	m	X	d	d	X	y	y	y	y

where X denotes the position of the delimiter [dash (–) or slash (/)]. As an example, if you wish to obtain the numeric value of the month, you must extract the fourth and fifth characters from the DATE$ string and convert that extracted two-character sequence into a numeric value. You can use the MID$ function to return the desired part of the DATE$ string and then use the VAL function to return the numerical value of the part you extracted. The following example illustrates the use of these two functions.

```
100 DATE$="6/17/85"
110 DAY$=MID$(DATE$,4,2) 'get 2 characters, beginning at 4th character
120 DAY=VAL(DAY$) 'convert to numeric value
130 PRINT "DAY IS ";DAY
140 TOGO=30-DAY 'now we can use it in a numeric computation
150 PRINT TOGO;" DAYS TILL PAYDAY"
RUN
DAY IS 17
 13 DAYS TILL PAYDAY
OK
```

In the preceding example, note that, although the date was set as 6/17/85, the day is stored internally in the fourth and fifth character positions of the string. Thus, you have to use the MID$ function to extract two characters, starting at the fourth character position in DATE$.

TIME$ Statement and Variable

Similar to DATE$, TIME$ can be used as a statement or as a variable. When used as a statement, it provides you with the ability to set the current time. The format for use in a statement is:

format$_{D/A}$: TIME$=var$

Here, the string variable can be provided in any one of the following forms:

hh	Sets the hour (0 to 23); minutes and seconds initialized to 00 (double zero)
hh:mm	Sets both the hour and minutes; minutes must be in the range of 0 to 59; seconds are initialized to 00 (double zero)
hh:mm:ss	Sets the hour, minutes, and seconds; seconds must be in the range 0 to 59

No matter the form used to set the time, it will be stored internally as an eight-character string. The storage positions include the two field delimiter characters as indicated.

h h : m m : s s

To retrieve the time, use TIME$ as a variable. The format when used as a variable is:

format$_{D/A}$: var$ = TIME$

The time will be returned as an eight-character string of the form hh:mm:ss. To manipulate the time as a numeric quantity will require you to extract the hours, minutes, and seconds from the string and convert them to numeric values. The following program segment illustrates how you can use the TIME$ statement and variable to determine the amount of time required to execute a program loop of 10,000 iterations.

```
LIST
100 TIME$="00"                  'initialize clock to zero
110 FOR I=1 TO 10000 :NEXT I
120 X$=TIME$
130 HR$=MID$(X$,1,2)            'get hours
140 HR=VAL(HR$)
150 MM$=MID$(X$,4,2)            'get minutes
160 MM=VAL(MM$)
170 SS$=MID$(X$,7,2)            'get seconds
180 SS=VAL(SS$)
190 PRINT "ELAPSED TIME =";HR;":";MM;":";SS
OK
RUN
ELAPSED TIME = 0 : 0 : 12
OK
```

SUBROUTINE INTERRUPTS AND EVENT TRAPPING

One of the most useful features of IBM BASIC is the ability to suspend program execution to service an external interrupt prior to resuming execution of the program. In comparison to other microcomputer-based systems that require programming at the assembly language level to obtain this capability, AT BASIC contains several subroutine statements that allow you to process interrupts in the BASIC language. The general form of these statements is:

format: ON event GOSUB line

where the event is caused by communications, function or cursor control key, light pen, or joystick activity. The line is the beginning line number of a BASIC subroutine that the program will branch to when the appropriate event occurs. For the branch to occur, the subroutine interrupt statement must be activated. This can be accomplished by the use of a series of BASIC statements that activates their associated subroutine interrupts. Similarly, a series of statements are contained in AT BASIC that can be used to deactivate subroutine interrupts. The use of these statements governs the ability of a program to respond to certain events that may or may not occur while the program is executed. In discussing subroutine interrupts, attention will be focused on function and cursor control keys, the light pen, and the joystick buttons, since communications processing will be covered in another chapter.

Function and Cursor Control Keys

The format of the subroutine interrupt that establishes a program line number for BASIC to branch to when the specified key is pressed is:

format$_A$: ON KEY (exprnm)GOSUB line

The numeric expression, exprnm, must be in the range of 1 to 14 and indicates the key to be trapped as follows:

1-10	Function keys F1 to F10
11	Cursor up
12	Cursor left
13	Cursor right
14	Cursor down
15-20	Keys defined by the form KEY n,CHR$(shift)+CHR$(scan code)

To activate the subroutine requires a KEY(exprnm)ON statement to be executed in the program. Once such a statement is executed, the indicated function and cursor control key subroutine interrupt will cause the program to branch to the indicated line if the specified key is pressed. Thus, the KEY(exprnm) ON statement activates the subroutine interrupt, while the ON KEY(exprnm) GOSUB line statement causes the actual interrupt to occur. You can disable trapping of the specified key by using 0 as the line number in the ON KEY statement.

Advanced BASIC contains three KEY(exprnm) statements whose formats are:

format$_A$: KEY(exprnm)ON
format$_A$: KEY(exprnm)OFF
format$_A$: KEY(exprnm)STOP

Similar to the ON KEY statement, the numeric expression must be in the range of 1 to 20 and indicates the specific function, cursor control key, or specially defined key to be operated on. Once a KEY(exprnm)ON statement is executed, every time the BASIC interpreter attempts to execute a new statement, it will check to see if the specified key was pressed. If it was, the interpreter will perform a subroutine interrupt to the line number specified in the ON KEY statement.

The KEY(exprnm)OFF statement disables event trapping and a subroutine interrupt will not occur even if the event takes place.

The KEY(exprnm)STOP statement can be used to temporarily suspend event trapping, since the event will be remembered and a subsequent KEY(exprnm)ON statement will cause the subroutine interrupt to take place based on the first key pressed after the KEY(exprnm)STOP statement was executed. Thus, the KEY(exprnm)STOP statement permits you to suspend event trapping to process the results obtained from servicing one subroutine interrupt without a second event being able to disrupt your processing action. When the actual subroutine branch occurs, an automatic KEY(exprnm)STOP is generated by advanced BASIC to preclude recursive traps. In addition, the RETURN from the subroutine will automatically cause a KEY(exprnm)ON to be executed, unless a KEY(exprnm)OFF was performed inside the interrupt routine. Thus, you will normally use a KEY(exprnm)STOP statement outside of the subroutine if you wish to perform additional processing after the RETURN but prior to allowing additional interrupts to be processed. The following program segment illustrates the use of several KEY(exprnm) and ON KEY(exprnm) statements.

```
4000 KEY OFF
4010 LOCATE 25,10
4020 PRINT "F1=SORT F2=PRINT REPORT"
4030 KEY(1) ON
4040 KEY(2) ON
4050 ON KEY(1) GOSUB 5000
4060 ON KEY(2) GOSUB 6000
4070 REM continue processing
.
5000 REM sort routine
5010 KEY(1) OFF:KEY(2) OFF
.
5990 RETURN
6000 REM print report routine
6010 KEY(1) OFF:KEY(2) OFF
.
6990 RETURN
```

In this example, the F1 and F2 keys are used to invoke a sort routine (F1) and a report printing routine (F2). Note that after the sort keys are turned off (line 4000) the message "F1 = SORT F2 = PRINT REPORT" is displayed on the 25th line to inform the operator of the use of these keys. Lines 4030 and 4040 activate the subroutine interrupts in lines 4050 and 4060. In each subroutine, both KEY(1) and KEY(2) are purposely turned off to prevent the operator from interrupting the invocation of one subroutine by pressing another of the activated keys. Now, modify and execute the preceding example to see how you can associate a key with predefined functions that will be invoked when the appropriate key is pressed. First, add a continuous loop to the program segment to represent the processing of an application. This loop is accomplished by the statement in line 4080. Next, add two PRINT statements, one in line 5020 and one in line 6020 that will be executed when the appropriate function keys are pressed. Thus, once the program is executed, pressing the F1 function key will cause a subroutine interrupt to line 5000, while pressing the F2 function key will cause a subroutine interrupt to line 6000. Note that the RETURN statements in lines 5990 and 6990 were changed to RETURN 4030. Thus, once the subroutine is completed, the function keys are again enabled. The listing of this program segment follows.

```
LIST
4000 KEY OFF
4010 LOCATE 25,10
4020 PRINT "F1=SORT F2=PRINT REPORT"
4030 KEY(1) ON
4040 KEY(2) ON
4050 ON KEY(1) GOSUB 5000
4060 ON KEY(2) GOSUB 6000
4070 REM continue processing
4080 GOTO 4080
5000 REM sort routine
5010 KEY(1) OFF:KEY(2) OFF
5020 PRINT "F1 KEY GETS US HERE"
5990 RETURN 4030
6000 REM print report routine
6010 KEY(1) OFF:KEY(2) OFF
6020 PRINT "F2 KEY GETS US HERE"
6990 RETURN 4030
Ok
```

Now, RUN the program. When you initially press the F2 key the program goes into execution. First the soft keys will be turned off, and the message telling you the new meaning of the F1 and F2 keys will be displayed on the 25th line of the screen. Then, nothing will happen as the program goes into an infinite loop in line 4080. If you press the F1 or F2 keys, subroutine interrupt will occur to line 5000 or 6000, depending on the key that was pressed. If you typed this program into your PC AT and pressed the F1 key, the message "F1 KEY GETS US HERE" will be displayed, since we added line 5020 to the program to visually ascertain that pressing that key will cause a subroutine interrupt to line 5000. Similarly, the message "F2 KEY GETS US HERE" will be displayed when the F2 key is pressed. The execution of this program followed by pressing the F1 and F2 keys in the sequence F1, F2, F2, F1, is shown below.

```
RUN

F1 KEY GETS US HERE
F2 KEY GETS US HERE
F2 KEY GETS US HERE
F1 KEY GETS US HERE

            F1=SORT F2=PRINT REPORT
```

As shown, subroutine interrupts provide you with the ability to greatly simplify operator interaction with the PC AT. You can write a program that could perform assorted functions based on the operator pressing certain keys that have been predefined to result in subroutine interrupts to the appropriate statements to perform those functions.

Light Pen

Similar to function and cursor key interrupt processing, the light pen must be activated for the ON PEN GOSUB branch to the indicated line number to occur. First, the three PEN statements will be examined, and then the subroutine interrupt those statements control will be reviewed.

The PEN ON statement enables the BASIC PEN read function. The format of this statement is:

format: PEN ON

Once the light pen is enabled, you can use the PEN function to read the status of the light pen and, if operating under advanced BASIC, it will permit BASIC to transfer control to the indicated interrupt subroutine line number when the pen is used. The format of the PEN function is:

format: varnm = PEN(exprnm)

where the numeric expression must be in the range 0 to 9. This function is used to read the light pen coordinates based on the value of the numeric expression as indicated in Table 9-3.

The following program segment illustrates how you can use an interrupt subroutine to read the light pen coordinates.

```
100 PEN ON
110 DIM A(9)
120 ON PEN GOSUB 5000
.
.
5000 FOR I=1 TO 9
5010 A(I)=PEN(I)
5020 NEXT I
5030 RETURN
```

This program segment enables the light pen and returns the values of the light pen coordinates in the appropriate elements of the array A when the pen is activated.

You can disable the PEN read function by the use of the PEN OFF statement whose format is:

format: PEN OFF

In addition to disabling the PEN read function, if you are operating under advanced BASIC, this statement will also inhibit the PEN subroutine in-

Table 9-3. Light Pen Function Return Values

FUNCTION VALUE (EXPRNM)	OPERATIONAL RESULT
0	Returns −1 if pen down since last poll, 0 if not
1	Returns the x coordinate where pen was last activated: $0 \le x \le 319$ in medium resolution, and $0 \le x \le 639$ in high resolution
2	Returns the y coordinate where pen was last activated: $0 \le y \le 199$
3	Returns the current pen switch value, −1 if down, 0 if up
4	Returns the last known valid x coordinate: $0 \le x \le 319$ in medium resolution, and $0 \le x \le 639$ in high resolution
5	Returns the last known valid y coordinate: $0 \le y \le 199$
6	Returns the character row position where pen was last activated: 0≤row≤24
7	Returns the character column position where pen was last activated: 0≤column≤40, or 0≤column≤80 depending on WIDTH
8	Returns the last known valid character row: 0≤row≤24
9	Returns the last known valid character column position: 0≤column≤40, or 0≤column≤80 depending on WIDTH

terrupt. You can also disable the trapping of the light pen by an ON PEN GOSUB 0 statement.

The PEN STOP statement is only available in advanced BASIC. Its format is:

format$_A$: PEN STOP

The execution of the PEN STOP statement results in the trapping of light pen activity becoming disabled; however, if the activity occurs, it will be remembered so that a subsequent PEN ON statement will result in a trap occurring.

Joystick

Two joysticks can be interfaced to the PC AT system unit. Each joystick has two buttons labeled A and B as well as the stick that can be moved to various X, Y positions. Prior to examining how you can develop the appropriate BASIC statements to conduct joystick event trapping, joystick function and statements necessary to perform joystick processing will be discussed.

BASIC contains a STICK function that can be used to obtain the X and Y coordinates of the two joysticks. The format of this function is:

format: varnm=STICK(exprnm)

The numeric function used in the function call must range between 0 and 3. The values returned from this function call are indicated in Table 9-4.

Table 9-4. Joystick Function Call Operational Result

CALLING ARGUMENT	OPERATIONAL RESULT
0	Returns the X coordinate for joystick A
1	Returns the Y coordinate for joystick A
2	Returns the X coordinate for joystick B
3	Returns the Y coordinate for joystick B

We can enable, disable, and temporarily suspend the trapping of the joystick buttons in advanced BASIC by the use of three STRIG statements.

The STRIG ON statement must be executed to enable a subroutine interrupt to occur through the use of a ON STRIG GOSUB statement. The format of the STRIG ON statement is:

format$_A$: STRIG(exprnm)ON

The numeric expression in the statement must evaluate to the value 0, 2, 4, or 6 and indicates the button to be trapped. A 0 indicates button A1 on the joystick, and a 2 indicates button B1. A 4 indicates button A2, while 6 indicates that button B2 is to be trapped. After a STRIG ON statement is executed, BASIC will check to see if the specified button has been pressed prior to executing the next program statement.

The execution of a STRIG OFF statement disables event trapping and the event will not be remembered even if it should occur. The format of this statement is:

format$_A$: STRIG(exprnm)OFF

Again, the numeric expression must evaluate to the value 0, 2, 4, or 6.

The STRIG STOP statement will temporarily suspend joystick event trapping. The format of this statement is:

format$_A$: STRIG(exprnm)STOP

Once the STRIG STOP statement is executed, no event trapping will occur; however, if a joystick button is pressed it will be remembered and the resulting trap will occur if a subsequent STRIG ON statement is executed.

The ON-STRIG-GOSUB statement causes the BASIC program to branch to a specific line number when one of the joystick buttons is pressed. For the branch to occur, a STRIG ON statement must be executed to activate the subroutine interrupt. The format of this statement is:

format$_A$: ON STRIG(exprnm)GOSUB line

The numeric expression must be evaluated to a value of 0 or 2 and indicates which joystick will cause a subroutine interrupt to occur. If the numeric expression results in a value of 0, the button on the first joystick will cause a subroutine interrupt while a value of 2 is used for the second joystick. An example of a joystick subroutine interrupt in a program segment follows:

```
100 STRIG(0) ON
110 ON STRIG(0) GOSUB 5000
.
.
5000 REM subroutine to process
5010 REM pressing of first button
5020 REM on the joystick
.
6000 RETURN
```

CHAPTER TEN
Data File Operations

FILE STRUCTURE

PC AT BASIC supports two types of files: sequential files and random-access files. Sequential files, as the name implies, contain data that can only be accessed or written sequentially. You can have sequential files on cassette or disk; hence, all versions of AT BASIC support sequential file operations. Cassette BASIC supports sequential operations on cassette, while disk and advanced BASIC support sequential operations on both cassette and diskette. Since there is no cassette port on the AT, our coverage of data file operations will focus on disk storage.

Random file access provides you with the capability to read information from a file or write information to the file without regard for the location of the information. In random-access processing, you will use a pointer that will specify the location from which information is to be read from a file or where it is to be written onto a file. Since only disk storage provides you with the capability to use random-access processing, random-access files are only applicable to disk and advanced BASIC.

FILE CONCEPTS

A file contains blocks of data known as records. Each record may contain one or more fields and each field in turn may contain one or more characters. The field normally represents one distinct piece of information, such as a name, address, telephone number, and so on. Thus, you can view a file as representing a collection of information that may reside on disk. In Fig. 10-1, the file structure of a file that could contain information for a

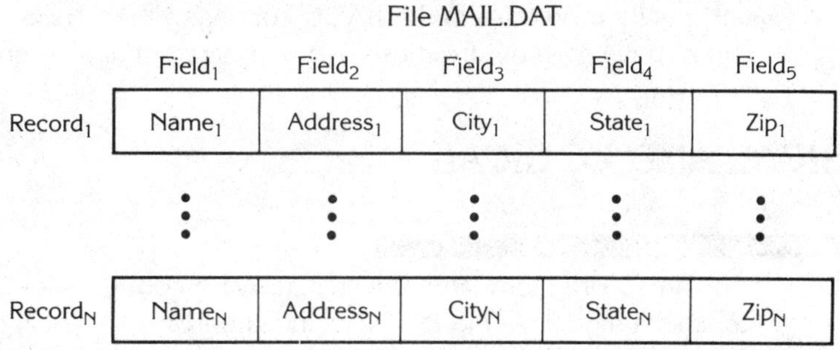

Fig. 10-1. Typical file structure.

program to generate mailing labels is illustrated. Note that if this is a sequential file, you must read record$_1$ through record$_{i-1}$ to access record$_1$. If this file were a random-access file, you could use a pointer to point directly to record$_i$ to read the information contained on that record directly.

The five fields represent one logical record. When data is actually stored on a disk, it is stored as a physical record. The amount of data stored on one such record will depend on the format you use to output data to the file.

I/O operations performed in BASIC require a file number. This is a unique number that will be associated with the actual file you wish to read data from or write data onto. The file number provides a physical path between subsequent file I/O statements and the file you wish to access. This path is established by the OPEN statement, which will be covered later in this chapter. The file number can be a number, variable, or expression. Its value must be equal to or greater than 1 and less than or equal to the maximum number of files permitted to be open at one time in the version of BASIC you are using. Cassette BASIC permits a maximum of four open files, while disk and advanced BASIC permit a maximum of three open files in the default mode. You can increase the maximum number of open files permitted in disk and advanced BASIC by invoking what is known as the F option in the BASIC command. The format of this optional parameter is:

```
/F:files
```

where 1=<files<=15.

When you bring up disk or advanced BASIC, you would use the F option at that time to specify the number of OPEN files your program requires that exceed three since, when omitted, the number of files the program can have OPEN at one time defaults to that value. If you require five files, your BASIC commands would be either of the following:

```
BASIC /F:5
BASICA /F:5
```

Since each sequential file requires 188 bytes of memory and random-access files require a minimum of 316 bytes, you should insure that you do not specify more files in the BASIC command than necessary. Otherwise, you will remove memory from use by the program that is reserved for files you are not using.

PHYSICAL AND LOGICAL DEVICES

In its originally announced hardware configuration, both the basic and enhanced models of the PC AT included only one physical diskette drive known as physical drive A. If you do not have a second diskette drive, BASIC permits you to refer to logical device B by using the device identifier B:. When you do so, upon executing the first statement in your program that references logical device B, DOS will issue the following prompt.

```
Insert diskette for drive B: and strike
any key when ready
```

Once you insert the appropriate diskette into physical drive A and strike any key on the keyboard, the program will perform its activity that referenced logical drive B on physical drive A.

If your PC AT is later expanded to two diskette drives, you will then have two physical drives. Thereafter, any reference in a program statement to logical device B will automatically cause DOS to perform the appropriate action on the diskette in physical drive B.

In this chapter we have included several examples that illustrate the use of drive B. From the preceding, it should be noted that the actions of these statements will occur on physical drive A unless your PC AT is expanded to two diskette drives.

SEQUENTIAL FILE STATEMENTS

OPEN Statement

The OPEN statement must be used prior to any I/O statements in a program because it establishes a path to the file that will be used by subsequent file reference statements. The format of this statement for sequential file operations is:

format: OPEN filespec[FOR $mode_1$]AS[#]filenum

where $mode_1$ is:

OUTPUT	to specify sequential output mode
INPUT	to specify sequential input mode

APPEND	to specify sequential output mode where output will be added to the end of the file; if the file does not exist, the file will be created and data will be treated as in the OUTPUT mode

The file number (filenum) must be less than or equal to 3 if you are in disk or advanced BASIC. If the /F option was in the BASIC command, the file number must be less than or equal to 15 and cannot exceed the number used in the /F option. When working with tree structured directories, you can include a path to the file in the file specification, since, if omitted, the current directory will be used. Some examples of the use of this statement and the operational result follow.

Statement	Operational result
100 OPEN "B:HISTORY.DAT" FOR OUTPUT AS #3	Permits output to the file named HISTORY with the extension DAT in the current directory on the diskette in drive B, using file number 3
200 OPEN "JAN.DAT" FOR INPUT AS #2	Permits input from the file named JAN with the extension DAT in the current directory on the diskette in the current drive using file number 2
300 OPEN "C:\SALES\DATA" FOR OUTPUT AS #1	Permits output to the file named DATA in the directory called SALES in drive C, using file number 1
400 OPEN "FEB.DAT" FOR APPEND AS #1	Permits the adding of data to the file named FEB with the extension DAT in the current directory on the current drive, using file number 1

Since you may wish to control the operational mode of data flow within your program, an alternate format of this statement is provided in BASIC. This format is:

format: OPEN $mode_2$,[#]filenum,filespec[LEN=reclen]

where $mode_2$ is a string expression whose first character indicates the I/O operation as follows:

O specifies sequential output mode
I specifies sequential input mode

If a record length (reclen) is not specified, BASIC will use a default record length of 128 bytes. TWo examples of this statement and their operational result follow.

Statement	Operational result
100 OPEN "1", #2, "B:JAN.DAT"	Permits input from the file named JAN with extension DAT on the diskette in drive B, using file number 2
200 OPEN "0", #1, "C:\SALES\DATA"	Permits output to the file named DATA in the directory called SALES on drive C, using file number 1

To see how you can use this second format of the OPEN statement to control data flow within a program consider the following program segment.

```
10 IF X<5 THEN A$="O" ELSE A$="I"
20 OPEN A$, #1, "JAN.DAT"
```

In the preceding example, when X is less than 5, the file JAN with the extension DAT will be opened for output. Note that this will destroy any existing data on the file if the file already exists. If X is not less than 5, the file will be opened for input. When you open a file for input, if the file does not exist, a "File not found" error will result.

When you process sequential files, you must execute an OPEN statement prior to using any of the following statements or the INPUT$ function: PRINT#, WRITE#, PRINT# USING, INPUT#, LINE INPUT#, and INPUT$.

CLOSE Statement

Once you have concluded your file operations, you may wish to terminate the path between your program and a particular file or files. You can use the CLOSE statement to conclude I/O to a device or file. The format of this statement is:

format: CLOSE[[#]filenum[,[#]filenum] . . .]

When used without specifying any file numbers, this statement will close all devices and files that were previously opened. If you specify one or more file numbers, only those specified will be closed. Examples of the use of this statement and the operational result follow.

Statement	Operational result
100 CLOSE	Causes all open devices and files to be closed
200 CLOSE #1,#3,#5	Causes the files and devices associated with file numbers 1, 3, and 5 to be closed
300 CLOSE #2,#4	Causes the files and devices associated with file numbers 2 and 4 to be closed

Once the CLOSE statement is executed, the association between a particular file or device and its file number will terminate. If the device or file was opened for sequential output, the contents of the information in the file buffer will be written to the file or device prior to the association terminating.

Since the execution of the END statement or the BASIC commands NEW, RESET, or SYSTEM will cause all open files and devices to be automatically closed, a logical question is why would you use this statement in place of the END statement or a command that performs the same function?

First, the CLOSE statement performs the function within a program. You can place it in your program to insure files are closed without having to worry about a program reaching an END statement or the operator keying in a BASIC command. Second, suppose you require access to a large number of files within your program. Since the default value of the number of files that can be opened at any one time in disk or advanced BASIC is three, what happens if you require access to four or more files? You could use the /F option in the disk or advanced BASIC command to permit up to 15 files to be open at any instant in time. Since each sequential file uses a buffer of 128 bytes, you may either run out of program memory as you open additional files or you could reach the maximum number of 15 files permitted to be open. In such situations, the CLOSE statement allows you to terminate the path between one or more file numbers and specified devices or files after you performed operations on each file. This allows you to reuse the file number to OPEN another device or file or you can reOPEN the previously CLOSEd device or file if you require access to it later in the program. Thus, the CLOSE statement permits you to conserve program memory and to access an almost infinite number of files from a program, although you can only have 15 such files opened at one time. The following program segment illustrates the use of the CLOSE statement.

```
LIST
100 OPEN "JAN.DAT" FOR INPUT AS #1
110 OPEN "FEB.DAT" FOR INPUT AS #2
120 OPEN "MAR.DAT" FOR INPUT AS #3
.
.
500 CLOSE #1, #2, #3
510 OPEN "APR.DAT" FOR INPUT AS #1
520 OPEN "MAY.DAT" FOR INPUT AS #2
530 OPEN "JUN.DAT" FOR INPUT AS #3
```

In the preceding example, due to memory limitations you may wish to only have three data files opened at any one time. Thus, after you close file numbers 1 through 3, you can reopen them to three new files and continue processing.

Now, let's examine the format and utilization of each of the statements and functions requiring the OPEN statement to write data onto and read data from files. Once this discussion is complete, you will then be able to create several programs that demonstrate sequential file processing.

PRINT# Statement

The PRINT# statement provides you with the capability to write data sequentially onto a file. The format of this statement is

format: PRINT#filenum,list of expressions

where filenum is the file number that was used when the file was opened for data output and list of expressions is a list of string and/or numeric expressions that will be written onto the file.

The PRINT# statement functions the same as a PRINT statement, with the exception that data is written to a file instead of being displayed on the screen. When you use the PRINT# statement to write data to a file you must be careful in your selection of delimiters used to separate each expression in the list of expressions contained in the statement. This is because different delimiters result in a different amount of blanks inserted between print fields. You can see this from the following example in which you will use the normal PRINT statement, since it will provide a screen display of the image of data written to a file using the PRINT# statement.

```
100 READ A,B,C
110 DATA 1,3,5
120 PRINT A,B,C
130 PRINT A;B;C
RUN
 1             3             5
 1 3 5
OK
```

In the preceding example, note that the commas used as delimiters between variables result in extra blanks being inserted between print fields. Since the same image of the data displayed on the screen with a PRINT statement is written to a file using a PRINT# statement, the blanks between print fields will be written to the file. Thus, the PRINT# statement does not compress data on the file.

To reduce the amount of required file space necessary to store data, you should use semicolons as delimiters when you have numeric expressions in your list. Since there is always at least one blank space between numeric expressions written to a file using semicolons as a separator, that space will serve to distinguish each numeric expression as a distinct entity when you input them from the file to the computer with an appropriate INPUT statement. Since the data written to sequential files is in sequential order, note that the following statements

```
100 PRINT #1,A
110 PRINT #1,B
120 PRINT #1,C
```

perform the same function as the statement

```
100 PRINT #1,A,B,C
```

Thus, in sequential file operations, you must be careful to insure that the program stores data in the same format that you will use for the retrieval of data.

When strings are written to a file, you may use semicolons to separate them from other string expressions in the list of expressions as well as to conserve file space when the data is written onto a file. Furthermore, you must insert the appropriate delimiter into the file; otherwise, two separate strings would be written to the file as one interconnected string. Thus, the following program segment

```
LIST
10 OPEN "MAILLIST.DAT" FOR OUTPUT AS #1
20 NAMEL$="HELD"
30 NAMEF$="GILBERT"
40 PRINT #1 NAMEL$;NAMEF$
```

would result in the interconnected string HELDGILBERT being written to the file. If you later attempt to read this record, you would have no way to read the data as two separate strings that represent a last and first name field. You can correct this situation by one of several methods that can be used to insert the appropriate delimiter into a file. The most obvious method to add the required delimiters is by inserting them into the PRINT# statement as indicated.

```
40 PRINT #1 NAMEL$;",";NAMEF$
```

The execution of this statement would cause the following data image to be written to the file:

```
HELD,GILBERT
```

This results in two distinct fields separated by a comma. The information in the record now can be read back into the PC AT as two distinct strings, each representing one field of information.

A second method that can be used to generate a required delimiter between strings is obtained by concatenation of each odd numbered string in a sequence of strings with a string representing a delimiter. This is illustrated below.

```
35 DELIMIT$=","
40 PRINT NAMEL$+DELIMIT$;NAMEF$
```

In line 40, the concatenation of the comma to the first string will result in the comma serving as a separator that will distinguish two separate strings for later input. Now that you can add the appropriate delimiter, a logical question is what do you do when one string naturally contains an imbedded comma? For example, suppose you wish to write the string ANAME$ to a file where

```
ANAME$="HELD,GILBERT"
```

Note that you cannot use NAME$, since it is a reserved word. The statement

```
PRINT #1,ANAME$
```

would write the following data image to the file:

```
HELD,GILBERT
```

When you attempt later to read the record from the file, your string variable used in an INPUT# statement will only read information from the record until the delimiter is reached. This will result in the string "HELD" being extracted from the record instead of both the last and first names as well as the comma used in the string. To write the string to the file so it will be read back as one string requires you to surround the string with double quotation marks. You can use the CHR$ function that converts an ASCII code to its character equivalent. Here, you would use the value 34 (see Appendix A), which would result in the one character string of a double quotation mark being written to the file each time a CHR$(34) function is encountered in the statement. Your previous statement would then be rewritten as follows:

```
PRINT #1 CHR$(34);ANAME$;CHR$(34)
```

The execution of this statement would cause the following data image to be written onto the file:

```
"HELD,GILBERT"
```

Since the information contained in a pair of double quotation signs is treated as one string, this will solve your problem of unintentionally reading only a portion of a string previously written to a file.

String processing can be a very valuable tool in storing information in an efficient manner. By concatenation of each field with a string variable containing a comma and then concatenating the result to the previous field, you can construct one string of variable length containing a last name, first name, middle initial, address, and so on, with each field separated from the next field by a comma. Once you read a string, you could develop a short subroutine that could easily break each part of the resulting stored string into its various components. Starting with a null string, you would then search the length of the retrieved string for a comma. Each character that is not a comma would be concatenated with the null string until a comma is encountered. Then, the appropriate string variable would be assigned the value of the concatenated string, that string would be set to a null value, and the search would resume for a second comma or the end of the string. By storing each data record on a file as one string, you can optimize your storage capacity.

When you mix both strings and numerics in a PRINT# statement, you must also insert appropriate delimiters into the PRINT# statement or you may obtain an error when you attempt to retrieve the stored data. To illustrate this point, consider the following example.

```
100 A$="GIL HELD"
110 YOB=1943
120 PRINT #1 A$;YOB
```

After executing these statements, the data would be stored sequentially as one string as indicated below.

```
GIL HELD 1943
```

If you later attempt to retrieve the stored information using the statement

```
INPUT #1,A$,YOB
```

the entire string "GIL HELD 1943" would be assigned to A$ and an "Input Past end" error would occur, since there would be no data on the file to assign to YOB. If you used a literal comma as a string delimiter in the PRINT# statement as follows

```
120 PRINT #1,A$;",";YOB
```

the data would have be written to the file as

```
GIL HELD, 1943
```

Then, the INPUT# statement would correctly assign GIL HELD to A$ and 1943 to YOB.

WRITE# Statement

Another mechanism that provides you with the capability to write data onto a sequential file is obtained by the use of the WRITE# statement. The format of this statement is indicated below.

format: WRITE# filenum,list of expressions

The format and the operational result of the WRITE# statement are similar to the PRINT# statement; however, several important differences result from the execution of these two statements. First, the WRITE# statement will automatically insert commas between items as they are written onto a sequential file as well as delimiting strings with quotation marks. Thus, whereas it is necessary to put explicit delimiters in the list of expressions when using the PRINT# statement, you can avoid this requirement by using the WRITE# statement. The PRINT# statement functions like all PRINT-related statements by placing a blank character in front of positive numbers as they are written to a file. This serves as an automatic separator between items written to a file, printed or placed on the screen using one of the appropriate PRINT statements. Since the WRITE# statement automatically inserts commas between items, no blank character is required in front of a positive number. After all items in the list of expressions are written, a carriage return/line feed sequence will be generated onto the file. The following use of the WRITE# statement

```
10 NAMEL$="HELD"
20 NAMEF$="GILBERT"
30 YOB=1943
40 WRITE #1 NAMEL$,NAMEF$,YOB
```

would write the following image to the file.

```
"HELD","GILBERT",1943
```

Now, consider the following example.

```
100 READ A,B,C,D$
110 DATA 1,3,5,IMAGE
120 WRITE #1 A,B,C,D$
```

The execution of this program segment preceded by the appropriate OPEN statement would write the following image to the file.

```
1,3,5,"IMAGE"
```

In developing programs in BASIC that use sequential files, you will normally prefer the WRITE# statement over the PRINT# statement. This is because it is easier to use the WRITE# statement to write data to a sequential file that a subsequent INPUT# statement can read.

PRINT# USING Statement

The PRINT# USING statement permits you to write to a file using a specified format. The PRINT# USING statement functions similarly to the PRINT USING and LPRINT USING statements, with the only difference among the three statements being that the PRINT USING statement displays strings or numbers on the screen and the LPRINT USING statement causes data to be printed in a specified format, while the PRINT# USING statement writes the data image specified by the format of the statement onto a file. The format of the PRINT# USING statement is indicated below:

format: PRINT#filenum,USING var$; list of expressions

The string variable following the keyword USING contains the formatting characters that define the field and format of strings or numbers that will be written onto the file. The use of these formatting characters was previously described in Chapter 9.

One of the primary uses of the PRINT# USING statement is to generate reports onto a diskette instead of a printer. If the system you are working on does not have a printer or perhaps does not have a letter quality printer, you can generate the report onto a file. A file "dump" program would then read the file and dump its image onto the printer, producing a hard copy of the report. Even if you have a printer, it is considerably faster to write data to a file than to a printer. Thus, you may wish to execute a program without tying up your printer for a long period of time. Several examples using this statement follow:

```
100 A=3.71
110 B=4.978
120 PRINT#1,USING "#.## #.####";A,B
```

result in the image

```
3.71 4.9780
```

being written onto the file opened with file number 1.

Changing line number 120 to

```
120 PRINT#1, USING ".## #.####";A,B
```

results in the print image

```
%3.71 4.9780
```

being written onto the file. The percent sign (%) in front of the first number indicates that the number to be printed is larger than the specified numeric field.

INPUT# Statement

The INPUT# statement provides you with the capability to read data items previously written to a sequential file. As data items are read, they will be assigned to program variables, permitting you to use those data items within your program. The format of this statement is:

format: INPUT# filenum, var[,var] . . .

The file number in the statement must be the number previously used when the file was opened for input. Unlike the conventional BASIC INPUT statement, no prompt message will be generated, nor will a question mark be printed when the INPUT# statement is executed.

When an INPUT# statement is executed, a type comparison is performed between the variable names in the statement and the type of data on the record to be read. If they do not match, a "Type mismatch" error will result. This is illustrated by the following example where it is assumed each record on the file contains three fields providing quantity-on-hand, cost, and an item description. The first two fields are numeric, while the third field is a string. Suppose our INPUT# statement used to read information from the file is as follows:

```
100 INPUT#1,QTY,COST,ITEM
```

Since the third variable was entered as a numeric type, a "Type mismatch" error would occur. You can correct this by modifying your statement changing ITEM to ITEM$. Thus,

```
100 INPUT#1,QTY,COST,ITEM$
```

would have three variable names that match the type of data in the file.

If you are reading numeric values from the file, all leading spaces, carriage return, and line feed characters will be ignored. The first character encountered that is not a space, carriage return, or line feed is assumed by BASIC to be the start of a number. Each number of the file is considered to be terminated when a space, carriage return, line feed, or comma is encountered. When a string variable is specified in the INPUT# statement, BASIC will scan the record for a string. Again, leading spaces, commas, carriage returns, and line feeds will be ignored. The first character encountered that is not a space, comma, carriage return, or line feed will be assumed to be the start of the string. When the first character of the string is a quotation mark ("), BASIC will assign all characters on the record between this quotation mark and a second quotation mark to the string variable in the INPUT# statement. This "quoted" string may not include a quotation mark within the string, since it would cause BASIC to misinterpret where the string ends.

When the first character in the string is not a quotation mark, the string is an "unquoted" string. Unquoted strings are terminated when a comma, carriage return, or line feed is encountered as data is read from a file record. For both "quoted" and "unquoted" strings, the maximum string length that can be read is 255 characters. The examples in Table 10-1 illustrate the resulting values of variables used in an INPUT# statement based on the indicated record information stored on the file.

The sequential file actually read by the INPUT# statement will depend on the file specification used in the OPEN statement that contains the matching file number used in the INPUT# statement. Although you will normally specify the diskette (A: or B:) or fixed disk (C: or D:) in the OPEN statement, you could specify the keyboard (KYBD:). Such a specification would result in the INPUT# statement reading data directly from the keyboard. Since the communications adapter is treated similarly to other devices, you can use the INPUT# statement to read a sequential data stream from that device.

Table 10-1. INPUT# Statement Variables

INPUT# STATEMENT	RECORD INFORMATION	VARIABLE ASSIGNMENTS
100 INPUT#,A,B	105.7 2089	A=105.7 B=2089
100 INPUT#A,B	105.7,2089	A=105.7 B=2089
100 INPUT#1,N$,X$,X	MACON,GA,25	N$="MACON" X$="GA" X=25
100 INPUT#1,N$,X	"MACON,GA",25	N$="MACON,GA" X=25
100 INPUT#1,N$,X	"MACON,GA" 25	N$="MACON,GA" X=25

INPUT$ Function

The INPUT$ function provides you with the capability to read a string of specified length from a file or from the keyboard. The format of this function is:

format: INPUT$(exprnm[,[#]filenum])

The numeric expression in the format defines the number of characters that will be returned when the function is invoked. The file number used in the function must be within the ranges previously discussed for disk file operations.

The following example illustrates the use of the INPUT$ function.

```
LIST
100 OPEN "KYBD:" FOR INPUT AS #1
110 X$=INPUT$(30,#1)
120 PRINT X$
RUN
LETS ENTER THIRTY CHARACTERS A
OK
```

When the INPUT$ function is executed, no characters will be displayed on the screen. If you wish to display the characters you entered, you should follow this function call by a PRINT statement as indicated in the previous example.

In line 110, 30 characters are read from the keyboard and assigned to the string variable X$. The PRINT statement in line 120 echoes the characters previously input to the screen. When the INPUT$ function requests data from the keyboard no prompt message nor a prompt question mark (?) is generated.

Therefore, it is good programming practice to prefix this statement with a PRINT statement that prompts the user for the required data.

The INPUT$ statement will read all characters up to the specified length of the string requested to include special control characters, with the exception of the Ctrl+Break, which will interrupt program execution. This ability to read strings regardless of their content makes this function valuable for reading ASCII codes that would otherwise be interpreted by the BASIC Editor as a request to perform a specific function. Thus, you could use this function to enter a backspace character from the keyboard into your program. When the INPUT$ function requests data from the keyboard, the function call will be automatically completed when the required number of characters are entered, alleviating the necessity of pressing the Enter key to terminate input. The following examples illustrate the use of this function and its operational result.

Function	**Operational result**
100 X$=INPUT$(50,#1)	Reads a string of 50 characters and assigns them to the string variable X$
100 Y$=INPUT$(30,#2)	Reads a string of 30 characters from file number 2 and assigns them to the string variable Y$

In the next example, you will use the INPUT$ function to read 1 character from the keyboard. This is similar to the INKEY$ variable, with the exception that program execution will be suspended while the INPUT$ function awaits a key to be pressed. In comparison, the INKEY$ variable will read the keyboard state at the time the variable is encountered. Thus:

```
100 OPEN "KYBD:" FOR INPUT AS #1
110 X$=INPUT$(1,#1)
120 IF X$="E" THEN END ELSE 500
.
500 REM program continues
```

is the equivalent of

```
100 X$=INKEY$
110 IF X$="E" THEN END
120 IF X$="" THEN 100 ELSE 500
.
500 REM program continues
```

LINE INPUT# Statement

The LINE INPUT# statement provides you with the capability to read an entire line of up to 254 characters from a file. The format of this statement is:

format: LINE INPUT#filenum, string

When used in sequential file processing, this statement causes all information to be read without regard to any delimiters except the carriage return/line feed sequence. The string read to include the carriage return/line feed sequence will be assigned as one entity to a string variable specified in the statement. The next execution of a LINE INPUT# statement will continue reading data from the file until the next carriage return/line feed sequence is encountered. This statement provides you with the ability to read programs stored in ASCII format. Since each LINE INPUT# statement reads an entire line of information stored on a file, this statement is very useful to input data from an ASCII file that you wish to transfer through the communications adapter to another computer.

The LINE INPUT# statement is useful if you previously created a file according to a particular format and now wish to examine its contents. Suppose you generated a report on a file using PRINT USING# statements. The following program segment would "dump" the formatted file to the printer.

```
100 OPEN "REPORT.DAT" FOR INPUT AS #1
110 LINE INPUT#1,X$
120 PRINT X$
130 GOTO 110
```

In the preceding example, what happens when you branch back to line 110 after you previously read the last record in the file? This will cause an "Input past end" error, which occurs when you attempt to read past the end-of-file mark. To avoid this error, you must use the EOF function to detect the occurrence of the end-of-file mark. When you detect the end-of-file mark, you will branch to a statement and avoid executing the input statement that would cause an "Input past end" error to occur. Let's examine the EOF function and then modify the file dump program to eliminate the "Input past end" error.

EOF Function

The EOF function provides you with the capability to test for an end-of-file condition. The format of this function is:

format: varnm = EOF(filenum)

The EOF function returns one of two values depending on whether or not the end-of-file mark has been reached on the specified file. A −1 (true) will be returned if the end-of-file mark is reached, while a 0 (zero) will be returned if the end-of-file mark has not been reached. Since attempting to read past the end-of-file will cause an error, you should prefix each file INPUT statement in a program with an end-of-file test. Thus, your file dump program should be modified as indicated below.

```
100 OPEN "REPORT.DAT" FOR INPUT AS #1
105 IF EOF(1) THEN 140
110 LINE INPUT#1,X$
```

```
120 PRINT X$
130 GOTO 105
140 CLOSE #1
```

There are two additional functions that can be used in sequential file operations—the LOC and LOF functions.

LOC Function

The LOC function returns the number of physical records that were read from or written onto a file since it was opened. The format of this function is:

format$_{D/A}$: varnm = LOC (filenum)

The number of physical records on a file is a function of the format you employ to record data on the file. In the following example, the numbers 1 to 512 were recorded first on the file named "JUNK.BAS", which resulted in 19 records of information, since a semicolon(;) was used after the variable 1 in line 105. In the next example, we removed the semicolon, which resulted in spaces being placed between the numbers. Here, the number of physical records required to record the same data increased to 27.

```
LIST
100 OPEN "B:JUNK.BAS" FOR OUTPUT AS #1
105 FOR I=1 TO 512:PRINT#1,I;:NEXT I
106 PRINT "RECORD#=";LOC(1)
140 CLOSE #1
Ok
RUN
RECORD#= 19
Ok
105 FOR I=1 TO 512:PRINT#1,I:NEXT I
RUN
RECORD#= 27
Ok
```

Since sequential files can be opened in only one mode at a time, you cannot easily update or delete information on such files. To change a piece of information previously written onto such a file requires you to read the file until you locate the information you wish to change or delete. Then, you must obtain the location of the record you wish to update or delete and close the file. After you reopen the file, you will read information from the old file onto a new file until you reach the point where you wish to update or delete a record. If you wish to update the record, you will INPUT the changes from the keyboard and skip the information on the old file, writing the new information and all remaining information from the old file onto the new file. If you wish to delete the record, you will simply transfer all information from the old file to the new file with the exception of the record you wish to delete. To accomplish this file manipulation, you must keep track of the physical records or the number of fields of the logical records you have processed until you reach the appropriate point where you wish to delete or modify information. Since working on a physical record basis requires you to know the number of bytes written to a file to form the record, it will be far easier to keep track of the number of fields of data you have processed. You will see how to do this when sequential file processing is discussed in the next section of this chapter.

LOF Function

The LOF function returns the length of the file in bytes. The format of this function is:

format$_{D/A}$: varnm = LOF(filenum)

You can use this function to determine the number of sectors on the diskette that a file occupies as shown by the following program segment.

```
LIST
100 OPEN "B:JUNK.BAS" FOR OUTPUT AS #1
105 FOR I=1 TO 512:PRINT#1,I:NEXT I
106 PRINT "RECORD#=";LOC(1)
107 X=LOF(1)
108 S=X/128
110 PRINT "FILE OCCUPIES ";S;" SECTORS"
140 CLOSE #1
Ok
RUN
RECORD#= 27
FILE OCCUPIES 27 SECTORS
Ok
```

SEQUENTIAL FILE PROCESSING

Now that file I/O statements and functions relevant to sequential files have been reviewed, let's use these statements and functions to construct a series of programs that use such files.

In each of the following examples, certain file-related processing steps will be used to create a sequential file and to access the data on that file. As a minimum, you should consider the following steps to insure correct sequential file processing.

1. Prior to writing data onto a file in output or append operations, insure that the file is open.
2. Write data onto a file using the PRINT#, WRITE#, or PRINT# USING statements. Remember that the PRINT# and PRINT# USING statements do not automatically write field delimiters onto the file.
3. If the file you are writing onto previously existed and was not opened in the APPEND mode, existing data on that file will be destroyed.
4. To access data on a file created by your program or opened by the program for output, you must close the file and reopen it for input.
5. Read data from sequential files using the INPUT# or LINE INPUT# statements.

6. To avoid an "Input past end" error when reading data from a file, use the EOF function to test for the end-of-file mark.

Suppose you wish to create a telephone directory and store the name and telephone number of your business associates and friends on a diskette. Let's first develop a program module that will input the appropriate information from the keyboard and write that information onto a diskette. Next, you will develop a retrieval module that will search the diskette file by name and retrieve the appropriate person's telephone number. Since you may wish to change information previously placed on the file, you will develop two additional program modules that will add information to the diskette or modify and delete information already on the diskette. You will also develop two program modules that will add new names and telephone numbers to your file and provide you with a hard-copy listing of the directory.

After each of these modules is examined, they will be combined into one program and a menu will be added to provide you with the capability of selecting any of the desired functions.

File Creation

The following program module creates a sequential file named "TELLIST" from information inputted from the keyboard.

```
LIST
100 OPEN "B:TELLIST.DAT" FOR OUTPUT AS #1
110 CLS
120 PRINT "TELEPHONE DIRECTORY CREATION - ENTER 0 TO EXIT"
130 INPUT "LAST NAME";N$
140 IF N$="0" THEN 190
150 INPUT "INITIAL(S)";I$
160 INPUT "TELEPHONE NUMBER";T$
170 WRITE#1,N$,I$,T$
180 GOTO 120
190 CLOSE#1
Ok
```

Note that the WRITE# statement was used in line 170 instead of a PRINT# statement, since the former automatically inserts commas between items. If the PRINT# statement was used, line 170 would be rewritten as

```
170 PRINT#1,N$;",";I$;",";T$
```

In addition, the WRITE# statement will automatically delimit strings with quotation marks, which is compatible to other non-IBM BASICs. Now, let's execute this program module and enter several names and telephone numbers as follows.

```
TELEPHONE DIRECTORY CREATION - ENTER 0 TO EXIT
LAST NAME? UNGER
INITIAL(S)? F.U.
TELEPHONE NUMBER? 444-4444
```

```
TELEPHONE DIRECTORY CREATION - ENTER 0 TO EXIT
LAST NAME? ROBERTSON
INITIAL(S)? X.Z.
TELEPHONE NUMBER? 111-1111
TELEPHONE DIRECTORY CREATION - ENTER 0 TO EXIT
LAST NAME? MAXWELL
INITIAL(S)? S
TELEPHONE NUMBER? 999-9999
TELEPHONE DIRECTORY CREATION - ENTER 0 TO EXIT
LAST NAME? HELD
INITIAL(S)? G.X.
TELEPHONE NUMBER? 000-0011
TELEPHONE DIRECTORY CREATION - ENTER 0 TO EXIT
LAST NAME? 0
OK
```

Now that the initial data has been entered on the file, let's develop a retrieval module. This module is listed below.

```
LIST
200 CLS
210 PRINT "TELEPHONE DIRECTORY RETRIEVAL"
220 OPEN "B:TELLIST.DAT" FOR INPUT AS #1
230 INPUT "ENTER LAST NAME";NAMEL$
240 IF EOF(1) THEN 340
250 INPUT#1,N$,I$,T$
260 IF NAMEL$<>N$ THEN 240
270 PRINT N$,I$,T$
280 PRINT "ANOTHER SEARCH Y/N"
290 A$=INKEY$
300 IF A$="N" THEN 360
310 IF A$<>"Y" THEN 290
320 CLOSE#1 :CLEAR
330 GOTO 220
340 PRINT "NAME NOT ON DIRECTORY"
350 GOTO 280
360 CLOSE#1
OK
```

In the telephone directory retrieval example, note that the end-of-file mark is tested for in line 240. If you encounter the end of the file, then the name you are searching for is not on the directory, and you will branch to line 340 and print the appropriate message on the display.

If you have successfully found the telephone number on the directory, the program module will let you specify if you wish another search. Since data stored on sequential files is placed in the order it was written to the file, you must reposition your pointer back to the beginning of the file unless you created the file in alphabetical order and search for names in alphabetical order. Since this was not done, you must first CLOSE the file and then reOPEN it to reread the file from the beginning. This mechanism is equivalent to a RESTORE# statement that is available on some BASICs but is unfortunately missing from IBM BASIC. The execution of this program module for the retrieval of the telephone numbers of several persons follows.

```
TELEPHONE DIRECTORY RETRIEVAL
ENTER LAST NAME? ROBERTSON
ROBERTSON      X.Z.          111-1111
```

```
ANOTHER SEARCH Y/N
ENTER LAST NAME? HOPKINS
NAME NOT ON DIRECTORY
ANOTHER SEARCH Y/N
ENTER LAST NAME? HELD
HELD           G.X.           000-0011
ANOTHER SEARCH Y/N
OK
```

Suppose you wish to add new information to the directory. To add information to a previously created sequential file requires you to open the file in the APPEND mode. This program module is listed below.

```
400 CLS
410 PRINT "DIRECTORY ADDITION"
420 OPEN "B:TELLIST.DAT" FOR APPEND AS #1
430 INPUT "LAST NAME";N$
440 INPUT "INITIAL(S)";I$
450 INPUT "TELEPHONE NUMBER";T$
460 WRITE #1,N$,I$,T$
470 PRINT "ENTER C TO CONTINUE E TO EXIT"
480 A$=INKEY$
490 IF A$="C" THEN 430
500 IF A$="E" THEN 510 ELSE 480
510 CLOSE#1
```

Now, let's add several names to the telephone directory. The execution of the previous program segment and the addition of three persons to the directory is shown below.

```
DIRECTORY ADDITION
LAST NAME? HERMAN
INITIAL(S)? Q.B.
TELEPHONE NUMBER? WEG-1212
ENTER C TO CONTINUE E TO EXIT
LAST NAME? ZORBA
INITIAL(S)? G.
TELEPHONE NUMBER? 555-5555
ENTER C TO CONTINUE E TO EXIT
LAST NAME? XRAY
INITIAL(S)? A.U.
TELEPHONE NUMBER? 765-4321
ENTER C TO CONTINUE E TO EXIT
OK
```

Now, let's examine how you can modify or delete information previously entered onto a sequential file. Since such files can only be opened for one mode of operation, you must first access the information you wish to modify or delete and obtain its position in the file. After obtaining the new information, if you wish to modify previously entered data you must then CLOSE the file and again read the information one field at a time, transferring the information to a new file until you reach the position where the information changed. At that point, you will WRITE the modified field or fields of information from memory onto the new file, skip the old field or fields of information, and continue writing the remaining fields from the old file onto the new file until you reach the end of the file. At this point, you will erase the old file and rename the new file, using the old file name. If you wish to delete one or more fields of information, you would follow the same procedure; however, you would skip the fields you wish to delete instead of writing those fields from memory onto the file when you modify a sequential file. This program module follows.

```
600 CLS
610 OPEN "B:TELLIST.DAT" FOR INPUT AS #1
620 OPEN "B:TEMP.DAT" FOR OUTPUT AS #2
630 PRINT "MODIFY/DELETE SECTION"
640 INPUT "ENTER LAST NAME ",LNAME$
650 FCOUNT=0
660 IF EOF(1) THEN 760
670 INPUT#1,N$,I$,T$
680 FCOUNT=FCOUNT+1       'physical record position
690 IF N$<>LNAME$ THEN 660
700 PRINT "FOR:";LNAME$;",";I$;" TELEPHONE# IS: ";T$
710 INPUT "DO YOU WISH TO (M)ODIFY OR (D)ELETE INFORMATION ";A$
720 IF A$<>"M" AND A$<>"D" THEN 710
730 IF A$="D" THEN 820
740 INPUT "ENTER NEW TELEPHONE# ";TEL$
750 GOTO 820
760 PRINT "NAME NOT ON DIRECTORY"
770 CLOSE
780 INPUT "(A)NOTHER TRY OR (E)XIT ";B$
790 IF B$<>"A" AND B$<>"E" THEN 780
800 IF B$="A" THEN 610
810 IF B$="E" THEN 990
820 CLOSE#1
830 OPEN "B:TELLIST.DAT" FOR INPUT AS #1
840 FOR I=1 TO FCOUNT-1     'read up to prior physical record to be changed
850 INPUT#1,N$,I$,T$
860 WRITE#2,N$,I$,T$
870 NEXT I
880 INPUT#1,N$,I$,T$         'read the record to be modified/deleted
890 IF A$="D" THEN 910       'if delete do not write on file
900 WRITE#2,LNAME$,I$,TEL$ 'if to be modified put new information on file
910 IF EOF(1) THEN 950        'get
920 INPUT#1,N$,I$,T$          'remainder
930 WRITE#2,N$,I$,T$          'of
940 GOTO 910                  'file
950 CLOSE
960 KILL "B:TELLIST.DAT"
970 NAME "B:TEMP.DAT" AS "B:TELLIST.DAT
980 GOTO 780
990 CLOSE
```

The execution of this program segment showing the results of asking for a name not on the directory is illustrated in the following.

```
MODIFY/DELETE SECTION
ENTER LAST NAME HOPKINS
NAME NOT ON DIRECTORY
(A)NOTHER TRY OR (E)XIT ? A
MODIFY/DELETE SECTION
ENTER LAST NAME ROBERTSON
FOR:ROBERTSON,X.Z. TELEPHONE# IS: 111-1111
DO YOU WISH TO (M)ODIFY OR (D)ELETE INFORMATION ? M
ENTER NEW TELEPHONE# ? 000-0000
(A)NOTHER TRY OR (E)XIT ? A
MODIFY/DELETE SECTION
ENTER LAST NAME ROBERTSON
```

```
FOR:ROBERTSON,X.Z. TELEPHONE# IS: 000-0000
DO YOU WISH TO (M)ODIFY OR (D)ELETE INFORMATION ? D
(A)NOTHER TRY OR (E)XIT ? A
MODIFY/DELETE SECTION
ENTER LAST NAME ROBERTSON
NAME NOT ON DIRECTORY
(A)NOTHER TRY OR (E)XIT ? E
```

Changing a telephone number and deleting a person from the directory is illustrated in this short sample. To improve operational efficiency, if you change or delete many pieces of information at one time, you should first place all change and deletion requests into arrays in memory. Then, you could sort the requests and perform all disk I/O operations at one time.

Now, you can combine each of the preceding modules into one program and add an appropriate menu to permit the operator to select the specific function he or she wishes to perform.

If you forgot to save each of the program segments using the A option, you can reload each segment and save it with that option. This will allow you to merge all of the segments together to facilitate constructing one program from the previous modules. The completed program listing follows.

```
5 CLS
10 PRINT "WELCOME TO THE TELEPHONE DIRECTORY PROGRAM"
20 PRINT "YOU MAY ACCESS THE FOLLOWING FUNCTIONS BY"
30 PRINT "ENTERING THE APPROPRIATE NUMBER WHEN ASKED"
40 PRINT "    ENTER 1 TO CREATE INITIAL DIRECTORY"
50 PRINT "    ENTER 2 TO RETRIEVE INFORMATION"
60 PRINT "    ENTER 3 TO ADD NEW NAMES TO DIRECTORY"
70 PRINT "    ENTER 4 TO MODIFY/DELETE ENTRIES ON DIRECTORY"
75 PRINT "    ENTER 5 TO EXIT THIS PROGRAM"
80 INPUT " ******* ENTER YOUR CHOICE ****** ",C
90 ON C GOTO 100,200,400,600,1010
92 PRINT " COME ON, READ THE DIRECTIONS- ENTER 1,2,3 OR 4"
94 GOTO 80
100 OPEN "B:TELLIST.DAT" FOR OUTPUT AS #1
110 CLS
120 PRINT "TELEPHONE DIRECTORY CREATION - ENTER 0 TO EXIT"
130 INPUT "LAST NAME";N$
140 IF N$="0" THEN 190
150 INPUT "INITIAL(S)";I$
160 INPUT "TELEPHONE NUMBER";T$
170 WRITE#1,N$,I$,T$
180 GOTO 120
190 CLOSE#1
195 GOTO 5
200 CLS
210 PRINT "TELEPHONE DIRECTORY RETRIEVAL"
220 OPEN "B:TELLIST.DAT" FOR INPUT AS #1
230 INPUT "ENTER LAST NAME";NAMEL$
240 IF EOF(1) THEN 340
250 INPUT#1,N$,I$,T$
260 IF NAMEL$<>N$ THEN 240
270 PRINT N$,I$,T$
280 PRINT "ANOTHER SEARCH Y/N"
290 A$=INKEY$
300 IF A$="N" THEN 360
```

```
310 IF A$<>"Y" THEN 290
320 CLOSE#1 :CLEAR
330 GOTO 220
340 PRINT "NAME NOT ON DIRECTORY"
350 GOTO 280
360 CLOSE#1
370 GOTO 5
400 CLS
410 PRINT "DIRECTORY ADDITION"
420 OPEN "B:TELLIST.DAT" FOR APPEND AS #1
430 INPUT "LAST NAME";N$
440 INPUT "INITIAL(S)";I$
450 INPUT "TELEPHONE NUMBER";T$
460 WRITE #1,N$,I$,T$
470 PRINT "ENTER C TO CONTINUE E TO EXIT"
480 A$=INKEY$
490 IF A$="C" THEN 430
500 IF A$="E" THEN 510 ELSE 480
510 CLOSE#1
520 GOTO 5
600 CLS
610 OPEN "B:TELLIST.DAT" FOR INPUT AS #1
620 OPEN "B:TEMP.DAT" FOR OUTPUT AS #2
630 PRINT "MODIFY/DELETE SECTION"
640 INPUT "ENTER LAST NAME ",LNAME$
650 FCOUNT=0
660 IF EOF(1) THEN 760
670 INPUT#1,N$,I$,T$
680 FCOUNT=FCOUNT+1       'physical record position
690 IF N$<>LNAME$ THEN 660
700 PRINT "FOR:";LNAME$;",";I$;" TELEPHONE# IS: ";T$
710 INPUT "DO YOU WISH TO (M)ODIFY OR (D)ELETE INFORMATION ";A$
720 IF A$<>"M" AND A$<>"D" THEN 710
730 IF A$="D" THEN 820
740 INPUT "ENTER NEW TELEPHONE# ";TEL$
750 GOTO 820
760 PRINT "NAME NOT ON DIRECTORY"
770 CLOSE
780 INPUT "(A)NOTHER TRY OR (E)XIT ";B$
790 IF B$<>"A" AND B$<>"E" THEN 780
800 IF B$="A" THEN 610
810 IF B$="E" THEN 990
820 CLOSE#1
830 OPEN "B:TELLIST.DAT" FOR INPUT AS #1
840 FOR I=1 TO FCOUNT-1    'read up to prior physical record to be changed
850 INPUT#1,N$,I$,T$
860 WRITE#2,N$,I$,T$
870 NEXT I
880 INPUT#1,N$,I$,T$       'read the record to be modified/deleted
890 IF A$="D" THEN 910     'if delete do not write on file
900 WRITE#2,LNAME$,I$,TEL$ 'if to be modified put new information on file
910 IF EOF(1) THEN 950     'get
920 INPUT#1,N$,I$,T$       'remainder
930 WRITE#2,N$,I$,T$       'of
940 GOTO 910               'file
950 CLOSE
960 KILL "B:TELLIST.DAT"
970 NAME "B:TEMP.DAT" AS "B:TELLIST.DAT"
980 GOTO 780
990 CLOSE
1000 GOTO 5
1010 END
```

The initial menu displayed on program execution is shown below.

```
WELCOME TO THE TELEPHONE DIRECTORY PROGRAM
YOU MAY ACCESS THE FOLLOWING FUNCTIONS BY
ENTERING THE APPROPRIATE NUMBER WHEN ASKED
   ENTER 1 TO CREATE INITIAL DIRECTORY
   ENTER 2 TO RETRIEVE INFORMATION
   ENTER 3 TO ADD NEW NAMES TO DIRECTORY
   ENTER 4 TO MODIFY/DELETE ENTRIES ON DIRECTORY
   ENTER 5 TO EXIT THIS PROGRAM
 ******* ENTER YOUR CHOICE ******
```

While the program can be made more efficient by sorting entries in alphabetical order and storing change and modification information in memory until all entries are completed prior to changing the directory file, this program should provide you with a mechanism to implement a practical and useful program to operate on your PC AT.

RANDOM FILE OVERVIEW

In comparison to sequential file processing, the use of random files offers several distinct advantages. Due to the nature of random files, data can be accessed randomly from any location on the file without having to read all prior information as required with sequential files. This random accessibility is due to data being stored on the diskette in distinct units of information called records. Here, a logical record is the exact same size as a physical record and each record in the file holds the same amount of information. This information content is defined in terms of characters when the file is created and the amount of information that can be stored in one record is referred to as the record length.

Each record in a random file is identified by a unique number that specifies its absolute location in the file. Thus, if you know the record number, you can immediately locate the record on the file. The smallest random file will consist of one record. Such files will automatically expand as records are added; however, they will not shrink. Thus, to remove unwanted records from random files and shrink the size of the file will require you to copy the records that are to be preserved onto a new random file.

A second major advantage of random files is the ability to perform both input and output on the same random file. This allows you to easily update data on the file without having to resort to multiple file operations as explained in the review of sequential file processing.

A third advantage of random files is one of storage space. Sequential files are stored as ASCII characters, whereas random files are stored in packed binary format. In most cases, the packed binary format will require less file space than an equivalent sequential file.

Similar to sequential file processing, there is a series of steps you must consider to perform operations on random files. These program steps are listed here.

1. Open the file for random access prior to performing any file reference operations.
2. Use the FIELD statement to allocate space in the random buffer for all variables that will be written onto or read from a random file.
3. Prior to writing to the random file the LSET or RSET statements must be used to first place the data to be written to the file into the random buffer. Since the random buffer can only contain string variables, the MKI$, MKS$ and MKD$ functions should be used to convert any integer, single-precision, or double-precision variable to a string if you wish to write data onto the file.
4. To record data on the random file, you must use the PUT statement to move data from the random buffer onto the random file.
5. If you wish to access data on the random file, you must use the GET statement to first move the desired record from the random file into the random buffer. Since the buffer only operates on strings, numeric values must be converted back to their appropriate numeric type by using the CVI, CVS, or CVD functions.

RANDOM FILE STATEMENTS AND FUNCTIONS

Prior to examining random file processing, the statements and functions associated with such files will be reviewed. The statements covered in this section include OPEN, CLOSE, FIELD, GET, LSET, RESET, and PUT. The functions are CVD, CVI, CVS, LOC, LOF, MKD$, MKI$, and MKS$.

OPEN Statement

Similar to sequential file processing, you must also open all random access files prior to their first reference within a program. Since each record in a random file holds the same amount of information, and the record number is used as the pointer to access records randomly, you must specify the record length in the OPEN statement. When working with tree structured directories, you can include a path in the file specification, since, if omitted, the current directory is assumed for use. The format of this statement is:

format$_{D/A}$: OPEN filespec AS[#]filenum[LEN=reclen]

Since both output onto and input from a random file can occur on the same file, the mode specifier used in sequential file operations can be omitted. The record length (reclen) is an integer expression that sets the record length of the random file. Its value can range from 1 to 32767, and, if not specified, a default value of 128 bytes will be used. The following examples illustrate the operational result of several versions of this statement.

Statement	Operational result
100 OPEN"JAN.DAT"AS#1 LEN=32	Opens the file JAN.DAT in the default directory on the diskette in the default drive as a random file with a record length of 32
200 OPEN"B:JAN.DAT"AS#1	Opens the file JAN.DAT on the diskette in drive B as a random file; the record length is the default value of 128
300 OPEN"C:\SALES\DATA"AS#1 LEN=40	Opens the file named DATA in the SALES directory on drive C as a random file with a record length of 40

CLOSE Statement

The CLOSE statement in random file processing has the same format and utilization as in sequential file processing. The execution of such a statement cause I/O to a random file to conclude.

FIELD Statement

The FIELD statement must be used in random file processing to allocate space in the random buffer for all variables that will be written onto or read from a random file. Thus, it must follow an OPEN statement but precede a GET or PUT statement. The format of this statement is:

format$_{D/A}$: FIELD[#]filenum,width AS var$[,width AS var$] . . .

where filenum is the file number under which the file was previously opened; width is a numeric expression that specifies the number of character positions that will be allocated to the string variable (var$); and var$ is a string variable that will be used for random file access.

The following examples illustrate the operational result of several versions of this statement that could be used in a BASIC program.

Statement	Operational result
100 FIELD#1,10 AS N$,20 AS Y$	Allocates the first 10 positions (bytes) in the random file buffer for file number 1 to the string variable N$ and the next 20 positions to Y$

Statement	Operational result
200 FIELD#2,15 AS TAX$, 15 AS PAY$	Allocates the first 15 positions (bytes) in the random file buffer for file number 2 to the string variable TAX$ and the next 15 positions to PAY$

The FIELD statement allocates space but does not actually place any data into the random file buffer. The actual placement of data into the buffer results from the execution of an LSET or RSET statement.

You can execute any number of FIELD statements with the same file number and each such statement will serve to redefine the buffer from the first character position. This capability will allow you to manipulate the extraction of data stored on a random file or to be written onto a random file. You can see one effect of this technique of containing multiple FIELD statements in a program by examining Fig. 10-2. Here, the first FIELD statement defines a name and address field consisting of 30 bytes per record. The second FIELD statement redefines the buffer. Here, the previous name field of 10 bytes is broken into three fields consisting of a last name (LNAME$) and two initial fields (IN1$ and IN2$). Once you use a variable name in a field statement, you should normally exclude that name from later use in an INPUT or LET statement with that variable name on the left side of the equality sign. This is because defining a variable name in a FIELD statement makes it point to the correct place in a random file and the use of that variable in another BASIC statement could remove it from functioning as a field specifier.

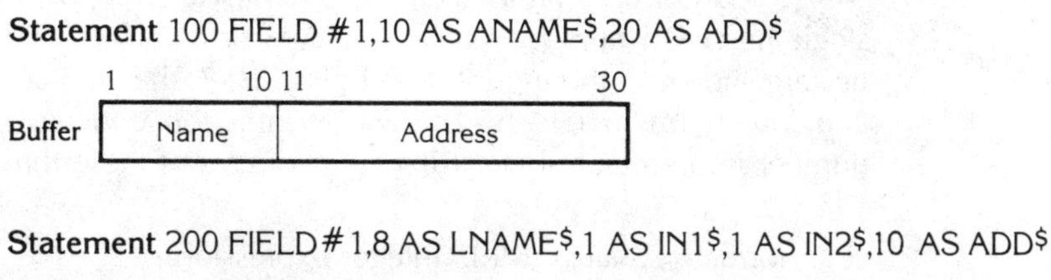

Fig. 10-2. Redefining the random buffer.

LSET and RSET Statements

These two statements provide you with the capability to move data from the PC AT's memory into a random file buffer prior to executing a PUT statement. The formats of these statements are:

format$_{D/A}$: LSET var$ = var$$_1$
format$_{D/A}$: RSET var$ = var$$_1$

Here, LSET left justifies the specified string variable $\text{var\$}_1$, while RSET performs a right justification function. The string variable, var$, on the left-hand side of the equality sign must be previously defined in a FIELD statement. If $\text{var\$}_1$ requires fewer bytes than were specified for the string variable, var$, then spaces will be added to pad the extra positions. If $\text{var\$}_1$ contains more bytes than were specified for the string variable, var$, then the extra characters are dropped from the right of $\text{var\$}_1$. Note that both LSET and RSET only operate on strings. Thus, if you wish to place numeric value into the random buffer, you must first convert those values to strings. You can perform this operation on numeric data through the use of the "make" functions, MKI$, MKS$, and MKD$ that convert numeric type values to string type values. The use of the MKI and MK$ functions is illustrated in Fig. 10-3.

```
100 FIELD #1,5 AS JCODE$,7 AS VALUE$
110 X$=MKI$(10412)
120 LSET JCODE$=X$
130 Y$=MKS$(137.52)
140 LSET VALUE$=X$
```

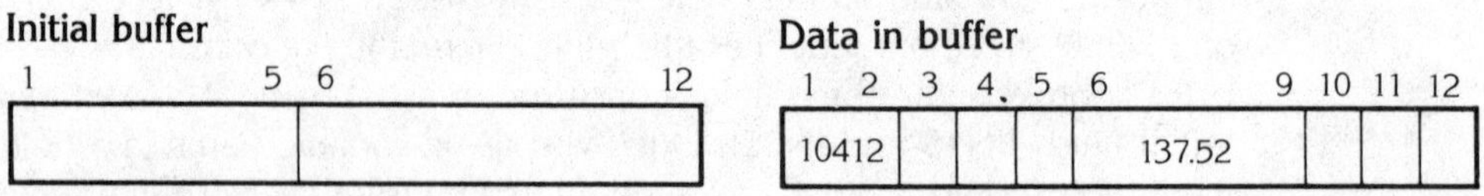

Fig. 10-3. Operational result of LSET statement.

Make String Functions

MKI$ converts an integer into a two-byte string, while MKS$ converts a single-precision number into a four-byte string. Thus, although numeric values are shown in the input buffer in Fig. 10-3, they are actually strings of two and four bytes in length. The MKD$ function converts a double-precision number into an eight-byte string. The formats of these three functions are:

format$_{D/A}$: var$ = MKI$(integer expression)
format$_{D/A}$: var$ = MKS$(single precision expression)
format$_{D/A}$: var$ = MKD$(double precision expression)

PUT Statement

The PUT statement provides you with the capability to write a record previously entered into the random buffer onto a random file. Thus, you must first use the OPEN and FIELD statements and one or more LSET or RSET statements prior to using this statement in a program. The format of this statement is:

format$_{D/A}$: PUT[#]filenum[,recnum]

where filenum is the file number under which the file was OPENed and recnum is the record number of the record to be written onto the file from the random buffer.

The record number specifies the position in the file where the contents of the random buffer will be written to and must be in the range 1 to 16 million. If the record number is omitted, the random buffer contents will be written onto the file using the next available record number after the last PUT statement.

The following program segment illustrates the use of the PUT statement. Note that you must first open the file, define the fields of the random buffer prior to using the PUT statement. Also note that the record specifier, CARDNO% in this example, must be an integer in the range 1 to 16 million.

```
100 OPEN "B:XRAY.DAT" AS #1 LEN=60
110 FIELD #1,30 AS X$,10 AS Y$,10 AS Z$,10 AS BOOM$
.
.
500 LSET X$=ADDRESS$
510 LSET Y$=MKI$(ZIP)
520 LSET Z$=MKS$(BALANCE)
530 LSET BOOM$=MKS$(CLIMIT)
.
.
750 PUT #1,CARDNO%
```

GET Statement

The GET statement is the complement of the PUT statement because its execution causes a record to be read from a random file into a random buffer. Prior to using this statement in a program, you must OPEN the file and use a FIELD statement to define the fields in the random buffer. The format of this statement is:

format$_{D/A}$: GET[#]filenum[,recnum]

where filenum is the file number under which the file was opened and recnum is the record number of the random file to be read into the random buffer. The record number range must be 1 to 16 million.

If the record number is omitted from the statement, the next record after the previous GET statement will be read into the buffer. The following program segment illustrates the use of this statement.

```
100 OPEN "B:XRAY.DAT" AS #1 LEN=60
110 FIELD #1,20 AS PARTNAME$,10 AS QTY$
120 INPUT "ENTER PART NUMBER ";PART%
130 GET #1,PART%
140 QTY=CVI(QTY$)SS$
150 PRINT "PART ";PARTNAME$;" QUANTITY ON HAND= ";QTY
160 TOTAL=TOTAL+QTY
```

The preceding example illustrates how you can use a part number to randomly access a record containing a part name consisting of 20 characters and a quantity on hand containing 10 characters from a random file. Note that the part number (PART%) is assigned as an integer, since it is used to specify the record number on the file where you wish to retrieve information from. Also note that, although the FIELD statement specifies each field as a string, you wish to use the quantity on hand (QTY$) as a numeric value.

Convert to Numeric Functions

Since you must convert string variable types to numeric variable types to perform numeric operations, the CVI function was used in line 140 of the program segment. This function is one of three "conversion to numeric" functions available in BASIC and results in the conversion of a two-byte string to an integer. The formats of these three functions are:

format$_{D/A}$: varnm=CVI(2-byte string)
format$_{D/A}$: varnm=CVS(4-byte string)
format$_{D/A}$: varnm=CVD(8-byte string)

LOC Function

When used with random files, the LOC function returns the record number of the last record that was read from or written onto a random file. You can use this function to obtain the current record number or you can use the function in a statement for testing purposes. Thus,

```
100 X=LOC(1)
```

returns the record number of the last record read or written onto a random file and assigns that number to the variable X. The statements

```
100 IF LOC(1)=20 THEN 120
110 PUT #2,LOC(1)
120 REM continue processing
```

could be used to skip record 20 when placing data of file number 2.

LOF Function

The LOF function is the same for both sequential and random file processing. That is, it returns the number of bytes allocated to the file.

RANDOM FILE PROCESSING

In this section, an "on-line charge authorization" program to illustrate random file processing techniques will be developed.

Suppose the credit department of a store wishes to develop an automated system that will access a customer's account number as sales are made in different departments of the store. This system will consist of a program that will verify that the customer has not exceeded his or her credit limit. For simplicity, assume that each customer record has the following format:

account number	credit limit	charges to date

Suppose account numbers vary from 40001 to 40100. Since using these account numbers as record numbers would waste a great amount of file space, you can transpose them into a range of record numbers more acceptable for random file processing. This transformation can be accomplished by subtracting 40000 from each account number. By doing so, you will use the record number as a transformed account number and for data storage purposes your record format then becomes:

credit limit	charges to date

Let's examine the BASIC statements necessary to perform the various processing functions you might require—such as file initialization, credit authorization, credit limit change, and generating a status report.

Your main menu segment might then be constructed as follows. Note that your option choice is assigned to the variable labeled AOPTION as OPTION is a reserved word.

```
100 OPEN "B:CREDIT.DAT" AS #1 LEN=20
110 FIELD #1,10 AS CL$,10 AS C$
120 PRINT "CREDIT AUTHORIZATION OPTIONS"
130 PRINT "  1  FILE INITIALIZATION"
140 PRINT "  2  CREDIT AUTHORIZATION"
150 PRINT "  3  CREDIT LIMIT CHANGE"
160 PRINT "  4  STATUS REPORT"
170 PRINT "  5  EXIT PROGRAM"
180 INPUT "***ENTER OPTION DESIRED*** ",AOPTION
190 IF AOPTION >=1 OR AOPTION <=5 THEN 220
200 PRINT "OPTION NUMBER INVALID"
210 GOTO 180
220 ON AOPTION GOSUB 300,500,700,900,1010
230 GOTO 120
```

Again for simplicity, assume each individual account number has the same initial limit. Since the charge balance will be zero, your program module will initialize the credit limit field of each record to a constant and the charges to date field to zero. The following statements perform this function.

```
230 GOTO 120
300 INPUT "IS THIS THE END OF THE MONTH -Y/N ";A$
310 IF A$ <>"Y" THEN RETURN
320 INPUT "ENTER CREDIT LIMIT ASSIGNMENT ",CREDIT
330 CREDIT$=MKS$(CREDIT)
340 LSET CL$=CREDIT$
350 CHARGE=0!
```

```
360 CHARGE$=MKS$(CHARGE)
370 LSET C$=CHARGE$
380 FOR RECN%=1 TO 100
390 PUT#1,RECN%
400 NEXT RECN%
410 RETURN
```

In the preceding program segment, note that you must convert numeric values to string values prior to placing such entries in the random buffer. This was accomplished by using the MKS$ function. You could also combine several pairs of statements. As an example, lines 330 and 340 could be replaced by the statement LSET CL$ = MKS$(CREDIT).

For the file authorization segment, you will first accept the account number and pending charge from the keyboard. Then, you will transpose the charge number into a valid record number and retrieve the credit limit and charges-to-date for that account. If the pending charge plus the charges-to-date do not exceed the credit limit, you will authorize the charge and update the charges-to-date field. Otherwise, the pending charge will not be approved and the charges-to-date field will not be modified. The statements required to perform these functions follow.

```
500 INPUT "ACCOUNT NUMBER ";ACCT
510 IF ACCT>=40001! AND ACCT<=40100! THEN 540
520 PRINT "INVALID ACCOUNT NUMBER"
530 RETURN
540 INPUT "AMOUNT OF PENDING CHARGE ";AMT
550 RECN%=INT(ACCT-40000!)
560 GET#1,RECN%
570 CL=CVS(CL$)    'convert to numeric
580 C=CVS(C$)      'ditto
590 NAMT=AMT+C
600 IF NAMT<=CL THEN 625
605 PRINT "*********************"
610 PRINT "CHARGE NOT AUTHORIZED"
615 PRINT "*********************"
620 RETURN
625 PRINT "*********************"
630 PRINT "CHARGE IS AUTHORIZED"
635 PRINT "*********************
640 LSET C$=MKS$(NAMT)    'update
650 PUT#1,RECN%           'charge-to-date
660 RETURN
```

Now, let's examine the program segment necessary to change the credit limit. Here, you will once again first accept the account number and transform it into an acceptable record number. Then you will retrieve the current credit limit and ask the operator to enter its new value. Then, you will update the record, changing the value of the credit limit. The following statements perform this function.

```
700 INPUT "ENTER ACCOUNT NUMBER ";ACCT
710 IF ACCT>=40001! AND ACCT<=40100! THEN 740
720 PRINT "INVALID ACCOUNT NUMBER"
730 RETURN
740 RECN%=INT(ACCT-40000!)
```

```
750 GET#1,RECN%
760 CL=CVS(CL$)
770 PRINT "FOR ACCOUNT# ";ACCT;" CREDIT LIMIT IS ";CL
780 INPUT "ENTER NEW CREDIT LIMIT ";CL
790 CL$=MKS$(CL)
800 PUT#1,RECN%
810 RETURN
```

Although you have a random file, you will process the file sequentially as you generate a status report that will list each account number, credit limit, and charges-to-date as well as print summary statistics. The next program segment shows the statements necessary to perform this function.

```
900 CSUM=0 :CTD=0
910 LPRINT "ACCOUNT #    CREDIT LIMIT   MONTHLY CHARGES TO DATE"
920 FOR RECN%=1 TO 100
930 GET#1,RECN%
940 CSUM=CSUM+CVS(CL$)
950 CTD=CTD+CVS(C$)
960 ACCT=40000!+RECN%
970 LPRINT USING"#######    ########,.##    ########,.##";ACCT,CVS(CL$),CVS(C$)
980 NEXT RECN%
990 LPRINT USING"TOTALS    #########,.## ##########,.##";CSUM,CTD
1000 RETURN
```

To provide a mechanism for an orderly exit from the program, you can include both a CLOSE and an END statement in line 1010 as follows:

```
1010 CLOSE:END
```

Thus, when the operator desires to exit from the program, the file will be closed automatically.

Now, let's run the program just created and use one or more program options in each program execution. First let's initialize the credit limit of all accounts to $500.00 The execution of the appropriate program option is shown below.

```
RUN
CREDIT AUTHORIZATION OPTIONS
  1  FILE INITIALIZATION
  2  CREDIT AUTHORIZATION
  3  CREDIT LIMIT CHANGE
  4  STATUS REPORT
  5  EXIT PROGRAM
***ENTER OPTION DESIRED*** 1
IS THIS THE END OF THE MONTH -Y\N ? Y
ENTER CREDIT LIMIT ASSIGNMENT 500.00
CREDIT AUTHORIZATION OPTIONS
  1  FILE INITIALIZATION
  2  CREDIT AUTHORIZATION
  3  CREDIT LIMIT CHANGE
  4  STATUS REPORT
  5  EXIT PROGRAM
***ENTER OPTION DESIRED*** 5
OK
```

Suppose after lunch our busy credit authorization center gets a call from the widget department that a customer with account number 40005 desires to charge the purchase of a widget costing $600. You now run the program again and find out that the charge is not authorized as indicated by the next portion of the display shown below.

```
RUN
CREDIT AUTHORIZATION OPTIONS
   1  FILE INITIALIZATION
   2  CREDIT AUTHORIZATION
   3  CREDIT LIMIT CHANGE
   4  STATUS REPORT
   5  EXIT PROGRAM
***ENTER OPTION DESIRED*** 2
ACCOUNT NUMBER ? 40005
AMOUNT OF PENDING CHARGE ? 600
**********************
CHARGE NOT AUTHORIZED
**********************
CREDIT AUTHORIZATION OPTIONS
   1  FILE INITIALIZATION
   2  CREDIT AUTHORIZATION
   3  CREDIT LIMIT CHANGE
   4  STATUS REPORT
   5  EXIT PROGRAM
***ENTER OPTION DESIRED*** 5
Ok
```

Since the widget salesperson knows the customer and can vouch for his bank balance, you call your manager who proceeds to raise the credit limit of the customer's account to $700. Now, when you enter option 3, the charge is authorized as shown below.

```
***ENTER OPTION DESIRED*** 3
ENTER ACCOUNT NUMBER ? 40005
FOR ACCOUNT# 40005 CREDIT LIMIT IS 500
ENTER NEW CREDIT LIMIT ? 700
CREDIT AUTHORIZATION OPTIONS
   1  FILE INITIALIZATION
   2  CREDIT AUTHORIZATION
   3  CREDIT LIMIT CHANGE
   4  STATUS REPORT
   5  EXIT PROGRAM
***ENTER OPTION DESIRED*** 2
ACCOUNT NUMBER ? 40005
AMOUNT OF PENDING CHARGE ? 600
***********************
CHARGE IS AUTHORIZED
***********************
```

To illustrate the result of selecting option 4, you have changed line number 920 so that RECN% will vary from 1 to 10 instead of 1 to 100. The execution of this option that provides a report summary for the first 10 account numbers follows.

```
ACCOUNT #     CREDIT LIMIT    MONTHLY CHARGES TO DATE
   40001         500.00               0.00
   40002         500.00               0.00
   40003         500.00               0.00
   40004         500.00               0.00
   40005         500.00             600.00
   40006         500.00               0.00
   40007         500.00               0.00
   40008         500.00               0.00
   40009         500.00               0.00
   40010         500.00               0.00
TOTALS         5,000.00             600.00
```

FILE ERROR CONDITIONS TO CONSIDER

There are a number of file error conditions you must consider in developing a program that manipulates files. Foremost among these conditions are "Disk full" (error number 61), "Too many files" (error number 67), and "Disk not Ready" (error number 71). You can use the error-handling procedures discussed in Chapter 7 to develop one or more error-handling routines to check for such conditions and display an appropriate message to the PC AT operator to take corrective action. Thus, on detection of error number 71, you could inform the operator that he or she either forgot to close the diskette drive door or failed to put the diskette in the drive. Appendix C lists BASIC error numbers and their associated messages and meanings.

CHAPTER ELEVEN

Text and Graphics Display Control

TEXT AND GRAPHICS MODE OVERVIEW

Although many types of display adapters can be used in the PC AT, two adapters represent a large majority of those used—the IBM monochrome display and printer adapter and the color/graphics monitor adapter. The monochrome display and printer adapter card is normally interfaced to the IBM monochrome display and, as such, only permits the display of textual information in black and white. The adapter card contains 4K, 8-bit bytes of onboard display memory. The use of this memory results in the PC AT's system memory being unaffected by the display of information. Although the AT permits a limited capability to use this hardware to draw pictures using line and block characters, no true graphics capability is obtainable.

In the text mode, alphanumeric characters are produced on the screen by special character generating circuitry contained in the monochrome display and printer adapter card. Although the location of the characters on the screen may change, their size and shape are fixed. Characters will be displayed in 25 horizontal lines, each line containing 80 character positions when the monochrome display is interfaced to the IBM monochrome display and printer adapter card.

The color/graphics monitor adapter card also contains circuitry to produce alphanumeric characters on the screen; however, such text can be displayed in color or in black and white. In addition, this adapter card contains the required circuitry to address individual picture elements (pixels) on the screen, resulting in full graphics capability. Although the IBM monochrome display cannot be directly interfaced to the color/graphics monitor adapter card due to design incompatibilities, a full range of black and white and color televisions and monitors can be connected to this adapter card. Three processing modes are available when you use the color/graphics adapter card—text mode, medium-resolution graphics mode, and high-resolution graphics mode. The BASIC SCREEN statement is used to select the desired operating mode when using the color/graphics adapter card. The use of this statement will be covered later in this chapter.

The color/graphics monitor adapter card contains 16K 8-bit bytes of on-board memory. This memory is subdivided into pages that can be written onto and/or displayed on an individual basis. This provides you with the capability to develop a program that generates multiple displays and selectively controls which display occurs on the screen at a given time.

Text mode processing using the color/graphics monitor adapter card is similar to processing using the IBM monochrome display and printer adapter card. The two significant differences are the availability of color processing and the selective page display capability one obtains from using the color/graphics monitor adapter card. Another area where differences may exist is in the number of characters displayed per line. If you are using a black and white or color television, you will normally set the width of the screen to 40 characters through the use of the BASIC WIDTH statement. This is required to obtain the clarity necessary to read the individual characters displayed on the screen. If you are using a black and white or color monitor, you can set the width of each line to 80 characters due to the better resolution capability of those monitors.

Medium-Resolution Graphics

In medium-resolution graphics, the screen is divided into 360 horizontal and 200 vertical pixels. These pixels are numbered from left to right and from top to bottom, as indicated in Fig. 11-1. Medium-resolution graphics mode allows the assignment of four possible colors. Color 0 is the background color and can be any of the 16 colors available while colors 1 through 3 are set by selecting one of two three-color sets known as palettes. Thus, one can obtain up to 4 colors on the screen at any one time. Color setting will be covered

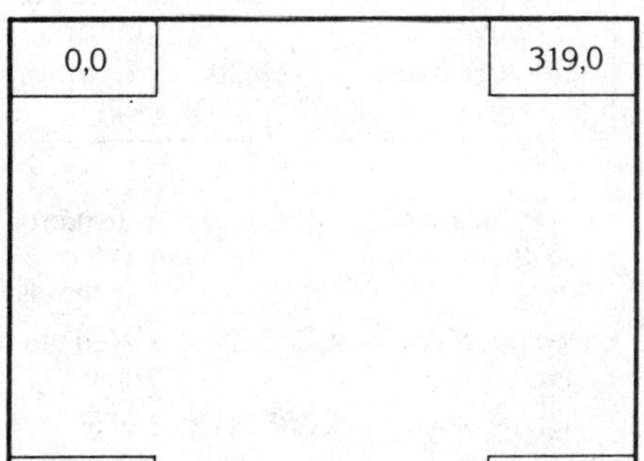

Fig. 11-1. Medium-resolution pixel addressing.

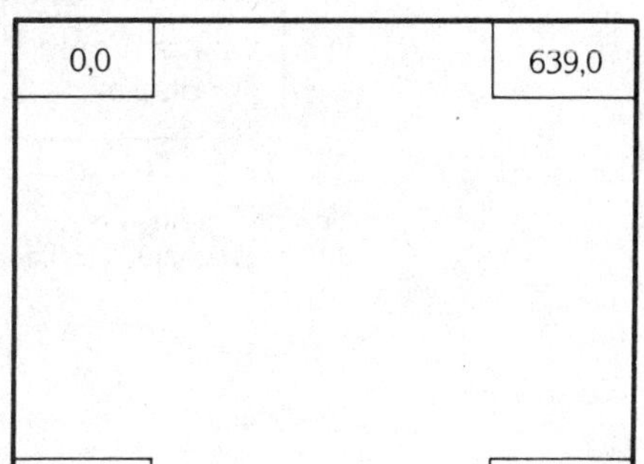

Fig. 11-2. High-resolution pixel addressing.

when the use of the BASIC COLOR statement is discussed later in this chapter.

High-Resolution Graphics

High-resolution graphics provides 640 horizontal and 200 vertical picture elements. Like medium-resolution graphics, these points are numbered starting with 0 at the upper left corner of the screen. The pixel addressing scheme for high-resolution graphics is illustrated in Fig. 11-2. Only two colors are available in high-resolution graphics mode—black and white.

Text Formats

Two text formats can be displayed in either graphics resolution mode—25 rows of 40 characters or 25 rows of 80 characters. Thus, although text can be displayed in graphics mode, unless one has a monitor connected to the color/graphics monitor adapter card, only a text mode of 25 lines by 40 columns should be used. This will permit a resolution of detail that will make each displayed character identifiable. If you attempt to use a text mode of 25 lines by 80 columns with a standard television, you will see that the lack of sharpness makes the characters indistinguishable from one another. The relationship of text and graphics processing to each adapter card and the various types of displays that can be used with the AT is illustrated in Fig. 11-3. This illustration also shows the appropriate WIDTH and SCREEN statements required to set the display width and obtain the desired text or graphics processing mode.

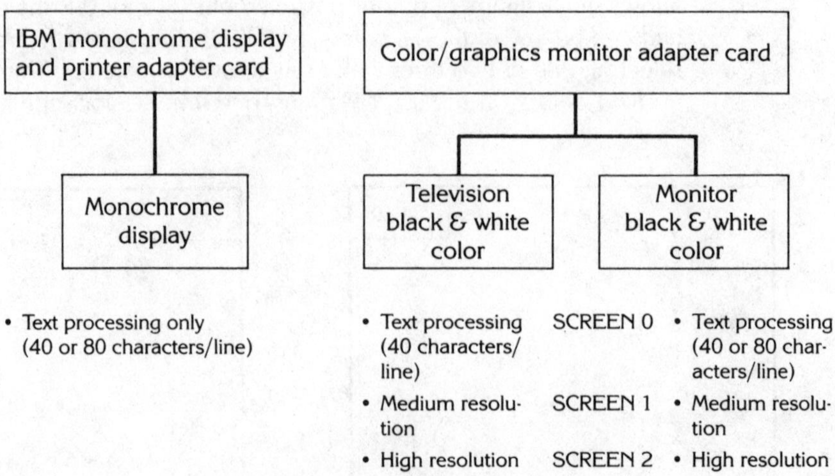

Fig. 11-3. Text and graphics mode processing relationship.

TEXT MODE PROCESSING

Monochrome Display and Printer Adapter

The IBM monochrome display and printer adapter contains 4,096 8-bit bytes of on-board memory. Since the display of 25 lines of 80 characters per line requires only 2,000 memory locations, a logical question is what purpose does the remaining on-board memory serve? The answer to this question is based on the AT using two 8-bit bytes per stored character in the adapter. The first character occupies an even address in the card's on-board memory and contains the ASCII code of the character to be displayed. The second character contains the attribute code for the preceding character and resides at an odd address in the card's on-board memory. Figure 11-4 illustrates the character storage within the IBM monochrome display and printer adapter card. By assigning an attribute value, you can assign such characteristics as underlining, high intensity, blinking, and invisibililty (white-on-white or black-on-black) to an individual character or to a group of characters. This attribute assignment is performed by the COLOR statement whose text mode format is:

format: COLOR foreground[,background]

The foreground parameter represents the character itself, while the background is the square box that surrounds the character when it is displayed. You can set the foreground and background of a character or group of characters in BASIC through the COLOR statement. Table 11-1 lists the

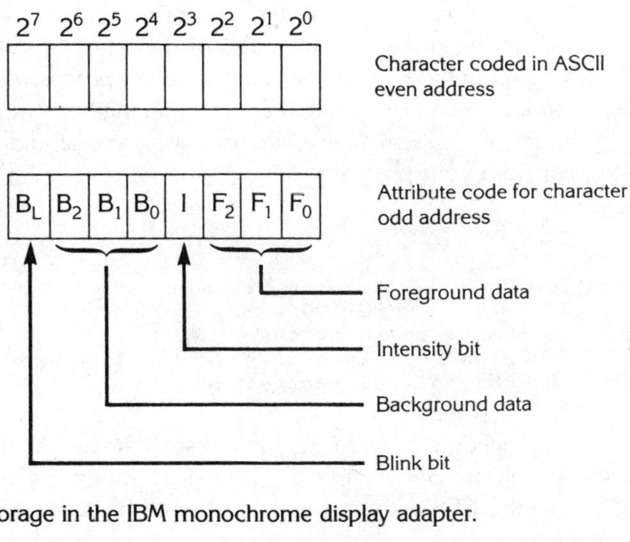

Fig. 11-4. Character storage in the IBM monochrome display adapter.

Table 11-1. Foreground and Background Operational Results Using the IBM Monochrome Display and Printer Adapter

FOREGROUND VALUES	OPERATIONAL RESULT
0, 2–7	White on black
1	Underlined
7	White
8, 10–15	High intensity white on black
9	High intensity underlined
16, 18–23	Blinking
17	Blinking, underlined
24, 26–31	High intensity, blinking
25	Blinking, underlined, high intensity
BACKGROUND	
0–6	Black
7	White

SPECIAL CASES

FOREGROUND VALUES	BACKGROUND VALUES	OPERATIONAL RESULT
X	X	Character is invisible
0, 8, 16, 24	0, 8	Not displayed
8, 16, 24	7	Black on white (inverse video)

foreground and background values and their operational results when you are using the IBM monochrome display and printer adapter card.

You can examine the utilization of the COLOR statement on the monochrome display by considering several typical processing requirements. Suppose you develop a program that contains a lengthy computation. Rather than have the PC AT appear idle to the operator, you could insert the following statements into your program.

```
100 CLS
110 LOCATE 12,35
120 COLOR 23 'turn on blinking
130 PRINT "COMPUTING"
140 REM do computations
500 COLOR 7 'return to normal white on black
510 REM continue processing
```

The preceding program segment first clears the display and positions the cursor at column 35 on line 12. Prior to printing the message "COMPUTING," use the COLOR statement to activate blinking. After the computation is completed, return the screen to its normal display of white on black by a second COLOR statement. Note that once you set a foreground or background attribute, that attribute will remain set until another COLOR statement is executed that changes the attribute.

If you wish to highlight information being displayed, you could use a foreground value of 1. This will result in the display of underlined characters on the screen. The following program segment illustrates this capability.

```
100 LOCATE 12,34
110 COLOR 1          'set underlining
120 PRINT "NATIONAL DEBT"
130 COLOR 7          'return to normal
```

When using underlining, you must first reposition the cursor to the position where you wish underlining to commence by using the LOCATE statement. If you used a TAB function within a PRINT statement, the resulting display would be very different. The statements:

```
110 COLOR 1          'set underlining
120 PRINT TAB(34)"NATIONAL DEBT"
130 COLOR 7          'return to normal
```

would cause character positions 1 through 34 on the display to be underlined in addition to the underlining of the message "NATIONAL DEBT."

You can display characters in their reverse image by using a foreground value of 8, 16, or 24 and a background value of 7. Thus, the program segment

```
100 COLOR 8,7  'inverse video -black on white
110 LOCATE 12,35
120 PRINT 'NATIONAL DEBT"
130 COLOR 7  'return to normal
```

would highlight the message "NATIONAL DEBT" in a reverse image.

Prior to discussing text mode processing using the color/graphics monitor adapter, a word of caution is in order concerning the use of COLOR statements. If the program executes a COLOR statement that causes the display to blink or underline characters, and you use the "Ctrl + Break key sequence prior to the execution of another COLOR statement that returns the screen to its normal mode, all subsequent characters that are displayed will be blinked or underlined. You can return to the normal display mode by executing a direct mode COLOR statement. Thus,

```
COLOR 7
```

entered without a line number would cause all future output to the screen to appear as standard white on black.

Color/Graphics Monitor Adapter

Unlike the monochrome display and printer adapter that permits only text mode, the color/graphics monitor adapter permits us to use one of three modes. Mode selection is accomplished by the use of the SCREEN statement. This statement is only meaningful when the color/graphics monitor adapter card is used. The format of this statement is:

format: SCREEN[mode][,[burst][,[apage][,vpage]]]

where mode is a numeric expression that results in an integer value of 0, 1, or 2 where mode 0 is text mode at a width of 40 or 80 colums based on the WIDTH statement, mode 1 is medium-resolution graphics of 320 by 200 pixels, and mode 2 is high-resolution graphics of 640 by 200 pixels; burst is a numeric expression that returns a true (1) or false (0) value that results in enabling or disabling color based on the mode as follows (not applicable to high-resolution graphics in in which there is only black and white);

Burst	Text mode	Medium-resolution mode
0	Disable color (b&w only)	Enable color
1	Enable color images	Disable color

apage is a numeric expression that represents the active page to be written to by output statements to the screen (this parameter is only valid in text mode and its range of values depends on the screen width as follows);

Active page values	Screen width
0–7	40
0–3	80

and vpage is a numeric expression that represents the page to be displayed on the screen (this parameter is only valid in text mode and its range is the same as the active page).

Prior to examining all aspects of the SCREEN statement, let's review the manner of character storage in the color/graphics monitor adapter card. This card contains 16K 8-bit bytes of on-board memory. In text mode, textual information is stored in the same manner as when you are using the monochrome display and printer adapter. That is, two bytes of on-board storage are used per stored character. The even address in memory is used to store the character to be displayed while the odd address contains its attribute. This storage scheme is shown in Fig. 11-5. The significant differences between storage of textual data on the two adapter cards is in the physical quantity of data that can be stored and the attributes that can be assigned to each character stored.

Since the color/graphics monitor adapter contains 16K bytes of on-board storage, up to 8,000 characters and their attributes can be stored in this card. With a 25-line by 80-character display requiring 2,000 character storage lo-

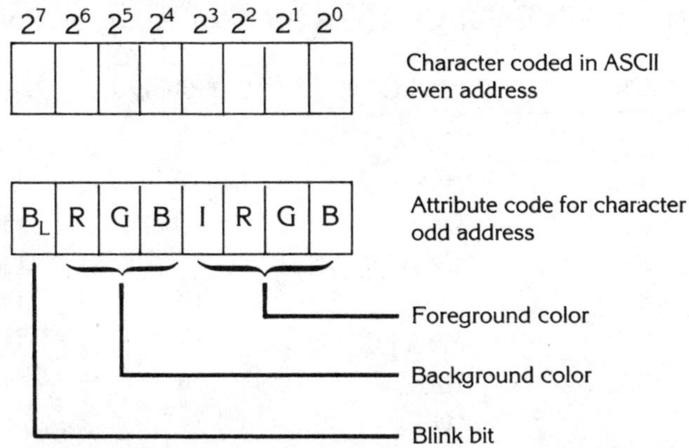

Fig. 11-5. Character storage in the color/graphics adapter.

cations, up to 4 pages (0 through 3) can be stored if your width is 80 characters per line. If your width is 40 characters per line, only 1,000 characters are on a screen and you can then store 8 pages (0 through 7) in the color/graphics monitor adapter card's memory.

The second significant difference between the two adapters in text mode processing is the character attributes. As indicated in Fig. 11-5, the color/graphics monitor adapter card permits the assignment of foreground and background colors. In addition, you can also specify the screen border color. When you are using the color/graphics monitor adapter card, the format and the operational result of the COLOR statement change from its previous use with the IBM monochrome display and printer adapter card. The format of this statement becomes:

format: COLOR[foreground][,[background][,border]]

The foreground value is a numeric expression in the range 0 to 31 that represents the color of the character or group of characters to be displayed. The background value is a numeric expression in the range 0 to 7 that represents the background color in the box in which the character is displayed.

The area on a television or monitor that is outside the area where characters are displayed is known as the border of the screen. You can set the color of this border area by specifying a numeric expression in the range 0 to 15 in the appropriate part of the COLOR statement.

Table 11-2 lists the values and resulting colors when you are using the color/graphics monitor adapter card in text mode. Note that the addition of 16 to any foreground color causes character blinking in the base color to occur.

If the foreground color equals the background color, the effect is the same as when the monochrome display and printer adapter card is used. That is, the character displayed will be invisible. When you use the COLOR statement, you may omit any parameter and the previous value will be used as the default value. This is illustrated by the following program segment.

Table 11-2. Color/Graphics Monitor Adapter Colors

COLOR #	COLOR	COLOR #	COLOR
0	Black	8	Gray
1	Blue	9	Light blue
2	Green	10	Light green
3	Cyan	11	Light cyan
4	Red	12	Light red
5	Magenta	13	Light magenta
6	Brown	14	Yellow
7	White	15	High-intensity white

```
100 SCREEN 1       'set text mode
110 COLOR 0,4,7    'set black foreground
                   'red background
                   'white border
500 COLOR ,,1      'change border to blue
```

Although you may omit any parameter from the COLOR statement, you should not terminate this statement with a comma because this will result in a "Missing operand" error.

To become familiar with the COLOR statement, let's examine the operational result of several program segments. Each of these program segments will be executed using the color/graphics monitor adapter card in text mode.

In the first example, information using a black foreground and white background will be displayed initially. If information is entered incorrectly in response to the prompt message, the AT will gain the operator's attention by printing an error message in red. The following program segment illustrates how you perform this color change. Note that line 1040 sets a black foreground, white background, and blue border. If a stock number at or below 100 is entered, the program segment changes the display color to red foreground (line 1080) and prints the messages "ILLEGAL VALUE, CONSULT MANUAL" and "AND REENTER DATA". Next, the foreground color is reset to black in line 1120 and the previous entry is erased from the screen (line 1140). When a valid stock number is entered, the program erases the previously displayed error messages (lines 1170 and 1180).

```
1000 SCREEN 0
1010 WIDTH 40
1020 CLS
1030 KEY OFF
1040 COLOR 0,7,1
1050 LOCATE 12,11
1060 INPUT "ENTER STOCK NUMBER ",S
1070 IF S>100 THEN 1160
1080 COLOR 4,7,1
1090 LOCATE 13,11
1100 PRINT "ILLEGAL VALUE,CONSULT MANUAL"
1110 PRINT TAB(13)"AND REENTER DATA"
1120 COLOR 0,7,1
```

```
1130 LOCATE 12,28
1140 PRINT SPC(12)
1150 GOTO 1050
1160 REM continue processing
1170 LOCATE 13,11:PRINT SPC(29)
1180 LOCATE 14,13:PRINT SPC(27)
```

The next example shows both the 16 color capability of the PC and how you can vary colors by using a variable in the COLOR statement. In this example, line 30 sets the foreground color to black and the background color to white. The FOR-NEXT loop varies the foreground color, resulting in each message being printed in a different color.

```
10 SCREEN 0:CLS:KEY OFF
20 REM Rainbow generation
30 COLOR 0,7,0
40 FOR I=0 TO 15
50 COLOR I,7,1 'change foreground color
60 PRINT"TEXT DISPLAY IN COLOR #;"I
70 NEXT I
```

Now that you have some background on the color processing capability of text mode operations, let's refocus our attention on the SCREEN statement. When a SCREEN statement is executed, the new screen mode is placed in effect, and the existing screen will be erased. In addition, the foreground color will be set to white, while the background and border colors will be set to black. Thus, in addition to setting the screen attributes that will be used by subsequent statements, the SCREEN statement automatically generates a COLOR 7,0,0 statement. You can use the SCREEN statement not only to place you into one of three processing modes but also to display one page of information while your program is constructing another page. This can be accomplished by manipulating the active and visual pages and switching to different visual pages by using a series of SCREEN statements. Prior to actually doing so, let's examine the operational results of the use of some versions of this statement.

Statement	**Operational result**
100 SCREEN 0,1	Selects text mode with color; active and visual pages default to zero
200 SCREEN 1,0	Selects medium–resolution graphics and enables color
300 SCREEN 0,1,1,2	Selects text mode with color, use active page 1, display page 2
400 SCREEN 2	Selects high-resolution graphics

Now, let's examine a program segment that shows how you can display one page of information while you are constructing subsequent pages for display. The following program segment initializes your display width to 40 columns and sets you into text mode with color enabled and the active page set equal to the visual page. This means that data output to the display will immediately appear on the screen. Next, the COLOR 20 statement sets the foreground color to red with an attribute of blinking and the message "COMPUTING" will be displayed in blinking red characters. The three FOR-NEXT loops in lines 160 to 240 fill each of seven active pages with 800 colored asterisks and the message "ENTER C TO CONTINUE, E TO EXIT". Each active page will contain a different colored sequence of asterisks and the previous denoted message. The FOR-NEXT loop bounding lines 275 and 320 will repeatedly ask the operator if he or she wishes to continue or exit. If the operator wishes to continue, the appropriate visual page is immediately displayed from the on-board memory of the color/graphics monitor adapter card.

```
90 KEY OFF
95 CLS
100 WIDTH 40 'set screen to 40
110 SCREEN 0,1,0,0 'set active=visual page
120 COLOR 20 'set foreground to RED & blinking
130 LOCATE 12,15
140 PRINT "COMPUTING"
150 COLOR 7 'RESET TO WHITE FOREGROUND
160 FOR X=1 TO 7
170 SCREEN ,,X,0 'fill active pages 1-7,display page 0
180 COLOR X      'using color x
190 FOR I=1 TO 20
200 FOR J=1 TO 40
210 PRINT "*";
220 NEXT J
230 NEXT I
235 LOCATE 25,8
236 PRINT "ENTER C TO CONTINUE, E TO EXIT"
240 NEXT X
271 SCREEN ,,0,0 'set active=visual to display
272 LOCATE 25,8
273 PRINT "ENTER C TO CONTINUE E TO EXIT"
275 FOR I=1 TO 7
280 A$=INKEY$
290 IF A$="E" THEN 330
300 IF A$<>"C" THEN 280
310 SCREEN ,,,I
320 NEXT I
330 SCREEN ,,0,0 'set active=visual
340 CLS
350 END
```

An important use of pages is to construct one or more "help" screens in the visual page and have the pressing of function keys display those pages.

GRAPHICS MODE PROCESSING

The SCREEN statement may be used to enter the desired graphics processing mode. Although graphics mode is a separate entity from text mode, text can be displayed in either of the two graphics modes. To do so requires that an appropriate statement be issued, such as a PRINT statement, which will result in the generation of the desired character or group of characters on the graphics screen. The key difference between text and graphics modes is the character set that can be displayed, the assignment of colors to output on the screen, and the capability to draw graphical representations.

In text mode, the entire character set of 256 characters can be displayed on the screen. In graphics mode, only the first 128 characters from the character set can be displayed. Since this character subset includes all upper- and lowercase letters, all punctuation characters, all digits and many symbols, this is not a significant limitation.

Concerning colors, in text mode each character can be assigned one of 16 colors. In graphics mode, colors are assigned by selecting one of two three-color sets known as palettes. Palette 0 results in cyan, magenta, and white colors, while the first palette produces green, red, and brown colors.

In medium-resolution graphics mode, 200 rows of 320 pixels permit a total of 64,000 pixels to be displayed. Since only 16K 8-bit bytes of storage are available in the color/graphics monitor adapter, each byte of onboard storage is used to represent four pixels. This representation of data storage for medium-resolution graphics is shown in Fig. 11-6. Here, 2-bit positions are used to represent each pixel. Each bit pair can have one of four possible values that are used to define the color number assigned to that pixel. As indicated, a color number assignment of 0 will assign any of 16 colors to the pixel. The color so assigned is the default color previously set in a COLOR statement and is the background color. Color numbers 1 through 3 will select one of six

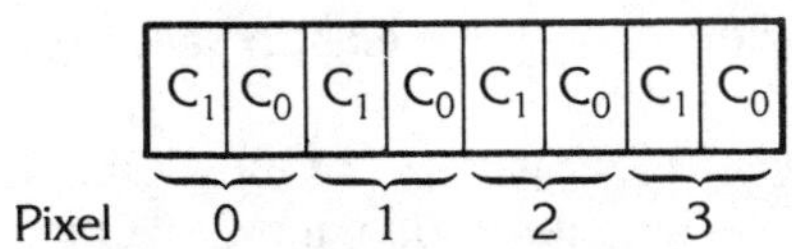

Color number assignment

C_1	C_0	Color number
0	0	0
0	1	1
1	0	2
1	1	3

Color assignment

Color number	Resulting color	
0	any of 16 colors	
	Palette 0	Palette 1
1	Green	Cyan
2	Red	Magenta
3	Brown	White

Fig. 11-6. Medium-resolution graphics storage in the color/graphics adapter.

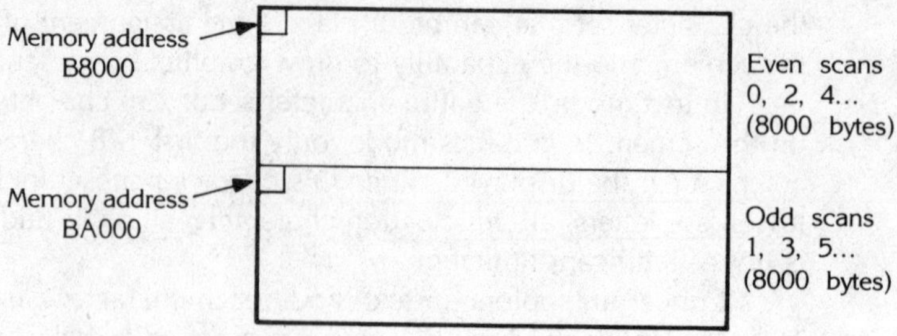

Fig. 11-7. Graphics storage map.

colors depending on the palette selected. Thus, a total of four colors can be displayed on the screen at any one time.

In high-resolution graphics, you can display 200 rows of 640 pixels or a total of 128,000 pixels. In this mode, 8 pixels are stored per character in the 16K byte on-board memory of the color/graphics monitor adapter card. Since no color information can be stored, only a black and white display is possible in high-resolution graphics. Figure 11-7 illustrates how graphic data is stored in the color/graphics monitor adapter. Note that the 16K byte memory is divided into even and odd scan areas and that address B8000 contains PEL information for the first four or eight picture elements in the upper left corner of the display area. If you are in medium-resolution graphics, then four pixels are stored per memory location, while eight pixels are stored in high-resolution graphics.

A new format and operation result of the COLOR statement occurs in medium-resolution graphics. In this mode, the COLOR statement sets a background color and a palette of three colors for use by such graphics statements as PSET, PRESET, LINE, CIRCLE, and PAINT, which will be covered later in this chapter. The format of the COLOR statement in medium-resolution graphics mode is:

format: COLOR[background][,[palette]]

Here, the background color is a numeric expression in the range 0 to 15 that specifies the background color. The values and resulting colors are listed in Table 11-2. As indicated in Fig. 11-6, the palette value is normally in the range 0 to 3 and selects the indicated palette of colors. If the numeric expression used for the palette parameter has a value of 0 or is an even number, palette 0 will be selected. If the palette value is 1 or an odd number, palette 1 will be selected.

Since high-resolution graphics only permits black and white, the COLOR statement cannot be used in this graphics mode.

Since all graphics statements are applicable to both graphics modes, each of the graphics statements will be examined with respect to medium-resolution graphics. In this way, you will become acquainted with the color-generating capability of this graphics mode.

Graphics Statements

The statements covered in this section are applicable only to graphics mode operations. That is, you must be using the color/graphics monitor adapter and precede the graphics statement by the execution of a SCREEN 1 or SCREEN 2 statement. SCREEN 1 will place you in medium-resolution graphics mode, while SCREEN 2 will place you in high-resolution graphics mode.

For each graphics statement, you can specify the location where you wish to draw on the screen in absolute or relative form. In absolute form, you will indicate the actual coordinates of the point or points on the screen where your graphics statement is to initiate operation. In relative form, you reference the last point referenced by providing offset values that BASIC will use to compute the new location. The relative form is indicated by the word STEP, followed by the X and Y offsets in parentheses. This offset indicator follows the graphics statement. Thus, if the last point referenced by a previous graphics statement was 100,100, STEP (50,−50) would reference location 150,50 on the screen.

PSET Statement

The PSET statement provides you with the ability to draw a point at a specified location on the screen. The format of this statement is:

format: PSET(x,y)[,color]

Here, x and y are the horizontal and vertical coordinates of the point to be set. The value of x can range from 0 to 199, while y can vary from 0 to 319 or 0 to 639, depending on whether you are in medium- or high-resolution graphics mode.

The actual color used for the setting of the point depends on the graphics mode you are in. In medium-resolution graphics mode, the range of the color parameter is 0 to 3. A zero value selects the background color defined by a COLOR statement, while a value of 1, 2, or 3 will select a color from the palette specified in a previous COLOR statement. As an example of the use of this statement, consider the following program segment.

```
10 KEY OFF
20 CLS
30 SCREEN 1
40 COLOR 9,1 'background is blue, palette is 1
50 PSET (50,50),2
```

Prior to discussing the execution result of the preceding statements, let's review the colors of the two palettes as indicated below.

Color	Palette 0	Palette 1
1	Green	Cyan
2	Red	Magenta
3	Brown	White

With palette 1 selected in line 40, the point at location 50,50 will be set in color 2 of palette 1, which is magenta. Now, let's take another example to investigate the use of this statement.

```
10 KEY OFF
20 CLS
30 SCREEN 1
40 COLOR 9,1 'background is blue, palette is 1
50 FOR I=50 TO 150
60 PSET(10,I),3
70 NEXT I
```

This program segment draws a line of points from position 10,50 to 10,150. Since color 3 of palette 1 is specified, the points are set in white. Each time PSET is executed, one pixel at the specified location is set. The size of the pixel set will be smaller in high resolution than medium resolution because there are more pixels on a high-resolution screen. Since high resolution only allows black and white, the color values in the PSET statement take on different meanings in that graphics mode. In high-resolution graphics, a color of 0 or 2 indicates black while a value of 1 or 3 indicates white.

PRESET Statement

The PRESET statement works almost the same way as PSET. The only difference is that if no color parameter is specified, the background color (0) will be used. This can result in a previously set point being erased. The format of this statement is:

format: PRESET(x,y)[,color]

The following program segment demonstrates one use of the PRESET statement. This program segment sets a vertical line and then erases every other pixel, resulting in a dashed line appearing on the screen. Once again, the line—in this case a dashed line—will appear in white on a blue background.

```
10 KEY OFF
20 CLS
30 SCREEN 1
40 COLOR 9,1 'background is blue, palette is 1
50 FOR I=50 TO 150 'set line of points
60 PSET(100,I)
70 NEXT I
80 FOR I=50 TO 150 STEP 2 'erase every other
90 PRESET(100,I)
100 NEXT I
```

Plotting with PSET and PRESET

For plotting applications, you can use the PSET and PRESET statements to plot many types of graphs. Prior to doing so, you must consider the relationship between the coordinates of the graphics screen and the coordinates of the application you wish to plot. Normally, you will require some type of conversion or transformation between the coordinates of the graphics screen and the coordinates of the application. This is best explained by examining

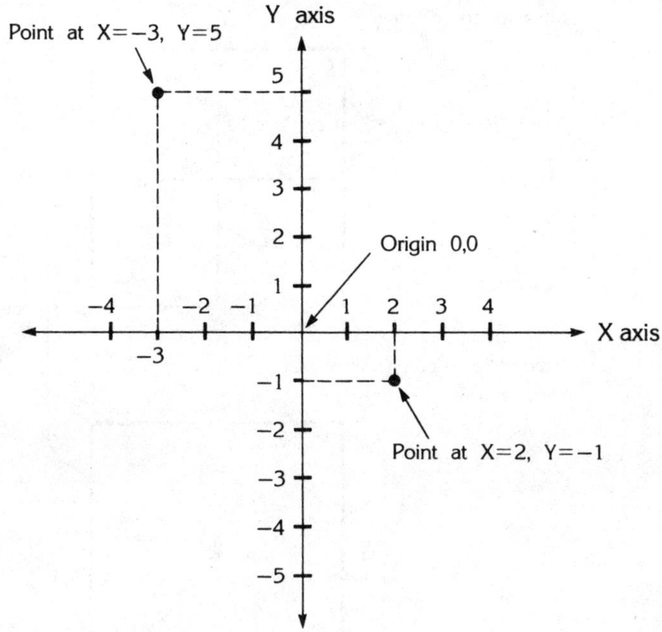

Fig. 11-8. Cartesian coordinate system.

the coordinate system used for most plotting applications—Cartesian coordinates.

In the system of Cartesian coordinates, the x-axis is the horizontal axis and the y-axis is the vertical axis. The x-axis increases in value to the right and decreases in value to the left. The y-axis increases in value in the up direction and decreases in value in the down direction. The point where the x and y axes intersect is known as the origin. At this point, both x and y are zero. Figure 11-8 illustrates a Cartesian coordinate system.

To convert from the x,y coordinate system to either graphics mode screen coordinate system is a fairly simple task. You must first determine the graphics mode you wish to use and where you wish to place the origin on the screen. Suppose you wish to use medium-resolution graphics and center the origin of your plot on the screen. The coordinate transformation required is illustrated in Fig. 11-9. Here, the Cartesian origin of 0,0 is transformed to 160,100. This centers the graph at the center of the medium-resolution graphics screen. Without considering the scaling of values, you would add 160 to every x value and 100 to every y value prior to plotting points on the medium-resolution graphics screen. Since the values to be plotted may exceed the number of horizontal and vertical points on the screen, you will normally have to scale the points you wish to plot. This will enable them to be displayed within the boundaries of the screen. To scale the x,y Cartesian coordinates to the AT's screen coordinates, you should follow the following procedures.

1. Determine the range of the horizontal values to be plotted. This requires the addition of the absolute value of the maximum negative x

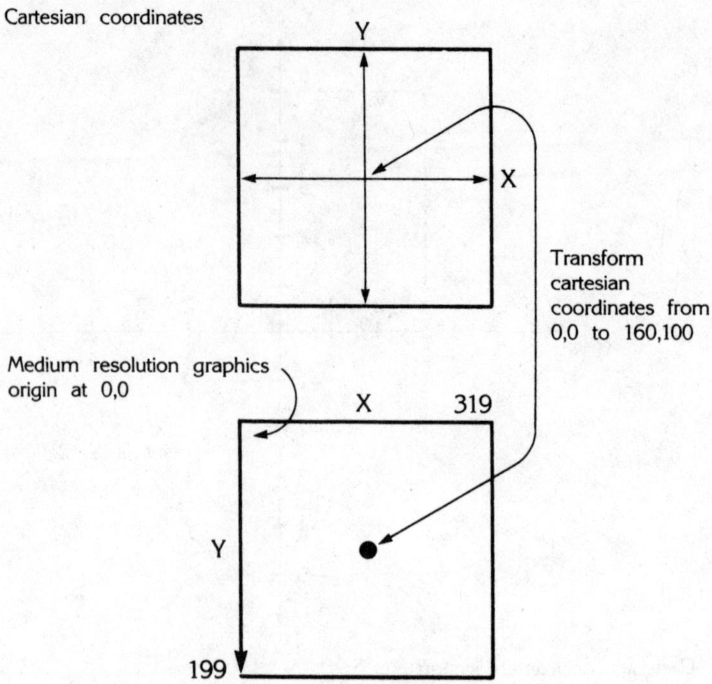

Fig. 11-9. Coördinate transformation.

value to the maximum positive x value. Thus, if the values of x go from −75 to 425, the range of x is 500. Let's call this value RX for the range of x.

2. Divide 320 by RX for medium-resolution graphics mode and 640 by RX for high-resolution graphics mode. The result of this division is the x axis scale factor to be denoted as SX. This is the number of x units for every horizontal pixel on the screen.
3. Determine the range of the vertical values to be plotted. This requires the addition of the absolute value of the maximum negative y value to the maximum y value. Thus, if the values of y range from −50 to +175, the range of y would be 225. Let's denote this range of y values as RY.
4. Divide 200 by RY for both medium- and high-resolution graphics mode. The result of this division is the y-axis scale factor to be denoted as SY. This is the number of y units for every vertical pixel on the screen.

Once you have scaled the x and y coordinates, you must decide on the location of the origin you want on the screen prior to plotting any values. The origin will have a horizontal location of 0 through 319 or 0 through 639, depending on whether you are to plot in medium- or high-resolution graphics mode. For both modes, the vertical location will range between 0 and 199. Let's call these coordinates CX and CY. Then, you can use the following two equations to transform the x and y data you wish displayed to the coordinates of the AT.

$$X = CX + X^*SX$$
$$Y = CY - Y^*SY$$

You can then use the PSET statement with the transformed x and y values to plot your data.

As an example of the use of coordinate transformations, let's plot the equation:

$$Y = aX^2$$

for the range of X between −20 and +20, using a value of 2 for a. Then, the range of X is 40 while the range of Y is 1,600. If you are using medium-resolution graphics, next divide 320 by 40 and 200 by 1,600 to obtain the vertical and horizontal axis scale factors. If you wish to center the plot in the middle of the medium-resolution graphics screen, CX will equal 160 and CY will equal 100. The following program segment would then plot your function, scaled to the coordinates of medium-resolution graphics, using the center of the screen as your origin.

```
Ok
10 KEY OFF
20 CLS
30 SCREEN 1
40 COLOR 9,1
50 CX=160:CY=100
110 SX=320/40:SY=200/1600
120 FOR I=-20 TO 20
130 X=CX+I*SX
140 IY=2*(I^2)
150 Y=CY-IY*SY
160 PSET(X,Y)
170 NEXT I
```

The display resulting from the execution of this program segment is shown in Fig. 11–10. You can change this point graph to approximate a line graph

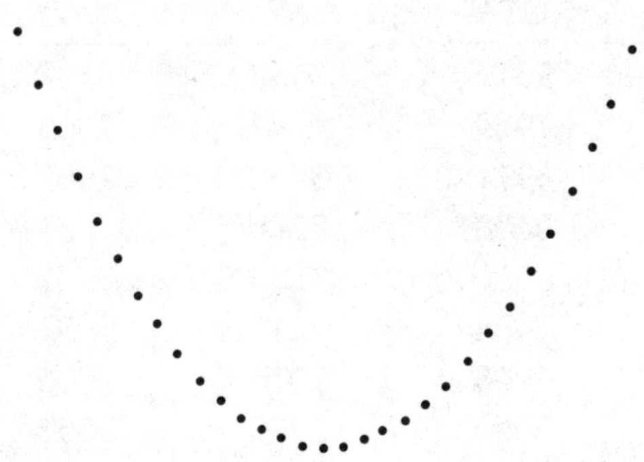

Fig. 11-10. Plotting by increments.

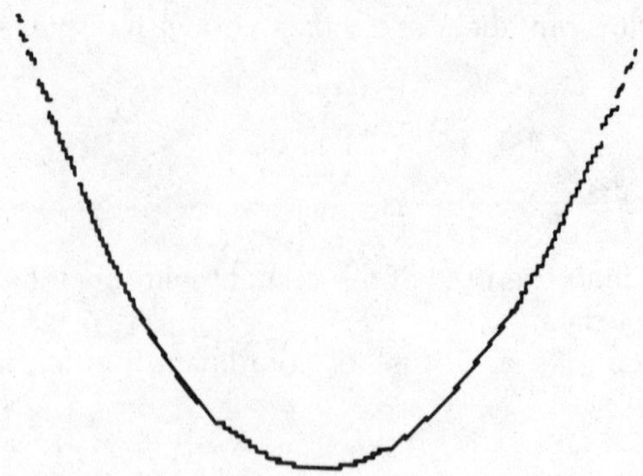

Fig. 11-11. Plotting by smaller increments.

by changing the step increment in line 120 from an implied value of 1 to a smaller increment. In Fig. 11-11, the results of executing this program with a STEP of .10 are shown.

Now, let's consider another plotting example. Suppose you wish to plot the data contained in Table 11-3 using the X-axis for the year and the Y-axis for expenditures. Here, you may wish to relocate the origin toward the lower left corner of the screen. If you wish to label the X and Y axis, you must consider the number of pixels per character so our labels do not interfere with the graph.

In medium-resolution graphics, the screen size is 320 by 200 pixels. If you are using a monitor, you can set the width to either 40 or 80 characters per column. If you use 40 characters per column, then each character will take up 320/40 or 8 pixel positions horizontally. Since you can display 25 lines in the 200 vertical pixels of the screen, each character occupies 200/25 or 8 vertical pixel positions. If you wish to display a four-column wide label on the Y-axis and a three-row high label on the X-axis, you cannot relocate

Table 11-3. Department of Defense Aircraft Expenditures (Millions of Dollars)

YEAR	TOTAL	AF	NAVY	ARMY
1980	9379	5417	3337	625
1979	7969	4587	2965	417
1978	6971	3989	2602	380
1977	6608	3586	2721	301
1976	6520	3323	3061	136
1975	5484	2211	3137	136
1974	5006	2078	2806	122
1973	5066	2396	2557	113
1972	5927	3191	2347	389
1971	6631	3960	2125	546

the origin of the graph to 0,199 but instead allow sufficient space for the labels. This means you must move the origin to a point a minimum of 32 pixels to the left and 24 pixels above the lower left corner of the screen. Since you may wish to use the 25th line for status information, you should relocate the origin 8 additional pixel elements above the origin for a total of 32 pixel elements. Since you will eventually draw the X and Y axes on the screen, you will also leave room for their construction. Thus, let's place the origin of your graph 40 pixels to the right and 40 pixels above the lower left corner of the screen at location 40,159. The format of the screen display is illustrated in Fig. 11-12.

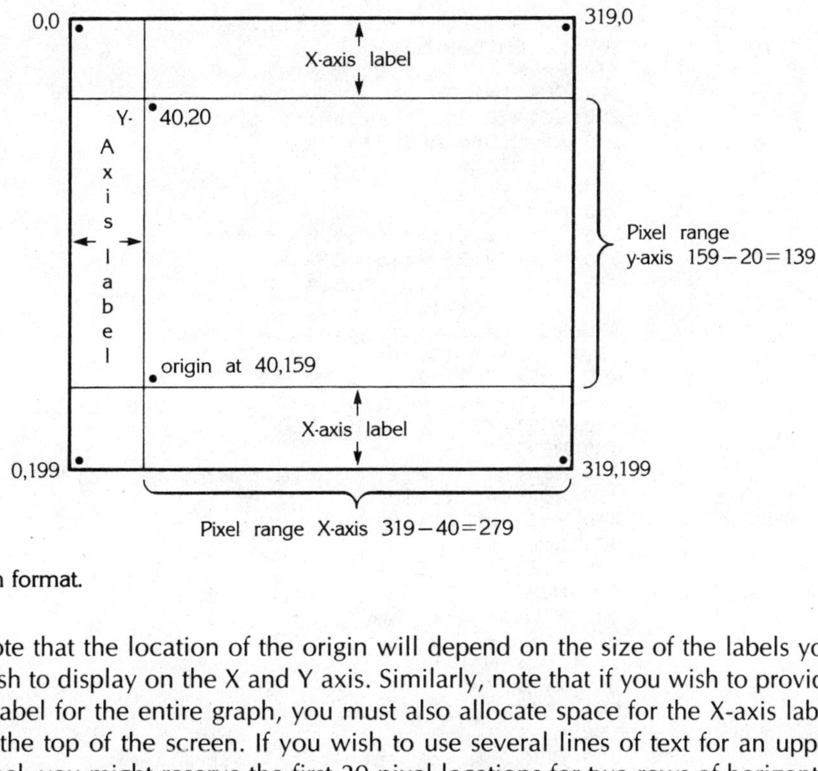

Fig. 11-12. Screen format.

Note that the location of the origin will depend on the size of the labels you wish to display on the X and Y axis. Similarly, note that if you wish to provide a label for the entire graph, you must also allocate space for the X-axis label at the top of the screen. If you wish to use several lines of text for an upper label, you might reserve the first 20 pixel locations for two rows of horizontal text to be displayed at the top of the screen. Now that you have decided on your display format and where to place the origin on the screen, let's execute the following program segment to display the required points and text.

```
5 CLS
10 KEY OFF
20 COLOR 9,0 'background blue,palette 0
30 SCREEN 1
40 LABEL1$="DEPARTMENT OF DEFENSE AIRCRAFT SPENDING"
50 LABEL2$="(MILLIONS OF DOLLARS)"
60 LABEL3$="EXPENDITURES"
70 FOR I=1 TO 10
80 READ Y(I)
90 NEXT I
```

```
100 DATA 71,72,73,74,75,76,77,78,79,80
110 FOR I=1 TO 10
120 READ T(I),AF(I),N(I),A(I)
130 NEXT I
140 DATA 9379,5417,3337,625,7969,4587,2965,417
150 DATA 6971.3989.2602.380.6608.3586.2721.301
160 DATA 6520,3323,3061,136,5484,2211,3137,136
170 DATA 5006,2078,2806,122,5066,2396,2557,113
180 DATA 5927,3191,2347,389,6631,3960,2125,546
190 REM plot labels
200 L=LEN(LABEL1$) 'get length
210 P=INT((40-L)/2)'center on row
215 IF P<0=0 THEN P=1
220 LOCATE 2,P:PRINT LABEL1$
230 L=LEN(LABEL2$)
240 P=INT((40-L)/2)
250 LOCATE 3,P:PRINT LABEL2$
260 L=LEN(LABEL3$)
270 P=INT((25-L)/2)
280 FOR I=1 TO L
290 LOCATE P,1 'place on column
300 X$=MID$(LABEL3$,I,1)
310 PRINT X$
320 P=P+1
330 NEXT I
340 REM now lets plot points
350 RX=(80-71)+1:SX=279/RX
360 RY=(9379-113)+1:SY=139/RY
370 CX=40:CY=169
380 REM lets plot points for total
390 FOR I=1 TO 10
400 Y=CY-T(I)*SY
410 X=CX+I*SX
420 PSET(X,Y),1
430 NEXT I
440 REM do it again for AIR FORCE
450 FOR I=1 TO 10
460 Y=CY-AF(I)*SY
470 X=CX+I*SX
480 PSET(X,Y),2
490 NEXT I
500 REM now for NAVY
510 FOR I=1 TO 10
520 Y=CY-N(I)*SY
530 X=CX+I*SX
540 PSET(X,Y),3
550 NEXT I
560 REM now for the land lubbers (ARMY)
570 COLOR 9,1 'first change palettes
580 FOR I=1 TO 10
590 Y=CY-A(I)*SY
600 X=CX+I*SX
610 PSET(X,Y),1
620 NEXT I
890 P=5
910 FOR I=1 TO 7
915 LOCATE 23,P
920 PRINT Y(I);
930 P=P+4
940 NEXT I
941 LOCATE 23,33:PRINT "78 79 80";
950 LOCATE 23,1
960 PRINT "YEAR"
970 GOTO 970
```

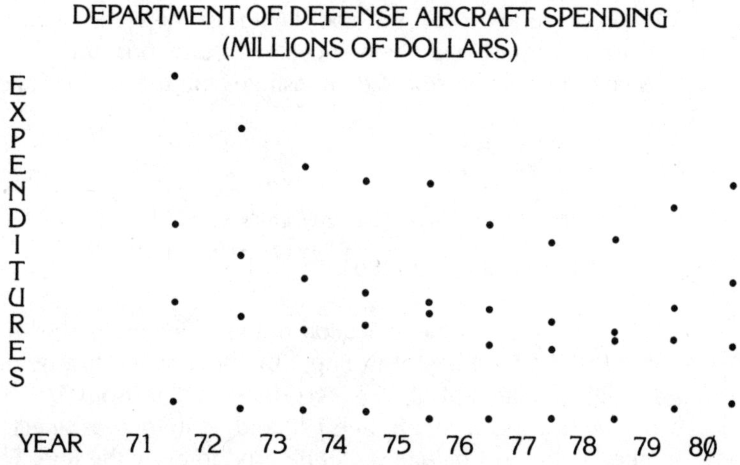

Fig. 11-13. Labeled point graph.

Note that when you execute this program, certain deficiencies in the graph become apparent as illustrated in Fig. 11-13. First, each point is plotted as a dot, and no dots are interconnected to show trend information, Next, although the years are displayed on the X-axis, a far better display method would be to insert "hash marks" to show the appropriate location of each year for the plot. Both of these omissions can be satisfied through the use of the LINE statement, which follows.

LINE Statement

The LINE statement provides you with the ability to draw a line between any two points on the screen. By using the various options of this statement, you may also draw a box and, optionally, fill the box with a selected color. The format of this statement is:

format: LINE[(X1,Y1)] – (X2,Y2)[,[color][,B[F]][,style]

where X1,Y1, and X2,Y2 are the coordinates of the line or box, which may be specified in either absolute or relative form; color is the color number in the range 0 to 3 that selects the color based on the graphics resolution; B causes a box to be drawn; BF causes a box to be drawn and filled with color; and style is a 16-bit integer mask that can be used to custom shape the line.

To understand the use of the LINE statement, let's construct and execute several program segments.

The simplest use of this statement is to draw a line from the last point referenced by a previous graphics statement to a new point using the default color. The format of this statement is:

format: LINE – (X2,Y2)

where X2 and Y2 are the coordinates of the screen you wish to draw a line to from the last point referenced by a previous graphics statement. The following program segment demonstrates the use of this statement.

```
100 SCREEN 1
110 KEY OFF
115 CLS
120 COLOR 9,0 'blue background,palette 0
130 PSET(10,10) 'draw point in default color
140 LINE-(150,150)
```

The result of the execution of this statement is shown in Fig. 11-14. Note that the PSET statement in line 130 above is the last point referenced so that the LINE statement in line 140 draws a line from 10,10 to 150,150. Since palette 0 was selected in line 120 and no color was selected in the LINE statement, color 3 of palette 0 will be used to draw the line. Thus, the line will be drawn in brown. Note that when using a blue background, the brown line will be a light shade of brown.

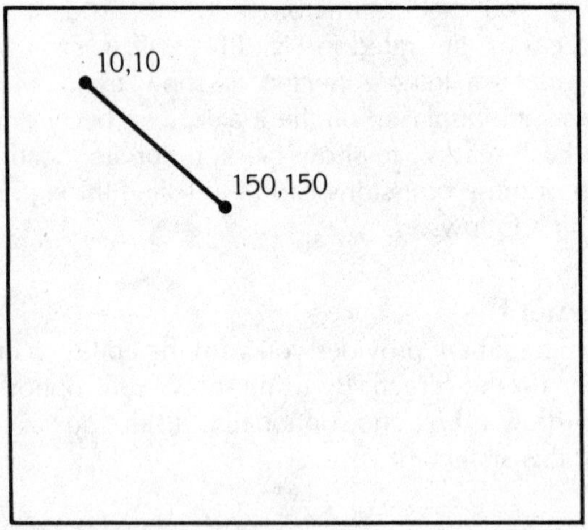

Fig. 11-14. LINE statement example.

You can include the starting and ending points within the LINE statement using the following format of this statement.

format: LINE(X1,Y1) – (X2,Y2)

In the following program segment, the PSET statement has been eliminated, since we no longer require the last point referenced when using this version of the LINE statement. Note that the execution of this program statement results in the same result as the previous program segment illustrated in Fig. 11-14.

```
100 SCREEN 1
110 KEY OFF
```

```
115 CLS
120 COLOR 9,0 'blue background,palette 0
130 LINE (10,10)-(150,150)
```

Now, let's examine how you can draw boxes with the LINE statement and fill such boxes with color.

When you use the LINE statement to draw a box, each pair of coordinates defines the opposite corners of the box. This is illustrated in Fig. 11-15. Note that the LINE statement draws a box from the horizontal line defined by the start point (X1,Y1) to the horizontal line defined by the end point (X2,Y2). The B parameter in the LINE statement in effect replaces four LINE commands by one statement to perform the equivalent function. Thus, the statements

```
100 SCREEN 1
110 KEY OFF
115 CLS
120 COLOR 9,0 'blue background,palette 0
130 LINE (50,50)-(150,150),2,B
```

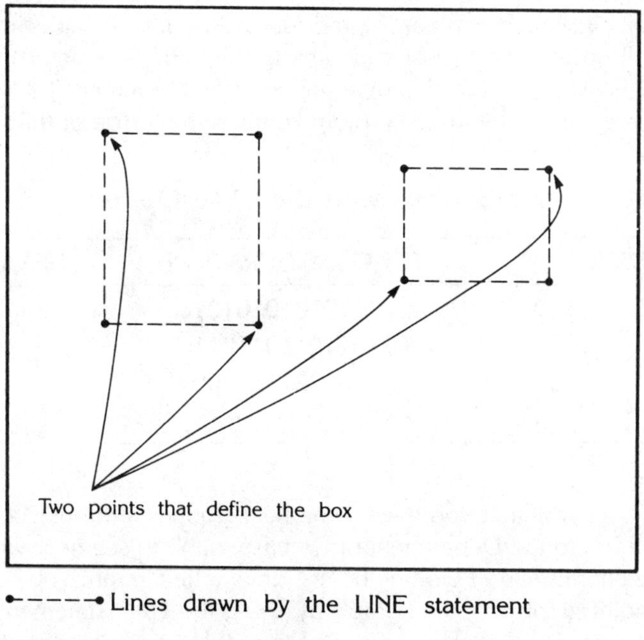

Fig. 11-15. Using the LINE statement to draw boxes.

will draw a rectangular box with the points (50,50) and (150,150) as the opposite corners. The box will be outlined in color 2 of palette 0 or red. You can also omit the color from the statement as shown by the following program segment.

```
100 SCREEN 1
110 KEY OFF
115 CLS
```

```
120 COLOR 9,0 'blue background,palette 0
130 LINE (50,50)-(150,150),,B
```

In this example, the default is the foreground color, color number 3.

By using the parameters BF in the LINE statement, you can draw the same rectangle as obtained with the B parameter; however, the interior points of the rectangle will now be filled with the selected color. To see the operational result of the LINE statement with the BF parameters, consider the following program segment.

```
100 SCREEN 1
110 KEY OFF
115 CLS
120 COLOR 9,0 'blue background,palette 0
130 LINE (10,10)-(150,30),1,BF
140 LINE (80,50)-(250,70),2,BF
150 LINE (180,90)-(300,110),3,BF
```

The last parameter you can include in the LINE statement allows you to customize the type of line you wish to draw. The style parameter option is 16 bits in length and can be represented by four hexadecimal characters. If the bit position is 1 (one), a point will be plotted, while a 0 (zero) bit causes the LINE statement to skip over the point on the screen. Table 11-4 shows several types of lines you can customize through the use of the style option.

Table 11-4. Customized Lines with the Style Option

LINE TYPE	BIT CONFIGURATION	HEXADECIMAL VALUE
-Δ-Δ-Δ-Δ-Δ-Δ-Δ-Δ	1010101010101010	&HAAAA
Δ--Δ--Δ--Δ--Δ--Δ	0110110110110110	&H3333
----ΔΔΔΔ----ΔΔΔΔ	1111000011110000	&HF0F0

where Δ is a space

Now that you have some background in the use of the LINE statement, return to the Department of Defense graph to see how you can use this statement. Instead of plotting points, draw a line graph. You can easily convert the point graph to a line graph by using the LINE statement to link each set of points. Thus, replace lines 380 to 430 by the following statements:

```
380 X=CX+SX:Y=CY-T(1)*SY
390 FOR I=1 TO 9
400 Y1=CY-T(I+1)*SY:X1=CX+(I+1)*SX
410 LINE (X,Y)-(X1,Y1),1
420 X=X1:Y=Y1
430 NEXT I
```

Here, line 380 obtains the first set of points that will be used in the LINE statement. The FOR-NEXT loop then obtains succeeding points and after each pair of points is used in the LINE statement, line 420 sets those points to the first pair of points to be used by the next LINE statement executed in the loop. Similarly, lines 440 to 490 are replaced by the following statements.

```
440 X=CX+SX:Y=CY-AF(1)*SY
450 FOR I=1 TO 9
460 Y1=CY-AF(I+1)*SY:X1=CX+(I+1)*SX
470 LINE (X,Y)-(X1,Y1),2
480 X=X1:Y=Y1
490 NEXT I
```

You can also replace lines 500 to 550 and lines 560 to 620 by similar statements.

Next, you can add the following statements to draw the X and Y axis and place hash marks along the X-axis.

```
332 REM draw x and y axis
333 LINE (40,20)-(40,169)
334 LINE (40,169)-(319,169)
970 FOR I=1 TO 10
971 X=CX+I*SX
972 LINE (X,167)-(X,171)
973 NEXT I
```

The reason lines 970 through 973 are used to draw the hash marks instead of continuing at line 335 is because the display of the years along the X-axis (lines 910 to 960) causes a box around each character to be placed on the screen, and this box would erase part of the hash marks. Executing your modified point graph will generate a line graph. The results from the execution of your modified program are shown in Fig. 11-16. You can use a similar procedure to place hash marks on the Y-axis and label values on that axis. In fact, this might be a nice exercise to test your knowledge of graphics processing. While this graph offers significant improvements over the previous point graph, there are still areas open for improvement. Prior to discussing such areas, let's cover the CIRCLE statement.

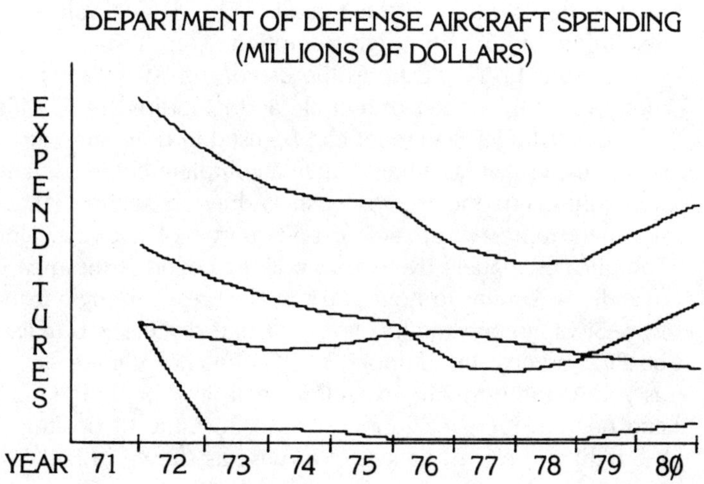

Fig. 11-16. A line graph.

CIRCLE Statement

The CIRCLE statement provides you with the capability to draw not only circles but also ellipses and arcs. The format of this statement is:

format$_A$: CIRCLE (Xctr, Yctr), radius[,color[,start,end[,aspect]]]

where Xctr and Yctr are the X and Y coordinates of the center of the circle; radius is the radius of the circle along its major axis, expressed in points; color is a numeric expression in the range 0 to 3 that specifies the color of the circle as follows;

Medium resolution		**High resolution**	
Color value	*Color*	*Color value*	*Color*
0	Background	0	Black
1–3	Selects color from the current palette (3 is default)	1	White (default)

start,end are the angles expressed in radians that specify where the circle or ellipse will begin and end (as shown below)

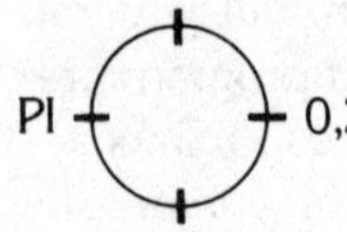

where PI=3.141593 (if start and end values are omitted, a complete circle or ellipse will be drawn); and aspect is a numeric expression that defines the ratio of the X-radius to the Y-radius. The default values are 5/6 for medium resolution and 5/12 for high resolution.

Figure 11-17 illustrates the use of the basic format of the CIRCLE statement where the center of a circle and its radius are specified.

The CIRCLE statement can be used to draw an entire circle or a portion of a circle known as an arc. Since a complete circle contains 360°, you would normally define the arc you wish to draw in degrees. That is, 0 to 90° would normally represent an arc of one-quarter of a circle. Unfortunately, BASIC complicates matters by requiring you to express the measurement of the arc in radians, similar to how you must express an angle using one of the built-in BASIC trigonometric functions. Thus, 0 degrees is 0 radians while 90° would be PI/2 radians. In addition, BASIC does not number the degrees of a circle as you would normally expect. Instead of 0° being the top point on the circle and degrees increasing clockwise to 360, the 0° position in BASIC starts on the right and moves counterclockwise as shown in Fig. 11-18.

From Fig. 11-18, note that one-half circle is PI radians, while a full circle is 2*PI or approximately 6.2831 radians.

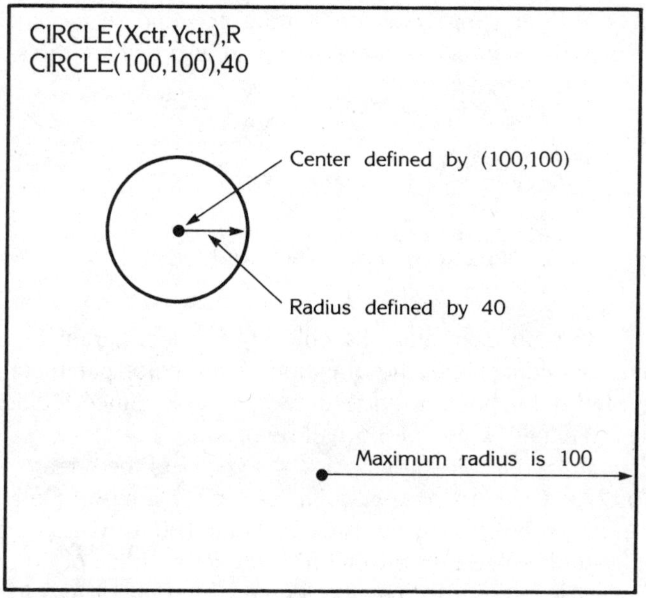

Fig. 11-17. CIRCLE statement format.

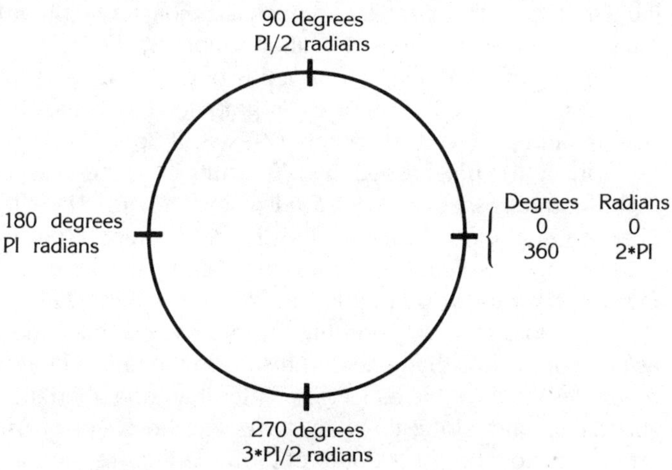

Fig. 11-18. Specifying arcs with the CIRCLE statement.

When positioning the center of a circle, you must consider which resolution you are in. This is because medium-resolution graphics provides a screen of 320 by 200 points, whereas in high-resolution graphics the screen consists of 640 by 200 points. You could use the following statements to draw a circle in the middle of a medium-resolution screen:

```
10 SCREEN 1
20 CLS
30 KEY OFF
40 CIRCLE (160,100),60
```

Note that omitting the starting and ending arc positions results in the display of a complete circle. You can also display the same circle using the following statements:

```
10 SCREEN 1
20 CLS
30 KEY OFF
40 PI=3.141593
50 CIRCLE (160,100),60,,0,PI*2
```

In both examples, the color and aspect parameters were omitted from the statement. Here, the omission of the color parameter results in the foreground color being used to draw the circle. Since the aspect was not specified, a default value of 5/6 will be used.

In high-resolution graphics, the center of the screen is located at 320,100. To draw a circle whose coordinates are centered on the high-resolution screen can be accomplished by using 320 and 100 as its X and Y center points.

In the medium-resolution example, a radius of 60 points was specified. Since the radius specifies the length of the major axis in points, how high is the circle? Although you would logically expect the circle to be as tall as it is wide, it is not, since the screen is not square. The aspect that is the ratio of the X-radius to the Y-radius compensates for the fact that the screen is wider than it is tall. In medium-resolution graphics, the default aspect ratio is 5/6. This means that a circle with a radius of 60 points is 50 points tall.

Since the medium-resolution graphics mode has 320 horizontal points (X-axis) and 200 vertical points (Y-axis), its pixel aspect is 320/200 or 8/5. Multiplying the pixel aspect by 5/6 results in a screen aspect of 4/3rds, which is the normal aspect ratio of a television picture. Thus, the aspect ratio provides a visual circle based on the standard screen aspect ratio of 4/3.

In high-resolution graphics, the default aspect ratio is 5/12. Here, a circle with a radius of 60 points would be 144 points tall.

For both medium- and high-resolution graphics, the default value of the aspect ratio is less than one and results in the radius being measured in points along the X-axis. If the aspect is greater than one, then the radius will be measured in points along the Y-axis. To see the effect of using different aspect ratios, consider an aspect ratio of .5 in medium-resolution graphics. Here, the height-to-width ratio of the circle to be drawn will be .5, and the circle would appear as a flattened circle, which is actually an ellipse. This is illustrated in the top portion of Fig. 11-19. Next, let us consider an aspect ratio of 2. Here, the circle would appear as an egg or an ellipse rotated 90°. This is illustrated in the bottom of Fig. 11-19.

Suppose that instead of a circle you wish to draw an arc. You can do so using the CIRCLE statement by simply specifying the points on the circle where the arc will start and end. Remember that these points must be specified in radians and not degrees. The following example illustrates how you can draw a 90° arc in the upper right quadrant. Here, your starting point is 0 radians and your ending point is PI/2 radians.

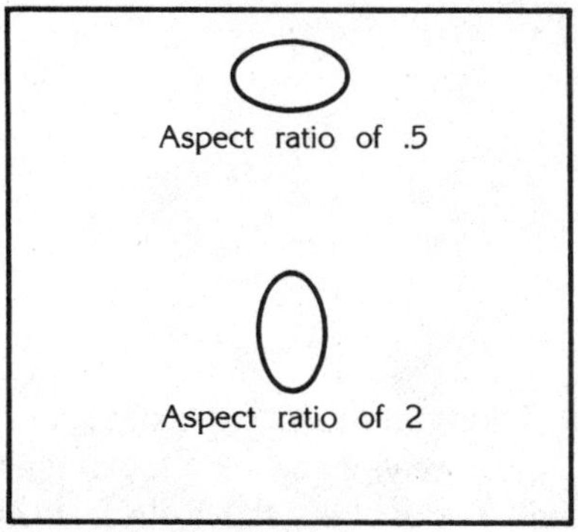

Fig. 11-19. Varying the aspect ratio.

```
10 SCREEN 1
20 CLS
30 KEY OFF
40 PI=3.141593
50 CIRCLE (160,100),60,1,0,PI/2
```

If you wish to draw a 90° arc in the upper left quadrant, you merely change your starting and ending points by shifting them 90° to the left. Here, your CIRCLE statement becomes:

```
50 CIRCLE (160,100),60,1,PI/2,PI
```

In both of these arc-drawing examples, a starting point that is less than an ending point has been specified. When this occurs, the specified arc is drawn counterclockwise. If your first arc point specifier is greater than the second, BASIC will draw the arc clockwise.

Although arcs are interesting, many times for an arc to be meaningful you will want to construct a wedge by connecting one or both endpoints of the arc to the center points that specify the arc. The lines used to connect the center points of the arc to its endpoints are the rays of the arc. You can draw these rays using the CIRCLE statement by specifying a negative endpoint for each ray you wish drawn. Since a −0 is not permitted in the CIRCLE statement, you can use a very small negative value, such as −.0001 to draw a line between the center point of the circle and an endpoint of an arc that is located at 0 radians.

As an example of the use of rays, consider the famous electronic character whom you will simulate on your screen using the following statements.

```
10 SCREEN 1
20 CLS
30 KEY OFF
40 PI=3.141593
50 CIRCLE (160,100),60,1,-PI/6,-1.75*PI
```

The execution of the CIRCLE statement draws a part of a circle similar to the following:

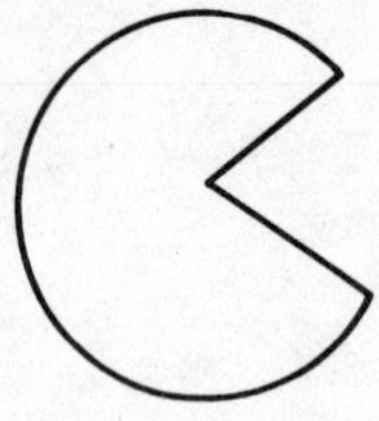

One of the features lacking in the CIRCLE statement is a mechanism to fill in the circle similar to the way you can fill a rectangle with the BF parameters in the LINE statement. Fortunately, the PAINT statement provides you with the capability to fill any area on the screen to include circles with a color. Prior to returning to the line graph, let's also cover the PAINT statement, so when you do return you can visually improve your graph significantly.

PAINT Statement

The PAINT statement allows you to fill in an area on the screen with color as well as to optionally color the boundary of the area. The format of this statement is:

format$_A$: PAINT(X,Y)[color[,boundary]]

where X,Y are the coordinates of a point within the area to be painted with color; color is the color to be painted with in the range 0 to 3 (this selects the color based on the graphics resolution as follows);

Medium resolution		**High resolution**	
Color value	*Color*	*Color value*	*Color*
0	Background	0	Black
1–3	Current palette defined by COLOR statement	1	White
Default	Foreground, color 3		

and boundary is the color of the edges of the figure you wish to paint, in the range 0 to 3.

To see the operational result of this statement, let's redraw the famous electronic character and color the character using the following program segment.

```
10 SCREEN 1
20 CLS
25 COLOR 9,0
30 KEY OFF
40 PI=3.141593
50 CIRCLE (160,100),60,1,-PI/6,-1.75*PI
60 PAINT (159,89),1
```

Since the starting point of the PAINT statement must be inside the figure to be painted, you specified the X and Y coordinates in line 60 just inside the center point boundary of the shape to be colored.

Now, let's return to the line chart example. You can highlight each of the points on the line graph by drawing a small circle centered at each point and filling in the circle with color. This can be accomplished by the addition of the following statement to your program at lines 411, 431, 471, 491, 531, 551, and 601.

```
CIRCLE (X,Y),2,3:PAINT (X,Y)
```

The execution of the line graph program with each point highlighted is shown in Fig. 11-20.

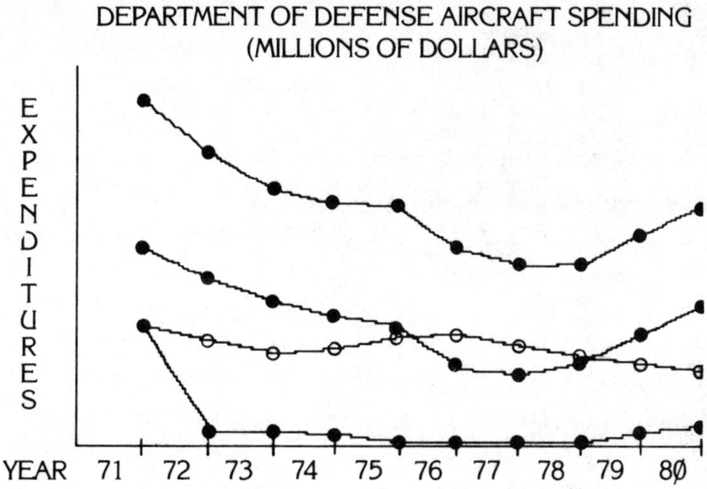

Fig. 11-20. Point highlighting.

The following listing shows the statements required to produce the line chart illustrated in Fig. 11-20. This listing is based on the original point chart and includes the program modifications covered to introduce hash marks on the X-axis, converting point displays into a line chart, and highlighting the points on the line chart.

```
5 CLS
10 KEY OFF
20 COLOR 9,0 'background blue,palette 0
30 SCREEN 1
40 LABEL1$="DEPARTMENT OF DEFENSE AIRCRAFT SPENDING"
50 LABEL2$="(MILLIONS OF DOLLARS)"
60 LABEL3$="EXPENDITURES"
70 FOR I=1 TO 10
80 READ Y(I)
90 NEXT I
100 DATA 71,72,73,74,75,76,77,78,79,80
110 FOR I=1 TO 10
```

```
120 READ T(I),AF(I),N(I),A(I)
130 NEXT I
140 DATA 9379,5417,3337,625,7969,4587,2965,417
150 DATA 6971,3989,2602,380,6608,3586,2721,301
160 DATA 6520,3323,3061,136,5484,2211,3137,136
170 DATA 5006,2078,2806,122,5066,2396,2557,113
180 DATA 5927,3191,2347,389,6631,3960,2125,546
190 REM plot labels
200 L=LEN(LABEL1$) 'get length
210 P=INT((40-L)/2)'center on row
215 IF P<0=0 THEN P=1
220 LOCATE 2,P:PRINT LABEL1$
230 L=LEN(LABEL2$)
240 P=INT((40-L)/2)
250 LOCATE 3,P:PRINT LABEL2$
260 L=LEN(LABEL3$)
270 P=INT((25-L)/2)
280 FOR I=1 TO L
290 LOCATE P,1 'place on column
300 X$=MID$(LABEL3$,I,1)
310 PRINT X$
320 P=P+1
330 NEXT I
332 REM draw x and y axis
333 LINE (40,20)-(40,169)
334 LINE (40,169)-(319,169)
340 REM now lets plot points
350 RX=(80-71)+1:SX=279/RX
360 RY=(9379-113)+1:SY=139/RY
370 CX=40:CY=169
380 X=CX+SX:Y=CY-T(1)*SY
390 FOR I=1 TO 9
400 Y1=CY-T(I+1)*SY:X1=CX+(I+1)*SX
410 LINE (X,Y)-(X1,Y1),1
411 CIRCLE (X,Y),2,3:PAINT (X,Y)
420 X=X1:Y=Y1
430 NEXT I
431 CIRCLE (X,Y),2,3:PAINT (X,Y)
440 X=CX+SX:Y=CY-AF(1)*SY
450 FOR I=1 TO 9
460 Y1=CY-AF(I+1)*SY:X1=CX+(I+1)*SX
470 LINE (X,Y)-(X1,Y1),2
471 CIRCLE (X,Y),2,3:PAINT (X,Y)
480 X=X1:Y=Y1
490 NEXT I
491 CIRCLE (X,Y),2,3:PAINT (X,Y)
500 X=CX+SX:Y=CY-N(1)*SY
510 FOR I=1 TO 9
520 Y1=CY-N(I+1)*SY:X1=CX+(I+1)*SX
530 LINE (X,Y)-(X1,Y1),3
531 CIRCLE (X,Y),2,3:PAINT (X,Y)
540 X=X1:Y=Y1
550 NEXT I
551 CIRCLE (X,Y),2,3:PAINT (X,Y)
560 X=CX+SX:Y=CY-N(1)*SY
580 FOR I=1 TO 9
590 Y1=CY-A(I+1)*SY:X1=CX+(I+1)*SX
600 LINE (X,Y)-(X1,Y1),1
601 CIRCLE (X,Y),2,3:PAINT (X,Y)
610 X=X1:Y=Y1
620 NEXT I
621 CIRCLE (X,Y),2,3:PAINT (X,Y)
890 P=5
910 FOR I=1 TO 7
```

```
915 LOCATE 23,P
920 PRINT Y(I);
930 P=P+4
940 NEXT I
941 LOCATE 23,33:PRINT "78 79 80";
950 LOCATE 23,1
960 PRINT "YEAR"
970 FOR I=1 TO 10
971 X=CX+I*SX
972 LINE (X,167)-(X,171)
973 NEXT I
975 GOTO 975
```

DRAW Statement

The DRAW statement provides you with the ability to predefine BASIC strings that specify the definition of an object to be displayed when the statement is executed. The format of this statement is:

format$_A$: DRAW string parameters

The string parameters consist of a series of one or more movement commands. The available movement commands are listed in Table 11-5.

For the first nine commands listed in Table 11-5, n specifies the distance to move. The actual number of points moved is n times the scaling factor,

Table 11-5. DRAW Statement Movement Commands

COMMAND	OPERATIONAL RESULT
Un	Moves up n points
Dn	Moves down n points
Ln	Moves left n points
Rn	Moves right n points
En	Moves diagonally up and right n points
Fn	Moves diagonally down and right n points
Gn	Moves diagonally down and left n points
Hn	Moves diagonally up and left n points
Mx,y	Moves to point (x,y) if absolute or moves (x,y) points from current position if relative and plots a point
Bx,y	Same as Mx,y but does not plot point
Nx,y	Same as Mx,y but returns to original position when finished
An	Sets angle as a multiple of 90° (n=0 to n=3)
Tn	Turns angle n° where n can range from −360 to +360
Cn	Sets color to n (0 to 3 in medium resolution, 0 to 1 in high resolution)
Sn	Sets scale factor (1≤n≤255)
X string$	Executes substring

which is set by the S command. The scale factor is obtained by the S command automatically dividing the value of n by 4. Thus, if n=1, the resulting scale factor would be 1/4. Similarly, if n=20, the resulting scale factor would be 5. The actual number of points moved by the U, D, L, R, E, F, G, H, and relative M commands is the scale factor multiplied by the distances given in those commands. If the S command is omitted, a default scale factor of 1 will be assumed.

The Mx,y command permits you to move absolute or relative. If X is preceded by a plus (+) or minus (−) sign, the move is relative to the last point referenced. Otherwise, the move is absolute, to the indicated X,Y point.

When a DRAW statement is executed, BASIC examines the string and interprets the single letter commands contained in the string. To help you visualize the effect of the movement commands, consider Fig. 11-21, which illustrates the directions on the screen resulting from executing the first eight commands listed in Table 11-5.

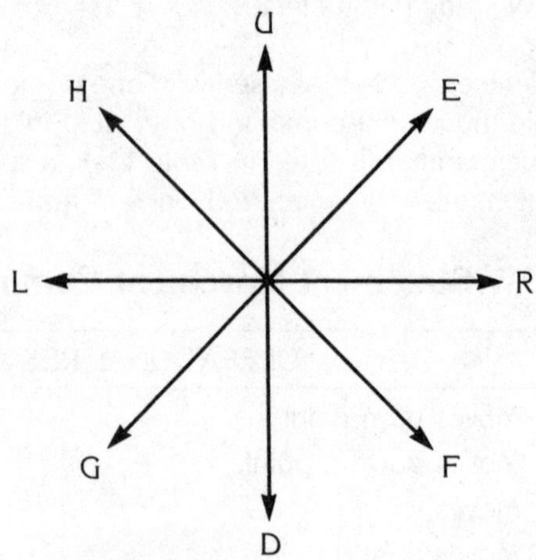

Fig. 11-21. DRAW command directions.

To see how the DRAW statement operates, consider the following program segment.

```
100 SCREEN 1
105 CLS
110 COLOR 9,0
120 PSET (50,50)
130 DRAW "U20R20D20L20"
140 A$="U50R50D50L50"
150 PSET (200,200)
160 DRAW A$
```

The execution of line 130 causes a line to be drawn up 20, right 20, and then down 20 positions on the screen. Since location (50,50) was the last point referenced, the drawing will commence at location 50,50. In line 140, a new set of movement commands is defined and set equal to the string A$. Then, after relocating the point reference in line 150, the next DRAW state-

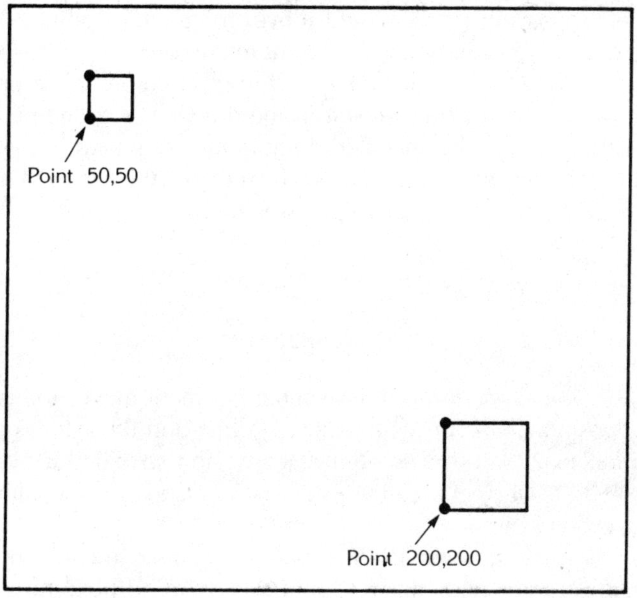

Fig. 11-22. DRAW statement example.

ment draws the string defined by A$. The result of this program segment is illustrated in Fig. 11-22.

It should be noted that you can also use semicolons or blanks as separators between the movement commands for clarity if you wish. Thus, as an example, line 130 could be rewritten as either of the two example shown below.

```
130 DRAW "U20 R20 D20 L20"
130 DRAW "U20; R20; D20; L20"
```

Now, let's cover each of the DRAW commands in detail to obtain an appreciation of the capability of this statement.

B command prefix. This command prefix results in the movement of the graphics point to a specified position on the screen. This is accomplished without a line being drawn between the last point referenced and the point specified by the X and Y coordinates of the command prefixed. Thus, the command

```
BM 100,50
```

when executed in a DRAW statement would move the graphics point to location 100,50 on the screen. You can also use relative movements as shown by the following example.

```
BM+30,-20
```

This command prefix would move the graphics point 30 pixels to the right and 20 pixels below the last point referenced.

M command. This command results in an absolute or relative move. This move may or may not result in the drawing of a line between the last point referenced and the specified point in the command. If the M command has a B prefix, no line will be drawn. To see how the B and M commands function, consider the following program segment.

```
100 SCREEN 1
110 KEY OFF:CLS
120 COLOR 9,0
130 DRAW "BM100,100M200,200"
```

The execution of this program segment moves the last point referenced to position 100,100 with drawing a line and then draws a line from that position to 200,200, since the M command specified a movement to location 200,200. Thus, you can use the M command to draw a line between any two specified points.

Other movement commands. The other movement commands are all relative commands that specify the number of pixel positions of relative displacement from the last point referenced. To see how these commands are used, consider the following program segment.

```
100 SCREEN 1
110 KEY OFF:CLS
120 COLOR 9,0
130 DRAW "BM40,80R50D30L40D50L10U80BM60,90R20D10L20U10"
135 PAINT (41,81)
140 DRAW "BM120,80R50D10L40D60R40D10L50U80"
145 PAINT (121,81)
```

Line 130 draws a capital P, while line number 140 draws a capital C. Next, highlight each letter by filling the drawn shape with color through the use of PAINT statements in lines 135 and 145. The result is a yellow PC on your display.

C command. This C command can be used in the DRAW statement to change the color of the following line. The format of this command is:

format: Cn

where n is an integer in the range 0 to 3 in medium-resolution graphics and 0 to 1 in high-resolution graphics. In medium-resolution graphics mode, a value of 0 selects the background color, while a value 1 to 3 results in the color from the palette selected by the COLOR statement being used for the next line drawn. Modify your previous program segment as follows to see the effect of this command.

```
100 SCREEN 1
110 KEY OFF:CLS
120 COLOR 9,0
130 DRAW "BM40,80R50D30L40D50L10U80C1BM60,90R20D10L20U10"
140 DRAW "C2BM120,80R50D10L40C3D60R40D10L50U80"
```

With the color in the DRAW command not initially specified, the default color, color 3 of palette 0, is used. This results in the outer boundary of the P colored in brown. Next, a color of 1 is specified by the C1 command in line 130. This changes the color of the inner portion of the character P to green. In line 140, the C2 command causes a portion of the C to be drawn in red, while the color command C3 causes the remainder of that character to be drawn in brown.

N command prefix. This command prefix can be viewed as an N final pixel movement prefix. This command may prefix any movement command and results in the location of the last point referenced not being updated. Figure 11-23 illustrates the operational result of the following program segment.

```
100 SCREEN 1
110 KEY OFF:CLS
120 COLOR 9,0
130 DRAW "BM160,100NE50NF50NG50NH50"
```

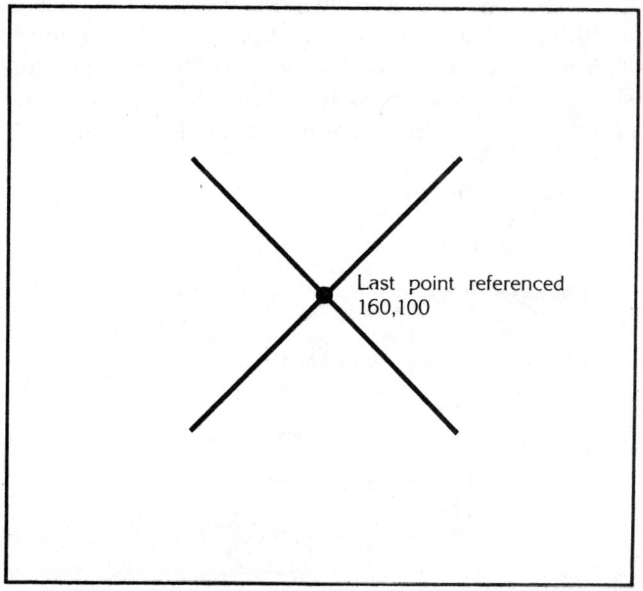

Fig. 11-23. N command operation.

Here, the commands NE, NF, NG, and NH result in lines drawn from location 160,100 50 pixels in length at 45, 135, 225, and 315° from the starting point. Since the N command prefixes E, F, G, and H, the last point referenced does not change.

Angle command. The A command sets an angle as a multiple of 90° that functions to rotate all subsequent lines in the draw command to the new position. The format of this command is:

format: An

where n is 0, 1, 2, or 3 and specifies rotations of 0, 90, 180, and 270°, respectively. To see how this command works, first construct a shape on the screen using the following program segment.

```
100 SCREEN 1
110 KEY OFF:CLS
120 COLOR 9,0
130 DRAW "BM160,50E5F5D45G5H5U45"
```

This program draws a sorry-looking propeller on the screen as illustrated in the upper portion of Fig. 11-24. Now rotate the propeller 90° by the following statement.

```
140 X$="BM160,50E5F5D45G5H5U45"
150 DRAW "A1"+X$
```

The execution of line 140 rotates the propeller 90° as shown in the right portion of Fig. 11-24. Note that the previously drawn propeller has not been erased. If you wish to simulate a rotating object, such as a propeller, you must erase the previously drawn object prior to rotating and drawing the new object. You can accomplish this by using the color command with color set to 0 since this will blank out a line. Thus, the following program segment would cause the propeller to appear to spin on the screen.

```
100 SCREEN 1
110 KEY OFF:CLS
120 COLOR 9,0
130 X$="BM160,50C1E5F5D45G5H5U45"
140 Y$="M160,50C0E5F5D45G5H5U45"
150 FOR I=1 TO 100:NEXT I 'time out
160 FOR J=0 TO 3 'rotate
170 P$=STR$(J):Q$=STR$(J) 'get string
180 DRAW "A"+P$+X$ 'rotate and draw
190 FOR I=1 TO 100:NEXT I 'time out
200 DRAW "A"+Q$+Y$'erase object previously drawn
210 NEXT J
220 DRAW "A2"+Y$
230 GOTO 150
```

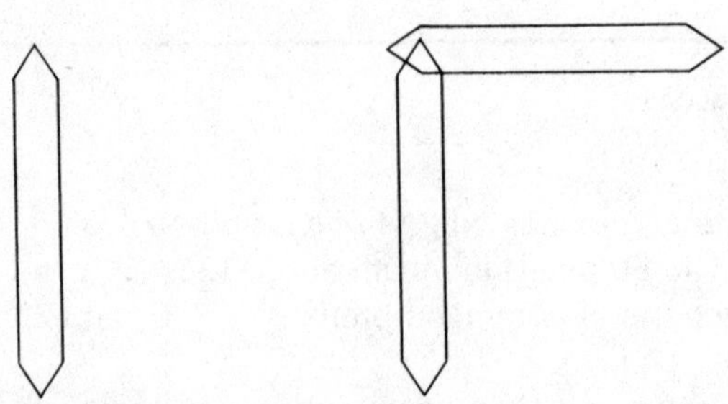

Fig. 11-24. Using the A command.

S command. This command is one of the most powerful commands for animation purposes. By being able to scale your drawings, you can obtain a visual depth perception by making objects appear greater or smaller in size. The format of this command is:

format: Sn

where n can range in value from 1 to 255. Here, the scale factor is n divided by 4 so that when n=1, the scale factor is 1/4. The scale factor multiplied by the number given in the U, D, L, R, E, F, G, and H commands results in the actual distance moved on the screen. To see how this command operates, a small program segment that uses a scale factor in a drawing will be examined.

To see how the scale factor works, let's define a string to be drawn and then vary the scale factor through the use of a FOR-NEXT loop as follows:

```
100 SCREEN 1
110 CLS:KEY OFF
120 COLOR 9,0
130 X$="BM2,2R4D4L4U4" 'form box
135 DRAW X$
140 FOR I=1 TO 200 STEP 4
150 Y$="S"+STR$(I)
160 DRAW Y$+X$
170 NEXT I
180 GOTO 180
```

The result of the execution of this program is shown in Fig. 11-25. Note that line 180 was included only to remove the Ok message from the screen.

Fig. 11-25. Using the S command.

X string command. This command causes a substring to be executed. This command allows you to execute a second string from within a string. This means that you can define any constant string and use it as a substring within a DRAW statement. Thus, you can use the DRAW statement to move positions while you draw certain predefined objects with the X command at each designated location. The following program segment illustrates one use of this command.

```
100 SCREEN 1
110 KEY OFF:CLS
120 COLOR 9,0
130 A$="R20D20L20U20"
140 DRAW "BM50,107XA$;BM150,107XA$;"
150 DRAW "BM50,123XA$;BM150,123XA$;"
```

In this example, the string A$ defines a square with a 20 pixel length. The DRAW statement in line 140 moves the last point referenced to two positions on the screen and executes the substring at each location. Line 150 performs a similar operation. Note that a semicolon must follow the execute substring variable. The result of the execution of this program segment is shown in Fig. 11-26. Using a little imagination, you can see that this illustration shows that you have drawn two screen doors.

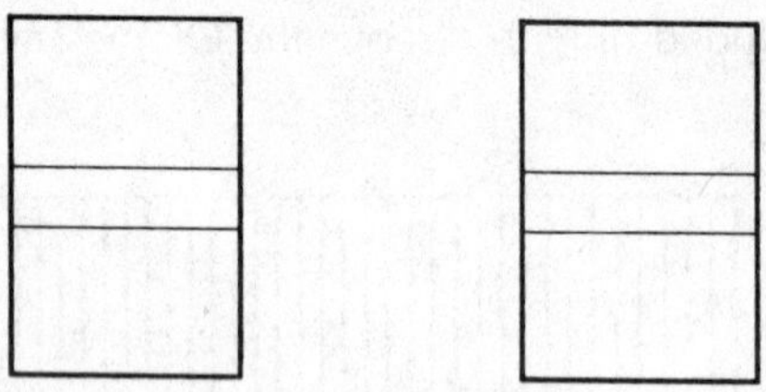

Fig. 11-26. Using the execute substring command.

GET Statement

The GET statement provides you with the ability to read points from a predefined area on the screen into an array. The complement to this statement is the PUT statement, which allows you to retrieve data from an array and place it onto a designated area on the screen.

The format of the GET statement is:

$format_A$: GET(X1,Y1) – (X2,Y2),array name

The two sets of X and Y coordinates define the rectangle from which the points will be read. The upper left corner is specified by (X1,Y1), while the lower right corner is specified by (X2,Y2), similar to the LINE statement when you wish to draw a box. The array name denotes the array into which the graphics data will be stored and must be previously dimensioned if it exceeds 11 elements. The number of elements required to be reserved for the array is:

4 + INT((X*bits per pixel + 7)/8)*Y

Here X and Y are the lengths of the horizontal and vertical sides of the rectangle and bits per pixel is 2 in medium-resolution graphics mode and 1 in high-resolution graphics.

To see the use of this statement, consider a rectangular area on the screen bounded by locations 10,50 and 40,80. The number of elements you must reserve for the array in medium-resolution graphics becomes:

4 + INT((31*1 + 7)/8)*31 = 128

Thus, the following program segment will move the graphics image inside the predefined rectangle into the array labeled X.

```
200 DIM X(127)
210 GET (10,50)-(40,80),X
```

The graphics image will remain in the array for later use by the PUT statement, which will now be covered.

PUT Statement

The PUT statement can be viewed as the complement of the GET statement, since it retrieves graphics data from an array and places it onto a designated area of the screen, The format of this statement is:

$format_A$: PUT(X1,Y1),array[,action]

Here, X1,Y1 define the upper left-hand corner of the location on the screen where the graphics image of the rectangle will be placed. The array name is the name of the numeric array that contains the information to be displayed. Action is an optional parameter that defines the operation to be performed on the graphics image prior to its display. Action may be PSET, PRESET, XOR, OR, or AND, while XOR is the default action.

By changing the upper left-hand coordinates in the statement, you can easily move objects around the screen. As an example of the use of this statement, consider the following program segment.

```
100 SCREEN 1
110 COLOR 9,0
120 KEY OFF:CLS
130 DRAW"BM10,10R10D10L10U10" 'DRAW SQUARE
140 DIM X(96)
150 GET (5,5)-(25,25),X
160 PUT(100,100),X,PSET
170 PUT(150,150),X,PSET
```

After a square is drawn in line 130, you can dimension the array that will hold the graphics image contained in the rectangular area you wish to store. Line 150 stores the image bounded by locations 5,5 and 25,25 in the array X. Line 160 replicates the stored image with the upper left-hand corner of the image at location 100,100, while line 170 also reproduces the stored image; however, this time the image is placed on the screen with location 150,150 as its upper left-hand corner.

The action parameters provide you with the ability to perform predefined operations on the data prior to its display. The PSET action option results in the transfer of the image defined in the GET statement with the colors and points set exactly as previously stored. When used as the action option, PSET results in the PUT statement being the exact complement of the GET statement.

The PRESET action option resets all the points that were set in the area bounded by the GET statement. This results in the display of a negative image on the screen.

The AND action option results in an AND operation on the points of the original rectangle of the GET statement and the points in the destination area defined by the PUT coordinate. If either point is reset, the resulting point will be reset, while if both points are set the resulting point will be set. This action option can be used to mask out areas within the rectangle formed by the PUT statement.

The OR action parameter performs an OR operation on the points of the original rectangle defined by the GET statement and the points in the destination area defined by the PUT coordinate. If either point is set, the resulting point is set, while if neither point is set the result will be reset.

The XOR action parameter performs an XOR operation on the points defined by the GET statement and the destination area on the screen defined by the PUT coordinate. When this action parameter is used, the points in the rectangular destination area will be inverted from where a point exists in the array image. A unique property of this parameter is that when an image is PUT against a background twice, the background will be restored to its original form. This allows you to move an object around the screen without affecting the background.

CHAPTER TWELVE

Batch and Shell Processing

COMPONENTS OF DOS

The PC AT's disk operating system contains four programs that can be viewed as the nucleus of DOS. These are the boot record, the IBMBIO and IBMDOS programs, and the COMMAND program.

The boot record is automatically loaded into the computer's memory each time DOS is initialized. The boot record is written onto every disk by the FORMAT program contained in DOS and serves as the disk initial program load. That is, after being loaded into memory, the boot record will load the rest of DOS.

The IBMBIO.COM program is an I/O device handler. This program is responsible for reading and writing data to and from the PC AT's memory and peripheral devices attached to the AT. Like the boot record, this program is placed on each disk formatted by the FORMAT program. As a hidden file, this file will not be listed when a DOS DIR command or BASIC FILES command is invoked. You can use the CHKDSK (check disk) command to determine the number of hidden files on a disk. Normally, the IBMBIO.COM and IBMDOS.COM are the only two files that are hidden from directory searches.

The IBMDOS.COM program is the second hidden file normally placed on a disk using the DOS FORMAT program. This program contains a file manager and a collection of service functions that are employed by programs developed to run under the control of DOS.

The last program that can be considered as part of the nucleus of DOS is the COMMAND.COM program. This program serves as a command processor, accepting commands that are used to run the appropriate programs. The COMMAND.COM program is extremely important, since this program provides the AT with its capability for automatic batch processing.

Every time DOS is initialized, the COMMAND.COM program will search the DOS disk for a file named AUTOEXEC.BAT. This file, if found, will be automatically executed whenever the system is initialized. The extension BAT designates a batch file and the filename AUTOEXEC designates the batch file that is automatically executed when DOS is initialized. By entering programs or commands into a file named AUTOEXEC.BAT, you can cause the AT to initiate a predefined sequence of operations every time DOS is initialized. Since such programs or commands will be executed in sequence, in effect you have generated a batch file of batch processing commands for the PC AT to execute.

If an AUTOEXEC.BAT file is on your DOS disk, this file will be immediately executed at the time of DOS initialization, and the normal DOS day and time prompt messages will be bypassed if you exclude DATE and TIME commands from your batch file. If no such file is on the DOS disk, the normal DOS prompts will be issued.

BATCH PROCESSING

You can execute a batch file by entering the name of the batch file at the DOS command level. Thus, the format required to execute a batch file is:

format$_{DOS}$: [d:][path]filename[parameters]

Here, the filename must have a filename extension of BAT. The optional parameters permit you to design a batch file that can perform different tasks based on operator-supplied data. Such parameters can be passed to the batch file when the file executes. If the drive specifier and path are not specified, the DOS default drive and current directory are used.

To obtain an understanding of the capability afforded by batch processing, let's develop a small example. By selective modifications to this example, you will obtain an appreciation of batch processing as well as an understanding of the utilization of other batch-processing commands.

Suppose you wish to have the capability to have several commands automatically performed. To obtain this capability, you can create a batch file whose invocation will cause DOS to execute such commands one at a time.

You can create a batch file by using the line editor program (EDLIN) or by using the COPY command, with the keyboard console as the file specification to transfer data directly from the console to the batch file. As indicated in the format for this command, the name BATCH is not part of the command, unless you want the name of the batch file to be BATCH.BAT.

To generate a batch file from the keyboard, you can enter the following version of the COPY command once you are at the DOS prompt level signified by the two-character sequence A> or C>, depending on whether DOS is on the first diskette drive or the first fixed disk.

```
A>COPY CON: BATCH.BAT
```

Although you would normally expect to use the device name KYBD:, you must use the DOS reserved name of CON:, since this name signifies to DOS that the console will be used as an input device. Thus, KYBD: is used as the device name within a BASIC program, while CON: is its equivalent at the DOS level.

The preceding command causes all entries from the keyboard to be copied onto the batch file named BATCH with the extension BAT. Note that only the extension BAT signifies to DOS that this is a batch file. Here, the filename is meaningless unless it is changed to AUTOEXEC.

Once the batch file is created, you can execute the commands in the file by simply entering the disk drive the batch file is located on and its file name.

As each command is executed, the DOS prompt characters and the command will be displayed on the screen. It should be noted that the use of the ECHO command allows you to enable or inhibit the display of batch commands as they are executed. In addition, DOS operational messages based on the results of the execution or attempted execution of a command will be displayed. As an example, such messages can range from "X File(s) copied" to "File not found" for file reference commands.

Two examples of batch file invocations and their operational results follow.

Example	**Operational result**
A>BATCH	Executes the commands in the file named BATCH located on the default drive
A>C:\SALES\RPT	Executes the commands in the batch file named RPT located in the SALES directory in drive C

Note that only the filename and not the extension is required when you wish to execute a batch file, although you can also include the extension if you so desire.

Now that you have initially described the methods to create and execute a batch file, let's actually construct such a file. This will permit you to obtain an idea about the capability of such files and how they operate.

Suppose you created a BASIC program that performs some type of processing function that requires program execution on a monthly cycle. The program and a data file named DATA1.DAT that serves as an input to the program are located on a master diskette labeled "MASTER". Each time the program is executed it creates a data file named DATA2.DAT. Suppose you wish to automatically run the program and have the output data file replace the input data file for the next execution cycle of the program. By creating a batch file, you can have the AT automatically perform the necessary commands to execute the program, copy files, and erase the unnecessary files from the master diskette. By performing these functions with a minimum of operator interaction, you can reduce the probability of operator error to a minimum.

The functions you wish to perform can be illustrated graphically as shown in Fig. 12-1.

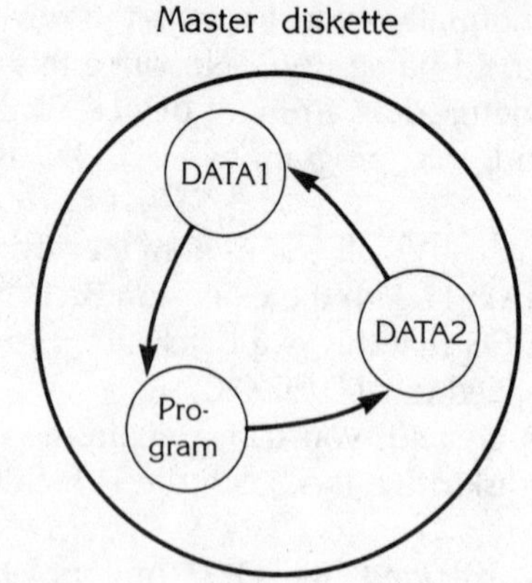

Fig. 12-1. Batch-processing function example.

You can tabulate the functions illustrated in Fig. 12-1. This tabulation will help you ascertain the DOS commands you must include in the batch file to perform the indicated operations. You can break the functions illustrated in Fig. 12-1 into three specific areas as indicated in the following.

1. Execute the program named PROGRAM on the master diskette.
2. Delete data files DATA1.DAT on the diskette in drive A.
3. Rename the data file DATA2.DAT on the diskette in drive A with the name DATA1.DAT.

Now that you know what functions have to be performed, let's equate the appropriate DOS command to each function.

If PROGRAM is written in advanced BASIC, then the command BASICA PROGRAM will tell DOS to load advanced BASIC and execute the program named PROGRAM. You can place this statement in a batch file by using the line editor or by using the COPY command directly from the keyboard. For the latter method, you would enter:

```
A>COPY CON: SUPER.BAT
BASICA PROGRAM
```

Here, you are creating a batch file named SUPER.BAT that will load advanced BASIC and execute the program file named PROGRAM when the batch file is invoked. You can delete the file named DATA1.DAT from the diskette in drive A by the following command.

```
ERASE DATA1.DAT
```

Finally, you can use the RENAME command to change the name of the DATA2.DAT file on the master diskette to DATA1.DAT. The command required to perform this function is:

```
RENAME DATA2.DAT DATA1.DAT
```

The commands previously covered can be entered in sequence into your batch file as shown below:

```
A>COPY CON: SUPER.BAT
BASICA PROGRAM
ERASE DATA1.DAT
RENAME DATA2.DAT DATA1.DAT
```

Once you have completed entering your commands, you can press the F6 key and the Enter key to generate an end-of-file mark. This key sequence also terminates the use of the keyboard as an input device to send data to the file.

Once the F6 (displayed as ^Z) and Enter keys are pressed, DOS will respond with the message:

```
^Z
            1 File(s) copied
A>
```

At this point, your batch file has been created and stored on the diskette in drive A. Now, you merely have to instruct the PC AT operator to initialize DOS and enter the batch command: SUPER. This will cause the batch program SUPER.BAT to be executed and each command in that file will be executed in sequence.

If any of your batch commands are invalid or reference nonexistent files, DOS will display an appropriate error message and resume execution at the next command in the batch file.

Now, suppose you wish to simplify the sequence of operations so the batch file is automatically executed whenever DOS is initialized. You can accomplish this by creating a special batch file called AUTOEXEC.BAT.

AUTOEXEC.BAT File

The AUTOEXEC.BAT file is a special batch file that will be automatically executed when DOS is initialized. As previously mentioned in this chapter, the command processor program, COMMAND.COM, will search the root directory of the DOS disk for a program file named AUTOEXEC.BAT. If this file is encountered on the disk, the command processor will automatically execute the file. Thus, creating a file named AUTOEXEC.BAT instead of the previous file named SUPER.BAT will cause the commands on the file to be executed automatically when DOS is initialized.

You can create the AUTOEXEC.BAT file similarly to the manner in which you created the SUPER.BAT file. That is, you can use the line editor (EDLIN) program or the COPY command, using the keyboard as the source file. For the latter you would enter.

```
A>COPY CON: AUTOEXEC.BAT
```

Then, you would enter the commands previously entered when you created the SUPER.BAT file and press the F6 and Enter keys to terminate the use of the keyboard as an input device and place an end-of-file mark on the AUTOEXEC.BAT file. Now, when the operator brings up DOS, the AUTOEXEC.BAT file will be automatically executed.

Although the batch file will now execute automatically, what happens if your batch file must access another disk? While you can assume that the program's operating instructions will cover this subject, a mechanism to prompt the operator would be desirable. You can obtain this capability through the use of the REM and PAUSE commands.

REM Command

The REM command provides you with the ability to display remarks from within a batch file. The format of this command is:

format$_{DOS}$: REM[remark]

You can have a string of up to 123 bytes in length in each REM command. When the REM command is executed within a batch file, the remark will be displayed and the next command will be executed. Obviously, this presents a problem if part of your batch file contained the following two commands:

```
REM Insert BACKUP diskette
COPY DATA2.DAT B:DATA2.DAT
```

Here, the message "Insert BACKUP diskette" would be displayed and quicker than a floppy diskette insertion the batch program would attempt to copy the file DATA2.DAT from the diskette in drive A to a second diskette. What is needed is a mechanism to delay the execution of the COPY command until the operator signifies that he or she has placed the appropriate diskette in the disk drive and is ready to proceed. This mechanism is obtained by the use of the PAUSE command.

PAUSE Command

The PAUSE command can be used in a batch file to suspend processing. The format of this command is:

format$_{DOS}$: PAUSE[remark]

In addition to suspending processing, this command causes the message "Strike a key when ready . . ." to be displayed. When the AT operator presses any key except Ctrl+Break, the batch file will resume processing at the next command in the file.

Pressing the Ctrl+Break key combination during the execution of a batch file will cause the message "Terminate batch job (Y/N)?" to be displayed. If you enter Y, the remaining commands in the batch file will be ignored and the DOS prompt will appear.

You can also include an optional remark in the PAUSE command. This remark will be displayed prior to the message "Strike a key when ready . . ." being displayed. This optional remark can be any string of characters up to 121 bytes in length.

Returning to the example, you could recode the previous two lines as follows:

```
REM Insert BACKUP diskette
PAUSE
COPY DATA2.DAT B:DATA2.DAT
```

The following examples show the operational result of the execution of the preceding REM and PAUSE commands. Note that both the DOS prompt characters as well as the commands are displayed as each command is executed.

```
A>REM Insert BACKUP diskette

A>PAUSE
Strike a key when ready . . .
```

Or, you can incorporate the remark into the PAUSE command as follows:

```
PAUSE Insert BACKUP diskette
COPY DATA2.DAT B:DATA2.DAT
```

You may occasionally create a lengthy batch file and use a liberal number of REM commands as a mechanism to internally document the file. In such cases, you may wish to inhibit the screen display of the REM statements as well as other DOS commands executed from the batch file. This can be accomplished by the use of the ECHO command.

ECHO Command

The ECHO command can be used to inhibit or enable the screen display of DOS commands executed from a batch file as well as display an initial message. The format of this command is:

$$\text{format}_{\text{DOS}}\text{: ECHO} \begin{Bmatrix} \text{ON} \\ \text{OFF} \end{Bmatrix} \text{[message]}$$

After power-on or a system reset is performed, the default value of ECHO is ECHO ON. Thus, if you wanted to stop the display of commands on the screen, you would enter the command ECHO OFF at the appropriate place in your batch file where you want command messages to be inhibited. Similarly, you could enter the ECHO ON command at a position in your batch file where you wish to have the execution of future batch commands in the batch file displayed.

Prior to using an AUTOEXEC file, you should consider whether or not any program in the batch file requires the use of the current date or time. This is because the execution of the AUTOEXEC.BAT bypasses the normal DOS prompt that requires the operator to enter the current date. While the clock/calendar on the PC AT may appear to alleviate the necessity of including the DATE and TIME commands, no allowance is made for daylight savings time changes, so you may wish to include these commands in your batch file. If one or more programs in the batch file requires such data, you can include the DATE and/or TIME commands in the AUTOEXEC.BAT file.

DATE Command

Since the date is recorded in the file directory every time you create or alter a file, you should include a DATE command in your batch file if any programs or commands result in the creation or modification of files. By entering the command DATE on one line of a batch file the message:

```
Current date is mm-dd-yy
Enter new date:
```

will be displayed when the command is executed. Processing will be suspended while the system awaits the entry of the new date.

If you wish, you can display a date by specifying the month, day, and year within the DATE command. While this will not set the date, it will show a date when the DATE command is executed. The following example shows the operational result of the execution of a DATE command that contains a date.

```
A>DATE 05-05-99
Current date is 00-00-80
Enter new date: 04-06-82
```

Here, the optional parameters of the command would be specified when you enter the DATE command into an AUTOEXEC.BAT file. The format of this command is:

format$_{DOS}$: DATE[mm-dd-yy]

TIME Command

Under DOS, both the date and time will be recorded in the directory whenever a file is created or modified. The format of the TIME command is:

format$_{DOS}$: TIME[hh:mm:ss.xx]

If you merely enter the command TIME into a batch file, the message

```
Current time is hh:mm:ss.xx
Enter new time:
```

will be displayed. This lets the AT operator enter the new time from the console. You can display a time by specifying the hours, minutes, seconds, and hundredths of a second in the command; however, the execution of this command will still require the operator to set the time or ignore the command by pressing the Enter key.

Batch-Processing Parameters

Since very few things are static in the real world, you can include dummy parameters within a batch file. These parameters can be supplied values by the operator when the file is executed. Up to 10 such dummy parameters, labeled %0 through %9 can be specified. As an example of the capability of dummy parameters, consider the following segment contained in a batch file.

```
COPY %1 %2
TYPE %3
```

Here, the dummy parameters %1, %2, and %3 will be sequentially specified by the operator when he or she executes the file. If the file containing the dummy parameters was created under the name SUPER.BAT, then the operator might enter

```
A>SUPER A:XRAY.BAS B:BOOM.DAT B:HIST.DAT
```

Here, A:XRAY.BAS is substituted for %1, B:BOOM.DAT is substituted for %2, and B:HIST.DAT is substituted for %3. The dummy parameter %0 is a special case, since it will always be replaced by the drive designator, if specified, as well as the filename of the batch file.

Conditional Execution

Two DOS batch commands provide you with the ability to conditionally execute DOS commands. The IF command permits the conditional execution of DOS commands, while the GOTO command permits you to branch to various locations within a batch file.

IF Command

The format of the IF command is:

format$_{DOS}$: IF [NOT] condition command

The condition parameter can be ERRORLEVEL number, string1 = = string2, or EXIST filespec. Thus, the IF command allows you to execute a batch command based on three types of conditions.

When the ERRORLEVEL number is specified, the command will be executed if the previous program executed from the batch file had an exit code equal to or higher than the ERRORLEVEL number. If string1 = = string2 is specified, the command will be executed only when the two strings are identical. The third option condition results in the command being executed only if the given filespec exists. You can see how to use the IF command by examining the GOTO command.

GOTO Command

The DOS GOTO command is very similar to the BASIC GOTO statement. Upon execution of the command in a batch file, control is transferred to the line following the one containing the specified label. The format of this command is:

format$_{DOS}$:GOTO label

Note that labels in a batch file must be preceded by a colon (:). Combining the IF and GOTO statements in an example illustrates the use of these two commands. Suppose a portion of your batch file is as follows:

```
PAUSE insert diskette labeled Junk
IF EXIST DATA2.DAT GOTO X
PAUSE wrong diskette inserted
:X
TYPE DATA2.DAT
```

The preceding batch file segment first displays the message "insert diskette labeled Junk" and suspends execution, displaying the message "Strike a key when ready . . ." Once a key is pressed, the batch program checks to see if the file DATA2.DAT exists, and if so, it branches to the command after the label X. Thus, if the desired file exists, it will be displayed by the execution of the TYPE command. If the file does not exist, the batch file will again suspend execution and display the message "wrong diskette inserted" and "Strike a key when ready . . .". Obviously, another loop could be constructed to permit the operator an endless number of chances to insert the diskette containing the desired file.

From the preceding discussion, you can see how batch files can be employed to string sequences of commands together. The primary use of such files is to simplify and reduce the scope of operator interaction with the PC AT. Normally, batch files should be considered by programmers as a mechanism to reduce the level of interaction required to execute a series of programs and operations by persons who may not have the knowledge and experience necessary to issue commands and follow a sequence of operational instructions.

Configuration File

One special type of batch file is a file named CONFIG.SYS. This configuration file contains commands that are used to configure your system. Then, each time you power-on your PC AT or perform a system reset, DOS will search the root directory of the drive from which it was initiated for this file. If found, this file will be read by DOS, and the various commands within the file will be interpreted. Commands in this file can be used to specify which country's date and time format will be used, the maximum number of drives that can be open at one time, the name of a file containing a device driver, and other configuration-related functions. When shipped in the United States, DOS has a configuration file containing one statement as illustrated below.

```
A>TYPE CONFIG.SYS
COUNTRY=001
```

Here, the statement COUNTRY=001 specifies the date and time format for the United States. To examine the use of the CONFIG.SYS file, let us assume you wish to create a virtual disk on your system. This will allow you to reserve a portion of RAM memory to be used as if it were a disk drive. Since a RAM disk provides a far faster file access or data transfer than an actual floppy disk (because the process is electrical rather than mechanical), its use in place of a second floppy can be highly advantageous for programs requiring numerous I/O operations.

To set up a virtual disk requires the use of the DEVICE statement in your configuration file. The format of this statement is:

format: DEVICE = [d:][path]VDISK.SYS [size][sector][entries]

where d: path is the drive and directory path containing the virtual disk; size specifies the virtual disk size in K bytes, with 64K used as a default value; sector is the sector size in bytes, with allowable sizes 128, 256, and 512 (here, the default value is 128) and entries specifies the number of directory entries (files) that the virtual disk can contain. The range of this parameter is 2 to 512 and has a default value of 64.

Suppose you wish to set up a virtual disk of 320K of RAM with a sector size of 512 bytes that can contain up to 64 files. To accomplish the preceding, you would enter the following statement into your configuration file.

```
DEVICE = VDISK.SYS 320 512 64
```

You can use either EDLIN or the COPY command to create the configuration file. Using the latter, you might enter the following two statements to set the time and date to the format for the United States and install your virtual disk.

```
A>COPY CON: CONFIG.SYS
COUNTRY=001
DEVICE=VDISK.SYS 320 512 64
^Z
        1 File(s) copied

A>
```

Note that like a batch file, the data entry to the CONFIG file is terminated by pressing either the F6 key or Ctrl+Z.

Now, you should test your PC AT to see if the virtual disk is installed the next time you power-on your system.

When you power-on your AT the next time or perform a system reset, the following message will appear, indicating that 320K bytes of memory was allocated to virtual disk D.

```
VDISK Version 1.0 virtual disk D:
   Buffer size:          320 KB
   Sector size:          512
Directory entries:   64

Current date is Sun 11-11-1984
Enter new date (mm-dd-yy):
```

Note that the virtual disk drive designator is based upon the first unused disk on your system. Thus, if you already have two disk drives called A: and B:, the virtual disk will be designated C:. Similarly, if you have drives A:, B:, and C:, the virtual disk will be designated D:.

To see how the virtual disk operates, consider the following example. Here, we will copy BASICA.COM to the virtual disk and then obtain a directory listing of drive D.

```
A>copy basica.* d:
BASICA.COM
            1 File(s) copied

A>dir d:

 Volume in drive D is VDISK V1.0
 Directory of D:\

BASICA      COM      26880      8-14-84      8:00a
            1 File(s)     296960 bytes free

A>
```

Figure 12-2 illustrates the relationship between the CONFIG.SYS file and an AUTOEXEC.BAT file with respect to the tasks DOS performs during its initialization process. Note that any CONFIG.SYS file on the system disk will be executed prior to any AUTOEXEC.BAT file. Also note that the date and time prompts will be bypassed by an AUTOEXEC.BAT file unless that file contains the DATE and TIME commands.

Now that you have reviewed the use of batch processing, you will use the previous material covered in this book to create a series of batch files and a BASIC program to simplify the utilization of tree structured directories.

FIXED DISK ORGANIZER PROGRAMS

Let us assume you have a fixed disk and wish to organize it into four directories under the root directory containing assorted programs as illustrated in Fig. 12-3. In the remainder of this chapter we will develop two methods to create a series of programs to organize a fixed disk.

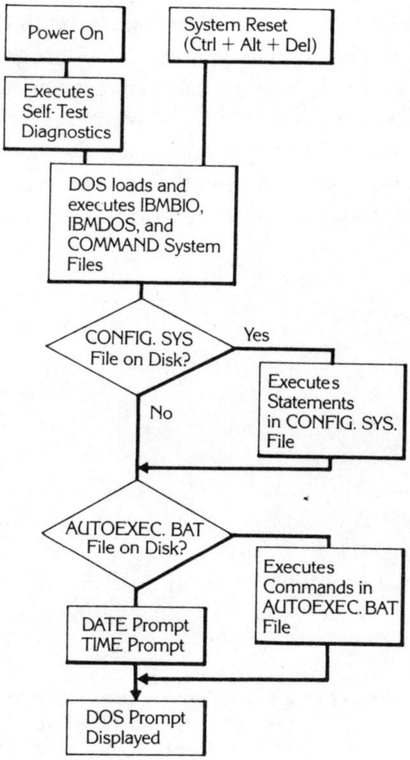

Fig. 12-2. DOS initialization process.

The first set of programs will illustrate the relationship between batch files on different directories using a tricky method to pass parameters from a BASIC program to a batch file. The second set of programs incorporates the use of the BASIC SHELL statement to simplify the fixed disk organization process. Either set of programs can be used to construct a comprehensive main menu driver that will display programs on the fixed disk and automatically change directories and execute a desired program based on a numeric response to the display prompt, returning you to the menu after you exit the previously requested program. The reason two methods are covered is that the SHELL statement is only applicable to BASIC version 3.0 and later versions of BASIC. Thus, some readers may select to use the first method to be covered for older PC systems that do not have BASIC 3.0. In addition, the first method requires a large number of batch files and illustrates the interaction of batch files on different directories.

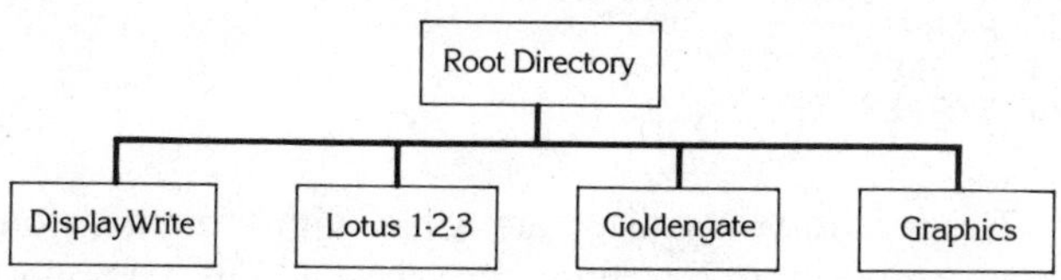

Fig. 12-3. Directory structure.

As illustrated in Fig. 12-3, you wish to place the IBM DisplayWrite program and its data files in one directory, Lotus 1-2-3 programs and files in another directory, and so on. Since persons unfamiliar with DOS and tree structured directories may use your PC AT, it would be nice to display a menu upon power-on or system reset that would place the operator in the root directory, switch him or her to the requested directory, and automatically place into execution each requested program. To do this, you must first create four directories as follows:

```
C>MKDIR\DISPLAY

C>MKDIR\LOTUS

C>MKDIR\GOLD

C>MKDIR\GRAPH
```

Next, you create a BASIC program and save it in the root directory under the name MAIN MENU. This program is listed below and requires some explanation as to your use of files 1.JNK through 5.JNK.

```
10 KEY OFF
15 CLS
20 PRINT "*****************************************************"
25 PRINT "*                  IBM PC AT MAIN MENU              *"
30 PRINT "*               DOS 3.X OPERATING SYSTEM            *"
35 PRINT "*****************************************************"
40 PRINT "*                                                   *"
45 PRINT "*               1 = IBM DisplayWrite II             *"
50 PRINT "*               2 = LOTUS 1-2-3                     *"
55 PRINT "*               3 = Cullinet Goldengate             *"
60 PRINT "*               4 = Decision Resources Sign-Master  *"
65 PRINT "*               5 = EXIT to DOS                     *"
70 PRINT "*****************************************************"
75 PRINT
80 INPUT "ENTER PROGRAM NUMBER DESIRED ",X
85 IF X>=1 AND X<=5 THEN 100
90 BEEP
95 GOTO 15
100 ON X GOTO 110,120,130,140,150
110 OPEN "1.JNK" FOR OUTPUT AS #1
115 GOTO 160
120 OPEN "2.JNK" FOR OUTPUT AS #1
125 GOTO 160
130 OPEN "3.JNK" FOR OUTPUT AS #1
135 GOTO 160
140 OPEN "4.JNK" FOR OUTPUT AS #1
145 GOTO 160
150 OPEN "5.JNK" FOR OUTPUT AS #1
160 PRINT #1,X
165 CLOSE
170 SYSTEM
```

The reason you will create a file with the extension .JNK based on the program you wish to execute is that the DOS IF statement only works with an error level number, a replaceable parameter, or the existence or nonexistence of a file. Since replaceable parameters result from the entry of parameters in a DOS command, there is no easy way to pass a variable from a BASIC program to a DOS batch file. Thus, by creating a file in BASIC, you can then have your batch file test for its existence, using the DOS IF statement. The batch file is illustrated in the following.

```
ECHO OFF
BASICA MAINMENU.BAS
IF EXIST 1.JNK GOTO DISPLAY
IF EXIST 2.JNK GOTO LOTUS
IF EXIST 3.JNK GOTO GOLD
IF EXIST 4.JNK GOTO SIGN
IF EXIST 5.JNK GOTO EXIT
:DISPLAY
CD\DISPLAY
DISPLAY.BAT
:LOTUS
CD\LOTUS
LOTUS.BAT
:GOLD
CD\GOLD
GOLD.BAT
:SIGN
CD\GRAPH
SIGN.BAT
:EXIT
ERASE 5.JNK
ECHO END BATCH JOB RETURN TO DOS
```

In the first line of the batch file, ECHO OFF turns off the display of all DOS commands. Next, advanced BASIC is executed, using the file MAINMENU, located in the root directory. Note that the BASIC program clears the screen and turns off the soft keys, resulting in your display screen appearing as illustrated below:

```
***************************************************
*               IBM PC AT MAIN MENU               *
*            DOS 3.X OPERATING SYSTEM             *
***************************************************
*                                                 *
*           1 = IBM DisplayWrite II               *
*           2 = LOTUS 1-2-3                       *
*           3 = Cullinet Goldengate               *
*           4 = Decision Resources Sign-Master    *
*           5 = EXIT to DOS                       *
***************************************************

ENTER PROGRAM NUMBER DESIRED
```

Depending on the program number entered, one of five files with the extension JNK will be created—1.JNK if program number 1 was selected, 2.JNK if program number 2 was selected, and so on. Note that the BASIC program uses the BEEP statement to generate a tone if a number other than 1 through 5 is entered and then clears the display and regenerates the screen display. Thus, you must enter a number corresponding to the five available options in the menu.

Once you select the desired program number, the appropriate file with the extension JNK is created in the root directory and the program terminates, passing control back to the batch file in the root directory. Here, lines 3 through 7 in the batch file use the IF command to test for the existence of the file with the JNK extension that was created by the BASIC program. Thus, if 1.JNK exists, the batch file branches to the label :DISPLAY.

Assuming you entered program number 1 when the BASIC program executed, the batch file would branch to the label :DISPLAY. At this point, the next line in the batch file changes the directory to DISPLAY and issues the command DISPLAY.BAT to execute the batch file in that directory. You would have previously entered a batch file named DISPLAY in that directory to execute the IBM DisplayWrite program as well as a command to change the directory back to the root. Since the file with the extension .JNK should be removed, you will also include the command CLEANUP in the batch file named DISPLAY, which will erase any file whose extension is .JNK and execute the AUTOEXEC file again. To demonstrate this concept, you will enter a one-line message in the DISPLAY file in order to see that you were transferred there correctly. Thus, the DISPLAY file in the directory \DISPLAY would contain the following statements:

```
C>TYPE DISPLAY.BAT
ECHO DISPLAYWRITE DOES ITS THING
CD\
CLEANUP

C>
```

Similarly, under the root directory, the BATCH file named CLEANUP would contain the following two DOS statements.

```
C>TYPE CLEANUP.BAT
ERASE *.JNK
AUTOEXEC.BAT

C>
```

Now when you turn power on or perform a system reset, the AUTOEXEC file loads BASIC and executes the BASIC program MAINMENU. If you select option 1, the file 1.JNK is created, which causes the batch file to branch to the label :DISPLAY. Next, the directory is changed to DISPLAY and the batch file DISPLAY.BAT is executed, which is verified by the following display.

```
**************************************************
*              IBM PC AT MAIN MENU               *
*            DOS 3.X OPERATING SYSTEM            *
**************************************************
*                                                *
*          1 = IBM DisplayWrite II               *
*          2 = LOTUS 1-2-3                       *
*          3 = Cullinet Goldengate               *
*          4 = Decision Resources Sign-Master    *
*          5 = EXIT to DOS                       *
**************************************************

ENTER PROGRAM NUMBER DESIRED 1
DISPLAYWRITE DOES ITS THING
```

After DisplayWrite executes (shown by the use of ECHO DISPLAY-WRITE DOES ITS THING in the batch file) and you exit this program, the batch statements CD\ and CLEANUP are executed. This causes the directory to change to the root directory and the batch file CLEANUP in that directory to execute. In turn, CLEANUP erases any file with the extension .JNK in the root directory and then executes AUTOEXEC again. Only by entering 5 when the program menu occurs can you exit this sequence. Figure 12-4 illustrates the relationship between the DISPLAY and root directories and the files on each directory. Note that all that remains is for you to create the appropriate batch CLEANUP program.

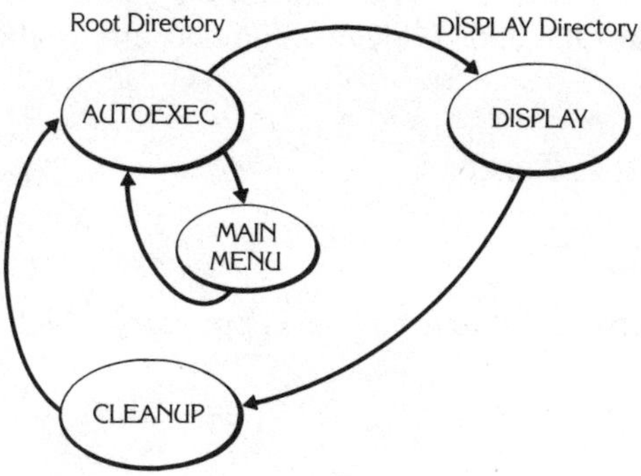

Fig. 12-4. File relationship.

SHELL Processing

In BASIC releases 3.0 and later, a SHELL statement is included which can be used to load and execute another program file, such as a file with .COM, .BAT, and .EXE extensions. The format of this BASIC statement is:

format$_A$: SHELL[command string]

The command string in the statement is a string expression containing the name of a program to be executed and any optional parameters you want to pass to that program. The following examples illustrate the use of the SHELL statement from within a BASIC program.

Example	**Operational Result**
100 SHELL "C\SALES\EST.BAT"	Executes the batch file EST in the SALES directory on drive C
120 SHELL"EST.BAT"	Executes the batch file EST in the current directory on the default drive

When a SHELL statement is used to execute another program, that program is known as a child process. When the child process completes execution, control is returned to the parent BASIC program containing the invoking

SHELL statement, at the statement following the SHELL statement. When control is passed from a parent BASIC program to a batch file, the batch file should contain EXIT as the last statement in the file to permit a return to the parent BASIC program. Now that you have a feeling for the utility of the BASIC SHELL statement, let us revise the previous fixed disk organizer program to take advantage of the BASIC SHELL statement.

In the root directory, you will again have an AUTOEXEC file, but now it only requires one statement to execute the BASIC program that contains the menu and uses SHELL statements to execute programs in the various subdirectories. Obviously, you can add additional DOS statements to this file, such as the ECHO OFF statement or TIME and DATE statements. In the following example, the ECHO OFF and BASICA statements are used in the AUTOEXEC file.

```
C>TYPE AUTOEXEC.BAT
ECHO OFF
BASICA MENU.BAS
```

Now let's examine the revised BASIC program, which is listed in the following.

```
10 KEY OFF
15 CLS
20 PRINT "*************************************************"
25 PRINT "*              IBM PC AT MAIN MENU              *"
30 PRINT "*            DOS 3.X OPERATING SYSTEM           *"
35 PRINT "*************************************************"
40 PRINT "*                                               *"
45 PRINT "*            1 = IBM DisplayWrite II            *"
50 PRINT "*            2 = LOTUS 1-2-3                    *"
55 PRINT "*            3 = Cullinet Goldengate            *"
60 PRINT "*            4 = Decision Resources Sign-Master *"
65 PRINT "*            5 = EXIT to DOS                    *"
70 PRINT "*************************************************"
75 PRINT
80 INPUT "ENTER PROGRAM NUMBER DESIRED ",X
85 IF X>=1 AND X<=5 THEN 100
90 BEEP
95 GOTO 15
100 ON X GOTO 110,120,130,140,150
110 SHELL "\DISPLAY\DISPLAY.BAT"
115 GOTO 160
120 SHELL "\LOTUS\LOTUS.BAT"
125 GOTO 160
130 SHELL "\GOLD\GOLD.BAT"
135 GOTO 160
140 SHELL "\GRAPH\SIGN.BAT"
145 GOTO 160
150 SYSTEM
160 GOTO 15
```

In the preceding program, the SHELL statements automatically transfer control to the appropriate batch file in the required directory if a program number between 1 and 4 is entered. If the number 5 is entered, the command SYSTEM returns you to DOS. Note that when control is passed back to the BASIC program from one of the batch files, the display is cleared and the main menu is redisplayed. Now, the only additional files required are one batch file under each of the four directories. Here, each batch file could simply execute the required program or perform additional functions if required. Also note that you could directly execute a .COM or .EXE file through the BASIC SHELL statement, thereby eliminating the requirement for a batch file in each directory. Thus, if the programs you wish to include in different directories are .EXE or .COM files, you could simply reference those files in the SHELL statement. In the following example, a batch file in the DISPLAY directory is used.

```
C>COPY CON: DISPLAY.BAT
ECHO OFF
ECHO DISPLAYWRITER DOES ITS THING
ECHO THEN BASIC PROGRAM RESUMES CONTROL
EXIT
^Z
        1 File(s) copied

C>CD\
```

Note that the batch file is terminated with EXIT, to pass control back to the parent BASIC program. If you are typing these files into your AT, don't forget to change back to the root directory prior to entering AUTOEXEC if you wish to test these programs. Otherwise, you would be in the DISPLAY directory, which does not contain the AUTOEXEC file. In the following example, you will enter the command AUTOEXEC to execute the batch file, which invokes BASIC and loads and executes the program MENU.BAS on the root directory. Upon entering 1 as the desired program number, the BASIC program transfers control to the batch file DISPLAY.BAT in the DISPLAY directory as illustrated here.

```
*************************************************
*              IBM PC AT MAIN MENU              *
*            DOS 3.X OPERATING SYSTEM           *
*************************************************
*                                               *
*           1 = IBM DisplayWrite II             *
*           2 = LOTUS 1-2-3                     *
*           3 = Cullinet Goldengate             *
*           4 = Decision Resources Sign-Master  *
*           5 = EXIT to DOS                     *
*************************************************

ENTER PROGRAM NUMBER DESIRED 1


C>ECHO OFF
DISPLAYWRITER DOES ITS THING
THEN BASIC PROGRAM RESUMES CONTROL
```

When the BASIC parent program (MENU.BAS) resumes control, the screen will be cleared and the menu will be redisplayed. The interaction of the previously created programs is illustrated in Fig. 12-5 for the root directory and the DISPLAY directory.

Note the simplicity of the file relationships in comparison to the previous example. Here, the AUTOEXEC batch file executes the BASIC program

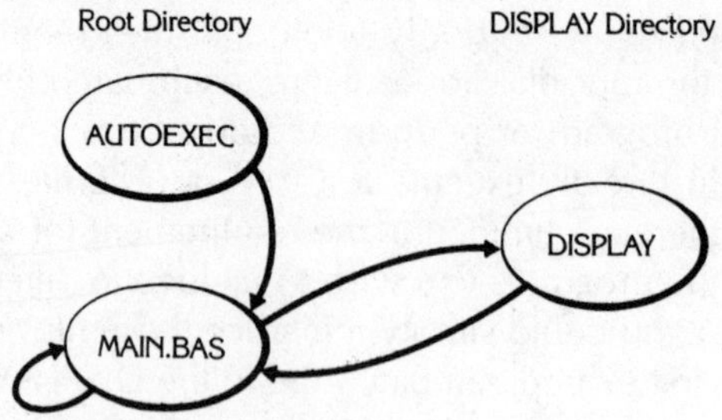

Fig. 12-5. File and directory relationship.

MAIN, which, under operator control, executes the required file in the appropriate directory.

Automatic Directory Listing

Now suppose that after several months of use your directories become filled with files. Every once in a while, it would be nice to obtain a listing of the contents of those directories. Although you could manually perform this operation, you can also create a batch file that will automatically perform directory listings. In addition, you can use the I/O redirection and piping features of DOS to your advantage by sorting each directory, printing the directories as a background operation, and automatically erasing any temporary files required to perform this operation. Your batch file would contain the following statements:

```
COPY CON: PDIR
DIR\DISPLAY|SORT>DIRSORT1.TXT
DIR\LOTUS|SORT>DIRSORT2.TXT
DIR\GOLD|SORT>DIRSORT3.TXT
DIR\GRAPH|SORT>DIRSORT4.TXT
PRINT DIRSORT1.TXT DIRSORT2.TXT DIRSORT3.TXT DIRSORT4.TXT
ERASE DISTORT?.TXT
^Z
```

Now, when you enter the command PDIR the four directories will be printed, each one in sorted order. By applying similar concepts, you can employ batch files to automate most tree-structured directory requirements you may have.

CHAPTER THIRTEEN
Introduction to TopView

TopView is a multitasking windowing environment that operates as an extension to IBM's disk operating system. This IBM software program provides the user of the AT with the capability to operate several programs at the same time, as well as to view the screen display of multiple programs concurrently through a process called windowing. As an extension to DOS, TopView permits the user to access many DOS commands while using one or more application programs. In addition, users can control the size of windows assigned to different programs, copy and paste information between programs, and automatically perform many DOS commands without having to know the syntax of the command.

By a technique known as time slicing, TopView will rapidly switch from one program to another without user intervention, permitting two or more application programs to operate at the same time. This multitasking capability permits you to run several programs or tasks at the same time, allowing each program or task to share such system resources as display, memory, and fixed disk and diskette storage, without interfering with each other. This capability allows you, for example, to initiate the recalculation of a large spreadsheet model and then to switch to a word processor program to compose a memorandum while the recalculation of the spreadsheet model is being performed.

INSTALLATION

Because of the amount of data transfer to and from memory when TopView is operated with several programs, it should be installed on a fixed disk, although it can also be operated from a diskette. To transfer TopView to a fixed disk, you must set the current drive and directory of your fixed disk to its root directory. Thus, you would enter C: or D:, depending on whether you wanted to install TopView on drive C or D. After entering CD\ to set the fixed disk to the root directory, you should place the TopView program diskette in drive A and, at the DOS prompt, enter the command A:FD. Once this command is entered, a batch file on the diskette will cause a subdirectory named TopView to be created on the fixed disk, after which the files on the diskette will be copied to the new subdirectory. During the file copy operation a message similar to that illustrated in Fig. 13-1 will be displayed.

```
Please wait.......

   A TopView subdirectory is being created on
   your fixed disk.  Files from your TopView
   diskette are being copied to your TopView
   subdirectory.
```

Fig. 13-1. TopView installation message.

Once the file copying operation is completed, your screen will clear and the message "TopView copy to fixed disk complete" will be displayed, after which the DOS prompt C> or D> will appear. At this point you can use the setup program to initialize the pointing device that will be used to control TopView operations. You can also copy a calculator program supplied on the TopView tutorial disk to your fixed disk. The following sequence illustrates the use of the COPY command to copy the calculator files from the tutorial disk to the fixed disk.

```
C>copy a:calc.* c:\
A:CALC.EXE
A:CALC.PIF
A:CALC.PLB
        3 File(s) copied

C>
```

To initialize the pointing device you will use with TopView requires the use of the SETUP command. Since TopView files are located in the subdirectory with that name, you should enter the command CD\TOPVIEW prior to entering the command SETUP. Once SETUP is entered, the screen display will appear as illustrated in Fig. 13-2.

After entering the number of the pointing device to be used with TopView, a "Setup Complete" message will be displayed and you will be provided with a choice of starting TopView or returning to DOS.

TopView can be started by entering 1 after the setup operation is completed or it can be started by entering the command TOPVIEW when you are logged onto the correct drive and subdirectory. Once TopView is started, a multitude of small windows superimposed upon one another will be dis-

```
TopView-Setup

                         Pointing Devices

        1.  Keyboard
        2.  PC Mouse by Mouse Systems *
                 Part Number 900120-214 (Serial Interface)
        3.  Microsoft Mouse for IBM Personal Computers *
                 Model Number 039-099    (Serial Interface)
        4.  Microsoft Mouse for IBM Personal Computers *
                 Model Number 037-099    (Parallel Interface)
        5.  Visi On Mouse  *
                 Part Number 69910-1011 (Serial Interface)
        6.  Other

        Type the number of your pointing device: [1]

                    Press ↵  Enter

   * Refer to your TopView User's Guide for warranty information.
```

Fig. 13-2. TopView setup menu.

played, along with a welcome message and a prompt asking for your selection as illustrated in Fig. 13-3.

At this point you can press the letter T to use the TopView tutorial, which is contained on a separate diskette that must be inserted into diskette drive A, or you can press the Enter key to work under the TopView environment. Since the tutorial will usually be used only once or perhaps a few times, its contents should normally not be copied to the fixed disk. Thus, if T is pressed to access

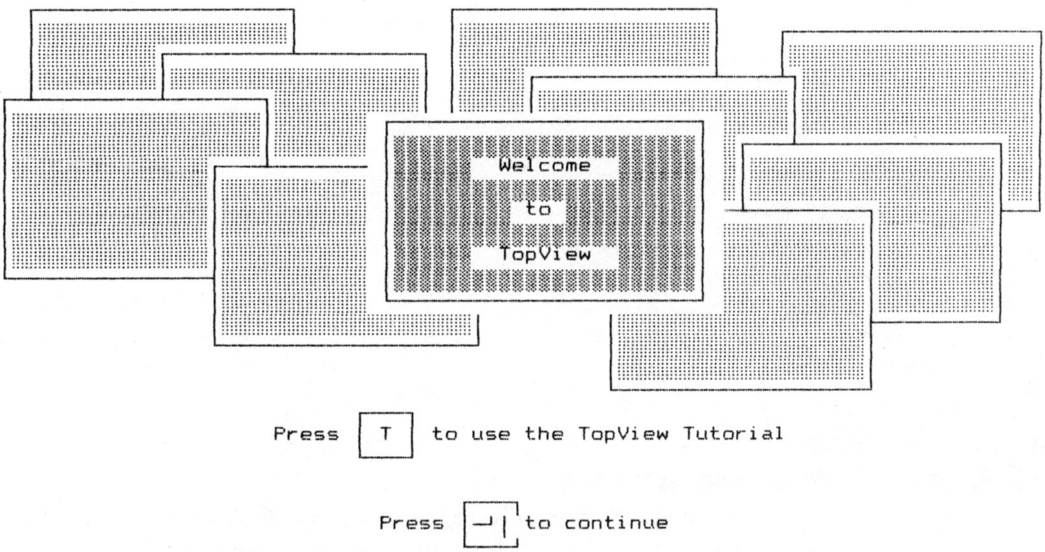

Fig. 13-3. TopView main menu.

the tutorial, you should first insert the TopView tutorial diskette into drive A before pressing the Enter key.

TopView Control Keys

Prior to actually examining the operation of TopView, let us review the keys that are used to perform TopView functions. First, the keyboard must be placed in the TopView mode. This is the normal mode of operation when TopView is initialized and results in a series of predefined functions being associated with the arrow keys, PgUp key, Home key, 5 key, and the plus and minus keys on the numeric keypad. To use these keys in their normal mode of operation you must press the Ctrl key, which serves as the mechanism to toggle between the TopView mode and the normal mode of keyboard operations. Each time you press the Ctrl key a short beep will sound to inform you that you are toggling in or out of the TopView mode of operation.

TopView Menu Key

The Alt key can be pressed to display the TopView menu as well as to toggle into the TopView mode. Pressing this key will cause a menu similar in appearance to the one illustrated in Fig. 13-4 to be displayed. This menu is divided into two sections, with the top section indicating functions that can be performed on your programs, while the bottom section indicates the TopView system functions that can be performed. When the TopView menu is displayed, the functions that can be selected at that particular point are preceded by a block. Thus, the TopView menu displayed in Fig. 13-4 would permit you to select all functions with the exception of Quit. Later in this chapter we will discuss each of the entries on the TopView menu.

```
----TopView----
   Scroll
 ■ Window
 ■ Scissors
 ■ Help
 ■ Suspend
   Quit
---------------
 ■ Switch
 ■ Programs
 ■ Exit
```

Fig. 13-4. TopView menu.

Pointer Control

Although the pointer normally appears as a rectangular block on the display, when it is positioned to an item on a TopView menu it will cause the item to be highlighted in inverse video. The four arrow keys can be used to move the pointer, with each arrow key moving the pointer one position in the direction of the arrow each time the key is pressed. By pressing the Ctrl key and an arrow key simultaneously, you can move the pointer several positions at a time. The actual number of positions moved by this two-key sequence can be controlled by the plus and minus keys—pressing the plus key can increase the number of positions that the pointer moves, while pressing the minus key will decrease the number of positions. By using the plus or minus keys, the pointer can be set to move horizontally between 2 and 24 positions and vertically between 1 and 12 positions in response to a Ctrl + arrow key sequence.

Operation Control Keys

When in the TopView mode of operation, the Home key is used to initiate a menu selection. Thus, you would first position the pointer onto the item in a menu to be selected and then press the Home key to make the menu selection. In IBM documentation the Home key is also referred to as Button 1.

When some menu items are selected, a second menu may be displayed that provides the user with the option of confirming or canceling the operation. The PgUp key can be used to cancel or end an operation and is referred to as Button 2 in IBM documentation.

Audio Control

Each time the pointer is moved on the screen a small beep will sound. This sound can be turned on or off by pressing the 5 key on the numeric keypad.

Table 13.1 summarizes the operation of the TopView control keys. It should be noted that once a word processing program, BASIC, or another pro-

Table 13-1. TopView Control Keys

KEY	FUNCTION
Ctrl	Toggles in and out of TopView mode
Alt	Displays or clears TopView menu from screen
Home	Initiates menu selection
PgUp	Cancels or ends an operation
Arrow	Moves pointer one position in direction of arrow
Ctrl + Arrow	Moves pointer several positions in direction of arrow
+	Increases the number of positions the pointer moves in response to a Ctrl + Arrow sequence
–	Decreases the number of positions the pointer moves in response to a Ctrl + Arrow sequence
5	Turns sound on or off when in the TopView mode of operation

gram is initiated that requires the use of such conventional keys as the arrow keys for cursor control, you must press the Ctrl key to toggle out of the TopView mode of operation. Otherwise, as an example, the left arrow key would move the TopView pointer instead of the program's cursor.

USING TOPVIEW

Since many of the features of TopView are best explained by example, let us examine several TopView operations.

The first time you execute TopView, its Start-a-Program menu will be displayed as illustrated in Fig. 13-5. This menu is similar to the TopView menu illustrated in Fig. 13-4 in that it is divided into two parts. The upper portion of the menu will initially have "DOS Services" as its only entry. Once programs are added to the TopView environment, subsequent displays of the Start-a-Program menu will list those programs in the upper portion of the menu. Each program or DOS Services can be selected by positioning the pointer over the appropriate entry and pressing the Home key. The lower portion of the Start-a-Program menu provides the mechanism for the TopView user to add or delete programs or to change program information. Prior to covering the operation of these functions let us look at how DOS Services are used.

Fig. 13-5. Start-a-Program menu.

DOS Services

DOS Services can be selected from the Start-a-Program menu by positioning the pointer over DOS Services and pressing the Home key. Once this is done a new screen display similar to the one illustrated in Fig. 13-6 will

```
┌DOS-Services┐ ┌DOS-Services-Directory──────────────────────────────┐
│ ▪ Copy     │ │ C:\*.*                                             │
│ ▪ Print    │ ├────────────────────────────────────────────────────┤
│ ▪ Type     │ │ Name       Ext      Size      Date        Time     │
│ ▪ Rename   │ ├────────────────────────────────────────────────────┤
│ ▪ Erase    │ │ ANSI       SYS      1664    10-20-83    12:00 pm   │
├────────────┤ │ ASSEMBLE        <DIR>        2-08-85     3:47 pm   │
│ ▪ Other    │ │ ASSIGN     COM       896    10-20-83    12:00 pm   │
└────────────┘ │ ASTCLOCK   COM      1598     2-23-84    12:31 pm   │
┌Sort-By─────┐ │ AUDIT      COM       982    10-05-84     4:07 pm   │
│ ▪ Name     │ │ AUTOEXEC   BAK        57     1-01-80     0:15 am   │
│ ▪ Ext      │ │ AUTOEXEC   BAT        96    11-06-84    10:20 am   │
│ ▪ Size     │ │ BACKUP     COM      3687    10-20-83    12:00 pm   │
│ ▪ Date/Time│ │ BASIC      COM     16256    10-20-83    12:00 pm   │
└────────────┘ │ BASICA     COM     26112    10-20-83    12:00 pm   │
               │ BAT        COM      9728     3-22-84     8:28 am   │
               │ CALC       EXE     56549    11-07-84    12:00 pm   │
               │ CALC       PIF       369    11-07-84    12:00 pm   │
               │ CALC       PLB      5133    11-07-84    12:00 pm   │
               │ CHKDSK     COM      6400    10-20-83    12:00 pm   │
               │ COMM       BAS      4352    10-20-83    12:00 pm   │
               │ COMMAND    COM     17792    10-20-83    12:00 pm   │
               │ COMP       COM      2534    10-20-83    12:00 pm   │
               │ CPDFDATA   BAK        51    10-05-84    10:12 am   │
               └────────────────────────────────────────────────────┘
```

Fig. 13-6. DOS Services menu.

appear. The window labeled DOS Services in the upper left corner of Fig. 13-6 provides the user with a mechanism to invoke several common DOS functions, including Copy, Print, Type, Rename, and Erase without having to remember the format of the DOS command. The DOS Services Directory window permits you to display all or part of the files in a directory. By moving the pointer into this window you can view different directories or scroll through the directory currently displayed if the number of entries in the directory exceeds the display area of the window.

When DOS Services is displayed, the cursor will be positioned at the top of the directory window. If you want to display a directory different from the root directory, you can enter any drive, path, and file specification. If the directory currently displayed contains <DIR> entries, you can move the pointer to that entry and press the Home key to display the files in that subdirectory. Thus, moving the pointer over ASSEMBLE in Fig. 13-6 and pressing the Home key would cause the entries in that subdirectory to be displayed.

Since TopView will display an "End of Directory" line to mark the end of the directory being displayed, the absence of this line in the DOS Services Directory window illustrated in Fig. 13-6 indicates that there are additional directory entries that are not displayed because the number of entries in the directory exceeds the number of lines in the window.

To display additional entries in the directory you can use the Scroll option from the TopView menu. To accomplish this you must first move the pointer into the directory window and then press the Alt key to display the TopView window. This is illustrated in Fig. 13-7.

Once the TopView menu is displayed, a block preceding Scroll will indicate that this option can be selected. If the pointer was not moved into the directory window, the block would not precede Scroll since you would not

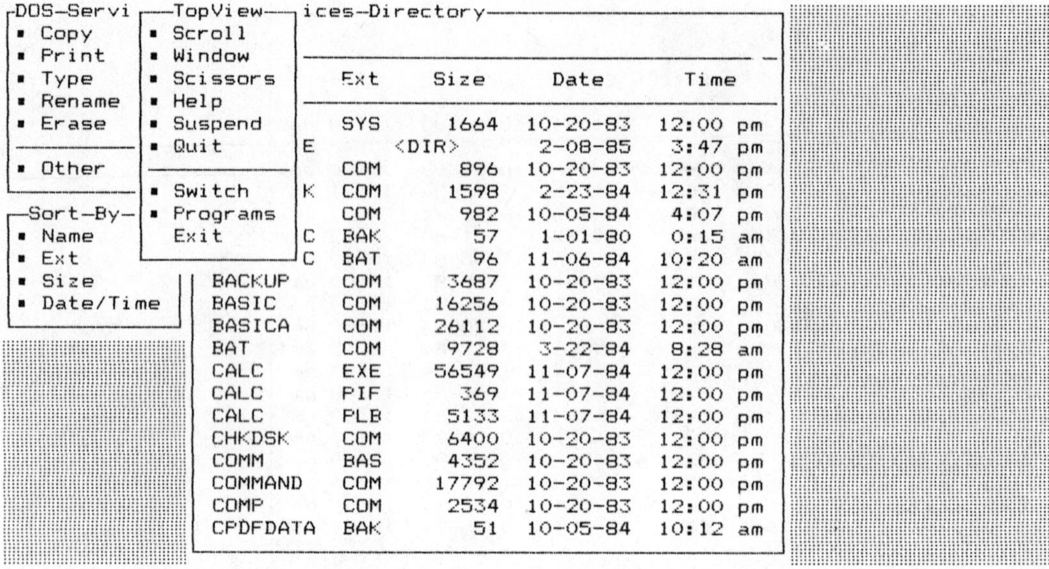

Fig. 13-7. Preparing to Scroll through a directory.

be pointing to a scrollable item. By positioning the pointer over Scroll and pressing the Home key, you will activate the Scroll option. Then you can press the arrow keys to control the direction of scrolling. By pressing Button 2, which is the PgUp key, you can terminate the Scroll option and your display will appear as previously illustrated in Fig. 13-6.

To invoke a DOS command you can move the pointer over the appropriate command in the DOS Services window and press the Home key. When you select Other, a window will appear over the DOS Services Directory that will provide room for 10 additional DOS commands. Since not all DOS commands are supported by TopView, the reader is cautioned to refer to the TopView manual to note the commands supported by the DOS Services Other option. If, for example, you wanted to display the filename AUTOEXEC.BAT (shown in Fig. 13-6), you would position the pointer over TYPE and select this command with the Home key. Then you would move the pointer over that file in the DOS Services Directory and also select it with the Home key.

ADDING APPLICATIONS

If you press the Alt key to display the TopView menu and select Programs, the Start-a-Program screen will be displayed. (This screen was previously illustrated in Fig. 13-5.) Since up to now no programs have been added to TopView, only DOS Services will be listed in the upper portion of that menu.

Suppose you previously copied your EasyWriter diskette to the fixed disk as illustrated below.

```
C>cd\

C>md\ew
```

```
C>cd\ew

C>copy a:*.* c:
A:COMMAND.COM
A:RECONFIG.BAT
A:TRANSFER.EXE
A:EW.COM
A:TARGET.COM
A:IBM88VMI.COM
A:CONFIG.COM
A:CONTARG.COM
A:EZWRITER.OPT
        9 File(s) copied

C>
```

Note that in this example you first changed to the root directory (cd\), made a directory labeled ew (md\ew), and then changed directories to that directory (cd\ew) prior to copying the files from the diskette in drive A to the fixed disk.

From the Start-a-Program window, position the pointer over the "Add a Program to Menu" option and press the Home key. Doing so will cause a new window labeled "Select a program to ADD to the Start a Program Menu" to be superimposed over the Start-a-Program window as illustrated in Fig. 13-8.

```
St Add-a-Program
   Select a program to  ADD  to the Start a Program Menu.

   • 3101 Emulator                        • Linker
   • Alarm Clock                          • Macro Assembler 1.0
   • BASIC                                • Multiplan 1.1
   • BASIC Compiler                       • Pascal Compiler 1.0 Pass  One
   • BASIC Prog. Dev. Sys. Editor         • Pascal Compiler 1.0 Pass  Two
   • BASIC Prog. Dev. Sys. Form           • Pascal Compiler 2.0 Pass  One
   • BASICA                               • Pascal Compiler 2.0 Pass  Two
   • COBOL Compiler                       • Pascal Compiler 2.0 Pass Three
   • DisplayWrite 1                       • PC Cluster
   • DisplayWrite 2 Version 1.1           • PCWriter
     DOS Services                         • PeachText
   • EasyWriter 1.15                      • Personal Communications Mgr.
   • FORTRAN Compiler 1.0 Pass One        • Personal Editor
   • FORTRAN Compiler 1.0 Pass Two        • Professional Editor
   • FORTRAN Compiler 2.0 Pass One        • Script/PC
   • FORTRAN Compiler 2.0 Pass Two        • Sort
   • IBM Filing Assistant                 • VisiCalc 1.2
   • IBM Graphing Assistant               • Word Proof
   • IBM Reporting Assistant
   • IBM Writing Assistant                • Other
```

Fig. 13-8. Adding a program to the Start-a-Program menu window.

Since EasyWriter version 1.15 is listed on the window, you can move the pointer over that entry and press the Home key to select that program. If you wanted to add a program that is not on the menu, you would move the pointer to Other and select that entry.

```
St Add-a-Program
   Select a program to  ADD  to the Start a Program Menu.

   ■ 3101 Emulator                          ■ Linker
   ■ Alarm Clock                            ■ Macro Assembler 1.0
   ■ BASIC                                  ■ Multiplan 1.1
   ■ BASIC Compiler                         ■ Pascal Compiler 1.0 Pass  One
   ■ BA Program-Location
   ■ BA
   ■ BA  Type the path (drive and directory), if different from below,
   ■ CO  where TopView can find  EasyWriter 1.15
   ■ Di
   ■ Di  Path: [c:\ew                                                   ]
     DO
   ■ Ea                 Press  ┘  Enter
   ■ FO
   ■ FO
   ■ FORTRAN Compiler 2.0 Pass One          ■ Script/PC
   ■ FORTRAN Compiler 2.0 Pass Two          ■ Sort
   ■ IBM Filing Assistant                   ■ VisiCalc 1.2
   ■ IBM Graphing Assistant                 ■ Word Proof
   ■ IBM Reporting Assistant
   ■ IBM Writing Assistant                  ■ Other
```

Fig. 13-9. Specifying the Path.

Once you select the program you wish to add, a new window labeled "Program Location" will be displayed. After the word Path in that window, you would enter C:\ew, since EasyWriter resides on drive C under the subdirectory ew. The completion of this screen with the Path C:\ew is illustrated in Fig. 13-9.

After EasyWriter is selected, a new window will be displayed telling you that the program was added (Fig. 13-10). Then Button 2, which is the PgUp

```
St Add-a-Program
   Select a program to  ADD  to the Start a Program Menu.

   ■ 3101 Emulator                          ■ Linker
   ■ Alarm Clock                            ■ Macro Assembler 1.0
   ■ BASIC                                  ■ Multiplan 1.1
   ■ BASIC Compiler                         ■ Pascal Compiler 1.0 Pass  One
   ■ BASIC Prog. Dev. Sys. Editor           ■ Pascal Compiler 1.0 Pass  Two
   ■ BASIC P Add-Status                                             ss  One
   ■ BASICA                                                         ss  Two
   ■ COBOL C  EasyWriter 1.15                      - added          ss Three
   ■ Display
   ■ Display  Press  Button 2 to quit  Add a Program
     DOS Ser
   ■ EasyWri                                                        s Mgr.
   ■ FORTRAN Compiler 1.0 Pass One          ■ Personal Editor
   ■ FORTRAN Compiler 1.0 Pass Two          ■ Professional Editor
   ■ FORTRAN Compiler 2.0 Pass One          ■ Script/PC
   ■ FORTRAN Compiler 2.0 Pass Two          ■ Sort
   ■ IBM Filing Assistant                   ■ VisiCalc 1.2
   ■ IBM Graphing Assistant                 ■ Word Proof
   ■ IBM Reporting Assistant
   ■ IBM Writing Assistant                  ■ Other
```

Fig. 13-10. Program addition verification.

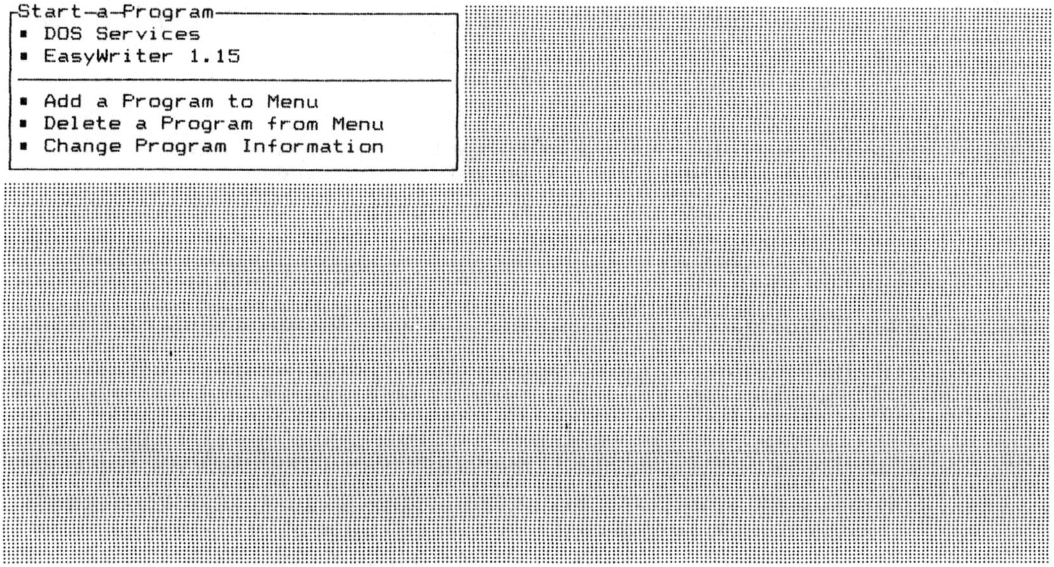

Fig. 13-11. Revised Start-a-Program window.

key, can be pressed to quit Add a Program. Once Button 2 is pressed the Start-a-Program window will reappear, with EasyWriter 1.15 added to the menu for selection as illustrated in Fig. 13-11.

It should be noted that one of the limitations of TopView is its inability to support batch files. Because EasyWriter normally uses drives A and B, you would normally use a batch file with an ASSIGN command to change the references to those drives to drive C or D if you have a fixed disk system and then invoke the EW.COM file. However, as batch files are not supported and the ASSIGN command cannot be invoked from TopView's DOS Services, you would have to use the command from DOS prior to starting TopView. Therefore, since the ASSIGN statement will affect all programs running in the system, IBM does not recommend its use. Thus, this is one of the idiosyncrasies of the present version of TopView that may force you to use diskettes with your fixed disk system.

MOVING DATA

Now that you have added EasyWriter to TopView, let us explore some additional features of this window environment by operating two programs and moving data from one program to the other. First, select EasyWriter from the menu in Fig. 13-11 by moving the pointer to that entry and pressing Button 1. After the EasyWriter menu appears, let us assume you enter the EasyWriter command E (to Edit) and entered the following two-line memorandum.

```
This is an example of using Easywriter and inserting the results
of a BASIC program computation into a memorandum.
```

Now suppose you wish to add the results of a BASIC program computation to your memorandum. If you press the Alt key, the TopView menu is displayed on your screen as illustrated in the following.

```
┌─TopView──┐ample of using Easywriter and inserting the results
│  Scroll  │ogram computation into a memorandum.
│■ Window  │
│■ Scissors│
│  Help    │
│■ Suspend │
│■ Quit    │
│──────────│
│■ Switch  │
│■ Programs│
│  Exit    │
└──────────┘
```

By moving the pointer to the Switch entry in the TopView menu and selecting that entry, you can move to another program. Since EasyWriter is currently the only program added to TopView, the result of selecting the Switch option will cause a box with EasyWriter and Start a Program to be displayed as illustrated in the following.

```
┌─Switch────────────┐f using Easywriter and inserting the results
│■ EasyWriter 1.15  │omputation into a memorandum.
│■ Start a Program  │
└───────────────────┘
```

If you select Start a Program, the window previously illustrated in Fig. 13-11 will be displayed. You can then select the "Add a Program to Menu" option, which will cause the window previously illustrated in Fig. 13-8 to be displayed. Next, you select BASICA and enter the path information to inform TopView of its location. Once the preceding functions are accomplished, the Start-a-Program window will appear superimposed over the active EasyWriter memorandum as illustrated below.

```
┌Start-a-Program─────────────────┐ter and inserting the results
│■ BASICA                        │ a memorandum.
│■ DOS Services                  │
│■ EasyWriter 1.15               │
│────────────────────────────────│
│■ Add a Program to Menu         │
│■ Delete a Program from Menu    │
│■ Change Program Information    │
└────────────────────────────────┘
```

Next, move the pointer to BASICA to select that program. After entering and executing a small BASIC program, assume your screen appears as shown in Fig. 13-12. (Note that the word "estimate" has been purposely misspelled; you will learn how to correct it later in the chapter.)

Now, suppose you want to copy the result of the budget summary computation to the memorandum you were preparing using EasyWriter. If you press the Alt key, the TopView menu will be displayed. A block preceding the Scissors entry indicates that that entry can be selected, as Fig. 13-13 illustrates.

```
The IBM Personal Computer Basic
Version A2.10 Copyright IBM Corp. 1981, 1982, 1983
26631 Bytes free

Ok
10 print "BUDGET SUMMARY"
20 print "---------------"
30 x=30
40 for i=2 to 10 step 2
50 print x*2000/i,i
60 next i
25 print "extimate","interest"
RUN
BUDGET SUMMARY
---------------
extimate      interest
 30000         2
 15000         4
 10000         6
 7500          8
 6000          10
Ok

1LIST   2RUN   3LOAD"   4SAVE"   5CONT 6,"LPT1 7TRON 8TROFF9KEY    0SCREEN
```

Fig. 13-12. BASIC program screen.

```
┌──TopView──┐nal Computer Basic
│  Scroll   │ Copyright IBM Corp. 1981, 1982, 1983
│ • Window  │ree
│ • Scissors│
│   Help    │
│ • Suspend │GET SUMMARY"
│   Quit    │------------"
│───────────│
│ • Switch  │ 10 step 2
│ • Programs│00/i,i
│   Exit    │
└───────────┘imate","interest"
RUN
BUDGET SUMMARY
---------------
extimate      interest
 30000         2
 15000         4
 10000         6
 7500          8
 6000          10
Ok
```

Fig. 13-13. Preparing to Copy instructions.

Note that several entries in the TopView window cannot be selected at this time: Scroll, Help, Quit, and Exit. Since there is no information to scroll, you cannot select that option. Many programs will be developed to run under TopView that will provide information on the current operation being performed by selecting Help. Unfortunately, BASIC does not provide help screens, as indicated by the absence of a block preceding that entry on the TopView menu.

To quit BASIC you would have to first enter the BASIC command SYSTEM. Since you have not done so, a block does not precede this option. Finally, since you have active programs in use, you cannot exit TopView until all active programs are terminated.

Once you select Scissors by moving the pointer to that entry and pressing the Home key, a submenu will be displayed with three options: Cut, Copy, and Paste. As illustrated in Fig. 13-14, you are only permitted to use the Copy option. Cut allows you to delete information from a window, which is not permitted under BASIC. Copy allows you to copy information from a window, while retaining the information in the original window, and is available for all non-graphics programs. The last option in the submenu, Paste, permits you to display information you previously copied or cut. Since you have not copied or cut information, no block precedes this entry.

```
┌─Scissors┐onal Computer Basic
│  Cut    │0 Copyright IBM Corp. 1981, 1982, 1983
│▪ Copy   │free
│  Paste  │
└─────────┘
10 print "BUDGET SUMMARY"
20 print "---------------"
30 x=30
40 for i=2 to 10 step 2
50 print x*2000/i,i
60 next i
25 print "extimate","interest"
RUN
BUDGET SUMMARY
---------------
extimate      interest
 30000          2
 15000          4
 10000          6
 7500           8
 6000           10
Ok

1LIST   2RUN   3LOAD"   4SAVE"   5CONT 6,"LPT1 7TRON 8TROFF9KEY     0SCREEN
```

Fig. 13-14. Selecting the Copy option.

After the Copy option is selected, you must move the pointer and press the Home key at the appropriate boundaries of the information to be copied. Thus, you would first move the pointer to the "B" in BUDGET and then press Button 1. Next, you use the right arrow key to move the pointer to the right until it is above the "t" in interest. As you move the pointer, a marked area will be displayed on the screen. If you want to copy the entire results of the BASIC program, you use the down arrow key to move the pointer to the row where interest is 10. When the marked area contains all the text you wish to copy, press Button 1 again and the following Confirm message appears.

```
┌─Copy──────┐
│ ▪ Confirm │
└───────────┘
```

If the area you selected is highlighted correctly, press Button 1 again, which causes the text to be stored in a Copy/Cut buffer storage area. If for some reason you marked the wrong area, press Button 2 to cancel the operation, press the Alt key to redisplay the TopView menu, select Scissors, and repeat the preceding operation.

When you have confirmed the Copy operation, you can redisplay the TopView menu by pressing the Alt key and select the Switch option, which permits you to move from one program to another. The display of the TopView menu is similar to the illustration in Fig. 13-13. Once Switch is selected, the Switch submenu will appear as illustrated in the following.

```
┌─Switch───────────────┐ puter B
│ ▪ BASICA             │ ght IBM
│ * EasyWriter 1.15    │
│ ▪ Start a Program    │
└──────────────────────┘
```

Since EasyWriter was suspended, an asterisk in the Switch submenu is used to indicate this fact. By positioning the pointer over EasyWriter and pressing Button 1, you will return to the EasyWriter screen. Then you can press the Alt key to display the TopView menu, resulting in the following display.

```
This is an example  ┌─TopView──┐ writer and inserting the results
of a BASIC program  │   Scroll │ nto a memorandum.
                    │ ▪ Window │
                    │ ▪ Scissors
                    │   Help   │
                    │ ▪ Suspend│
                    │ ▪ Quit   │
                    │──────────│
                    │ ▪ Switch │
                    │ ▪ Programs
                    │   Exit   │
                    └──────────┘
```

When you select Scissors from the TopView menu, the Scissors submenu will be displayed superimposed over your EasyWriter memorandum as indicated in the example that follows. Note that both Copy and Paste information can be selected at this time. You can copy information from the short EasyWriter memorandum you prepared into the Copy/Cut storage area the same way you previously copied the results of the BASIC program. Since you already have data in the Copy/Cut storage area as a result of the previous Copy operation, Paste is also preceded by a block.

```
This is an example  ┌──Scissors┐ywriter and inserting the results
of a BASIC program  │  Cut     │into a memorandum.
                    │▪ Copy    │
                    │▪ Paste   │
                    └──────────┘
```

When you select Paste, a window will appear containing the information you previously copied from the BASIC program. You can position the window by moving the pointer, since the window will move with the pointer. Once you have positioned the window at its appropriate location, you can press Button 1 to paste the information. This will cause a Confirm submenu to be displayed. After you press Button 1 again to confirm the Paste operation your memorandum will appear as illustrated in Fig. 13-15.

```
This is an example of using Easywriter and inserting the results
of a BASIC program computation into a memorandum.
                    BUDGET SUMMARY
                    ---------------
                    extimate        interest
                     30000            2
                     15000            4
                     10000            6
                     7500             8
                     6000             10
```

Fig. 13-15. Result of Paste operation.

Since you are now operating EasyWriter under TopView, you can press the F10 key to access the EasyWriter File System to save this memorandum if you so desire. You may even use the editing capability of EasyWriter to change "extimate" to "estimate." Prior to doing so, however, you should press the Ctrl key to toggle the keyboard out of the TopView mode. Then you can use the arrow keys to control cursor movements and position the cursor over the letter "x" and change it to "s."

EXITING TOPVIEW

Before exiting TopView you must terminate any programs running under its environment. Thus, you enter the letter "X" from the EasyWriter File System, which causes EasyWriter to exit to DOS and terminates that program. Then you enter the command SYSTEM to terminate BASIC as illustrated below.

```
Ok
system                   ┌BASICA─Ended──────────────────────────────────────────┐
                         │  Press Button 2 to End this Window and Continue ...  │
                         └──────────────────────────────────────────────────────┘
```

Once all applications under TopView have been terminated, press the Alt key and a block preceding the Exit entry in the TopView menu appears. If you select the Exit option, an Exit submenu is displayed with the sole entry "Confirm." Press Button 1 again and you will exit from TopView and the DOS prompt will be displayed.

OTHER OPTIONS TO CONSIDER

If you select the Window option in the TopView menu, you can change the size or position of a program's window. It also results in the display of a submenu labeled Window, which contains five options as illustrated in Fig. 13-16.

```
xample o┌──Window──┐ywriter and in
rogram c│  Move    │into a memoran
        │▪ Size    │ARY
        │  Zoom    │----
        │  Unzoom  │    interest
        │──────────│     2
        │▪ Hide    │     4
        └──────────┘     6
```

Fig. 13-16. Window submenu.

Like the TopView menu, the entries in the Window submenu that can be selected at any particular point are indicated by a block preceding the entry. Thus, Size and Hide could be selected at the time the Window submenu shown in Fig. 13-16 was displayed.

The Move option enables you to move a window once the pointer is within the window. Since a window must be smaller than the size of the screen to be moved, you must first use the Size option to reduce the size of the window prior to moving it. To adjust the size of a window, select the Size option and by moving the appropriate arrow keys, you can reduce or expand the size of the window. Once the size of the window is satisfactory, press Button 2 to terminate the sizing process.

Zoom can be used to return a sized window to its full size; Unzoom restores a zoomed window back to its previous size and location. The last option in the window submenu, Hide, removes a window from view. Once they are hidden, such programs will have a dash next to their name if the Switch option is selected from the TopView menu. To view a hidden program, you must select Switch from the TopView menu and then select the program name from the Switch submenu that will be displayed.

APPENDIX A ASCII Code Representation

All the ASCII codes in decimal and their associated characters are listed here. The column labeled "control character" lists the standard interpretations of ASCII codes 0 through 31 when they are used for control functions or data communications control. In addition to these 32 characters, ASCII code 127 is normally used as a pad or time fill character in asynchronous communications and should be disregarded when received by the PC AT, or one may receive a series of little houses on the display, since ASCII 127 is the graphic symbol ⌂. To do this, one can simply test for this character and not display it when it is encountered.

ASCII value	Character	Control character	ASCII value	Character
000	(null)	NUL	032	(space)
001	☺	SOH	033	!
002	●	STX	034	"
003	♥	ETX	035	#
004	♦	EOT	036	$
005	♣	ENQ	037	%
006	♠	ACK	038	&
007	(beep)	BEL	039	'
008	(backspace)	BS	040	(
009	(tab)	HT	041	)
010	(line feed)	LF	042	*
011	(home)	VT	043	+
012	(form feed)	FF	044	,
013	(carriage return)	CR	045	-
014	♫	SO	046	.
015	☼	SI	047	/
016	►	DLE	048	0
017	◄	DC1	049	1
018	↕	DC2	050	2
019	!!	DC3	051	3

ASCII value	Character	Control character	ASCII value	Character
020	¶	DC4	052	4
021	§	NAK	053	5
022	▬	SYN	054	6
023	↨	ETB	055	7
024	↑	CAN	056	8
025	↓	EM	057	9
026	→	SUB	058	:
027	←	ESC	059	;
028	(cursor right)	FS	060	<
029	(cursor left)	GS	061	=
030	(cursor up)	RS	062	>
031	(cursor down)	US	063	?

ASCII value	Character	ASCII value	Character
064	@	106	j
065	A	107	k
066	B	108	l
067	C	109	m
068	D	110	n
069	E	111	o
070	F	112	p
071	G	113	q
072	H	114	r
073	I	115	s
074	J	116	t
075	K	117	u
076	L	118	v
077	M	119	w
078	N	120	x
079	O	121	y
080	P	122	z
081	Q	123	{
082	R	124	¦
083	S	125	}
084	T	126	~
085	U	127	⌂
086	V	128	Ç
087	W	129	ü
088	X	130	é
089	Y	131	â
090	Z	132	ä
091	[	133	à
092	\	134	å
093	]	135	ç
094	^	136	ê
095	_	137	ë
096	'	138	è
097	a	139	ï
098	b	140	î
099	c	141	ì
100	d	142	Ä
101	e	143	Å
102	f	144	É
103	g	145	æ
104	h	146	Æ
105	i	147	ô

ASCII value	Character	ASCII value	Character
148	ö	202	╩
149	ò	203	╦
150	û	204	╠
151	ù	205	═
152	ÿ	206	╬
153	Ö	207	╧
154	Ü	208	╨
155	¢	209	╤
156	£	210	╥
157	¥	211	╙
158	Pts	212	╘
159	ƒ	213	╒
160	á	214	╓
161	í	215	╫
162	ó	216	╪
163	ú	217	┘
164	ñ	218	┌
165	Ñ	219	█
166	ª	220	▄
167	º	221	▌
168	¿	222	▐
169	⌐	223	▀
170	¬	224	∝
171	½	225	β
172	¼	226	Γ
173	¡	227	π
174	«	228	Σ
175	»	229	σ
176	░	230	μ
177	▒	231	τ
178	▓	232	Φ
179	│	233	Θ
180	┤	234	Ω
181	╡	235	δ
182	╢	236	∞
183	╖	237	Ø
184	╕	238	∈
185	╣	239	∩
186	║	240	≡
187	╗	241	±
188	╝	242	≥
189	╜	243	≤
190	╛	244	⌠
191	┐	245	⌡
192	└	246	÷
193	┴	247	≈
194	┬	248	°
195	├	249	•
196	─	250	·
197	┼	251	√
198	╞	252	^{n}
199	╟	253	^{2}
200	╚	254	■
201	╔	255	(blank 'FF')

APPENDIX B

Extended Character Codes

There are certain keys and key combinations that are not represented in standard ASCII code on the IBM AT. For such keys and key combinations, an extended code will be returned when the INKEY$ variable is used in a BASIC program. A null character (ASCII code 000) will be returned as the first character of a two-character string, while the second character will contain the code that defines the extended character.

To determine if an extended character code was received by INKEY$, you must then examine the second character to determine the actual key pressed as illustrated by the following program segment.

```
100 A$=INKEY$:IF A$=""THEN 100              'Cycle until key pressed
110 IF LEN(A$)=1 THEN 200                   'Not extended code
120 IF VAL(RIGHT$(A$,1))=71 THEN 150        'Home pressed
130 IF VAL(RIGHT$(A$,1))=72 THEN 160        'Cursor Up pressed
.
.
.
```

The decimal values of the ASCII codes for the second character of the AT's extended codes and the key(s) associated with those codes follow:

Second Code	Meaning
3	NUL (null character)
15	← (shift tab)
16-25	Alt Q, W, E, R, T, Y, U, I, O, P
30-38	Alt A, S, D, F, G, H, J, K, L
44-50	Alt Z, X, C, V, B, N, M
59-68	Function keys F1-F10 (when disabled as soft keys)
71	Home

Second Code	Meaning
72	Home
73	PgUp
75	PgUp
77	PgDn
79	End
80	End
81	PgDn
82	Ins
83	Del
84-93	F11-F20 (uppercase F1-F10)
94-103	F21-F30 (Ctrl F1-F10)
104-113	F31-F40 (Alt F1-F10)
114	PrtSc
115	Ctrl-PgUp (previous word)
116	Ctrl-PgDn (next word)
117	Ctrl-End
118	Ctrl-PgDn
119	Ctrl-Home
120-131	Alt 1, 2, 3, 4, 5, 6, 7, 8, 9, 0, -,=
132	Ctrl-PgUp

APPENDIX C

BASIC Error Messages

Number	Message	Number	Message
1	NEXT without FOR	30	WEND without WHILE
2	Syntax error	50	FIELD overflow
3	RETURN without GOSUB	51	Internal error
4	Out of data	52	Bad file number
5	Illegal function call	53	File not found
6	Overflow	54	Bad file mode
7	Out of memory	55	File already open
8	Undefined line number	57	Device I/O error
9	Subscript out of range	58	File already exists
10	Duplicate definition	61	Disk full
11	Division by zero	62	Input past end
12	Illegal direct	63	Bad record number
13	Type mismatch	64	Bad file name
14	Out of string space	66	Direct statement in file
15	String too long	67	Too many files
16	String formula too complex	68	Device unavailable
17	Can't continue	69	Communications buffer overflow
18	Undefined user function	70	Disk write protect
19	No RESUME	71	Disk not ready
20	RESUME without error	72	Disk media error
22	Missing operand	73	Avanced feature
23	Line buffer overflow	74	Rename across disks
24	Device timeout	75	Path/file access error
25	Device fault	76	Path not found
26	FOR without NEXT	—	Unprintable error
27	Out of paper	—	Incorrect DOS version
29	WHILE without WEND		

APPENDIX D Programming Tips and Techniques

DATA ENTRY

There are two areas you should focus your attention on when writing software that other people can be expected to use. The first area is providing menus for the user to easily enter the required data and select the various options he or she may desire with as few keystrokes as possible. The second area that unfortunately is overlooked by many programmers is making your program as idiot-proof as possible. It is this area that will be focused on in this section.

What happens if your program has the following statement

```
100 INPUT "ENTER VALUES ",VA,X$
```

and the operator enters too few or too many items? Here, the system message "Redo from start" would be displayed as shown by the following example.

```
100 INPUT "ENTER VALUES ",VA,X$
RUN
ENTER VALUES 3
?Redo from start
ENTER VALUES
```

Now, suppose the operator inadvertently enters a string for a numeric value. Here, the same error message would be displayed as shown by the following example.

```
ENTER VALUES X,Y
?Redo from start
ENTER VALUES
```

If a numeric is entered for a string, however, the system will not generate an error message, since this is perfectly valid, although it may not have been the intention of the operator to do so.

You can eliminate such errors causing a program termination by inputting a line of data to the system using the LINE INPUT statement. This statement reads the input of an entire line of up to 255 characters from the keyboard into the specified string. Once the data is contained in the string, you can then manipulate it internally to test for the number of entries you required and the range of values the entries must fall in. If such entries fail your test, you can then display one or more error messages and provide the operator with another chance to enter the data without the program halting execution with the display of some nebulous error message that will not be meaningful to most casual users of computers. The following program segment demonstrates one use of the LINE INPUT statement for error control purposes. Here, we read the data input as a string and convert it to a numeric by the use of the VAL statement.

```
LIST
90 LOCATE 10,10:PRINT SPC(70) :LOCATE 10,10
100 LINE INPUT "PAY RATE ",P$
110 P=VAL(P$)
120 IF P>0 THEN 150
130 BEEP
140 GOTO 90
150 REM program continues
Ok
```

Since you expect the number to be greater than zero, you test it for this value. If it is greater than zero, the program will branch to line 150 and continue processing. If P was entered as a string, the function call will return a value of 0 for P. If P was entered as a negative number, the function call will return the negative number. For either case, this will trigger your error processing, which in this example is limited to generating a short beep on the speaker with the BEEP statement, relocating the cursor to column 10 line 10, clearing that line and repositioning the cursor to location 10,10. Then, the program will request the entry of the data a second time. For this example, we may feel that the display of an error message is not required and that a beep and redisplay of the question is sufficient. Now, suppose you wish to add a short message when an error occurs. Rather than display the error message on the next line, you can use the 25th line of the display for this purpose. To do so you must first turn off the soft keys with a KEY OFF statement and then you can display your error message on the 25th line as shown by the execution of the following program segment.

```
LIST
10 X=10
20 LOCATE X,10:PRINT SPC(70):LOCATE X,10
30 LINE INPUT "PAY RATE ",P$
40 P=VAL(P$)
50 IF P>0 THEN 140
60 BEEP
70 KEY OFF
```

```
80 LOCATE 25,20
90 PRINT "NUMBER MUST BE POSITIVE -PRESS C TO CONTINUE"
100 A$=INKEY$:IF A$<>"C"THEN 100
110 KEY ON
120 X=X-1
130 GOTO 20
140 REM program continues
Ok
```

Entering a string value for PAY RATE produces the error message on line 25 as shown in the following.

```
PAY RATE Z




            NUMBER MUST BE POSITIVE -PRESS C TO CONTINUE
```

In this example, the message "NUMBER MUST BE POSITIVE-PRESS C TO CONTINUE" will be displayed on the status line. Once the operator enters an uppercase C, that line will be cleared. Note that the program will branch back to the current row location less one each time the error message is displayed. This is to compensate for the screen scrolling when the 25th line is used to display information.

Now, suppose you desire to input two data elements on the same line. You can still use the LINE INPUT statement; however, you must perform some additional processing to determine if two data elements were entered. Here, you would code a routine to search the string variable into which an entire line of data from the keyboard was assigned to. The following statements could be used as a separator. Note that if a comma was not included in the input, this program segment will branch to line 500. At this location in the program, you could have a routine that displays an error message informing the operator that two values, separated by a comma, must be entered.

```
LIST
100 X$="" 'null string
110 LOCATE 10,20:PRINT SPC(60):LOCATE 10,20
120 LINE INPUT "ENTER 2 VALUES ",P$
130 X$="" 'null string
140 FOR I=1 TO LEN(P$)
150 IF MID$(P$,I,1)="," THEN 180
160 X$=X$+MID$(P$,I,1)
```

```
170 NEXT I
175 IF I=LEN(P$) THEN 500
180 Y$=""
190 FOR J=I+1 TO LEN(P$)
200 Y$=Y$+MID$(P$J,1)
210 NEXT J
300 PRINT TAB(15)"ENTERED DATA IS:"X$ " AND " Y$
500 REM error message
OK
```

In the preceding example, the string P$ will be divided into two parts if the string contains a comma. All characters to the left of the comma will be placed in the string X$, while all characters to the right of the comma will be placed in the string Y$. Once you have divided your string into its appropriate parts, you can then compare each part to the expected value or range of values and generate one or more error messages if it does not fall within the expected range.

Line 300 in the example was inserted to display the result of the string manipulation process. This result is shown below.

```
RUN



                    ENTER 2 VALUES 123.45,BANG
                ENTERED DATA IS:123.45 AND BANG
Ok
```

COMPUTATIONAL AND STORAGE EFFICIENCY

From both a computational and data storage perspective, you should use the lowest type variable in your program statement and each variable name should contain a minimum number of characters. The rationale behind this is best understood by examining how variables are stored in BASIC. As illustrated in Fig. D-1, an integer variable requires a minimum of 6 bytes of storage while a double-precision variable requires a minimum of 12 bytes of storage. This is because a one- or two-character variable name will require 1 byte to define its type and 3 bytes to define its name. Thus, an integer variable will require 2 bytes to represent its data value or a total of 6 bytes of storage.

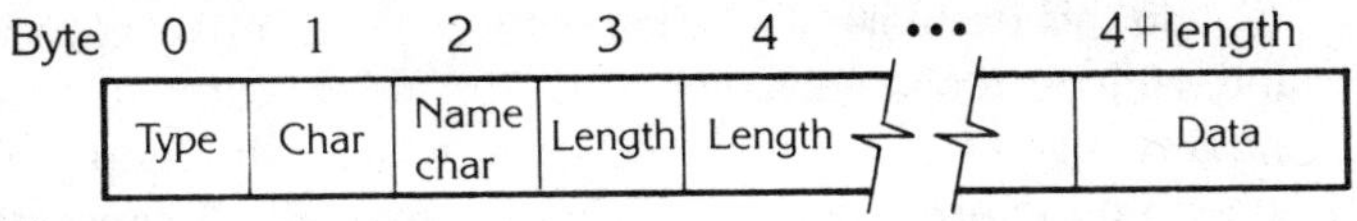

Fig. D-1. Variable storage in BASIC.

Similarly, a double-precision variable will require 1 byte to define its type, a minimum of 3 bytes to define its name, and 8 bytes to store its value.

Based on the preceding, the variable STATETAX would require 4 more bytes of storage than the variable STAX and 5 more bytes than the variable S. From a memory perspective, this means you should abbreviate variable names when possible, especially when your program becomes lengthy.

Concerning arithmetic operational speed, when possible you should use the lowest-type variable. That is, integers are preferred over single-precision variables, which in turn are preferred over double-precision variables. This is because integer arithmetic is performed faster than single-precision arithmetic, which is performed faster than double-precision arithmetic. You can speed up the execution of FOR-NEXT loops by using integer counters. This is demonstrated by the following program segment that displays the time required to execute two loops. The first loop uses an integer counter, while the second loop uses a single-precision counter, since not specifying a variable type causes a default to single precision.

```
Ok
10 TIMES$="00"
20 DEFINT I
30 FOR I=0 TO 10000
40 NEXT I
50 PRINT TIME$
60 TIME$="00"
70 FOR J=0 TO 10000
80 NEXT J
90 PRINT TIME$
RUN
00:00:09
00:00:12
Ok
```

Note that using an integer in the execution time results in an increase in loop execution speed of 25%.

Concerning the use of loops in BASIC, you should remove all unnecessary statements from such loops to include nonexecutable statements. Doing so will optimize the execution of the loop. You can see this by examining the following program segment.

```
100 SUM=0
110 FOR I=1 TO 500
120 REM get sum of elements
130 SUM=SUM+A(I)
140 K=B/C+Q
150 NEXT I
```

In this example, the statement K=B/C+Q has no relationship to the loop and will be repeatedly executed 500 times without changing its value. By moving line 140 to a position before or after the loop, you will considerably speed up the execution of the loop by removing unnecessary statements from the loop. Similarly, line 120 contains a nonexecutable REM statement, which BASIC will spend a small amount of time to identify as such. By containing this remark within a loop, BASIC will perform this examination 500 times. By moving the remark statement outside of the loop, BASIC will perform this examination only one time.

FILE MANIPULATION

One of the key problems associated with random and sequential file processing is in transforming a search argument into an appropriate value for pointing to a particular physical or logical record on a file. As an example, consider social security numbers. Although a social security number is required for most payroll and job accounting programs, its range of values excludes it from being directly used as a record number in random file processing. This is because the social security number can range from 000000000 to 999999999 and exceeds the maximum value of 16 million permitted for a record number in random file processing. Since personnel usually have random social security numbers, no transformation is normally possible to reduce this number to an acceptable record number.

If you wish to use the employee social security number as a pointer to the appropriate record in a random file, you can create a file containing social security numbers and record numbers as illustrated in Fig. D-2. Here, you would search through the SSN file until you match the current social security number with a social security number on the file. The record number associated with the social security number would then give you the exact position on your main data file where you can locate the appropriate information you seek or if you wish to modify some existing information on the record.

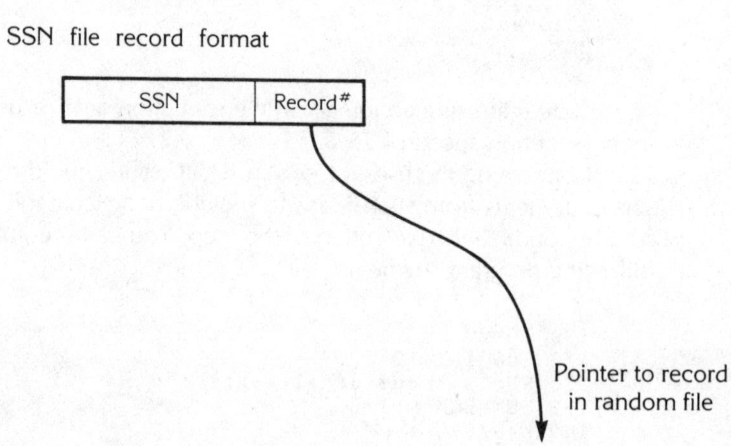

Fig. D-2. Using a record lookup file.

In addition to social security numbers, you can use the record lookup file concept for numerous day-to-day file processing problems. As an example, if you desire to develop a client insurance program, you could use the client's policy number and record number on a record lookup file. Then, when you wish to retrieve or update information, your program would first search the record lookup file to obtain the record number that indicates where on the client insurance file that policyholder's information is located.

MEMORY AND MACHINE PORT REFERENCING

AT BASIC contains three statements and a function that can be used to read and set the contents of memory or to send or receive a byte of data to or from a machine port. Prior to examining how you can perform certain desirable functions on the PC AT by using key address locations, these memory and port-related statements and functions will be reviewed.

Memory Reference

The PEEK function and POKE statement can be used to read the contents of a byte from memory or to write a byte of data into a memory location. The format of the PEEK function is:

format: varnm = PEEK(varnm)

Here, the calling argument is an integer in the range 0 to 65535 and represents the memory location where you wish to read a byte of data from. The value returned from the PEEK function will be an integer in the range 0 to 255 that represents the value of that byte of memory. Some examples of the operational result of this function follow.

Function	**Operational result**
10 X=PEEK(&H410)	Assigns the value of memory location hexadecimal 410 to the variable X
10 DEF SEG=&HB800 20 X=PEEK(1)	Assigns the value of memory location hexadecimal B8001 to the variable X

The complement of the PEEK function is the POKE statement. The format of this statement is:

format: POKE $varnm_1$,$varnm_2$

The first numeric variable, $varnm_1$, must be in the range 0 to 65535. This variable specifies the memory address into which the data defined by the second numeric variable, $varnm_2$, will be written into memory. The actual data to be POKEd must be in the range 0 to 255 and represents an ASCII character code of one of the characters in the AT's character set. The operational result from several POKE statements follows:

Statement	Operational result
10 POKE &HB8000,88	Writes the character X(ASCII88) into memory at location hexadecimal B8000
10 DEF SEG=&HB000 20 FOR I=0 TO 10 30 POKE 1,88 40 NEXT I	Writes the characters X into memory locations hexadecimal B80000 through B8000E

In the second example, 1 is offset by hexadecimal B80000 positions. The extra zero results from the address in the DEF SEG statement being shifted 4 bit positions to the left to form the segment address for the subsequent operation. This program segment would result in a string of 10 Xs in the upper left-hand portion of your display.

The PEEK function and POKE statement can be used in a program to check and/or change the status of various keys on the keyboard. In addition, this function and statement pair can be used to perform other operations that are triggered through references to key memory locations. These key memory locations are described in the IBM PC AT Technical Reference Manual. To understand how to use these memory locations within a program, let us examine what is known as the "equipment flag," which is found at memory location &H417. The bit configuration of this 8-bit byte is illustrated in Fig. D-3.

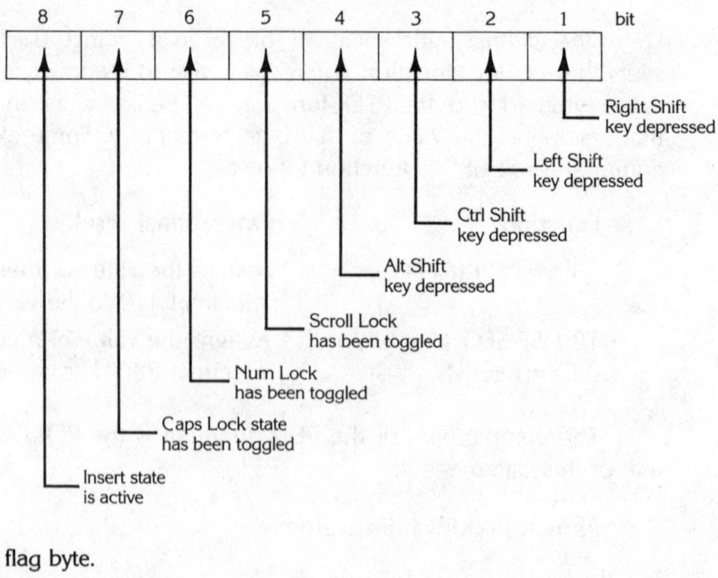

Fig. D-3. Equipment flag byte.

To toggle Caps Lock you must change the value of bit 7 in the equipment flag at location &H417. You can toggle that bit position by setting a "mask" for that position and then using the XOR operator, XORing location &H417 with the mask as illustrated below.

	X	X	X	X	X	X	X	X	Location &H417
Mask	0	1	0	0	0	0	0	0	XOR &H40
	X	C	X	X	X	X	X	X	Result

where:

X = any bit value (0 or 1)
C = complement state of original bit

In the preceding illustration, note that &H40 is binary 01000000, which is the mask. By using a "1" in bit position 7 the XOR operator will only change the value of bit position 7, leaving bit positions 1 through 6 and 8 in their original state. If you now enter the following two-line BASIC program into your AT, each time you execute the program the state of CapsLock will change. This is shown by the green light emitting diode on your keyboard which will be turned on and off.

```
OK
10 DEF SEG=0
20 POKE &H417,PEEK(&H417) XOR &H40
RUN
OK
```

You can use the preceding program to toggle the other keys by simply changing the mask value. Table D-1 lists the mask values for the 8 keys in the equipment flag.

Table D-1. Equipment Flag Mask Values

KEY	MASK
Ins State	&H80
Caps Lock	&H40
Num Lock	&H20
Scroll	&H10
Alt + Shift	&H08
Ctrl + Shift	&H04
Left + Shift	&H02
Right + Shift	&H01

Machine Port Reference

BASIC contains a function and a statement that can be used to read a byte from a machine port or to output a byte of data to a machine port. The INP function can be used to read a byte of data, while the OUT statement provides you with the capability to transmit a byte of data. Both the function and statement require you to know the location of the machine port you wish to read data from or transmit data to.

The format of the INP statement is:

format: varnm=INP(varnm)

The argument in the function must be in the range 0 to 65535. This function returns a byte of information that is read from the designated port number in the argument of the function.

The format of the OUT statement is:

format: OUT $varnm_1$,$varnm_2$

where $varnm_1$ is a numeric variable in the range 0 to 65535 that indicates the port number to which a byte of information will be transmitted, and $varnm_2$ is a numeric variable in the range of 0 to 255 that is the data to be transmitted.

The INP function and OUT statement can be used to check the status and control the different modes of operation supported by the controllers contained in the keyboard, CRT, and other devices attached to the AT. Again, the reader is referred to the IBM PC AT Technical Reference Manual for a listing of the addresses of machine ports and the associated value that equates to a predefined function.

Index